Learning Real Estate Finance

Terrence M. Clauretie
University of Nevada, Las Vegas

and

G. Stacy Sirmans
Florida State University

SOUTH-WESTERN
THOMSON LEARNING™

Australia · Canada · Mexico · Singapore · Spain · United Kingdom · United States

Learning Real Estate Finance, 1e, by Terrence M. Clauretie and G. Stacy Sirmans
Executive Publisher: Dave Shaut
Senior Acquisitions Editor: Scott Person
Developmental Editor: Sara Froelicher
Production Editor: Amy McGuire
Marketing Manager: Mark Linton
Online Editor: Edward Stubenrauch
Manufacturing Coordinator: Charlene Taylor
Internal Design: Daniel Van/DPS Associates, Inc.
Design Project Manager: Rik Moore
Cover Design and Photo Illustration: Rik Moore
Photo Sources: Rik Moore and PhotoDisc, Inc.
Production House/Compositor: DPS Associates, Inc.
Printer: Phoenix Color, Inc.

Printed in the United States of America
1 2 3 4 5 05 04 03 02 01

For more information contact South-Western/Thomson Learning, 5191 Natorp Boulevard, Mason, Ohio, 45050 or find us on the Internet at http://www.swcollege.com

For permission to use material from this text or product, contact us by
- **telephone: 1-800-730-2214**
- **fax: 1-800-730-2215**
- **web: http://www.thomsonrights.com**

Library of Congress Cataloging-in-Publication Data

Clauretie, Terrence M.
Learning real estate finance / Terrence M. Clauretie, G. Stacy Sirmans.—1st ed.
p. cm.
Includes index.
ISBN 0-324-14363-X
1. Mortgage loans—United States. 2. Residential real estate—United States—Finance. 3. Real property—United States—Finance. 4. Housing—United States—Finance I. Sirmans, G. Stacy. II. Title
HG2040.5.U5 C587 2001 2001042657
332.7'2—dc21

CONTENTS

Part II The Instruments of Residential Real Estate Finance 107

To our families with love and appreciation.

T. M. C.
G. S. S.

PREFACE

This text is written with the beginning real estate student in mind. No experience in the field of real estate finance is necessary to study with this text. The material focuses primarily on residential real estate finance, but some topics of commercial real estate finance, such as the time value of money, are introduced.

The book is divided into four parts; Part I is "About Real Estate Finance." After a brief review of the importance of real estate's contribution to the economy in terms of economic activity and employment in Chapter 1, we take a look at how funds flow through the economy in support of financing and investment in real estate. In Chapter 2 we examine how funds saved by some sectors of the economy are transferred to other sectors in need of financing activities. In Chapter 3 we discuss the secondary mortgage market, which holds a dominant position in the residential finance arena. After reviewing the concept of interest rates and the role that risk plays in determining interest rates in Chapter 4, we delve into the important concept of the time value of money in Chapter 5. This chapter is important for understanding how mortgages work. The appendix that follows Chapter 5 includes financial tables for your review and comprehension. We encourage you to spend some time with this chapter and to study it with a calculator in hand. The time value of money is one of the essential tools of finance and the foundation of much of the material that follows.

Part II covers the instruments of real estate finance. Chapter 6 looks at the early history of residential finance and the creation of the familiar long-term, fixed-rate mortgage. Chapter 7 explores the legal instruments used in real estate finance, including the promissory note and the deed-of-trust. The workings of the fixed-rate mortgage are explored in Chapter 8. Here, again, you are encouraged to read this chapter in a thorough fashion with calculator in hand. Chapter 9, a study of alternative mortgage instruments that differ from the long-term fixed-rate mortgage, completes Part II. Popular mortgages such as the adjustable rate mortgage are mentioned here, along with other mortgages available to the public.

Part III explores the process of creating a residential mortgage. Chapter 10 looks at how lenders evaluate the borrower while Chapter 11 looks at how lenders evaluate the property to be financed and used as collateral for the loan.

Chapter 12 discusses the process of closing the loan and the role of mortgage insurance and title insurance. The final chapter in this section, Chapter 13, is titled "Modern Finance" and covers tax-deferred exchanges and installment sales. Both these topics are important for real estate professionals.

The final section of the text, Part IV, covers the regulation and support of residential real estate transactions by the federal government. Chapter 14 covers regulation while Chapter 15 looks at support. There are two basic areas of regulation discussed. One covers the requirement that lenders give sufficient information to consumers to make informed decisions concerning their financing activities (RESPA and Truth-in-Lending). The other area covers discrimination in housing and mortgage lending. Regulation in this area is aimed at preventing discrimination on the basis of race, gender, national origin, religion, or familial status. The final chapter discusses various government programs that provide economic support to the residential real estate market.

Features in this text that assist in the study and comprehension of real estate finance include real-life examples titled "Sidebar Examples," "Mortgage Math" scenarios to further discussion of important equations, and key term definitions at the end of each chapter. Some chapters conclude with suggested reading and related web sites for further study. An answer section to help check your knowledge and understanding for "Problems to Solve" is at the back of this text.

PART I

About Real Estate Finance

Part I provides an introduction to the world of real estate finance. You will discover the important role that real estate finance plays in the larger picture of the U.S. economy. You will also develop an understanding of sources of funds and how they flow in this economy.

An important aspect of real estate finance that we develop here is the concept of *risk*. We view risk as affecting almost all real estate financial transactions, and a clear understanding of risk is crucial to learning other aspects of this field.

This part also addresses the time value of money. This topic, heavy with calculations and formulas, is often relegated (by other authors and other publishers) to an end-of-book appendix. However, we deem the understanding of these calculations so important that we have included the appendix here, along with other material that provides foundational understandings of real estate finance.

Chapter 1

Real Estate and the U.S. Economy

Chapter Outline

Introduction
Real Estate Assets: Single-Family Houses
Real Estate Assets: Commercial Real Estate
The Nation's Mortgages
Financing America's Housing
Financing U.S. Commercial Properties
Annual Activity
Employment in the Real Estate Industry
Summary
Key Terms and Definitions
Review Questions

Learning Objectives

After reading this chapter you will be able to:

- Describe the role of real estate activity in the U.S. economy.
- Cite mortgage and other financial data that indicate the importance of real estate in the economy.
- State how many people work in various aspects of real estate.

Key Terms

mortgage activity
mortgage debt
real estate employment

Introduction

The importance of real estate activity to the U.S. economy is enormous. Whether you consider how much real estate is currently owned, how much new construction is added each year, or how many people are employed in the real estate sector, the conclusion is clear: Real estate and real estate activity are a vital part of our economic life.

Real Estate Assets: Single-Family Houses

Family homes (single-family houses) represent nearly a fourth of the assets of U.S. households ($10.238 trillion of a total $43.218 trillion). About 40 percent of that $10.238 trillion worth of single-family residences is financed—the **mortgage activity** amounts to $4.0551 trillion. Figure 1-1 shows the distribution of household assets. Table 1-1 shows the balance sheet of the household sector of the economy.[1]

[1] The federal government also includes nonprofit entities in these data, but for single-family residences, the figures reflect ownership by the household sector.

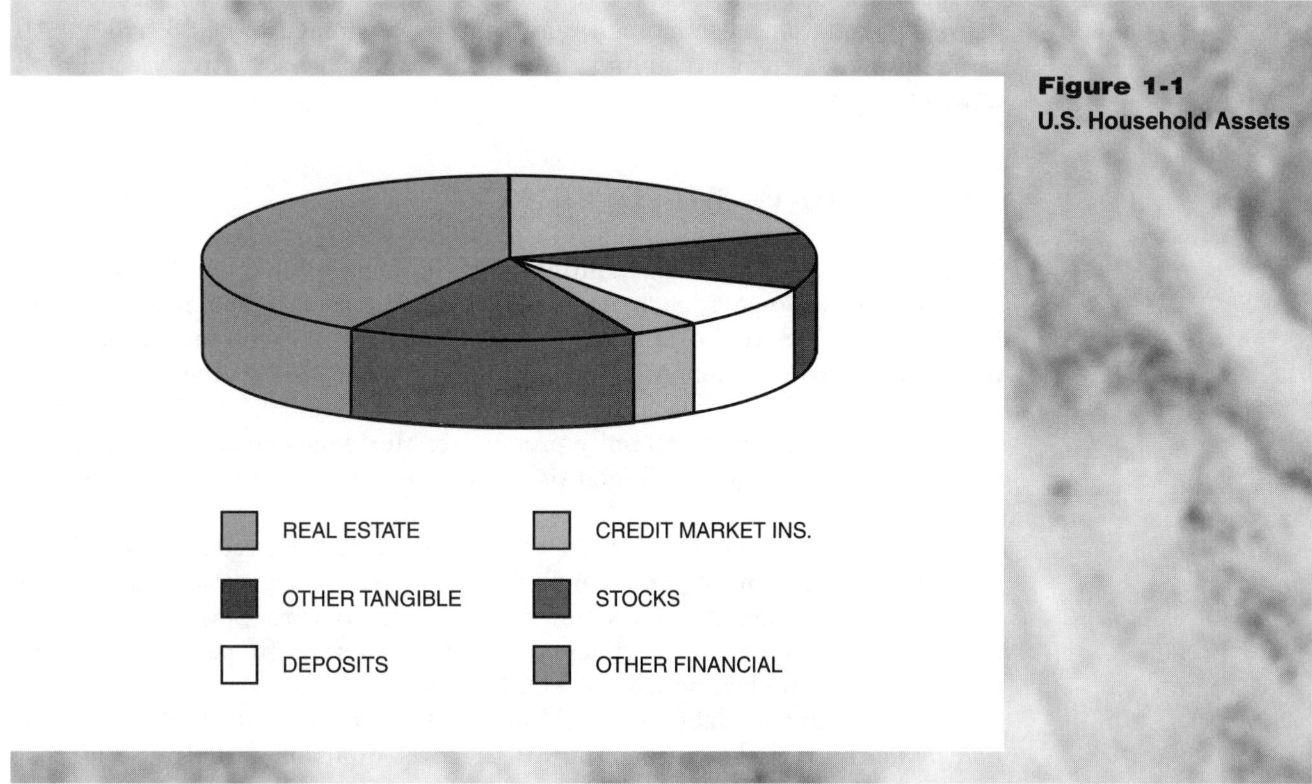

Figure 1-1
U.S. Household Assets

Table 1-1
Balance Sheet of the Household Sector, 1998

	Billions of Dollars
Assets	$43,218.3[a]
Tangible assets	12,953.7
Real estate	10,238.0[b]
Financial assets	30,264.6
Deposits	4,154.6
Credit market instruments	1,673.9
Corporate equities	6,299.9
Other	12,381.4
Liabilities	6,195.5
Residential mortgage	4,055.1
Net worth	37,022.8

[a]Includes nonprofit entities.
[b]Home ownership of household sector.
Source: Federal Reserve System, Flow of Funds Accounts.

Real Estate Assets: Commercial Real Estate

The value of the nation's real estate is not limited to houses. Commercial real estate consists of office buildings, warehouses, retail facilities, hospitals, senior facilities, recreational facilities, hotels, restaurants, and so on. The total value of the nation's commercial real estate is estimated to be $6 trillion. All U.S. real estate, commercial and residential, can be conservatively estimated at $16 trillion.

The Nation's Mortgages

Much real estate, both residential and commercial, has to be financed. Although some property is owned without debt or a mortgage, mortgage dollars financing U.S. real estate add up to *trillions*. In 1999 the total **mortgage debt** was $5.8571 trillion. As shown in Figure 1-2, $4.2762 trillion (73 percent) of this amount was in loans on single-family homes and $351.1 billion (6.5 percent) was in loans on multifamily properties. Mortgages on commercial properties (office buildings, retail facilities, hotels, and the like) amounted to $988 billion (see Table 1-2).

Who owes all this debt? In 1999, the household sector owed $4.2762 trillion in mortgage debt, mostly on single-family houses. Corporations owe some amount on single-family homes, but this is relatively rare. Corporations owed another $339.3 billion in mortgage debt on commercial properties, and nonfarm, noncorporate business owed $1,068.6 billion.

Who was all this debt owed to? Table 1-3 shows that, of the $5.8571 trillion in mortgage debt outstanding in the first quarter of 1999, the largest

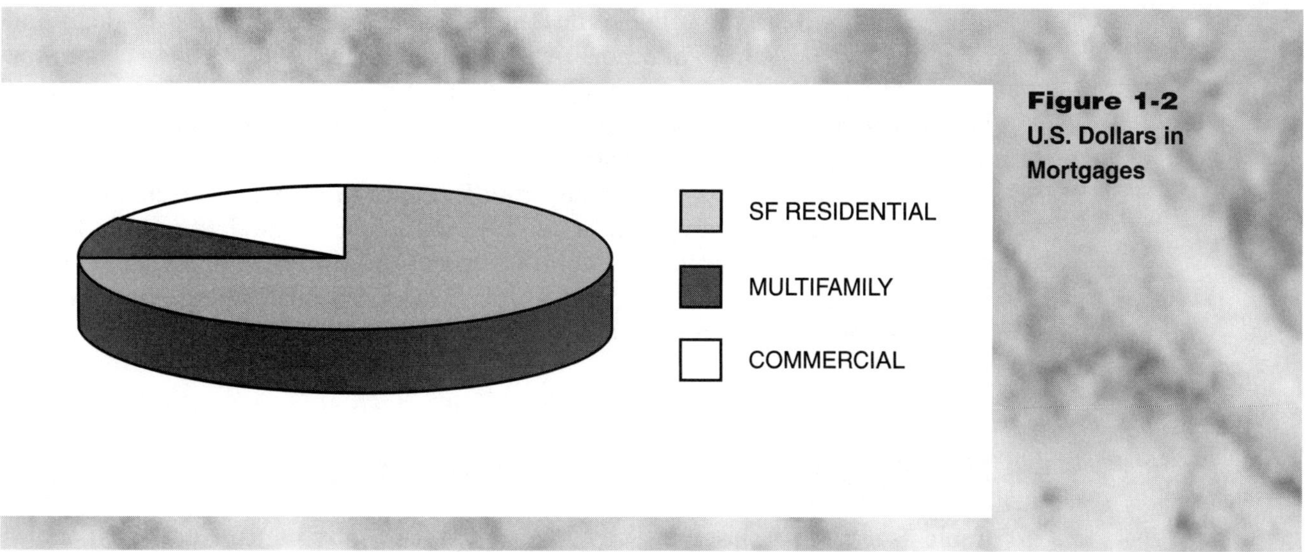

Figure 1-2
U.S. Dollars in Mortgages

share, $2.1114 trillion, was owed to federally related mortgage pools. Federally related mortgage pools (discussed further in Chapter 3) are semi-private corporations sponsored by the federal government. They issue bonds and, with the money received from selling the bonds, purchase mortgages from originators such as savings and loan associations and mortgage bankers.

Another $1.3371 trillion in mortgage debt was held by (owed to) commercial banks. This debt includes a mix of residential and commercial loans that commercial banks made and held in their own investment portfolios. (When a commercial bank or a savings and loan association makes a loan and keeps the loan on its books it is said to have originated a mortgage loan and held it in its

Table 1-2
U.S. Mortgages, 1996-1999 (billions of dollars)

	1996	1997	1998	1999[a]
Total mortgages	$4900.1	$5213.2	$5722.5	$5857.1
Mortgages on:				
Homes	3721.2	3957.0	4324.8	4421.7
Multifamily properties	294.8	310.5	341.3	351.1
Commercial properties	797.0	855.4	960.9	988.0
Farms	87.1	90.3	95.5	96.3
Total liabilities owed by:				
Household sector	3564.0	3803.9	4177.1	4276.2
Corporate	282.4	290.6	329.1	339.3
Nonfarm, noncorporate	934.6	981.6	1049.2	1068.6
Farm	87.1	90.3	95.5	96.3

[a]The 1999 figures are estimates for the entire year based on the first quarter results.
Source: Federal Reserve System, Flow of Funds Accounts.

own portfolio. If, on the other hand, the financial institution makes a loan and then resells that loan to another investor or lender, it is said to have originated a loan and sold it off, not keeping it in its portfolio.) Savings institutions, that is, savings and loan associations, mutual savings banks, and credit unions, held another $646.4 billion of the total.

When a family sells their house and finances part of the purchase (called seller financing or taking back a second), we say that the debt is held by the "household sector." Notice in Table 1-3 that the household sector held $99.9 billion in mortgage debt in 1999. This is a decrease from previous years, whereas debt owed to federally related mortgage pools and other sources has increased.

Financing America's Housing

Table 1-4 takes a closer look at the mortgages that finance America's single-family residences. Of the $4.4217 trillion in mortgages on single-family homes in 1999, less than 2 percent ($78.3 billion) was incurred by the household sector. Federally related mortgage pools held nearly half ($2.0612 trillion) of this, followed by commercial banks with $783.3 billion and savings institutions billion. About 40 percent of the total value of single-family residences, estimated at $10.238 trillion, was financed by mortgage debt.

As shown in Table 1-4 and Figure 1-3, the amount of mortgage debt held by (owed to) households steadily declined in the latter half of the 1990s, while debt held by federally related mortgage pools increased significantly.

Whereas about 40 percent of the value of the nation's homes is financed, only $351.1 billion or 25 percent of the value of multifamily housing is financed. Table 1-5 shows that owners of multifamily housing obtained this financing almost equally from commercial banks, savings institutions, and federally related mortgage pools. The proportion of financing is less than that for financing of single-family housing because much multifamily housing is purchased with all equity funds.

Table 1-3
Mortgage Holdings, 1996–1999 (billions of dollars)

	1996	1997	1998	1999[a]
Mortgages held by:				
Household sector	$ 107.9	$ 105.1	$ 102.1	$ 99.9
Commercial banks	1145.4	1245.3	1337.5	1337.1
Savings institutions	628.3	631.8	644.2	646.4
Life insurance companies	208.2	206.8	213.6	215.3
Federally related pools	1711.4	1825.8	2018.4	2111.4
Other	1098.9	1198.4	1406.7	1447.0
Total	4900.1	5213.2	5722.5	5857.1

[a]The 1999 figures are estimates for the entire year based on the first quarter results.
Source: Federal Reserve System, Flow of Funds Accounts.

Table 1-4
Home Mortgages, 1996–1999 (billions of dollars)

	1996	1997	1998	1999[a]
Held by:				
Household sector	$ 86.9	$ 83.6	$ 80.6	$ 78.3
Commercial banks	677.6	745.5	797.7	783.3
Savings institutions	513.7	520.7	533.5	534.2
Life insurance companies	7.0	7.2	6.6	6.6
Federally related pools	1678.9	1788.0	1970.2	2061.2
Other[b]	757.1	812.0	936.2	958.1
Total	3721.2	3957.0	4324.8	4421.7

[a]The 1999 figures are estimates for the entire year based on the first quarter results.
[b]Includes trusts, estates, business entities, pension funds, etc.
Source: Federal Reserve System, Flow of Funds Accounts.

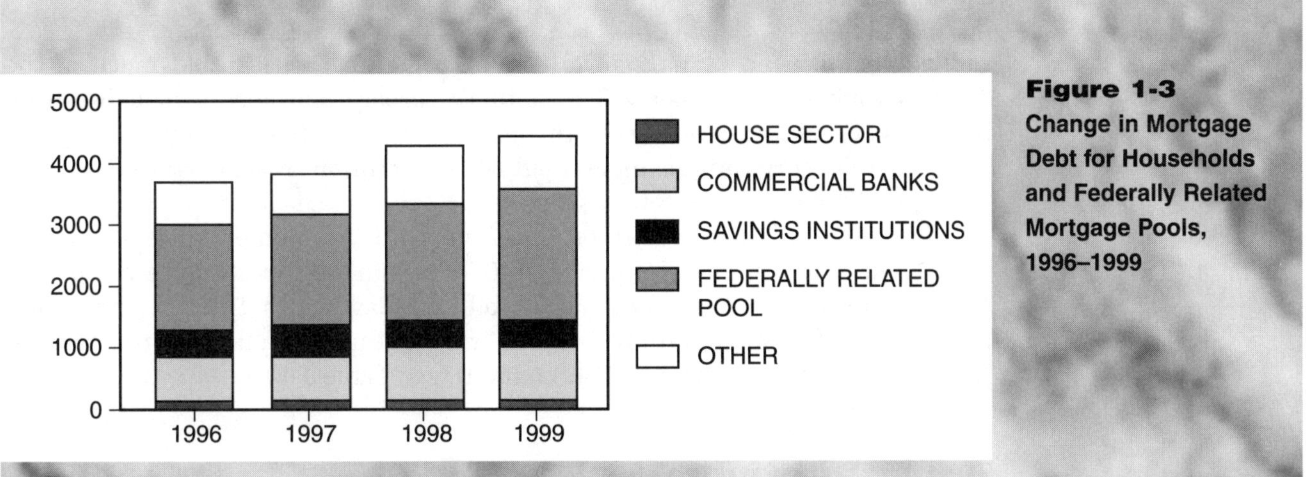

Figure 1-3
Change in Mortgage Debt for Households and Federally Related Mortgage Pools, 1996–1999

Table 1-5
Multifamily Mortgages, 1996–1999 (billions of dollars)

	1996	1997	1998	1999[a]
Held by:				
Household sector	$ 1.5	$ 1.5	$ 1.5	$ 1.4
Commercial banks	45.5	49.7	53.1	56.4
Savings institutions	61.6	59.5	57.1	57.0
Life insurance companies	30.8	30.4	31.5	31.0
Federally related pools	32.5	37.8	48.3	50.2
Other	122.9	131.6	149.8	155.1
Total	294.8	310.5	341.3	351.1

[a]The 1999 figures are estimates for the entire year based on the first quarter results.
Source: Federal Reserve System, Flow of Funds Accounts.

Table 1-6
Commercial Mortgages, 1996–1999 (billions of dollars)

	1996	1997	1998	1999[a]
Held by:				
Household sector	$ 3.6	$ 3.5	$ 3.4	$ 3.4
Commercial banks	397.5	423.1	457.6	467.9
Savings institutions	52.7	51.3	53.2	54.8
Life insurance companies	160.3	158.8	164.0	166.1
Federally related pools	0	0	0	0
Other	182.9	218.7	282.7	295.8
Total	797.0	855.4	960.9	988.0

[a]The 1999 figures are estimates for the entire year based on the first quarter results.
Source: Federal Reserve System, Flow of Funds Accounts.

Financing U.S. Commercial Properties

Individuals, pension plans, and other noncorporate entities hold much of the nation's commercial property. The nation's corporations also own substantial amounts of real estate as part of the assets they need to carry out their operations. In 1998 corporations alone held $4.2027 trillion in real estate as part of their $14.3733 trillion in total assets.

Nearly half of the $988 billion that financed U.S. commercial real estate in 1999 came from commercial banks ($467.9 billion). Life insurance companies financed another 16.6 percent ($166.1 billion). Savings institutions, traditionally lenders for single-family housing rather than commercial real estate, financed less than 2 percent ($54.8 billion) (see Table 1-6).

Annual Activity

Now that we have a picture of the size of the real estate sector and outstanding real estate debt, we can look at *annual* lending activity. In other words, how much does the level of debt used to finance real estate change each year?

For each year from 1996 through 1999, the mortgage debt of the country has increased for all types of real estate. Table 1-7 shows the change for each of these years over the previous year. In 1999, $571.1 billion—including $420.4 billion for single-family residences and $39.3 billion for multifamily residences—was added to the total mortgage debt in the country. Commercial real estate was financed, at least in part, with an additional $108.3 billion. Much of the commercial real estate is acquired with equity capital, so this debt does not reflect total sales activity. Of the $571.1 billion in additional mortgage debt, commercial banks provided only $26.3 billion (4.6 percent) and federally related mortgage pools provided $372 billion.

Table 1-8 shows the annual additions to single-family home mortgage debt in more detail. Although the net activity for 1999 followed the trend of previous years and increased by $420.4 billion, the source of those funds shifted

Table 1-7
Mortgage Activity, Annual Net Change, 1996–1999 (billions of dollars)

	1996	1997	1998	1999[a]
Total activity	$294.6	$313.1	$509.2	$571.1
Single-family	243.0	235.8	367.8	420.4
Multifamily	14.1	15.7	30.8	39.3
Commercial	34.9	58.4	105.5	108.3
Provided by:				
Commercial banks	55.2	99.9	92.2	26.3
Federally related pools	141.1	114.4	192.6	372.0

[a]The 1999 figures are estimates for the entire year based on the first quarter results.
Source: Federal Reserve System, Flow of Funds Accounts.

substantially. Federally related mortgage pools provided $364.2 billion, nearly 87 percent, of 1999's $420.4 billion in additional home mortgage debt and very nearly double what these pools had provided in 1998. On the other hand, savings institutions provided only $2.8 billion, a substantial reduction from the amounts they had provided in earlier years. Commercial banks *reduced* their holdings of residential loans in 1999 by $30.1 billion—they actually sold off more home loans than they originated.

Table 1-9 presents the changes in commercial mortgages. Of the $108.3 billion estimated additional funding for commercial facilities in 1999, $41.1 billion came from commercial banks and $49.7 billion came from asset-backed security (ABS) issuers.

Employment in the Real Estate Industry

Employment in the real estate industry provides further evidence of the significance of real estate in our economy. Data from the 1992 census (the most

Table 1-8
Home Mortgage Activity, 1996–1999 (billions of dollars)

	1996	1997	1998	1999[a]
Total activity	$243.0	$235.8	$367.8	$420.4
Commercial banks	31.1	67.9	52.2	−30.1
Savings institutions	31.4	7.0	12.8	2.8
Life insurance companies	−1.9	0.2	−0.6	0.2
Federally related pools	135.5	109.1	182.2	364.2

[a]The 1999 figures are estimates for the entire year based on the first quarter results.
Source: Federal Reserve System, Flow of Funds Accounts.

Table 1-9
Commercial Mortgage Activity, 1996–1999 (billions of dollars)

	1996	1997	1998	1999[a]
Total activity	$34.9	$58.4	$105.5	$108.3
Commercial banks	20.2	25.7	34.5	41.1
Life insurance companies	–5.6	–1.5	5.2	8.2
REITs[b]	–1.0	2.2	2.5	2.8
ABS issuers	20.1	30.3	58.3	49.7

[a]The 1999 figures are estimates for the entire year based on the first quarter results.
[b]Real Estate Investment Trust (corporations that issue stock and buy real estate assets)
Source: Federal Reserve System, Flow of Funds Accounts.

recent data available) reveal that 1,231,471 employees in 229,493 establishments were working in the real estate industry (see Table 1-10). Some of the larger categories of employment were real estate operators of nonresidential buildings, operators of apartment buildings, real estate agents and managers, and real estate property managers. In 1992, there were more than 38,000 real estate appraisers alone.

One of the largest employment sectors of the real estate industry is real estate agents and brokers. In 1992, the real estate industry employed 646,561 real estate agents and managers in 106,552 establishments. Residential real estate agents and brokers accounted for much of this. The 1992 data from the census (see Table 1-11) show that 148,548 residential real estate agents and brokers worked in 43,435 establishments (offices or agencies). These figures are low, since many real estate sales agents are independent contractors and are,

Table 1-10
Real Estate Related Employment, 1992

	Establishments	Revenue	Paid Employees
All real estate	229,493	$141,673,252	1,231,471
Real estate operators	102,887	74,069,546	462,564
Nonresidential	32,905	36,868,690	168,138
Apartments	48,330	29,373,795	228,270
Other	21,652	7,827,061	66,156
Real estate agents and managers	106,552	53,747,026	646,561
Residential	43,435	20,900,833	148,548
Nonresidential	9,383	4,911,422	46,100
Property managers	38,592	21,610,020	376,941
Residential	13,732	8,001,327	179,311
Nonresidential	9,448	6,092,754	107,220
Appraisers	10,015	2,981,854	38,080
Land developers	15,338	11,519,338	88,604

Source: U.S. Department of Commerce, Bureau of the Census.

Table 1-11
Residential Real Estate Agents and Brokers, 1992

	Establishments	Revenue (in thousands)	Paid Employees
Operating entire year			
Revenue of:			
$25 million or more	15	$ 590,566	3,585
$1 to $25 million	4,817	10,334,534	57,584
Up to $1 million	32,980	9,015,985	80,753
Not operating entire year	5,623	959,748	6,626
Total	43,435	20,900,833	148,548

Source: U.S. Department of Commerce, Bureau of the Census.

therefore, not included in these employment figures. Consider, for example, that membership in the National Association of Realtors (NAR) in 1999 was 720,000 of whom 590,000 were residential agents—and not all holders of a real estate license are members of NAR.

Table 1-12 shows revenues per establishment and per employee in various real estate segments. Table 1-13 takes a closer look at employment in offices of residential agents and brokers. Most residential sales operations are small. Of the offices that operated in 1992 (43,435) about one-fourth employed only one person. Only 62 firms employed more than 99 persons. (Recall, however, that the agents themselves may not be included in these totals.)

Table 1-12
Revenue per Establishment and Employee, 1992

	Revenue Per	
	Establishment	Employee
Real estate operators		
Nonresidential	$1,120,459	$219,276
Apartment	607,776	128,680
Real estate agents		
Residential	481,198	140,701
Nonresidential	523,438	106,538
Property Managers		
Residential	582,677	44,623
Nonresidential	644,872	56,825
Appraisers	297,739	78,305
Developers	751,033	130,009

Source: U.S. Department of Commerce, Bureau of the Census.

Table 1-13
Offices of Residential Real Estate Agents and Brokers, 1992

Employees	Establishments	Revenue (in thousands)	Paid
Operating entire year			
No employees	1,926	$ 348,140	0
One employee	13,335	2,394,934	13,335
Two employees	7,915	2,546,718	15,830
3-49 employees	14,444	13,016,015	92,786
50-99 employees	130	752,246	8,730
More than 99 employees	62	883,032	11,241
Not operating entire year	5,623	959,748	6,626
Total	43,435	20,900,833	148,548

Source: U.S. Department of Commerce, Bureau of the Census.

Finally, a look at how real estate firms are organized (see Table 1-14) shows that 124,457 of a total of 208,697 real estate firms operate from a corporate structure. Of 38,339 residential sales firms, 27,044 are operated from a corporate structure. The limited liability afforded by incorporation makes it an attractive option.

Summary

Just look around you. Look at your daily activities. You cannot help but see reminders of real estate activity in newspapers, magazines, television, signs on homes and buildings, construction sites, and elsewhere. Construction spending,

Table 1-14 **Ownership Structure of Real Estate Firms, 1992**

	Firms	Establishments	Revenue (in thousands)	Paid Employees
All types	208,697	229,493	$141,673,252	1,231,471
Corporate	124,457	141,033	92,141,697	895,025
Individual proprietorships	38,717	39,456	11,160,511	100,508
Partnerships	41,434	44,623	36,771,950	218,042
Other	4,090	4,381	1,599,094	17,896
Residential real estate agents	38,339	43,435	20,900,833	148,548
Corporate	27,044	31,699	17,523,411	123,453
Individual proprietorships	9,400	9,460	1,807,889	15,707
Partnerships	1,802	2,152	1,491,057	8,917
Other	93	124	78,476	471

Source: U.S. Department of Commerce, Bureau of the Census.

income, employment, loans: All are part of real estate's role in our economy—and our lives. Understanding real estate finance contributes to understanding how our economy works. The remainder of this text describes how that real estate is financed.

Key Terms and Definitions

mortgage activity—Origination of loans by lenders and the purchase and sale of those loans in the secondary mortgage market.

mortgage debt—Amount of loans made for the purchase of real estate property.

real estate employment—Total persons employed in the real estate industry, which includes brokers, salespersons, lenders, title companies, appraisers, and so forth.

Review Questions

1. Why is real estate activity important to the U.S. economy?
2. What part (percentage) of our household assets was accounted for by homes in 1999?
3. What was the total value of the mortgages on America's homes in 1999?
4. Describe the trend of household-held mortgage debt in the latter half of the 1990s.
5. In 1992, how many paid employees worked in real estate-related industries?

Chapter 2

Flow and Sources of Real Estate Funds

Chapter Outline

Learning Objectives

After reading this chapter you will be able to:

- Describe how funds flow from those individuals and institutions with an excess of funds to those with a lack or deficit of funds and a need to borrow.
- List key sources of funds in real estate finance.
- Describe how these sources operate.

Key Terms

capital market
debt instrument
deficit entity
direct transfer of funds
equity interest
fiduciary
money market
primary market
secondary market
securities market
security
surplus entity
thrifts

Introduction

Most real estate activity uses borrowed funds in one way or another. How funds move from entities with excess funds (**surplus entities**) to those needing funds (**deficit entities**) affects the timing, volume, and types of real estate activities. This chapter reviews how funds flow in the economy.

The Financing Process

The basic financing process is shown in Figure 2-1. Entities that need funds (deficit entities) are shown on the right. They need funds because their spending requirements are greater than their income and savings. The entities on the left-hand side of Figure 2-1 have more funds than required to meet their current needs. These surplus entities lend funds or purchase equity interests.

Some entities obtain funds by borrowing from the entities that provide or "advance" funds. When they borrow funds, they create or take on debt. Entities borrow funds by using a **debt instrument**, such as a bond, a mortgage, or a promissory note.

Another way in which entities obtain funds is by selling some ownership in themselves to investors. They sell an **equity interest** in their business, for example, by selling stock.

Entities that need to acquire funds include households, businesses, and governments (local, state, and federal). Households borrow funds to acquire durable goods, such as automobiles and appliances. The biggest need of households for funds, by far, is to buy a home, usually through what is generally called a mortgage. Businesses need funds to purchase long-term assets, such as plant and equipment, among other things. Governments need to obtain funds when government spending exceeds tax revenues.

Households cannot easily sell an equity interest in their residence, so they acquire funds by borrowing. Businesses acquire funds both by borrowing (issuing bonds, for example) and by selling an equity interest (issuing stock). Governments, like households, acquire funds by borrowing: The federal government issues Treasury bonds; state and local governments issue municipal bonds.

Households, businesses, and governments are also the entities that have funds available for lending or for buying equity interests. Households that already own a residence, for example, may have more income than they need to meet their spending requirements. They save the excess income in banks,

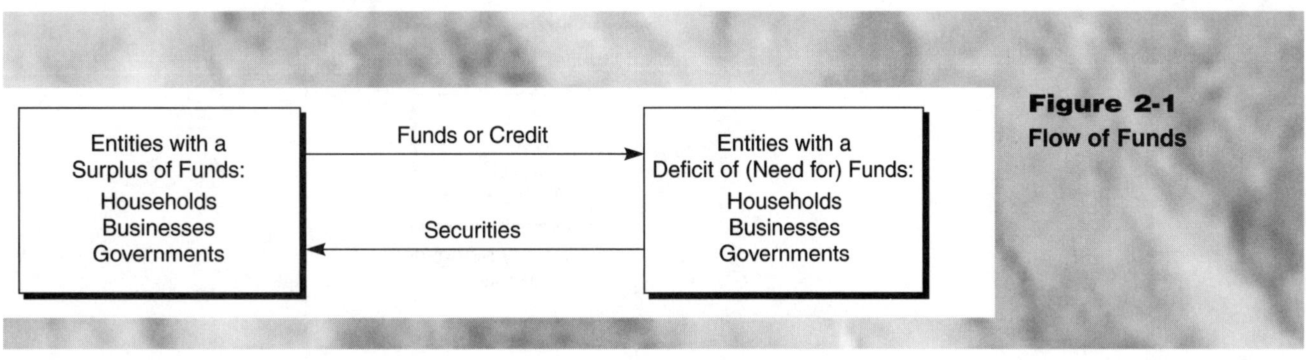

Figure 2-1
Flow of Funds

thrifts, insurance companies, and other financial institutions. These institutions invest the funds in mortgages, government bonds, or in equity interest of businesses. Figure 2-2 shows a more complete picture of the transfer of funds from entities that have a surplus to those that have a need or deficit. Table 2-1 shows the 2000 volume of funds transferred in the process depicted in Figure 2-2. Table 2.1 shows that the gross savings and investment in the United States for the year 2000 was $1.844 trillion.

How Funds Are Transferred

Funds can be transferred from surplus entities to deficit entities in three ways: direct transfer, transfer through an intermediary, and transfer through a securities market (stocks and bonds, for example.)

Direct Transfer

Direct transfer of funds occurs when a surplus entity advances the funds directly to a deficit entity. When relatives loan family members the funds to

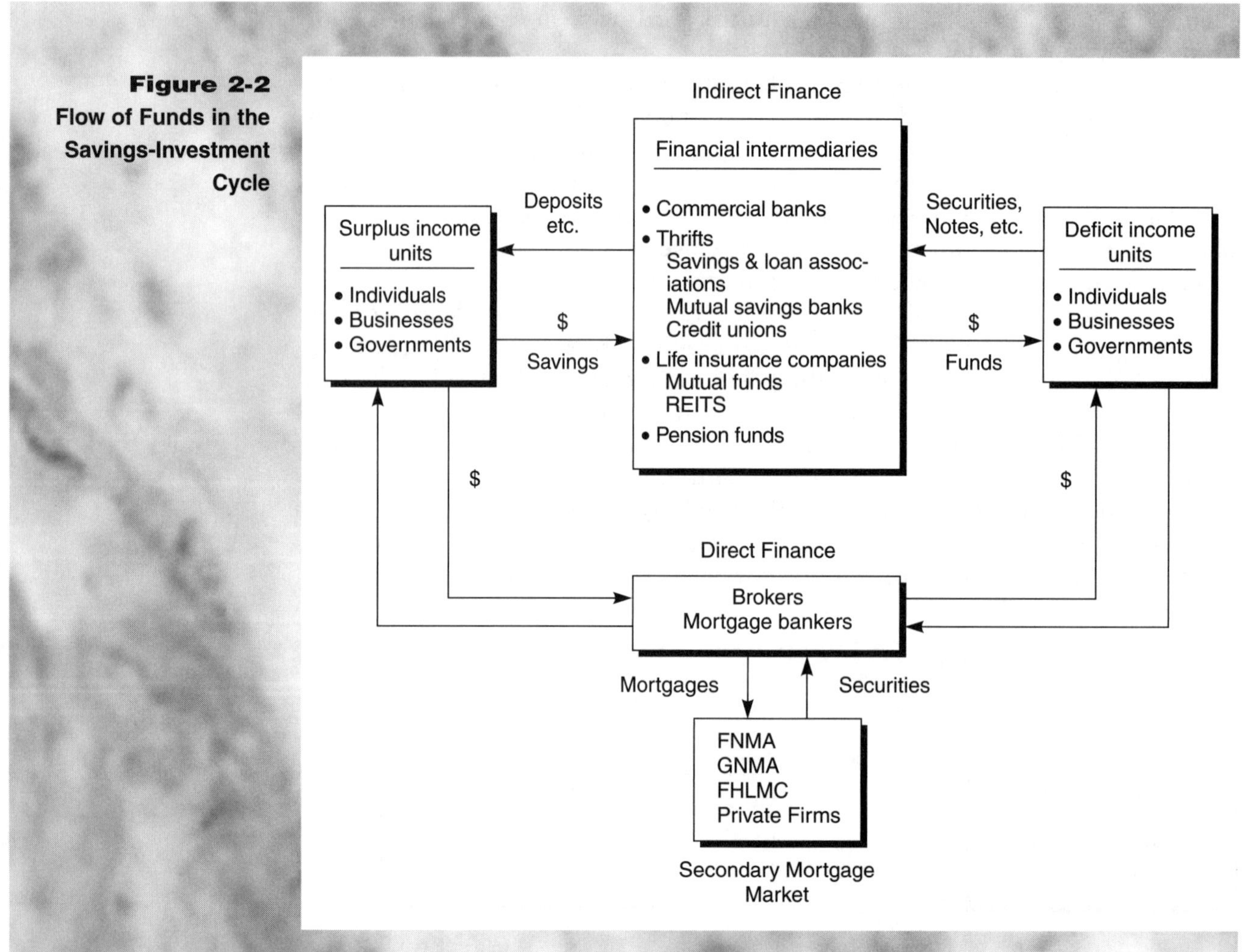

Figure 2-2
Flow of Funds in the Savings-Investment Cycle

Table 2-1
U.S. Gross Saving and Investment, 2000 (billions of dollars)

Gross total saving			$1,844.6
Gross private savings		$1,328.9	
Personal savings	$ 20.6		
Business savings			
Undistributed profits	278.5		
Consumption of fixed capital	731.1		
Noncorporate consumption of fixed capital	298.7		
Gross government saving		515.7	
Gross total investment			1,772.0
Gross private domestic investment		1,852.6	
Gross government investment		331.9	
Net foreign investment		(412.5)	
Statistical discrepancy			72.6

purchase a home, for example, they are making a direct transfer of funds. If a home seller loans funds to the buyer of the home, sometimes called *seller-provided financing* or *seller take-back*, the transfer of funds is direct.

A member of the household sector also makes a direct transfer when he or she purchases a bond issued by a corporation or by a government entity. A corporation that purchases a federal Treasury bond is making a direct transfer of funds to the federal government. There are numerous other examples of surplus entities transferring or "advancing" funds directly to deficit entities.

Transfers Through Intermediaries

Surplus entities can also advance funds to deficit entities through financial intermediaries or financial **fiduciaries**. Intermediaries facilitate the flow of funds in the financial system. For a fee, they take on risk (see Chapter 4) and/or offer lending services.

Intermediaries include commercial banks, savings and loan associations, savings banks, credit unions, life insurance companies, mutual funds, and pension funds. Savings and loan associations, savings banks, and credit unions together are called **thrifts** because they obtain most of their funds from the savings accounts of their depositors. Commercial banks obtain funds from other sources, such as issuing commercial paper and bonds, and are not considered to be thrifts.

When someone places funds in a savings account at a commercial bank or a thrift, he or she obtains an asset called a deposit. This deposit is a liability of the commercial bank or thrift—it owes the amount of the deposit back to the depositor. The commercial bank or thrift can transfer those funds to a household, a business, or a government—the ultimate deficit entities. In this circumstance, the funds go from the surplus entity to the intermediary and then to the deficit entity. The intermediary stands in the middle, between the surplus and deficit units, as shown in Figure 2-3.

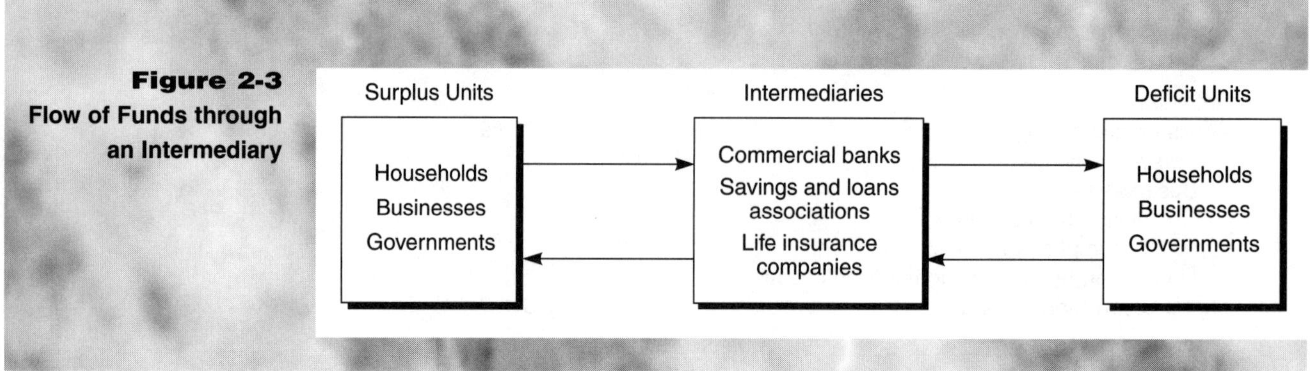

Figure 2-3
Flow of Funds through an Intermediary

Intermediaries pay interest to the depositors and charge interest to borrowers. As you would expect, the rate of interest that they pay is somewhat less than the rate they charge. For example, a business may pay a bank 8 percent annually on a loan, while the bank pays only 5 percent to its depositors. Likewise, someone who obtains a mortgage from a thrift may pay 7 percent annually on the mortgage, while the thrift pays 5 percent to depositors and keeps the difference. The thrift uses that interest rate differential, usually about two percentage points, to cover operating costs and provide a return to investors. The differential also compensates them for risk that they have undertaken in making loans. Chapter 4 describes such risks in more detail.

Commercial Banks

One of the most familiar intermediaries is the commercial bank. Commercial banks act as lenders and as depositories for a variety of activities. Most of the funds that these banks use for making loans come from their customers' checking accounts, called *demand deposits*. Other sources of their funds include their customers' savings accounts, loans from other banks, and the investments of their owners.

Commercial banks loan funds to individuals, businesses, and the government. These banks are an important source of real estate loans on commercial properties, investment properties, and single-family or multifamily residential properties. They also make construction loans, home improvement loans, and loans on mobile homes.

In recent years, commercial banks have been more active in making home equity loans, that is, loans that use the borrowers' equity in their home as collateral. Home equity loans remain popular with borrowers because the interest on these loans is tax deductible. Borrowers use their home equity loans for various purposes, including but not limited to buying other property.

Many commercial banks have subsidiaries that do nothing but make residential mortgage loans. They are more or less separate entities established for the purpose of making such loans.

The Federal Reserve System supervises commercial banks, and the Federal Deposit Insurance Corporation (FDIC) insures their customers' deposits.

Thrifts

Thrifts, the largest single source of residential mortgages, include mutual savings banks, credit unions, and savings and loan associations. Prior to the early 1980s, thrifts could accept only time (savings) deposits, not demand deposits (checking accounts). Now thrifts compete with the commercial banks for demand deposits. Beginning in 1982, deregulation of thrifts allowed them to broaden their investments to include more commercial real estate investments.

Mutual Savings Banks Mutual savings banks were established in the mid-19th century to serve the growing class of industrial workers. Mutual savings banks are owned as cooperatives, rather than stock companies. Cooperatives must be approved by state law. A dozen or so states, mostly in the East, allow this form of ownership.

Most of the assets, more than 70 percent, are savings deposits. The U.S. Government's Office of Thrift Supervision governs the activities of these banks. The FDIC insures the deposits in mutual savings banks, like those in commercial banks. [Prior to 1990 the Federal Savings and Loan Insurance Corporation (FSLIC) insured their deposits.] Mutual savings banks distribute their profits to their depositors in the form of interest or dividends.

Credit Unions Credit unions are restricted to serving members with a particular affiliation, such as the employees of a corporation, a government office, or other entity. They were created in 1970 under the National Credit Union Administration (NCUA) and are supervised by the National Credit Union Association Board (NCUAB). They are not governed by local, state, or federal banking regulations, and so may have more flexibility in the investment of their funds. Deposits in credit unions are insured by the federally insured National Credit Union Share Insurance Fund.

Although financing of residential real estate is not their primary activity, credit unions are actively investing in this market as well as in construction, home improvement, and home equity loans.

Savings Associations Like mutual savings banks, savings associations (also called savings and loan associations) are governed by the Office of Thrift Supervision, and the FDIC insures their deposits. They can be organized as mutual companies or as stock companies. Savings associations must be chartered by the federal government or by their state government.

Early savings associations were actually called *building and loan associations*. They formed specifically to make loans to their depositors for residential construction.

Insurance Companies

Life insurance companies control approximately 12 percent of the nation's savings and are a significant participant in real estate finance. Insurance companies receive periodic payments or lump-sum payments (both called "premiums") from policyholders, which may include individuals or organizations. In return, the insurance company promises to make certain payments back to the policyholder if specific events happen.

Because these companies need to build up a reserve of funds to have available for payments to policyholders under the specified conditions, they tend to make long-term investments. They are more concerned with long-term stability than with short-term flexibility or liquidity. Insurance companies invest their premiums in securities such as long-term commercial mortgages and other large projects. Commercial mortgages are loans on commercial real estate properties—office buildings, apartment complexes, retail outlets, and industrial facilities. Sometimes they obtain an equity position on projects they finance. Such arrangements, sometimes called *participation financing*, can enhance the company's profitability and control over the investment.

Increasingly, insurance companies are investing in residential real estate. However, these investments tend to take the form of purchasing blocks of residential mortgages or participating in the secondary mortgage market rather than originating individual single-family home loans.

States regulate life and casualty insurance companies through a department of insurance. Raising the cost of insurance premiums requires permission from the department of insurance. The decision to allow premium increases is often based on how much interest or return the insurance companies are receiving on their investments. The department of insurance also considers how much money the insurance company needs to be able to pay present and future claims. If the return on their investments is very low, then the insurance companies need to increase premiums so they can continue to pay policyholders' claims.

Pension Funds

Pension funds pool the contributions of employees and invest in long-term assets such as stocks, bonds, and real estate. Like insurance companies, pension funds need to build a reserve of funds to meet future needs of the contributors.

These funds enjoy a consistent stream of incoming funds. Retirement contributions are made on a regular basis, often through payroll deduction plans. This, together with the fact that payments to retirees are made in increments rather than as lump-sum payments, results in a substantial amount of capital to invest.

In the past, managers of pension funds invested little in real estate finance. However, during the last decade of the 20th century, when returns on other investments were relatively low, the managers began to make moderate investments in real estate securities, including real estate investment trusts.

Investment Companies

Investment companies combine the small investments made by individuals and organizations and invest in a diversified portfolio of stocks, bonds, or other well-defined types of assets. Many companies invest only in stocks, and some of these specialize only in growth stocks, income stock, or stock in companies in certain industries. Some investment companies, called *real estate investment trusts* (REITs), specialize in real estate properties or mortgages on real estate properties. Others invest in mortgage-type securities such as Government National Mortgage Association (GNMA) bonds.

Finance Companies

Finally, there is a special intermediary termed a *finance company*. A finance company makes a type of loan called a *consumer loan*. That is, they specialize in making loans to consumers rather than businesses. Consumer loans include consumer credit and home loans. Finance companies obtain the funds that they loan from private equity sources such as a parent corporation. An example of a finance company would be General Motors Acceptance Corporation for automobile loans and GMAC Mortgage for home loans.

Transfer of Funds through Securities Markets

Securities of various types are exchanged between sellers and buyers in the **securities market**. Securities exchanged in this market are, for the most part, bonds and stocks (equities), but they also include futures, options, and other securities. Usually brokers represent the buyers and sellers in the exchange process.

The securities market has two submarkets: the **money market** and the **capital market**. Securities with a maturity of a year or less are exchanged in the money market. One of the largest components of the money market is the exchange of Treasury bills. Another large component is the market for commercial paper. Commercial paper consists of short-term (usually less than 270 days), unsecured debt obligations of financially strong corporations and commercial banks. Long-term securities—long-term bonds and all stocks—are exchanged in the capital market.

The money market and the capital market are each divided into a **primary market** and a **secondary market**. The primary market is where a security is first offered for sale. The secondary market is where securities are subsequently bought and sold. For example, if a corporation needs to raise money to purchase a large asset, it may issue new stock. (The stock may have been authorized, but not issued.) When it sells this new stock for the very first time, it is sold in the primary market. If the buyer of this stock later decides to resell this stock to another investor, this second and all subsequent transactions take place in the secondary market.

How are funds transferred from surplus entities to deficit entities via the capital market? A homebuyer's mortgage is one example. When an entity such as a savings and loan association originates a mortgage to a homebuyer, the homebuyer is issuing a debt obligation, called a *promissory note*. The savings and loan association buys this note (mortgage) when it advances funds to the homebuyer. In this case the note (mortgage) origination is taking place in the primary market. Remember, the buyer's note is new. The buyer has never issued this promissory note before.

If the savings and loan association decides to sell the note (mortgage) to another institution, this second sale would take place in the secondary market.

The institution that purchases the mortgage in the secondary market, for example, the Federal National Mortgage Association (FNMA), may have obtained the necessary funds by issuing bonds to investors. FNMA will issue bonds to investors and use the mortgages as collateral. This is why the bonds that are issued by FNMA are termed *mortgage-backed bonds*.

In reality, investors in the bonds are the ultimate source of the funds used by a homebuyer to purchase a residence. This is an example of how funds are transferred through the capital market via mortgage-backed bonds.

Summary

The flow of funds from entities with a surplus of funds to entities that need those funds is essential to the real estate industry. Surplus entities include households, businesses, and government. Deficit entities also include households, businesses, and government. Deficit entities either borrow funds or sell something that will bring in money, usually an interest in themselves in the form of stock.

Funds are transferred in one of three ways: direct transfer, transfer through an intermediary, or transfer through a securities market. A direct transfer refers to the movement of funds straight from the surplus entity to the deficit entity, as in the direct loan of money from one family member to another. A transfer through an intermediary refers to a transfer that is facilitated by a commercial bank, savings and loan association, savings bank, credit union, etc. A transfer through a securities market, either through the money market or the capital market, refers to a transfer in which the ultimate source of the funds is a securities issue, such as mortgage-backed bonds issued by FNMA.

Key Terms and Definitions

capital market—A market where securities (stocks and bonds) with maturities greater than one year are traded.

debt instrument—A security such as a promissory note or a bond that outlines the terms of the loan.

deficit entity—A household, business, or government that has current expenditures in excess of current income and must obtain funds from surplus entities.

direct transfer of funds—The transfer of funds from a surplus entity to a deficit entity without the use of an intermediary.

equity interest—Ownership in a business, usually through ownership of stock.

fiduciary—A person in a position of trust and confidence for another.

money market—The market where short-term (less than one year) debt obligations are exchanged.

primary market—The market where financial securities are first originated

secondary market—The market where existing securities are exchanged.

securities market—A market where securities such as corporate stocks and bonds, government bonds, and mortgages are bought and sold.

security—An instrument that memorializes the transfer of funds.

surplus entity—A household, business, or government that has current income in excess of current expenditures and will transfer the excess to deficit entities.

thrifts—Savings and loan associations, mutual savings banks, and credit unions.

Review Questions

1. What is a deficit entity?
2. What is a surplus entity?
3. Name two basic ways in which deficit entities obtain funds.
4. How can a government be both a deficit entity and a surplus entity?
5. Name the three basic ways in which funds are transferred from surplus entities to deficit entities, and give an example of each.
6. What is a financial intermediary or fiduciary? What do financial intermediaries do?
7. List six examples of financial intermediaries.
8. What is the single largest source of residential mortgages?
9. What is a home equity loan?
10. How do life insurance companies get funds with which to make investments?
11. In which securities market are securities with a maturity of one year or less exchanged?
12. What is a *mortgage-backed bond*?

Chapter 3

The Secondary Mortgage Market

Chapter Outline

Learning Objectives

After reading this chapter, you will be able to:

- Explain why the secondary mortgage market exists and how it developed.
- Describe how the secondary market works.
- List the major secondary mortgage market agencies.
- Indicate the size of this market relative to all real estate lending.

Key Terms

collateralized
collateralized mortgage obligation (CMO)
conforming mortgage
credit enhancement
Farmers Home Administration (FmHA)
Federal Agricultural Mortgage Corporation (FAMC)
federal credit agency
Federal Financing Bank (FFB)
Federal Home Loan Mortgage Corporation (FHLMC)
Federal National Mortgage Association (FNMA)
Financial Accounting Standards Board (FASB)
Government National Mortgage Association (GNMA)
government-sponsored enterprise
grantor trust
guaranteed mortgage certificate (GMC)
interest only (IO)
mark-to-market
mortgage-backed bond (MBB)
mortgage-backed security (MSR)
mortgage-related security
participation certificate (PC)
pass-through security
prepayment
principal only (PO)
private mortgage insurance (PMI)
real estate mortgage investment conduit (REMIC)
secondary mortgage market
senior/subordinated pass-through
tranche

Introduction

A **secondary mortgage market** is one in which existing mortgages are bought and sold. This is very different from the primary mortgage market, where mortgages originate. Mortgages are originated by the initial lenders, such as thrifts (savings and loan associations, savings banks, and credit unions) or mortgage bankers. Some thrifts and all mortgage bankers then sell these loans in the secondary market. By definition, the owner of a mortgage that was purchased in the secondary market did not originate the loan.

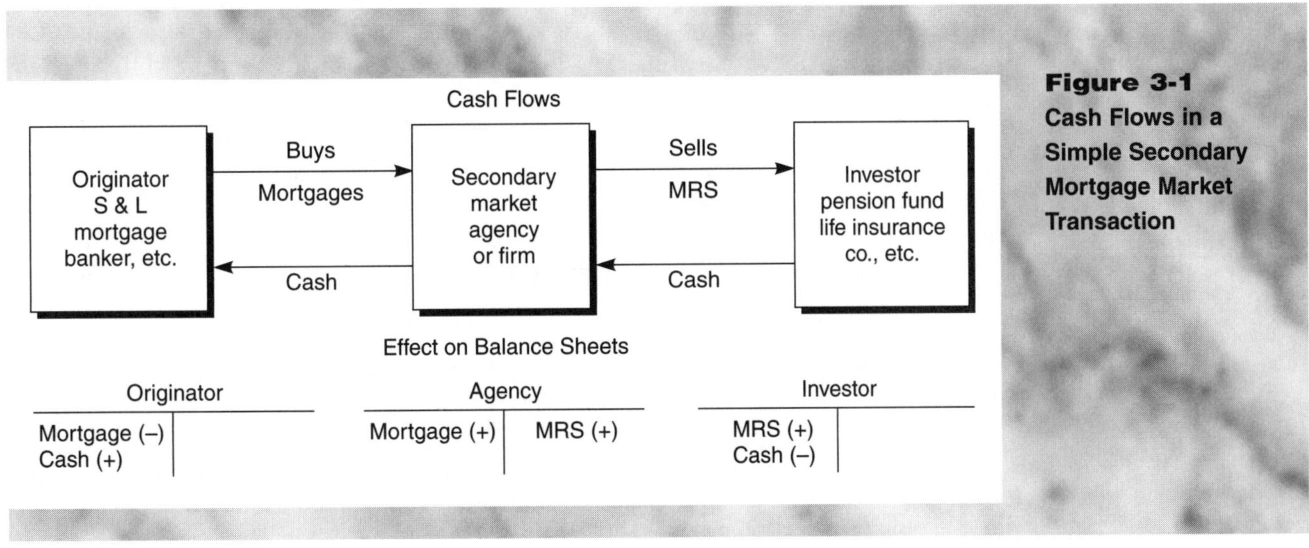

Figure 3-1 Cash Flows in a Simple Secondary Mortgage Market Transaction

The agencies and firms that purchase mortgages in the secondary market most often raise the funds required for the purchase by issuing bonds or other types of debt instruments. They pledge the mortgages (now their assets) as collateral for the debt they issue. The debt issue is termed a **mortgage-related security** because it is backed, or **collateralized**, by mortgages. Mortgage-related securities, sometimes referred to as **mortgage-backed securities**, are themselves bought and sold and are considered part of the secondary mortgage market.

Figure 3-1 shows an example of how funds might flow in this market. The investors who purchase the bonds (mortgage-related securities) from the secondary mortgage market agency or firm are the ultimate source of the funds. The agency or firm then uses the funds obtained from the investors to purchase mortgages from, for example, a savings and loan association (thrift). The savings and loan association uses the funds to originate mortgages.[1] (The transactions occur in the reverse order and take some time, however). The key actions to the flow are that, ultimately, investors supply the funds and homeowners use them to purchase residences. As a result, the amount of funds flowing into mortgages is not limited to the amount that savings and loan associations, thrifts, and banks can raise through deposits alone.

Why Does the Secondary Mortgage Market Exist?

Picture Jimmy Stewart as the beleaguered savings and loan association president in *It's a Wonderful Life*, fending off a mob of depositors eager to get their money. Either because of rumors of fiscal mismanagement of the institution or just a need for liquidity in times of unemployment, a "run" on the bank was exactly the sort of dramatic occurrence that moviegoers could relate to. In *It's a Wonderful Life*, Jimmy Stewart tried to persuade anxious depositors that their funds were safe—safely tied up in residential loans to their neighbors. Such ugly scenes were not far from reality in times when financial institutions faced severe liquidity problems that resulted from an inability to sell some of their assets quickly. In the depression years of the 1930s, other than stocks and bonds held by commercial banks, a large proportion of the assets of lending institutions, particularly thrifts, was tied up in illiquid mortgage loans. Up until as recently as the late 1960s, many thrifts had difficulty selling their mortgage assets. There were two reasons for this.

First, the financial institutions' mortgage assets were not homogeneous. The portfolio of a thrift would consist of many different loans with different interest rates, dates of maturity, and loan-to-value ratios. Selling $25 or $50 million worth of loans with such different characteristics could be very difficult. Second, potential buyers were concerned with the default risk, particularly of

---

[1]Note that the process has created a series of assets and liabilities even though there is only one source (investors) and only one use (homeowners) of funds. The homeowner's asset (residence is partially offset by a liability (mortgage). The mortgage is an asset to the secondary market entity and is offset by a liability (mortgage-related security). The mortgage-related security is, in turn, an asset for the investor. There is no limit to the number of assets and liabilities that can be created in the secondary mortgage market. The investor, for example, might fund the purchase of the mortgage-related securities by issuing its own form of debt and using the mortgage-related securities as collateral. In this case, two mortgage-related securities would ultimately be backed by the mortgages.

conventional loans. Investors nationwide had little or no ability to judge the soundness of loans underwritten by a thrift.

As a result of the inability to buy and sell mortgages, a mismatch of the supply and demand for capital persisted. The mismatch took two forms. First, there was a *regional mismatch*. This occurred when capital (in the form of deposits) was in greater supply in one region, yet the demand for mortgages was greater in another region. A more stable region with moderate housing growth ended up with an excess supply of savings, whereas a rapidly growing area with significant additions to the housing stock experienced a deficiency of capital. A secondary market for mortgages resolved this mismatch by allowing thrifts in capital-surplus areas to take their excess deposits and purchase mortgages from thrifts in capital-deficit areas. Second, an *institutional mismatch* occurred in the sense that traditional mortgage lenders may have had insufficient funds to meet the mortgage demand, and other nonmortgage intermediaries may have had a need to invest funds in long-term assets. This occurred, for example, when individuals began to place more of their savings in pension funds and less in thrifts and banks. The latter have less funds with which to originate mortgages, while the former have a need to invest in long-term assets. The secondary mortgage market offered a solution by facilitating the sale of mortgages from the thrifts and banks to the pension funds.

The secondary mortgage market developed because it solved these problems. Other developments stimulated this market in the 1970s and 1980s. During this time, life insurance companies gradually reduced their presence in the mortgage market, and their correspondent mortgage bankers needed new purchasers of the loans they originated. Also, as pension funds grew, they developed a need for long-term investments. Thrifts were particularly vulnerable to interest rate risk; pension funds and long-term investors could handle this risk better. Furthermore, some secondary market firms began to purchase mortgages, either because of their risk preference or their ability to issue mortgage-related securities that matched the maturity of the mortgages they purchased. By the 1980s numerous thrifts, attempting to avoid interest rate risk, sold so many of the loans they originated that essentially they became mortgage bankers. Investors in mortgage-backed securities, however, did not wish to take on default risk. The federal government's willingness to support the secondary mortgage market through guarantees of timely and full payment contributed to its growth as well.

The federal government encouraged the development of the secondary mortgage market by overriding state laws that had hindered its development. Many state laws limited investment in mortgage-backed securities by state-regulated investors, such as life insurance companies and pension funds. Some states also had tough securities registration requirements (blue-sky laws). In 1984 Congress passed the Secondary Mortgage Market Enhancement Act (SMMEA) to overcome these obstacles. This act removed state-imposed limits on the types and quantities of mortgage-backed securities that investors could purchase. At the same time, it exempted mortgage securities from state securities registration requirements. (The charters of Freddie Mac and Fannie Mae, discussed later in this chapter, exempt them from the registration laws as well.)

At the time the act was passed, Congress gave the states the option of taking back the authority for setting limits on investments by state-regulated investors if the state legislatures voted to override SMMEA within seven years.[2]

Mortgage-Related Securities

The key to a successful secondary market for mortgages is the creation of mortgage-related securities (MRSs) that are acceptable to investors. Securities must have certain features to be acceptable: a form of **credit enhancement**, ability to avoid double taxation, and ability to tailor cash flows to investors' needs.

- *Credit enhancement.* Mortgage-related securities have less default risk than the underlying mortgages that serve as collateral. This means that if I hold a mortgage-related security I have less risk from default than if I held the mortgage pool that backs up the mortgage-related securities. Table 3-1 shows some of the methods that MRSs use to enhance credit. Private rating agencies such as Standard & Poor's, Moody's, and Duff and Phelps rate the safety of many MRSs. State law prohibits many investors, such as pension funds, from investing in securities that have less than an investment-grade rating. As a result, a strong rating will broaden the market for the MRS and make it more liquid.
- *Double taxation.* MRSs need to avoid double taxation. A secondary market entity that issues MRSs and uses the funds to purchase mortgages will have interest revenue, which it passes through to the investors in the MRSs. MRS issuers must make sure that their revenues and the cash flows to the investors are not *both* taxed—otherwise, the double taxation will offset any benefits of the arrangement.

[2]By October 1991, the deadline for the override, 21 states had voted to override the preemption from state investment laws and another 5 opted to override the preemptions on the blue-sky laws. The remaining states, about one-half, are bound by the provisions of SMMEA.

Table 3-1 Mortgage-Related Securities

	Typical Credit Enhancement	Extent to Which Cash Flows Are Rearranged
Pass-through	FHA/VA loans in pool Agency guarantee	None
Mortgage-backed bonds	Agency equity Pool insurance	Moderate
Mortgage pay-through bonds	Agency equity Pool insurance	Moderate
Collateralized mortgage obligation	Agency equity Pool insurance Letter of credit	Substantial
Debt of agency	FHA/VA loans in pool	Moderate

- *Investor-friendly cash flows.* MRSs need to tailor their cash flows to fit investors' needs. Many investors do not desire to invest in securities whose cash flows exactly replicate those of mortgages, which can contain unexpected *prepayments*. This is especially so when interest rates drop and many mortgagors refinance (prepay) their mortgage. If the cash flows from the mortgages can be rearranged in amount and timing and then distributed to the MRS investors, the market for them will be larger and more liquid.

Types of Mortgage-Related Securities

These are the three principal types of mortgage-related securities:

1. Mortgage pass-through securities
2. Mortgage-backed bonds
3. Collateralized mortgage obligations

Mortgage Pass-Through Securities

Pass-through securities were the first popular MRS. The early successful ones were promoted by the Government National Mortgage Association (GNMA), a government agency within the Department of Housing and Urban Development, (HUD) in the mid to late 1960s. With a pass-through security, investors are said to have an "undivided interest" in the pool of mortgages, that is, the investor has an "ownership" position in the mortgages. This means they will receive the mortgage payments (principal and interest) and any prepayments just as though they were the lender.

Investors are attracted to the relatively high-yield, liquidity, and risk-free quality of pass-throughs. Many, however, do not like the uncertainty of the timing of the cash flows, due to unpredictable prepayments of mortgages. Also, mortgages prepay more quickly when interest rates drop, so that the prepayments must be reinvested at lower market rates. Investors in pass-throughs face the same callability risk as mortgage lenders. For these reasons, other MRSs have been developed to avoid the uncertainty surrounding the timing of the cash flows.

SIDEBAR

Pass-Through Example

In Figure 3-1, a thrift (or other originator) groups or packages together, say, 100 fixed-rate loans of $100,000 each, all with the same maturity and contract rate of interest—assume 30 years at 10 percent. It will next issue $10 million in bonds to obtain the cash to finance the mortgages. The bonds may have a minimum denomination of $25,000. Four hundred such bonds will be backed by the pool of mortgages. The bonds promise a 9.5 percent yield. Note that the mortgage originator earns 10 percent on the mortgages and pays 9.5 percent to investors in the bonds. The originator who services the loan and the agency that provides for credit enhancement will share the difference, 0.5 percent. In the case of GNMA bonds, that agency guarantees the timely payment of interest and principal and collects a small fee. Additional enhancement is gained by the provision that the mortgages are held by a trustee. Investors are satisfied with the 9.5 percent yield because of the credit enhancement and the high yield relative to other "safe" investments.

Assume that an investor buys two bonds ($50,000). At the end of the first month, the mortgagors will remit their payments. If all do so, then the total payments on the $10 million in mortgages will be $87,756.27, of which $83,333.33 will be interest and the remainder, $4,422.94, will be principal. The investors will receive this principal (prorated) and interest at 9.5 percent, or $83,589.61 ($4,422.94 + 0.095/12 × $10,000,000). The investor holding two bonds will receive one-half of 1 percent (2/400) of this amount, or $417.95, of which $22.11 will be principal reduction. The principal balance of his two bonds at the end of the first month will be $49,977.89. The investor will receive the same amount the following month, assuming that no mortgagor in the pool decides to prepay his or her entire loan.

If during a given month one or more mortgagors repay their loans, say, because of a move to a new residence, the entire amount of the prepayment will be prorated and divided to the investors in the pass-through bonds. In that month the investors' checks will be unexpectedly large and the principal balance of the bond will be reduced more quickly than normal. Essentially, bond investors have a small section of a larger portfolio of loans and receive cash flows that replicate those of a mortgage originator that retains loans in its portfolio.

Some pass-throughs (private or non-GNMA) are rated by Standard & Poor's, Moody's, and Duff and Phelps. Those agencies evaluate the credit risk of the collateral by reviewing the types of property, their location, and loan-to-value ratios. They also rate the capability of the issuer to make cash advances to cover the principal and interest on delinquent and defaulted properties.

Some lenders have pools of mortgages that carry neither FHA/VA nor **private mortgage insurance (PMI)**. These pools are difficult to securitize into pass-throughs because of their default risk. Often the lenders do not wish to purchase pool insurance[3] but prefer instead to self-insure the loans. A pass-through structure that allows for their securitization is the **senior/subordinated pass-through**. In this arrangement, the lender creates two securities from a pool of mortgages, one having the priority of receiving payments from the pool. From a $100 million pool of mortgages, the lender may create a senior pass-through with a principal balance of $94 million. Because the $94 million pool is secured by $100 million in mortgages, it can be described as overcollateralized.

The lender will typically sell the senior security and retain the rights to the cash flows on the subordinated security (the remaining $6 million, in this example). This overcollateralization enhances the safety of the senior security and gives it investment-grade quality, because cash flows from $100 million in mortgages are available to meet the payments on only $94 million in pass-throughs. This allows a moderate number of delinquencies and defaults from the pool to occur before the payments on the senior pass-throughs are threatened. Instead of insurance or government guarantees, the overcollateralization provides the credit enhancement.

Properly constructed senior securities will receive an investment-grade rating from the rating agencies. The agencies will assign an appropriate level of subordination, considering the level of credit risk inherent in the pool. The credit risk is determined by considering the likely amount and timing of defaults, the time required to resolve defaults, and the likely recovery from foreclosures. If an investment grade is assigned, the securities will trade at prices that yield 20 to 40 basis points less than whole-loan pass-throughs (those without overcollateralization). If the pool suffers a significant number of defaults early in its life, then some payments on the senior security may be missed. Increased levels of overcollateralization, however, reduce this risk.

Mortgage-Backed Bonds

Mortgage-backed bonds (MBBs) are mortgage-related securities that promise payments similar to corporate bonds. That is, they promise semi-annual payments of interest only until maturity, with the face value due at maturity. The issuer of the bonds owns the mortgages, so the investors in the bonds have no ownership interest in the mortgages. Issuers are primarily private financial firms. MBBs are usually, but not always, backed by conventional residential and commercial mortgages. The maturity on the bonds will be less than that on the mortgages, and the yield will be slightly below that on the mortgages. Credit enhancement is accomplished through overcollateralization. This means that the face value of the pool of mortgages will be greater than that of the bonds. The issuer makes up the difference with the equity contribution.

[3] Pool insurance is private mortgage insurance on the entire pool, not the individual mortgages. Usually only a small percent—say, 10 percent—of the pool is insured.

Uncertainty surrounding the achievement of the preceding scenario is the reason for the overcollateralization. If funds are insufficient to pay off the principal on the bonds, then some of the mortgages will have to be sold. This would be true if there were fewer prepayments of mortgages than expected, if there were a large number of defaults, or if the interest rate earned on the reserve fund dropped to a low level. The mortgages are usually placed in the hands of a trustee who will mark-to-market any changes in the value of the mortgages and make sure that the agreed-on overcollateralization is maintained (125 percent, in this example). **Mark-to-market** refers to valuing the mortgages on a frequent basis as a result of the changes in interest rates. A rise in rates, for example, will cause the market value of mortgages to fall, thus endangering the value of the collateral. If the overcollateralization falls below the agreed-on limit, the trustee will require that the issuer purchase additional mortgages from its own sources and add them to the pool.

SIDEBAR

Mortgage-Backed Bonds Example

Figure 3-2 shows an example where an issuer sells $100 million in MBBs, adds an additional $25 million, and purchases $125 million in conventional mortgages. The issuer will attempt to estimate the cash flows coming in from the pool of mortgages, but there will be some uncertainty due to prepayments. Also, the maturity of the MBBs will be less than that of the mortgages, but likely longer than the average life of a mortgage. For example, the maturity on the MBBs may be 15 years and that on the mortgages 30 years. However, because of prepayments, the average life of the mortgages may be, say, 12 years. A small percentage of mortgages will last the full 30 years, of course. Finally, there is some danger that some of the mortgages may default, and if they are without FHA/VA or private mortgage insurance, the MBB issuer will sustain a loss on such loans.

If all goes well, the issuer will take the monthly interest and principal payments from the pool of mortgages and invest them in a fund that earns interest. Then, semi-annually, the issuer will remit interest payments to the bondholders from this fund. Any prepayments of mortgages are added to the fund. The fund should continue to grow since interest, principal, and prepayments from the pool of mortgages will be larger than the interest payments on the bonds. At the maturity date, the fund should be large enough to pay the face value of the bonds. Any residual will be returned to the issuer as a return on the $25 million equity investment.

Rating agencies such as Standard & Poor's, Moody's, and Duff and Phelps rate the MBBs. They consider a number of factors:

1. *The quality of the mortgages in the pool.* Mortgage quality will be affected by insurance status (FHA/VA or PMI), their loan-to-value ratios, whether they are residential or commercial, whether they are first or second mortgages, and so forth.

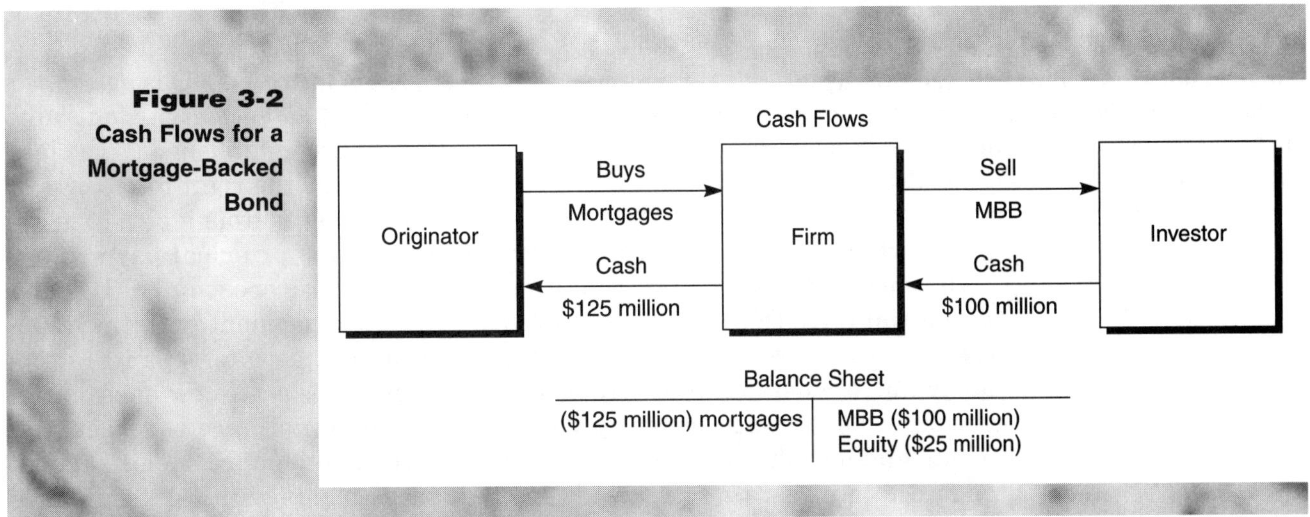

Figure 3-2 Cash Flows for a Mortgage-Backed Bond

2. *The interest rate spread between that on the mortgages and that on the MBBs.* The greater the spread, the higher the safety.
3. *The likely rate of prepayments of the mortgages.* Low-interest mortgages are less likely to prepay if interest rates have risen, for example.
4. *The geographic diversification of the mortgages in the pool.*
5. *The amount of overcollateralization.*

All of these considerations affect the rating and, therefore, the amount of overcollateralization chosen by the issuer. The extra $25 million in mortgages in our example is a buffer against the uncertainty of the rate of prepayment and the risk of default. Some issuers will enhance the credit rating of the MBBs further by providing for pool insurance or a letter of credit from a large commercial bank.

SIDEBAR

Collateralized Mortgage Obligations Example

In this example, an issuer sells $100 million in CMOs, adds $6 million of its own equity funds, and purchases $106 million of 10 percent mortgages (see Table 3-2). The CMO is overcollateralized by $6 million, or 6 percent, of the issue. The CMO has three bond-like tranches and a residual class. The Tranche A bonds earn the lowest rate, 9.25 percent. The other tranches earn somewhat more because of their longer maturity, which results from the order in which cash flows received from the mortgages are distributed to the various tranches. Tranche A bondholders are paid first. In addition to interest, Tranche A bondholders receive (1) any scheduled amortization of the mortgages, (2) any prepayments of the mortgages, and (3) deferred interest earned by the Tranche Z bondholders but transferred to the Tranche A bondholders. The principal amount of the Tranche A bonds is reduced by these three items. If there are many prepayments, the maturity of the Tranche A bonds will be shortened. For this reason, the maturity of these bonds is stated as a range of 5 to 9 years. Tranche B bondholders receive interest payments only, but no repayment or prepayment of principal until the Tranche A bondholders are completely paid. After the Tranche A holders are paid, the Tranche B holders receive all repayments and prepayments of principal, as well as interest deferred and transferred from Tranche Z. This pattern is followed for the remaining tranches. In any year, payments not given to any of the tranches result in a residual that accrues to the equity interest of the issuer.

Collateralized Mortgage Obligations

Collateralized mortgage obligations (CMOs) go the farthest in rearranging the uncertain cash flows from a pool of mortgages into those desired by investors. CMO restructuring of cash flows is the most complicated of all mortgage-related securities. The object of CMOs is to rearrange mortgage cash flows into several different bond-like securities with different maturities. The different bond classes are called **tranches**. A typical CMO will have three or four tranches. Because the cash flows from the mortgage pool are uncertain, a CMO flows residual cash flows into a tranche, which is often "owned" by the issuer of the CMO. Thus, the issuer needs to have an equity interest in the CMO. The cash flows that accrue to residual are a return on equity. The basic structure of a CMO is presented in Table 3-2.

A special form of CMO is a *stripped mortgage-backed security*. Generally, two classes are established. One class of investors has the right to receive all interest payments from a pool of mortgages, while the other has the right to receive all the principal payments—both scheduled amortization and prepayments. The **interest-only (IO)** and **principal-only (PO)** securities have some peculiar payment patterns, especially when interest rates are volatile. For example, as interest rates drop, many homeowners refinance their existing mortgages with new ones, extinguishing the existing mortgage. The holder of the PO will receive larger payments and a swifter reduction in his or her principal balance. He or she will be forced to invest these proceeds in other investments with a lower rate of

Table 3-2 Structure of a Collateralized Mortgage Obligation

Assets	Liabilities	Maturity (years)	Coupon (%)	Amount
Mortgages $106,000,000	Tranche A	5-9	9.25	$ 30,000,000
Yield 10%	Tranche B	9-14	9.50	30,000,000
	Tranche C	12-17	10.00	25,000,000
	Tranche Z	28-30	10.50	15,000,000
	Equity			6,000,000
Total				$106,000,000

return (remember, interest rates have fallen). The holder of the IO, meanwhile, will see his or her payments (on the terminated mortgages) stop entirely.

Tax and Accounting Issues of Mortgage-Related Securities

Secondary mortgage market agencies and firms that issue MRSs backed by pools of loans have always wrestled with the issue of double taxation. Essentially, cash flows from the mortgages to the agency or firm and then to the investors. If the cash flows are taxable when received by the agency, and then again by the investors, the tax burden would be so great as to eliminate the advantages of securitization of mortgages. Avoidance of the double taxation was accomplished in the early years by the creation of a **grantor trust** to own the mortgages. The grantor trust worked especially well for pass-through securities. If the provisions of a qualified grantor trust are met, then the trust is not taxed, only the investor in the pass-through. To qualify, a grantor trust must (1) have a limited life, (2) be self-liquidating (no assets remain after investors are paid off), and (3) require no active management of the assets after they are placed in trust. One can see why a pass-through easily fits these requirements.

When CMOs were developed to meet the cash flow demands of investors, tax and accounting problems developed. Many CMO issuers transferred (sold) the underlying loans to a trust in order to gain the favorable tax treatment and also to remove the loans from their balance sheet (as was the case with pass-throughs). Many thrifts, and certainly mortgage bankers, did not want to carry the loans as assets and MRSs as liabilities on their balance sheets (however, some originators did want to treat CMOs as a financing). Transfer to a trust appeared to solve both problems.

The Internal Revenue Service and the accounting profession complicated this arrangement, however. In March 1985, the **Financial Accounting Standards Board** ruled that an issuer must treat a CMO as a financing (debt), even when the loans are transferred to a trust, if the issuer holds more than a "nominal" residual interest in the collateral. But requirements by the rating agencies for overcollateralization create residual interests that are not nominal. In addition, the size of the residual may increase if prepayments are slower than expected or if reinvestment income exceeds expectations. Some CMO issuers responded by creating a second trust to own the residuals (an owner's trust). Investors could purchase certificates of beneficial interest in that trust.

But this did not solve the tax problem. The IRS ruled that CMOs using the trust arrangement were similar to a corporation retaining control and having an equity interest (the residual). The trust arrangement also required active management, because the cash flows not currently distributed to security holders had to be reinvested for later delivery. A few originators who did not mind avoiding the trust arrangement carried the mortgages as assets and the CMOs as debt. For them, the problems were not as severe. The residual interest meant that they could not borrow against the full amount of the debt, however.

Because of these problems, secondary mortgage market participants urged Congress to consider remedial legislation. It came as part of the Tax Reform Act of 1986. The legislation established the **real estate mortgage investment conduit (REMIC)** as an entity that could issue CMOs and not be subject to double taxation. A partnership, trust, or other corporation may elect REMIC status and maintain separate records relative to the mortgage pool and management of the funds related to the pool. For tax purposes, income is recorded as received from the pool of mortgages and deductions are allowed for interest paid (on the CMO tranches) to investors and for other pool-related expenses. The net income can then be passed through to the owner of the residual (usually the CMO issuer) as income or loss.

An agency, trust, or firm retains this favorable tax status as long as it does not engage in any prohibited transactions, including (1) receiving income from any asset that is not a "qualified mortgage," (2) receiving fees or compensation for services (other than servicing income from the mortgage portfolio), or (3) buying or selling mortgages out of the pool (except as the pool is liquidated if all proceeds are disbursed within 90 days).

If desired, the user of a REMIC can avoid reporting the mortgages as assets and the CMOs as liabilities; the REMIC is a stand-alone activity. The issuer will report a gain or loss on the "sale" of the mortgages into the REMIC trust, however. If the issuer wants to avoid a loss on the "sale," it will simply report the residual interest owned in the REMIC as an asset. Figure 3-3 shows how REMIC transactions work.

Secondary Mortgage Market Agencies and Firms

Several agencies issue mortgage-related securities or have done so in the past. These agencies include the following:

1. Federal National Mortgage Association (FNMA, Fannie Mae)
2. Government National Mortgage Association (GNMA, Ginnie Mae)
3. Federal Home Loan Mortgage Corporation (FHLMC, Freddie Mac)
4. Federal credit agencies
5. State and local credit agencies
6. Private firms

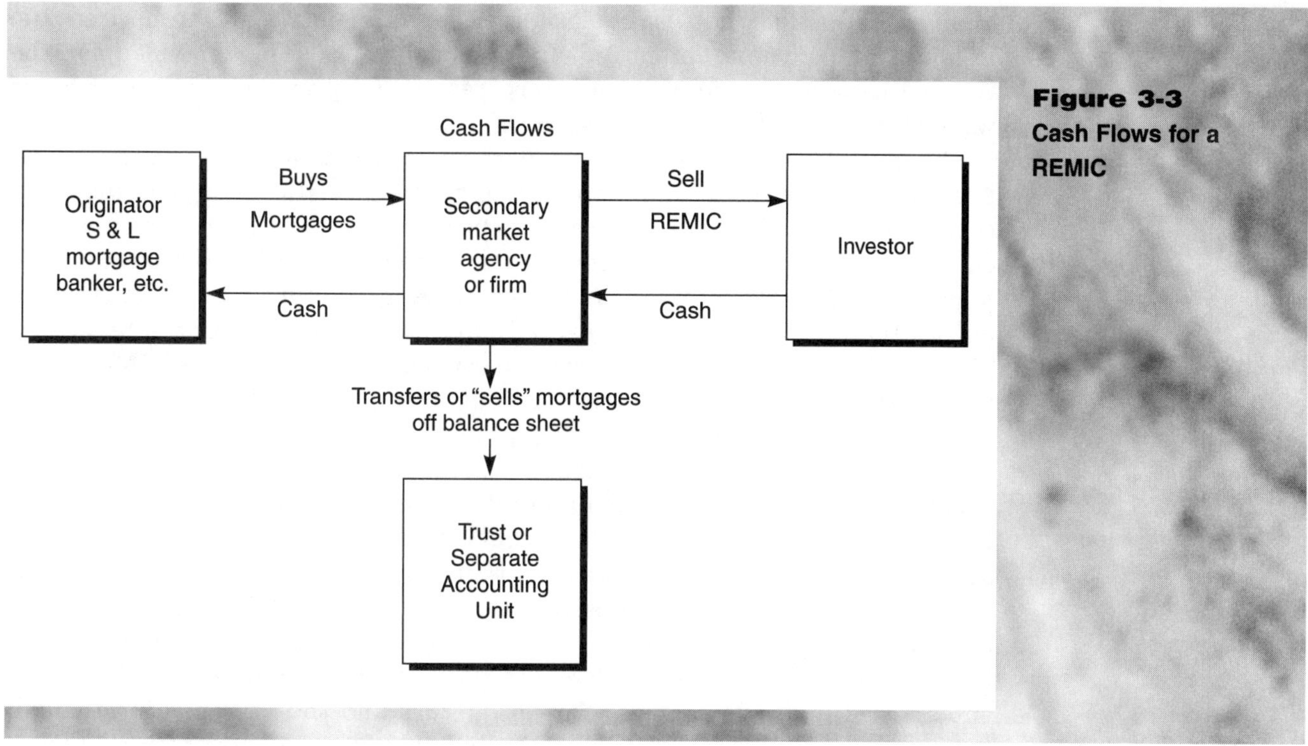

Figure 3-3
Cash Flows for a REMIC

Federal National Mortgage Association

Congress established the **Federal National Mortgage Association (FNMA** or "Fannie Mae") in 1938 as a subsidiary of the Reconstruction Finance Corporation (RFC). The main purpose was to form secondary market support for Federal Housing Administration (FHA) and, later, Veterans Administration (VA) loans. Up until the 1980s, the FHA and VA set a limit on the rate of interest lenders could charge on these loans in attempts to keep housing affordable. As interest rates rose, lenders were reluctant to originate FHA and VA loans because they would have to charge high points. Additionally, the value of existing loans declined with rising rates. Fannie Mae's purpose was to stand ready to purchase these loans at face value from originators. This would replenish their funds for new originations. Even though the loans' values were less than face value, Fannie Mae hoped to sell them back later at face value or at a gain when interest rates dropped. In a sense, Fannie Mae's purpose was to ride the interest rate cycle and take on interest rate risk. Fannie Mae obtained the funds to purchase mortgages by issuing long-term bonds. However, it faced substantial interest rate risk and in the early days relied on the Treasury to cover losses.

In 1950 the agency was transferred to the Housing and Home Finance Agency (an agency that was created in 1942 and later made part of HUD). Its life there was short; it was rechartered and became a separate agency in 1954. The recharter assigned three tasks to Fannie Mae: (1) continued enhancement of the secondary mortgage market for FHA and VA loans, (2) liquidation of properties and mortgages acquired by default, and (3) management of a subsidized loan program. The recharter also contained a provision that transformed

Fannie Mae into what is essentially a private entity—it authorized the issuance of nonvoting preferred and common stock. This provided for the restructuring of Fannie Mae as a corporation and provided additional funds with which it could purchase mortgages.

Fannie Mae supports the secondary mortgage market by issuing mortgage-related securities and purchasing mortgages. Its credit enhancement comes from the ability of Fannie Mae to borrow from the U.S. Treasury, and its equity results from the sale of common and preferred stock. Originally, Fannie Mae was authorized to purchase FHA and VA loans, but in 1970 Congress, in an act that established the Federal Home Loan Mortgage Corporation (see below), allowed the agency to purchase conventional loans. Fannie Mae holds most of these loans in its own portfolio but occasionally sells some of its inventory to control its interest rate risk exposure.

In the 1970s Fannie Mae issued mostly short-term debt, so it faced the same sort of maturity mismatch and interest rate risk problem as thrifts did. It was, essentially, a large thrift with liability obligations that matured within short periods of time and with assets that matured only after extended periods. When market interest rates rise, this structure (maturity mismatch) can be dangerous. The institution must make higher interest payments on its liabilities that are maturing and being renewed at the higher rate while its revenue is tied to assets that have yet to mature and thus are making the old, lower rate. In 1981 its portfolio of $61.4 billion dollars in long-term mortgages was financed partially by $21.2 billion dollars in short-term debt. The amount of liquidating assets within one year was $3.6 billion, which produced a one year maturity gap of $17.6 billion. This gap represented 29 percent of the agency's assets.

During the mid-1980s FNMA reduced its interest rate risk by issuing pass-throughs and collateralized mortgage obligations and by purchasing adjustable-rate mortgages. By the end of 1988, the liquidating assets and maturing liabilities within one year were equal ($36 billion each), so that the one-year maturity gap was zero. Since that time, the agency has had a more balanced portfolio of assets and liabilities. Table 3-3 shows the recent activity of FNMA.

Fannie Mae held about $415 billion in mortgages in its own portfolio at the end of 1998. The portfolio was financed with $205.4 billion in short-term debt and $254.9 billion in long-term debt. Fannie Mae made nearly $30 billion in interest income and expended $25.9 billion in interest expense in 1998 leaving net interest income of slightly over $4.1 billion. After accounting for other income and expenses Fannie Mae had net income after taxes of $3.446 billion in that year.

Government National Mortgage Association

In 1968 Congress passed the Housing and Urban Development Act. Among other things the act established the **Government National Mortgage Association** (**GNMA** or "Ginnie Mae") and placed it in the newly formed Department of HUD. Ginnie Mae relieved FNMA of two functions: the management and liquidation of previously originated (FNMA) mortgages and the loan subsidization program. Under the latter program, termed the special assistance function (SAF), Ginnie Mae subsidizes the cost of housing for low-income families.

Table 3-3
Federal National Mortgage Association Financial Activity for Year Ending 1998 (in Millions of Dollars)

Part A: Balance Sheet	
Assets	
Mortgage Portfolio	$415,223
Other Assets	69,791
Total Assets	485,014
Liabilities	
Debentures, Notes, Bonds	
Payable in One Year	205,413
Payable after One Year	254,878
Total	460,291
Other Liabilities	4,008
Total Liabilities	469,561
Equity	15,453
Part B: Income Statement	
Interest Income	$ 29,995
Interest Expense	25,885
Net Interest Income	4,110
Guarantee Fees	1,229
Miscellaneous Income	275
Administrative Expense	(708)
Provision for Losses and Foreclosed Property Expense	(311)
Other Expense	(50)
Net Income Before Tax	4,645
Taxes	(1,201)
Net Income	3,446

A typical arrangement, called a *tandem plan*, authorizes Ginnie Mae to make low-interest loans to qualified families. Ginnie Mae then sells the loans at a discount to Fannie Mae. The discount allows FNMA to earn a market yield. Ginnie Mae absorbs the loss—the difference between the amount of the loan originated and the discounted price received from FNMA. This is Ginnie Mae's only primary market activity. These two functions were never a large part of Ginnie Mae's operations, however. Rather, the agency has an important third function: support of the secondary mortgage market.

Ginnie Mae's secondary mortgage market operations support the FHA and VA (and, to a small extent, the Farmers Home Administration) loan market by guaranteeing pass-through securities. Credit enhancement on the pass-throughs comes from two sources: underlying loans guaranteed against default by the FHA and the VA and the Ginnie Mae guarantee of timely payment of interest and principal. So, even if there is a default on some of the loans in the pool, the pass-through investors will not have to wait until a claim is made to the FHA or the VA in order to obtain payment. The originator of the mortgages is required to make monthly payments to the investors in the pass-throughs and then seek reimbursement from the FHA, VA, or Farmer's Home Administration

(FmHA). If the originator cannot make the payment, Ginnie Mae will.[4] In 1998 Ginnie Mae had revenue in the form of guaranteed fees of $355.3 million. In that year it paid out $7.6 million in default expenses—which shows how profitable the guarantee can be for Ginnie Mae.

Ginnie Mae itself neither purchases mortgages nor issues securities. A balance sheet of Ginnie Mae would show that for its pass-through activity it holds no mortgages and issues no debt. The agency's activities can be understood by considering its early operations in support of the FHA and VA loan market. Later modifications in operations have been minor. Figure 3-4 shows a typical early Ginnie Mae arrangement as a process in stages.

In stage 1, a mortgage originator, say, a mortgage banker, obtains a line of credit from a commercial bank with which to make mortgage loans. As the loans are made, the line of credit is taken down and the loans are pledged as collateral for take-down. This is termed *warehousing*. In this fashion, the originator accumulates a pool of mortgages, say, $100 million in total value. All mortgages must have the same maturity (within a year) and the same rate of interest, and be guaranteed by either the FHA, VA, or FmHA. Next, the originator will request that the pool be qualified for a pass-through security to be issued. Ginnie Mae will qualify the pool if it meets the restrictions mentioned, as well as some other minor conditions. The originator must pay a nonrefundable fee ($500 on the first $1.5 million and $200 for each additional million in the pool) with its request for qualification.

In stage 2, the originator issues the pass-through securities, which are sold through securities dealers and investment banking firms.[5] Buyers include banks, thrifts, pension funds, life insurance companies, and individual investors. The originator pays off the line of credit with the funds obtained from the sale of the securities. The mortgages are then transferred to a trustee who makes sure that the pass-through investors are paid in the event that the mortgage is prepaid.

In stage 3, principal and interest payments are made to the investor. The principal of the investor's security is reduced by the amount of the scheduled amortization and any prepayments. The pass-through will bear a rate of interest that is 0.5 percent less than that on the mortgages. If the rate on the mortgages is 10 percent, then that on the pass-through will be 9.5 percent. The difference is split between the originator (44 basis points) for servicing the loans and Ginnie Mae (6 basis points) for its guarantee of timely payments. Ginnie Mae uses these funds to make payments (on defaulted loans) to the pass-through investors in the event the originator cannot.

In 1983, Ginnie Mae loosened the provision that all mortgages in a pool had to have the same interest rate. Under the Ginnie Mae II program, loans can be mixed as long as the difference in rates among the mortgages is no greater than 1 percent. The program also allows seasoned or existing mortgages to be included in the pool.

---

[4] In the early years of operation, GNMA had two programs: a straight pass-through, which provided for the payment of interest and principal only if paid by the mortgagors; and a partially modified pass-through, which provided for interest payment (but not principal) whether or not collected. Recent GNMA programs are all fully modified pass-throughs that pay interest and principal whether or not collected.

[5] They were sold through an organization called the Ginnie Mae Dealers Association that was merged into the Public Securities Association (PSA) in 1982.

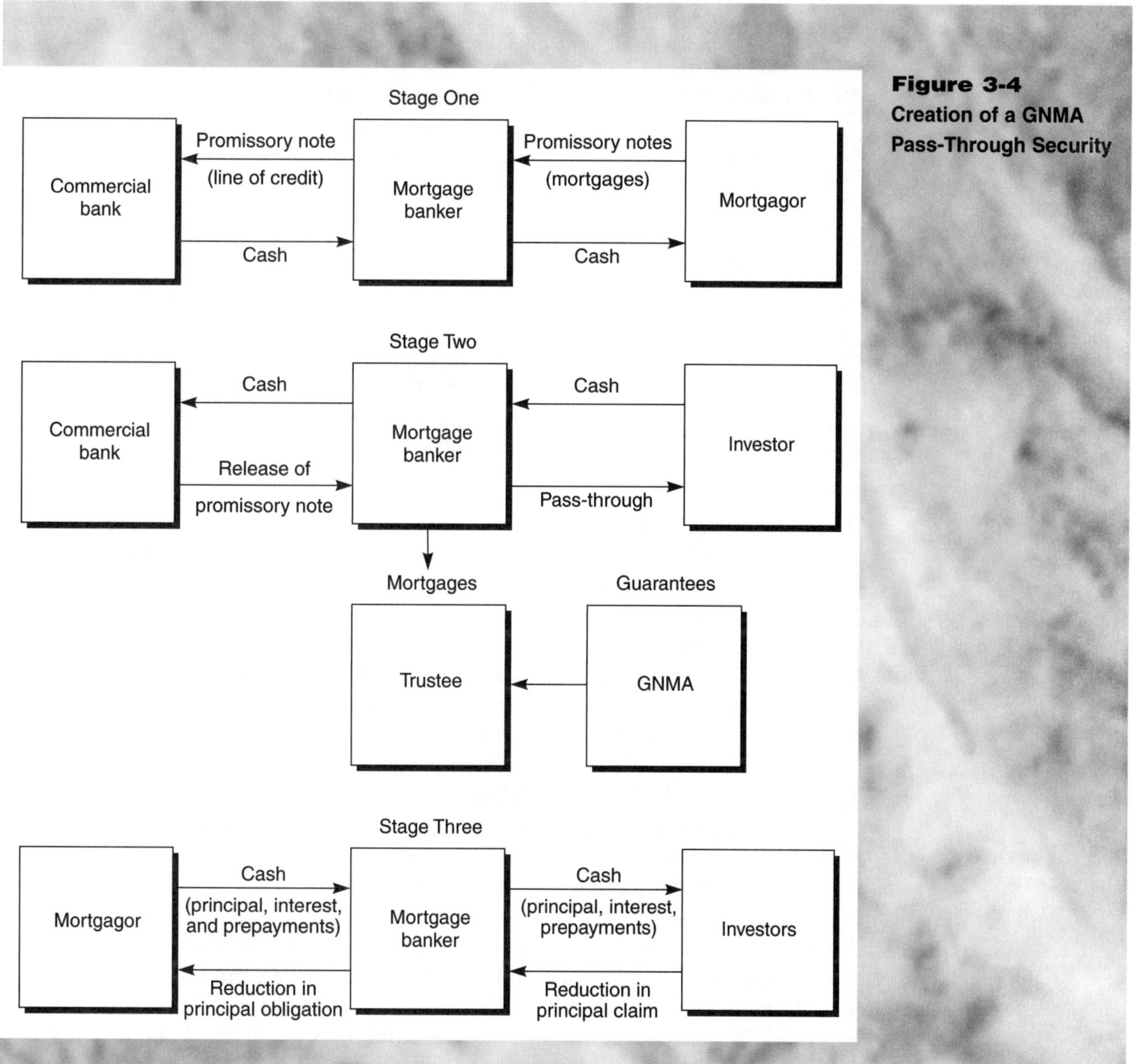

Figure 3-4
Creation of a GNMA Pass-Through Security

Table 3-4 shows the recent activity of the GNMA. In 1996 GNMA issued $105.3 billion in securities. This brought the total cumulative amount of issues to $1.207 trillion dollars. After accounting for repayments the total amount of GNMA securities left outstanding at the end of 1996 was $506.2 billion.

Federal Home Loan Mortgage Corporation

In 1970 mortgage-backed securities backed by pools of FHA- and VA-insured loans were well established. However, 65 percent of all one to four-family mortgages originated in that year were *conventional*. Furthermore, thrifts made most of the loans in the conventional market, and 70 percent of the loans they originated were conventional. Mortgage bankers, on the other hand, made most of the loans in the FHA/VA market, and 94 percent of their loans were FHA/VA.

Table 3-4 Ginnie Mae Securities Activities (in Billions of Dollars)

Year	New Securities Issued	Cumulative Issuance	Securities Outstanding
1986	$101.3	$ 368.0	$212.1
1987	94.9	462.9	317.6
1988	55.3	518.2	340.5
1989	57.3	575.5	369.8
1990	64.4	639.9	403.6
1991	62.8	702.3	425.3
1992	81.9	784.1	419.5
1993	138.1	922.1	417.7
1994	111.3	1,036.5	451.5
1995	72.9	1,106.1	472.3
1996	105.3	1,027.0	506.2

Thus, up to 1970, the government support of the secondary mortgage market aided the FHA/VA sector and mortgage bankers. In 1970, conventional lenders and thrifts were experiencing interest rate risk and their need for government support became obvious.

In 1970 Congress passed the Emergency Home Finance Act. Title III of this act chartered the **Federal Home Loan Mortgage Corporation** (**FHLMC** or "Freddie Mac"). The act authorized Freddie Mac, the corporation, to purchase both conventional and FHA/VA loans. It also authorized the purchase of conventional loans by Fannie Mae. As a result, the two agencies could purchase both FHA/VA and conventional loans. To date, Freddie Mac has specialized in conventional mortgages and Fannie Mae in FHA/VA mortgages. Freddie Mac's initial capital came from the sale of $100 million in nonvoting common stock that was sold to the 12 district Federal Home Loan Banks. It also issued 15 million shares of preferred stock at the end of 1984 to the Federal Home Loan Banks who, in turn, issued them to their members, the thrifts. This issuance was part of the effort to help troubled thrifts survive in the mid-1980s. Freddie Mac stock is traded on the New York Stock Exchange.

Freddie Mac obtains its funds by issuing a wide variety of debt and mortgage-related securities, including the following:

- *Discount notes and debentures.* Freddie Mac issues debentures in minimum denominations of $10,000 and increments of $5,000. It also issues discount notes (maturity of one year or less) with a minimum denomination of $25,000 and increments of $1.
- *Mortgage participation certificates.* The Freddie Mac **participation certificate (PC)** is the corporation's pass-through security. First sold in 1971, pools now consist of conventional fixed-rate, 30-year mortgages, 15-year mortgages, adjustable-rate mortgages, and multifamily mortgages. The corporation guarantees the timely payment of interest and principal.
- *Collateralized mortgage obligations.* First issued in 1983, Freddie Mac CMOs are available in several classes with varying stated maturities. Semi-annual principal payments are allocated to each class of the CMO in the order of the stated maturity. No principal is paid to an investor in a class until earlier

maturity classes are retired. Holders of each class of CMOs receive semi-annual interest payments on the unpaid principal balance of their bonds at the coupon rate for the class. Interest on the accrual class is paid out only upon the full payment of all other classes of bonds. Although they are the general obligation of Freddie Mac, each CMO is backed by its own pool of mortgages, which is owned by, and held in, its own portfolio.

- *Guaranteed mortgage certificates.* Issued early on, **guaranteed mortgage certificates (GMCs)** have not been sold directly by Freddie Mac since 1979. They represent an undivided interest in a pool of mortgages owned by Freddie Mac. The certificates pay a guaranteed minimum principal annually and interest semi-annually.

Table 3-5 shows the recent activity of the Federal Home Loan Mortgage Corporation. The bulk of the mortgages that are purchased by Freddie Mac are pooled and "sold" (held in trust) as backing for PCs, the agency's pass-through security. This is termed their "sold" portfolio, and the values of the securities or the underlying mortgages do not appear on the balance sheet. As of the end of 1998, Freddie Mac had $646,459,000,000 in PCs, backed by the same amount of mortgages.

Federal Credit Agencies

Several **federal credit agencies** support, in part, the primary and secondary mortgage market, as discussed in the following subsections.

Farm Credit System

In 1987 Congress passed the Agricultural Credit Act to consolidate and coordinate the activities of three agriculturally related systems: the Federal Land Banks, the Federal Intermediate Credit Banks, and the Banks for Cooperatives. The first two were merged into a system of 37 farm credit banks and the latter renamed the Federal Credit Banks. The farm credit system is divided into 12 farm credit districts. The farm credit banks make direct loans for agricultural purposes, including the purchase of rural homes. The banks obtain their funds by issuing securities through the Credit Banks Funding Corporation located in New York City. The securities are called Farm Credit Systemwide Obligations and consist of both discount notes and long-term bonds.

Farm Credit Assistance Financial Corporation

This agency was approved pursuant to the Agricultural Credit Act in early 1988. Its purpose was to provide capital to farm credit banks that were experiencing financial difficulty. It was authorized to issue up to $2.8 billion of uncollateralized debt guaranteed by the U.S. Treasury. The guaranteed debt securities have maturities of 15 years and may be issued no later than September 1992.

Federal Agricultural Mortgage Corporation

The **Federal Agricultural Mortgage Corporation** (**FAMC** or "Farmer Mac") is the third creation of the Agricultural Credit Act, the FAMC was intended to act similarly to GNMA and FNMA, but for farm mortgages. This institution, housed in the Farm Credit System, examines pools of farm mortgages, places a guarantee on the timely payment of principal and interest, and permits underwriters to sell pass-throughs in the secondary market. Unlike the

Table 3-5
Federal Home Loan Mortgage Corporation Financial Activity (in millions) 1999

Part A: Balance Sheet	
Interest Earning Assets	
Mortgage	$ 54,577
Guaranteed Mortgage Securities, net	239,285
Total Retained Portfolio	293,862
Cash and Investments	53,085
Reverse Repurchases	5,182
Total Interest Earning	352,129
Other	6,359
Total	358,488
Interest Bearing Liabilities	
Debt Securities	
Short Term	44,516
Long Term	283,900
Subordinated Borrowings	147
Other	9,299
Total Interest Bearing	337,862
Other	9,501
Stockholder's Equity	11,125
Total	358,488
Part B: Components of Revenue	
Net Interest Income on Earning Assets	2,540
Management and Guarantee Income	1,405
Other Income	110
Total Revenue	4,055
Credit-related Expenses	159
Administrative Expenses	655
Housing Tax Credit Partnerships	80
Total Non-Interest Expense	894
Net Income	2,223
Earnings Per Share	2.97
Return on Common Equity	25.5%

full guarantee of timely payments granted by GNMA, FAMC guarantees the timely payment of 90 percent of the principal and interest payments. Credit enhancement (funds to allow the guarantee of payments) comes from three sources: (1) a $1.5 billion line of credit from the Treasury; (2) $20 million in equity raised by selling stock to banks, insurance companies, and farm system institutions: and (3) the fees the agency charges for the guarantee. FAMC charges 50 basis points plus an annual fee of one-half of 1 percent of the outstanding pool balance.

Farmers Home Administration

The **Farmers Home Administration (FMHA)**, housed in the Department of Agriculture, extends loans to rural areas for farms, houses, and community facilities. Until 1975 the agency raised some funds through the sale of certificates of beneficial ownership (CBOs). Current sources of funds include a line of credit with the Treasury and the sale of its loans to the private sector or to trusts, which in turn create pass-through securities. The direct loans made by FmHA are restricted to areas with a population of less than 10,000 and to low- and moderate-income families. Maximum income limits (adjusted family income) are set and vary by section of the country and size of the family. The loans made by the agency are typically below-market-rate loans. They are sold at a discount, with the agency bearing the loss.

Financing Corporation

The Federal Home Loan Bank Board chartered the Financing Corporation (FICO) in 1987, pursuant to the Competitive Equality Banking Act of the same year. It was formed to help solve the deepening crisis of widespread insolvency among thrifts. The purpose of FICO was to recapitalize the Federal Savings and Loan Insurance Corporation (FSLIC) [later replaced by the Savings Association Insurance Fund (SAIF)], which was in danger of insolvency itself as a result of the costly resolutions of many failed thrifts. FICO was authorized to issue $3 billion in nonvoting capital stock and up to $10.825 billion (no more than $3.75 billion in any one year) in debt securities. The proceeds are to be transferred to the FSLIC for use in resolving problems with failed thrifts. The bonds are not guaranteed by either the U.S. government or the FSLIC. Since 1989 the annual level of debt for this agency has been $8.17 billion.

Federal Financing Bank

The **Federal Financing Bank (FFB)** bank was established by the Federal Financing Bank Act of 1973 to consolidate and reduce the government's cost of financing a variety of federal agencies and other borrowers whose obligations are guaranteed by the federal government. The bank issues debt to obtain funds with which to purchase the obligations of two dozen or so federal agencies. Most of the mortgage- and housing-related agency obligations are excluded. Examples of agencies whose obligations are purchased include the TVA, REA, NASA, SBA, postal service, and many others. Two housing-related obligations that the bank can purchase are those issued by HUD to support Section 108 guaranteed loans and low-rent public housing. In 1993 the bank had $127.3 billion in debt outstanding.

State and Local Credit Agencies

State housing finance agencies (HFAs) fund FHA-insured and VA-guaranteed loans that are packaged into securities guaranteed by GNMA. They also participate in affordable housing initiatives offered by Freddie Mac and Fannie Mae. In 1989, HFAs originated approximately $9 billion in collateralized mortgage obligations through the secondary mortgage market.

Private Firms

Numerous private firms have entered the secondary mortgage market. Once the government agencies demonstrated the need for the market and Congress passed enabling legislation, many private firms saw a profit in securitizing mortgages. The private companies do everything that the government-related agencies do. They both purchase mortgages for securitization and create mortgage-backed securities. Credit enhancement comes from pool insurance or overcollateralization or both. The mortgage-related securities that they issue are rated by the rating agencies. Many of the private firms specialize in loans that the government agencies either cannot or do not wish to securitize, such as nonconforming and jumbo loans. Some large thrifts or other financial institutions create subsidiaries to carry on the specialized function of mortgage securitization. More recently, several large investment bankers such as First Boston Corporation and Salomon Brothers have been active in issuing CMOs and REMICs.

Secondary Mortgage Market Activity

Table 3-6 shows the trading volume in mortgage securities from 1990 through 1998. Transactions refer to purchases and sales of mortgage-backed securities. The transaction turnover ratio is the ratio of mortgage-backed security transactions to outstanding Freddie Mac, Fannie Mae, and Ginnie Mae securities. For example, a typical security traded 8.4 times in 1998 as compared to only 5.2 times in 1990. In 1998, $15.803 trillion in securities were transacted.

Table 3-7 shows the securitized mortgage debt outstanding in 1990 and 1998. Securitized mortgage debt refers to mortgages that have been sold to the secondary mortgage market and financed by the issuance of a mortgage-related security. In 1998, 89 percent of all outstanding FHA/VA/RHS mortgages had been securitized, where RHS stands for the Rural Housing Service.

Table 3-8 shows the single-class mortgage security issuance by the three federal secondary mortgage market agencies. Single-class securities are passthroughs and mortgage-backed bonds. As an example, in 1998, Freddie Mac

Table 3-6
Mortgage Security Trading Volume Amounts (in Billions of Dollars)

Year	Transactions	Transaction Turnover Ratio
1990	$ 4,992	5.2
1991	6,206	5.6
1992	8,727	7.1
1993	11,758	8.9
1994	10,531	7.3
1995	7,477	4.9
1996	9,609	5.8
1997	12,130	6.8
1998	15,803	8.4

Source: Federal Home Loan Mortgage Corporation

Table 3-7 Securitized Mortgage Debt Outstanding Amounts (in Billions of Dollars)

	Total Mortgage Debt Outstanding	GSE Securitized	Private Label Securitized	Percent Securitized
1990				
Single family				
Conventional	$2,185	$715	$55	35%
FHA/VA/RHS	489	429	0	88
Total	2,674	1,144	55	45
Multifamily				
Conventional	230	26	1	12
FHA/RHS	57	31	0	55
Total	287	57	1	20
1998				
Single family				
Conventional	3,565	1,526	364	53
FHA/VA/RHS	630	564	0	89
Total	4,196	2,090	364	59
Multifamily				
Conventional	264	39	38	29
FHA/VA	63	32	0	51
Total	327	71	38	33

Source: Federal Home Loan Mortgage Corporation

issued $250.6 billion in single-class securities backed up by $242.4 billion in conventional fixed rate mortgages, $7.2 billion in conventional adjustable rate mortgages, $97 million in FHA and VA single-family mortgages, and $937 million in multifamily mortgages.

Table 3-9 shows the same information as Table 3-8 except for the issuance of multiclass securities. Multiclass securities are CMOs and REMICs. In 1998, Freddie Mac issued $135.2 billion in multiclass securities.

Taken together, the tables indicate the extent to which the secondary mortgage market, especially the three federal agencies, has grown in importance. This market is so large that virtually every residential mortgage originated (except for those on very expensive properties) is designed to be sold in the secondary mortgage market. That is, residential mortgages are designed to conform to the requirements of the three federal agencies. For that reason they are referred to as **conforming mortgages.**

Regulation of Government Sponsored Enterprises

Government-sponsored enterprises (GSE) is a term used to describe FNMA and FHLMC. These agencies are not official departments or branches of the U.S. government. Yet they were originated through federal legislation,

Table 3-8 Single-Class Mortgage Security Issuance (in Millions of Dollars)

	Conventional Fixed rate, SF	Conventional ARMS, SF	FHA/VA SF	Multi-Family	Total
Freddie Mac					
1990	$ 55,398	$16,194	$ 406	$ 1,817	$ 73,815
1991	84,622	7,574	144	0	92,340
1992	163,960	15,181	61	5	179,207
1993	187,876	20,052	20	0	207,948
1994	100,297	16,591	14	209	117,111
1995	71,253	14,267	2	355	85,877
1996	112,433	6,446	53	770	119,702
1997	104,733	8,990	35	500	114,258
1998	242,378	7,152	97	937	250,564
Fannie Mae					
1990	$ 84,171	$11,703	$ 132	$ 689	$ 96,695
1991	97,919	12,411	1,158	1,415	112,903
1992	180,766	12,108	303	850	194,027
1993	205,920	14,300	265	959	221,444
1994	112,879	15,305	201	2,237	130,622
1995	86,834	18,807	630	4,187	110,458
1996	128,393	15,273	535	5,668	149,869
1997	122,110	20,834	671	5,814	149,429
1998	297,754	14,008	3,358	11,028	326,148
	FHA & VA Fixed Rate, SF	**FHA ARMS, SF**	**Mobile Homes**	**FHA Multifamily**	**Total**
Ginnie Mae					
1990	$ 61,781	$ 716	$ 598	$ 1,300	$ 64,395
1991	57,477	3,516	653	984	62,630
1992	69,371	11,211	434	901	81,917
1993	115,299	20,208	454	2,028	137,989
1994	115,383	28,798	139	1,944	146,264
1995	47,883	22,712	86	2,084	72,765
1996	75,533	22,963	56	2,363	100,915
1997	70,705	30,933	28	2,481	104,147
1998	137,047	10,030	3	3,125	150,205

Source: Federal Home Loan Mortgage Corporation

and in the eyes of the investing public appear to enjoy the backing of the federal government. In fact, while the federal government does not guarantee the obligations of these two GSEs, Congress has expressed the feeling that in the event of default, they may be required to expend federal dollars to pay off investors who may have purchased their obligations. Because of this perceived obligation, there has been a recent move in Congress to pass legislation requiring some sort of federal regulation of the GSEs. The regulation would address the risk that the agencies face and would focus on the amount of capital they have.

These two agencies operate in ways similar to, but not exactly as, thrifts. They issue debt to purchase long-term mortgages. Some of the debt is short

Table 3-9
Multiclass Mortgage Security Insurance (in Millions of Dollars)

	Freddie Mac	Fannie Mae	Ginnie Mae
1990	$ 40,479	$ 60,917	$ 0
1991	72,032	101,805	0
1992	131,284	154,781	0
1993	143,336	167,992	0
1994	73,131	56,316	3,111
1995	15,372	8,191	2,226
1996	34,145	26,559	7,863
1997	84,366	74,812	8,415
1998	135,162	76,332	13,099

Source: Federal Home Loan Mortgage Corporation

term. Thus, the agencies face interest rate risk. In addition, any uninsured mortgages held by the agencies would pose a threat of default risk. Finally, the GSEs also face management and operating risk if the management of the GSEs fails to operate them efficiently.

In 1992 Congress passed the Federal Housing Enterprise Financial Safety and Soundness Act. This act set capital guidelines for Fannie Mae and Freddie Mac and, to monitor those guidelines, established the Office of Secondary Market Examination and Oversight (OSMEO) within the Department of Housing and Urban Development. The act sets two levels of capital guidelines, minimum and critical. In addition, it authorizes the Director of OSMEO to establish a third, and more rigorous, risk-based guideline. Under this guideline the director will simulate a 10-year "stress" period (high default rates) that includes large movements of interest rates. The capital sufficient to meet the default risk during this stress period establishes this guideline.

While the director establishes the risk-based guideline, the act sets the minimum and critical guidelines. The minimum capital is equal to 2.5 percent of the aggregate on-balance sheets assets plus 0.45 percent of the unpaid principal balance of mortgage-backed securities plus 0.45 percent of the off-balance sheet obligations of the enterprise. The critical capital level is established at 1.25, 0.25, and 0.25 percent of the same items. An enterprise is deemed adequately capitalized if its capital exceeds the rigorous risk-based capital guideline. It is deemed undercapitalized if its capital is less than the risk-based but greater than the minimum. It is considered significantly undercapitalized if its capital is less than the minimum but above the critical guideline. Finally, an enterprise is considered critically undercapitalized if its capital is less than the critical guideline. In the latter case, it must submit a capital restoration plan and can be placed into conservatorship. In addition, the director of OSMEO can limit the growth and activities of the enterprise.

In short, because the GSEs enjoy the apparent support and backing of the federal government, they are likely to be regulated just as thrifts and commercial banks are.

Summary

The secondary mortgage market is one in which existing mortgages are bought and sold. Purchased mortgages are "repackaged" and their cash flows converted into various types of mortgage-related securities, such as mortgage-backed bonds and collateralized mortgage obligations. These mortgage-related securities are also bought and sold in the secondary mortgage market. The secondary market exists to facilitate the flow of funds from areas or institutions with a surplus to areas or institutions with a deficit. The flow is facilitated by the creation of liquid, default-free, mortgage-related securities. The secondary market also allows originators of mortgages to shift interest rate risk to investors who are in a better position to handle the risks. Players that facilitate transactions in the secondary market include government agencies, such as the Government National Mortgage Association and the Federal National Mortgage Association, as well as private firms, such as First Boston or Salomon Brothers. These agencies and firms specialize in rearranging the cash flows from pools of mortgages into debt instruments that appeal to investors.

The federal government has actively supported the secondary mortgage market by its guarantee of some bonds (GNMA), its line of credit from the Treasury (FNMA), and legislation that facilitates the formation of conduits (REMICs) that have favorable tax rules. The secondary mortgage market has been so successful in meeting the needs of its participants that by 1998, 59 percent of all single-family residential mortgage debt has been securitized.

Because two agencies, FNMA and FHLMC, were established by federal legislation and enjoy the perception of federal backing, legislation was passed aimed at regulating these government-sponsored enterprises in terms of capital requirements reflecting their credit, interest rate, and management risks.

Key Terms and Definitions

collateralize—A security that has another asset that "backs" or guarantees payment of interest and principal.

collateralized mortgage obligation (CMO)—A multiple-class, pay-through bond, first issued by the FHLMC in June 1983. CMOs are secured by a pool of mortgages or a portfolio of pass-through securities. The CMO provides a type of call protection and pays principal and interest semiannually rather than monthly, as a pass-through security does.

conforming mortgage—A mortgage whose terms, such as its loan-to-value ratio and amount, must conform to the requirements of the three federal agencies before those agencies will agree to purchase them.

credit enhancement—The process whereby the issuer of a mortgage-related security adds support to the underlying assets by contributing capital or overcollateralizing the assets.

Farmers Home Administration (FmHA)—An agency within the Department of Agriculture that operates principally under the Consolidated Farm and Rural Development Act of 1921 and Title V of the Housing Act of 1949. This agency provides residential property financing to farmers and other qualified borrowers who are unable to obtain loans elsewhere.

Federal Agricultural Mortgage Corporation (FAMC)—A corporation created by the Agricultural Credit Act and intended to act similarly to the GNMA and FNMA, but for farm mortgages.

federal credit agency—Federally sponsored and/or supported agency that supports various activities such as housing or agriculture through credit availability.

Federal Financing Bank (FFB)—A federal bank established by the federal Financing Bank Act of 1973 to consolidate and reduce the government's cost of financing a variety of federal agencies and other borrowers whose obligations are guaranteed by the federal government.

Federal Home Loan Mortgage Corporation (FHLMC)—A private corporation authorized by Congress with an independent board of directors to provide secondary mortgage market support for conventional mortgages. It also sells participation certificates secured by pools of conventional mortgage loans. Popularly known as Freddie Mac, it is under the oversight of HUD.

Federal National Mortgage Association (FNMA)—A privately owned corporation created by Congress to support the secondary mortgage market. It purchases and sells residential mortgages insured by the FHA or guaranteed by the VA, as well as conventional home mortgages. Popularly known as Fannie Mae, it is under the oversight of HUD.

Financial Accounting Standards Board (FASB)—An independent, private entity that establishes standards for financial accounting and reporting and derives its authority from the SEC.

Government National Mortgage Association (GNMA)—Nicknamed Ginnie Mae, this HUD agency operates as a participant in the secondary mortgage market. It is involved with special government financing programs for urban renewal projects, elderly housing, and other high-risk mortgages. GNMA also carries out the liquidation and special assistance functions performed by the Federal National Mortgage Association prior to its reorganization in 1968. The association is involved with the mortgage securities pool and the tandem plan.

government-sponsored enterprise (GSE)—Refers to the three federal housing agencies: GNMA, FNMA, and FHLMC.

grantor trust—When the owner of real property, called the grantor, conveys title of the property to a trust.

guaranteed mortgage certificate (GMC)—A bond-like instrument issued by Freddie Mac that represents ownership in a large pool of residential mortgages. Principal is returned annually and interest is paid semi-annually.

interest only (IO)—A security that gives the owner the right to all of the interest payments from a pool of mortgages.

mark-to-market—A procedure where an asset (or liability, but usually an asset) is revalued periodically (can be as frequently as daily) on the books of the holder.

mortgage-backed bond (MBB)—A bond or debt instrument that is backed by a pool (large group) of mortgages and for which the cash flow of the mortgages serves as the source of repayment.

mortgage-backed security (MBS)—A security purchased by investors that is secured by mortgages. Such securities are also known as pass-through securities since the debt service paid by the borrower is passed through to the purchaser of the security.

mortgage-related security—A security backed or collateralized by a pool of mortgages.

participation certificate (PC)—Mortgage-backed security issued by FHLMC that is backed by mortgages purchased from eligible sellers. Called PC because seller retains some interest (5 or 10 percent) in the mortgages sold to FHLMC.

pass-through security—A security issued by the Government National Mortgage Association that provides for the interest and principal to pass through to the holder of the security.

prepayment—The payment or pay-off of the balance of a mortgage before the end of its term.

principal only (PO)—A security that gives the owner the right to all of the principal payments (both scheduled amortization and prepayments) from a pool of mortgages.

private mortgage insurance (PMI)—Insurance written by a private (nongovernmental) company protecting the mortgage lender against loss caused by a mortgage default or foreclosure.

real estate mortgage investment conduit (REMIC)—A type of mortgage-backed security that allows for income to be taxed only to the holders of the bond and not to the entity holding the mortgages.

secondary mortgage market—A market where existing mortgages are bought and sold. It contrasts with the primary mortgage market, where mortgages are originated.

senior/subordinated pass-through—A mortgage pass-through security issued in two classes. The subordinated class absorbs the payment risk for both classes.

tranche—Refers to a class of securities within a CMO. Each class will have a different interest rate and maturity date.

Review Questions

1. What are the benefits of a well-organized secondary mortgage market? List at least three.
2. What are forms of a supply and demand mismatch solved by the secondary mortgage market?
3. What are mortgage-related securities?
4. What are desirable characteristics of mortgage-related securities?
5. List and give a brief description of the types of mortgage-related securities.
6. What are the advantages of a collateralized mortgage obligation over a straight pass-through security?
7. Explain what credit enhancement is, and list a few ways in which it is accomplished in the secondary mortgage market.

8. What is a stripped mortgage-backed security?
9. Explain what a REMIC is and why Congress passed legislation to provide for them.
10. Compare and contrast the three primary federally sponsored agencies (GNMA, FNMA, FHLMC). Include in your comparison the types of mortgages they purchase and the types of securities they issue.

Suggested Reading

Anders, George. "How a Home Mortgage Got into A Huge Pool That Lured Investors." *The Wall Street Journal*, August 17, 1988.

Dougherty, Ann J. "The (Next-to-The) Last Word in Financial Innovation." *Secondary Mortgage Markets*, 6 (Spring 1989).

Federal Home Loan Mortgage Corporation. *A Citizen's Guide to the Secondary Mortgage Market*, Publication No. 67. FHLMC, December 1988.

Federal Home Loan Mortgage Corporation. *Secondary Mortgage Markets*, McLean, VA: Mortgage Market Review, 1994.

Lore, Kenneth G. *Mortgage-Backed Securities*. New York: Clark Boardman Company, 1987.

McElhone, Josephine. "The Bare Facts About Strips." *Secondary Mortgage Markets*, 4 (Summer 1987).

U.S. Department of Housing and Urban Development. *GNMA: Ginnie Mae Investment Facts*, Publication HUD-1047-GNMA. Government National Mortgage Association, 1986.

Related Web Sites

Much more information can be obtained by visiting the web sites for the Federal Home Loan Mortgage corporation and the Federal National Mortgage Corporation: http://www.freddiemac.com and http://www.fanniemae.com, respectively.

Chapter 4

Interest Rates and Risk

Chapter Outline

Learning Objectives

After reading this chapter you will be able to:

- Describe how *interest rates* (also called the *yield* or the *rate of return*) are determined in the financial markets.
- Describe or explain the concept of *risk*.
- Name the types of risk associated with different types of financial instruments.
- Explain why investors in securities require a higher rate of return when different elements of risk are associated with different securities.

Key Terms

callability risk
default risk
inflation risk
liquidity risk
maturity risk
maturity value
rate or return
real rate of interest

Introduction

A clear grasp of the nature of interest rates and the factors that affect them is essential to understanding real estate finance. Investments have different types and levels of risk associated with them. These risks affect the interest rates of investments.

This chapter discusses interest rates and various types of risk that affect them.

Interest Rates

The term *interest rate* is often used interchangeably with other such terms as *percent of interest*, *yield*, *return*, or *rate of return*. The term **rate of return** is more descriptive than interest rate, and often refers to the percent of interest that is *earned on an investment*.

The example of a simple investment, say, a one-year Treasury bill, illustrates the rate of return concept. A one-year Treasury bill is an obligation (bond) of the U.S. Treasury that matures in one year. If the **maturity value** (also called the *face value*) of a one-year Treasury bill is $100, then the owner of the bill will receive $100 when the bill matures in one year.

An investor who pays $95 for a $100 one-year Treasury bill today and keeps it until maturity will make a $5 gain on the investment. In this case the investor's rate of return was $5/$95, or 5.26 percent. When Treasury bills are priced as in this example of a one-year bill, the yield, return, or interest rate is 5.26 percent annually. (Note that, in the case of a Treasury bill, no interest payments are received by the investor between the date of purchase, today, and the date of maturity, one year from today.)

If the investor pays less than $95 for the bill (and it still pays $100 on maturity), the yield is higher. For example, if the investor pays $92 for the bill, gain on the investment is $8 and the yield will be $8/$92, or 8.696 percent annually. In other words, given the certain payout of $100 a year from today, the investor can make a higher return by paying less for the bill.

The Auction Process

Treasury bills and other, longer term, Treasury obligations (called *notes* and *bonds*) are traded in an auction environment. Potential investors bid against one another for the right to own these bills, notes, or bonds. As potential investors bid higher and higher prices, the yield that they will obtain gets smaller. The federal government wants investors to pay a high price, which reduces the interest it pays, or its cost of borrowing funds. Potential investors will not bid up the price relentlessly, however. Once a price that establishes a reasonable yield has been reached, the bidding process stops. The Treasury then delivers the bills—at a price that established a reasonable yield for investors.

This auction process is how markets for most assets work. When investors contemplate the purchase of a corporate bond, corporate stock, real estate investment trust, municipal bond, an apartment complex, an office building, or any other asset, they expect other bidders to be involved. The presence of other bidders ensures that no single investor is able to obtain an asset at a bargain price and make excess returns on the investment.

In determining how much to pay for an asset (and thereby determining the expected return on the investment), an investor will consider many aspects of the asset, including its *risk*. Generally, the higher the level of perceived risk of an asset, the higher the return required by investors in the asset.

Risk

Different elements of risk are associated with various investments. Elements of risk include inflation or purchasing power risk, default risk, maturity risk, callability risk, and liquidity risk. We discuss each of these in turn.

Inflation or Purchasing Power Risk

Inflation can partially or wholly reduce the return on an investment. Although we expect some level of inflation, we cannot be certain of the exact inflation rate over different periods in the future. If someone invests in short-term Treasury obligations anticipating only low inflation or no inflation at all, and then substantial inflation occurs unexpectedly, the return will be lower than the investor had planned to receive, and the investor has suffered from **inflation risk**.

For example, Ms. Clark believed that inflation during the next year would be nonexistent, so she decided to invest at a 3 percent rate of return. She purchased one-year Treasury bills that yielded that rate, 3 percent. Unexpectedly, the rate of inflation during the next year was actually 5 percent, and Ms. Clark actually lost purchasing power and her real return was negative. Her investment paid 3 percent, but inflation ate up 5 percent.

Here's another example. Assume that you can purchase, today, certain real items at $1 each. The items are real in the sense that you can see, feel, and touch these items. If you instead invest $100 today at a 3 percent annual rate of interest, then one year from today your investment will be worth $103—3 percent more than the amount invested. If there has been absolutely no increase in prices whatsoever, then those same real items will still cost $1 and you will be able to purchase 103 of them next year when your investment matures. But, if 5 percent inflation occurs during the next year, then each of the items will cost $1.05 and, since you only have $103 you will only be able to purchase about 98 ($103/1.05) of the items. In exchange for giving up the purchase of 100 of the items today, you are rewarded with the ability to buy only 98 next year. This is not a good deal. Also, it is precisely why investors require to be compensated for expected inflation over the life of the investment.

Expected rates of inflation are just that: expected. Investors have no certainty today about what the actual rate of inflation will be next year. In addition, the more distant in the future that an investment will mature, the more difficult it becomes to predict the annual rate of inflation. Nonetheless, investors still require compensation for any expected inflation (in addition to the real rate of return).

The **real rate of interest** can be defined as that rate which would exist on totally risk-free bonds in a completely inflation-free economy. It is also defined as the nominal rate on riskless bonds less the amount of inflation. So, for example, if you obtain an 8 percent (nominal) return on a financial instrument over a one-year period, and if the rate of inflation turned out to be 5 percent over this same period, then your real return (return adjusted for loss in purchasing power) would be 3 percent.

Figure 4-1 compares annual inflation rates with one-year T-bill rates for the years 1980 through 1998. For the most part, the two rates go up and down together. The difference between the T-bill rate and the inflation rate is the real rate of return. The average real rate of return on one-year T-bills during this period was in the neighborhood of 3 percent. The year with the highest real rate of return was 1985, in which the one-year T-bill paid nearly 11 percent while inflation remained steady at about 4 percent, giving investors a real return of about 7 percent. Notice, however, that in 1981, when inflation hit over 13 percent, even T-bills paying 12 percent meant a loss in purchasing power for their investors.

SIDEBAR

Inflation Component of Interest Rate
Economist Irving Fisher once theorized that the rate of interest we observe on financial instruments (bills, bonds, etc.) includes a component for expected inflation. He developed the following equation:

$$i = r + ei$$

where

i is the rate of interest we observe on financial instruments, also called the *nominal rate*

r is the real rate of interest

ei is expected inflation.

Inflation Risk and Real Estate Finance. Mortgage lenders are investors. When they lend money, they are, essentially, purchasing a bond called a personal note or mortgage. If mortgage lenders expect high rates of inflation, they will require a higher rate of return on their mortgage loans. In such cases, they will charge a higher rate of interest. This occurred in the late 1970s and early 1980s: When inflation was exceeding 10 percent, mortgage lenders charged high interest rates on mortgages. Because of inflation risk, interest rates skyrocketed, housing affordability dropped to all-time lows, new home sales declined, and real estate salespeople left the profession.

Default Risk

Default risk is defined as the degree of probability that a borrower (bond issuer) will fail to pay either the interest (when due) or the principal amount

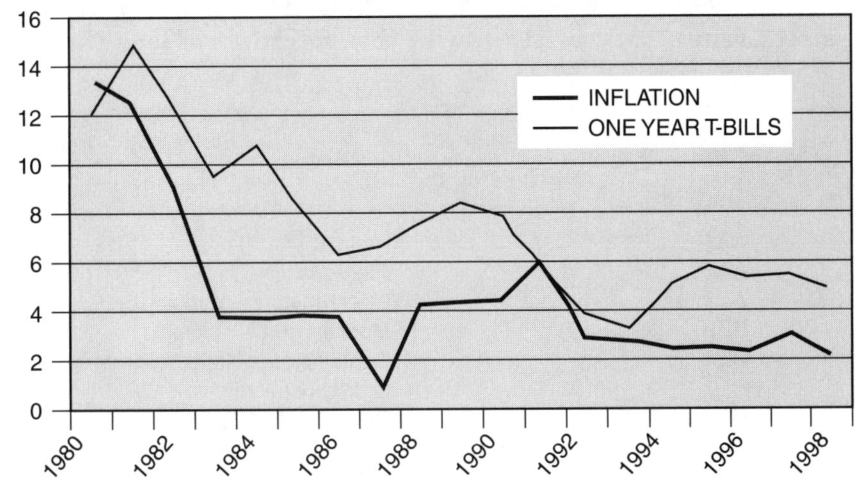

Figure 4-1
Inflation and One-Year T-Bill Rates, 1980–1998

of the debt or both. Because the federal government can print money and tax citizens, the Treasury is not expected to default on its obligations, so Treasury bills do not have default risk. All other borrowers, however, including states and municipalities, can default on their bonds. Therefore, all other securities are subject to default risk. Investors require a higher rate of return for higher default risk.

Risk of default varies by borrower. Financially strong borrowers, such as large, established corporations and fiscally sound state and local governments, are able to issue bonds that have only a slight probability of default. The rates of return for these bonds are only slightly higher than for comparable Treasury bonds.

Some agencies, Standard & Poor's, for example, rate bond issuers' obligations (bonds) in terms of default risk. Table 4-1 shows Standard & Poor's rating categories or levels. This agency, which is one of three or four nationally known bond rating agencies, rates the bonds of corporations, state and local governments, commercial mortgage-backed bonds (CMBBs), and other types of debt securities.

Investors require higher rates of return for investing in bonds and other debt securities that have higher default risks (lower ratings). Figure 4-2 shows the rate of return on bonds of various ratings from 1980 to 1998. Notice that the rates tend to move together, but lower rated bonds always have a higher return.

Default Risk and Real Estate Finance. The effects of default risk in real estate finance are not difficult to see. Homebuyers who have a poor credit history or inconsistent earnings history are likely to pay a higher rate of interest on their home loan than buyers whose financial history is strong. The buyer with the poor financial background is paying for the default risk that the lender is assuming by making the loan.

Maturity Risk

Maturity risk is the probability that interest rates will rise during the period of an investment. When this happens, investors who have committed themselves to a lower rate are at a disadvantage relative to investors in shorter term bonds. In other words, someone who has purchased a long-term investment at, say, 3 percent return, may be stuck with that return for a long time, even if

Table 4-1
Standard & Poor's Ratings Categories

Rating	Description
AAA	Highest quality
AA	High quality
A	Upper medium grade
BBB	Medium grade
BB	Contains speculative elements
B	Outright speculative
CCC and CC	Default definitely possible
C	Default, only partial recovery likely
DDD-D	Default, little recovery likely

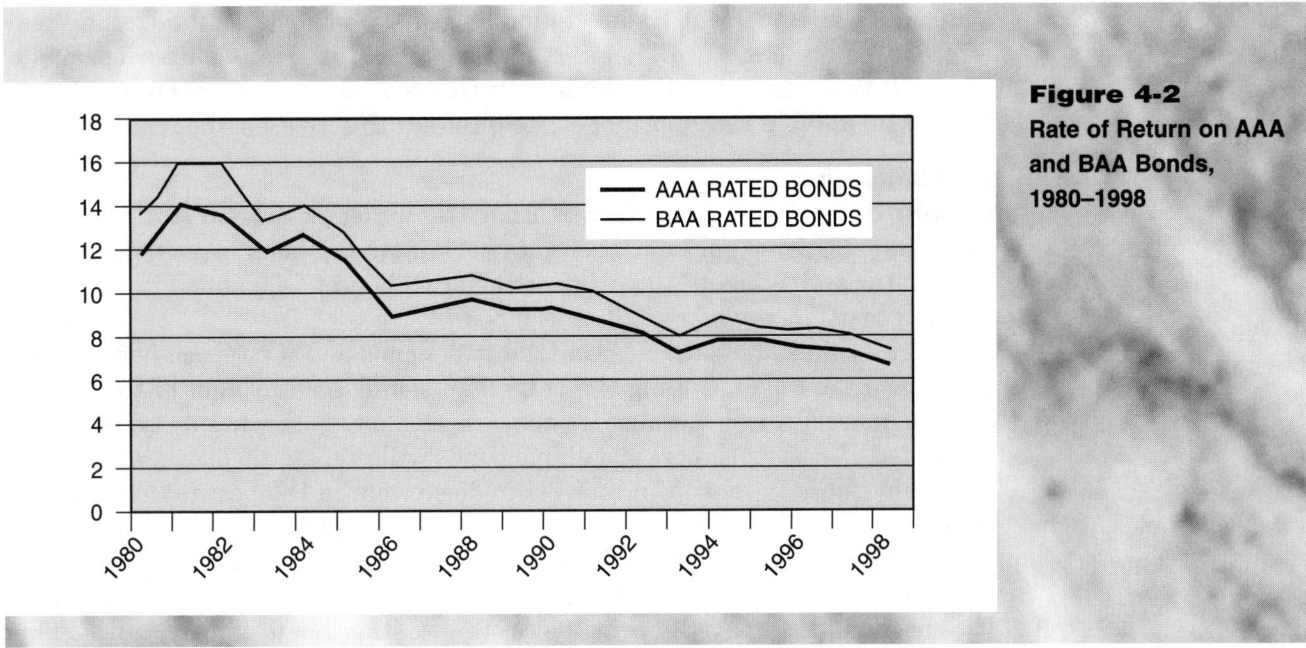

Figure 4-2
Rate of Return on AAA and BAA Bonds, 1980–1998

interest rates increase dramatically. That's the risk—the maturity risk—the investor takes when making a long-term investment.

Let's compare the purchase of two securities. Investor A buys a Treasury bill that matures in 1 year. At the end of the year, this investor receives the principal back, plus interest. Investor B buys a Treasury bond with a maturity of 10 years. This investor may receive interest payments each year and will receive the principal at maturity, that is, 10 years later.

Now assume that both bonds have a yield (return) of 6 percent annually. What will be the relative positions of Investor A and Investor B in one year? Who will be better off? Investor A receives the entire principal amount and can reinvest it at the prevailing rates at the end of that one-year period. If rates have increased, say, to 9 percent, Investor A has an advantage—he or she can reinvest the funds at the higher rate. Investor B has a bond earning an annual rate of return of 6 percent with nine more years to maturity.

Why doesn't Investor B sell the longer term bond and reinvest at a higher rate? This is, indeed, possible. However, the bond will sell at a price that is lower than the principal amount. Potential investors will not pay the full amount for the bond because it gives a low rate of interest in a high interest rate market. Investor B will take a financial loss whether he or she retains the bond or sells it.

The risk faced by Investor B in this case is called maturity risk. Because the bond has a longer maturity, Investor B faces the risk that interest rates can change (in this case, rise) and place him at a disadvantage relative to investors who invested in short-term bonds. So why would an investor purchase long-term bonds? Longer term bonds pay a somewhat higher yield to begin with. In the present example, Investor A may receive 6 percent on the one-year Treasury bond, while Investor B may actually receive 7 percent. The higher interest is compensation for maturity risk—the risk that interest rates may increase.

SIDEBAR

Default Risk Component of Interest Rate

The nominal return on, say, a corporate bond, can be described by the following formula:

$$i = r + ei + dr$$

where *dr* stands for default risk, and the other variables are as defined earlier.

Maturity Risk and Real Estate Finance. Many home loans and other real estate loans are long term. Lenders making fixed-rate loans for periods of 10, 15, or 30 years are accepting high maturity risk. Some newer types of loans, such as adjustable-rate mortgages, help reduce this risk for the lender.

SIDEBAR

Maturity Risk and Interest Rates

The following equation describes maturity risk, the risk for long-term bonds subject to default risk:

$$i = r + ei + dr + mr$$

where *mr* stands for maturity risk.

Callability Risk

Callability risk refers to the risk that the issuer of a bond (the borrower) might pay the principal (and, therefore, terminate the bond) prior to its scheduled maturity. Paying off the principal before a bond is scheduled to mature is referred to as *prepaying* or *calling* the bond.

Not all bonds are "callable." Callability depends on the contract between the issuer and the buyer. Calling the bond may sound good in light of the discussion on maturity risk because it appears as though the maturity would be shortened. However, issuers of callable bonds will prepay the principal ahead of time only if it is in their own interest to do so—not in the best interests of the buyer.

Bond issuers are most likely to call a bond when interest rates fall below the bond's rate. They can issue a new bond at a lower rate of interest and then use those funds to pay the principal of the existing bond, that is, call it. This may result in their owing the same amount, that is, the principal of the new bond may be the same as the previous one, but they are paying a lower rate of interest.

The investor whose bond is called receives the principal back earlier than expected. Now this investor must look for another investment, which will probably return a lower rate of interest. Note that if interest rates rise the issuer of the callable bond will not call it, and the bond buyer will have a bond paying a lower rate than the market is paying.

So why would anyone buy a callable bond? The answer is the same as in the case of the longer maturity bond. A callable bond must offer a slightly higher rate of interest at the beginning of the bond's life in order to be attractive to potential investors. While noncallable bonds may have a rate of, say, 7 percent, a callable bond may have a rate of 8 percent.

SIDEBAR

Callability Risk and Interest Rates

For a long-term corporate, callable bond, the rate may be defined as:

$$i = r + ei + dr + mr + cr$$

where *cr* stands for callability risk.

Callability Risk and Real Estate Finance. A good example of a callable bond is a mortgage on a residence. A lender who makes a mortgage loan is actually purchasing the homebuyer's bond (promissory note). In the case of a long-term fixed-rate mortgage, the homebuyer promises to make 30 years of payments at a specified rate of interest. If mortgage rates drop, the homeowner may refinance the mortgage—essentially, she calls the bond. The homeowner takes out a new mortgage (issues a new bond) at a lower rate and pays off the old mortgage. The lender must now reinvest the funds (make another loan) at the current lower rate of interest.

Because a mortgage has callability risk, a lender will charge a slightly higher rate of interest at the beginning of the loan. This is why FHA mortgages, which have no default risk but are callable, have a slightly higher rate than long-term Treasury bonds, which also have no default risk but are not callable.

Lenders can prevent refinancing (calling the old loan) by having a sufficient prepayment penalty. Most residential mortgages, however, do not have a prepayment penalty, usually because of federal and state laws. However, those with a prepayment penalty have a lower interest rate than those without.

Liquidity Risk

Liquidity refers to the ability of an investor to resell a security. In other words, liquidity means the ease with which an investor can convert an asset into cash without suffering a loss in the asset's current value. A Treasury bill can be sold for its full value within a day because the daily market for this type of security is large and active. Therefore, the liquidity of a Treasury bill is very high. This is also true of the stocks and bonds of major corporations, which is observable in the activity of the New York Stock Exchange and the New York Bond Exchange.

Other types of securities may be difficult to sell quickly because they lack a large active market. They have a lack of liquidity or low liquidity. This is the case for oil and gas limited partnerships, real estate limited partnerships, the municipal bonds of very small municipalities, and so forth.

Investors usually require an addition to a rate of return to compensate for an investment's **liquidity risk**, that is, its lack of liquidity. They are taking the risk that, in the event they would suddenly need to convert the investment into cash, they would not be able to do so quickly or without suffering a loss.

> **SIDEBAR**
>
> **Liquidity and Interest Rates**
>
> $i = r + ei + dr + mr + cr + lr$
>
> where *lr* stands for liquidity risk.

Liquidity Risk and Real Estate Finance. A home is not very liquid. Although the owners could sell it next week at auction, they might have to take a loss. To sell a residence at its full value, owners make a leisurely sale that usually takes some time, depending on market conditions.

Risk and Rates of Return

Different types of risk affect rates of return, and we expect greater risk to be associated with higher rates of return. Figure 4-3 shows the annual rate of return on a selection of securities from 1980 through 1998. It also shows the

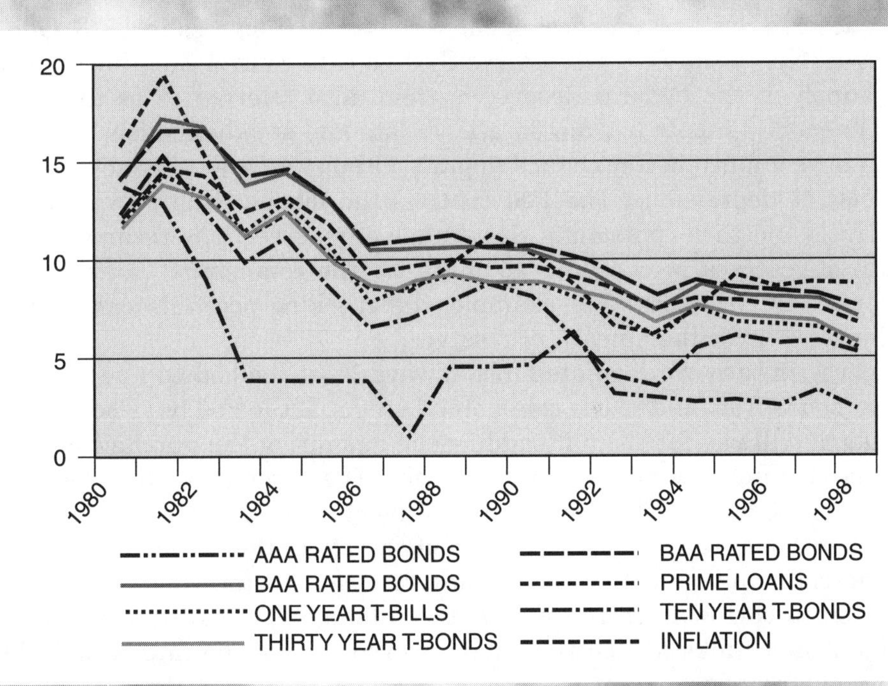

Figure 4-3
Annual Rate of Return on Various Securities, 1980–1998

annual inflation rate for those years. Notice that the annual rates of return move together and follow the rate of inflation. As inflation has moderated during the last two decades, so have the return rates on various securities. This illustrates that the first component in any rate of return is the expected rate of inflation.

The security with the least risk is the one-year T-bill, which has no default, maturity, callability, or liquidity risk. As you would expect, therefore, the one-year T-bill has the lowest return of any security precisely because it represents the least risk for investors.

Securities with higher risk also have higher annual rates of return. Note, for example, that the return on the riskier BAA-rated corporate bonds is higher than the return on the less risky AAA-rated corporate bonds.

The return on conventional 30-year mortgages ("prime loans") is higher than on 30-year Treasury bonds. Why? Conventional mortgages carry a callability risk that the Treasury bonds do not.

The Federal Reserve System and Interest Rates

In the United States the commercial banking system is responsible for "creating" most of our money supply. This may seem, at first, strange because we generally think of money as coins from the U.S. Mint or currency from the U.S. Treasury (actually, the Bureau of Engraving and Printing). In reality, we use checking accounts much more frequently to purchase items or pay bills. Thus, checking accounts, or demand deposits as they are also called, represent about 80 to 85 percent of our money "supply."

This is where the Federal Reserve System comes in. The commercial banking system that creates the bulk of our money supply is regulated by the Federal Reserve System, a federal agency created by Congress in 1913. One of the central roles of the Federal Reserve System is to control the growth of the money supply. If the Federal Reserve System (also referred to as the "Fed") allows the money supply to grow in a moderate and steady fashion, the economy will have a much better chance to grow without experiencing severe business cycles or depressions. The Fed controls the money supply by setting a reserve ratio and then controlling the volume of reserves. The reserve ratio is the ratio of reserves to checking accounts for the commercial banks. If the reserve ratio is 20 percent, for example, the checking accounts cannot total more than five times the amount of reserves.

Reserves, in turn are regulated in two ways. First the Fed will buy and sell Treasury bonds from and to the commercial banks. If the Fed buys bonds from the banks, it will pay for them by adding the amount of the purchase price to the reserve account (at the Fed) of the banks. The reverse is true when they sell bonds to the banks. The buying and selling of bonds is referred to as *open-market operations*. The second way the Fed can affect the amount of reserves at commercial banks is by setting the interest rate on the reserves that the banks wish to borrow from the Fed. If the interest rate, called the discount rate, is low then banks will borrow more reserves, and if the rate is high then banks will borrow fewer reserves.

The activities of the Fed have an impact on the general level of interest rates (including mortgage rates) and serve to set U.S. monetary policy. If the Fed raises the discount rate, then banks will borrow fewer reserves. With lower reserves, the banks will be able to lend less money (in the form of checking accounts) and will ration their available loan limit by raising rates on their loans to consumers, mortgages being one example. You should note that the rise in interest rates may be temporary, however. If the reduced growth in the money supply leads to less inflation and reduced expectations of future inflation, then the ultimate effect on interest rates may be to lower them. In any event you should be aware of the importance of the Fed and its impact on the money supply, the economy, and interest rates.

Summary

The term *rate of return* refers to the percent of interest that is earned on an investment. In other words, it is the ratio of the amount earned on an investment to the amount initially invested.

Investments have various types of risk associated with them. These include inflation or purchasing power risk, default risk, maturity risk, callability risk, and liquidity risk. Real estate investments have some degree of all of these risks. Investors require a higher rate of return on investments with higher risk.

Key Terms and Definitions

callability risk–The risk that a debt instrument, including a mortgage, will be paid off prior to maturity if the market rate of interest falls.

default risk—The risk of incurring a loss on a loan as a result of a default.

inflation risk—The risk that inflation will cause a decline in the purchasing power of the future dollars to be received from an investment.

liquidity risk—The risk that an asset may not be easily and rapidly sold for cash at its current value.

maturity risk—The increase in risk due to the increase in the maturity of a debt obligation due to possible changes in interest rates or inflation rates.

maturity value—The value of an investment when it matures, such as the face value of a bond at maturity.

rate of return—Expressed as a percentage and usually on an annual basis represents the interest received from an investment.

real rate of interest—The nominal interest received less the rate of inflation. Example: If you receive 8 percent annual interest on a bond but inflation is 5 percent annually, your real rate received is 3 percent annually.

Review Questions

1. Describe how interest rates are determined in the auction process.
2. Define risk as it applies to investments.
3. Define rate of return.
4. What is the rate of return on a one-year Treasury bill that is purchased for $940 today and pays $1000 when it matures?
5. How can inflation reduce the return on an investment? Give an example.
6. If Irwin invests in a one-year Treasury bill that yields 3 percent, and the rate of inflation during the year of the investment is also 3 percent, what is Irwin's financial outcome at the end of the year?
7. Define and give an example of *real return.*
8. What is default risk?
9. Why do borrowers with a poor credit record often pay a higher interest rate than borrowers with a good credit history?
10. Describe maturity risk.
11. The Houghs are considering refinancing their home because mortgage rates have fallen. What type of risk does this represent to the holder of their mortgage?
12. A mortgage is a liability to the homebuyer, but an asset to the lender. Explain.

Problems to Solve (Answers may be checked against the Answer section)

1. If the real default-free rate of return is 2 percent and expected inflation during the next year is 5 percent, what will the nominal yield be on a one-year Treasury security?
2. The nominal yield on a one-year Treasury security is 8 percent. Expected inflation during the next year is 5 percent. What does this say about the real rate of return on default-free securities?
3. In Problem 1, assume that the one-year Treasury security was not very liquid and that the liquidity risk premium was 2 percent. What would be the nominal return on the security in that situation?

Chapter 5

The Time Value of Money

Chapter Outline

Learning Objectives

After reading this chapter you will be able to:

- Describe the basic mechanics of the time value of money.
- Perform calculations related to discounting and compounding.

Key Terms

annuity
annuity due
compounding
compounding annually
discounting
future value of an annuity
ordinary annuity

Introduction

"Money has time value." So says the marketplace of borrowers and lenders. What does this mean for you, an individual lender or borrower? Two things: (1) To compare dollars that fall in different periods (such as different years) you must "adjust for time"; and (2) the market is willing to compensate investors for time.

Is $1 today the same as $1 in one year? We cannot answer this unless we know how the $1 will be or could be invested. What interest, dividend, or price appreciation can that dollar earn in that year? Consider this often-used example: Would you prefer to receive $1 today or $1 a year from now? Because you can immediately invest $1 taken today at some interest rate, the preferred choice is to take the dollar now. If today's rate is 5 percent, you could invest your $1.00 for one year starting today and have $1.05 at the end of the year. This is "adjusting for time."

This reasoning would apply as long as interest rates other than zero can be earned in the market. If the interest rate is zero, the value of money is constant across time, and the time value of money theory is irrelevant. Again, take the example of receiving $1 today or $1 at the end of one year. If you take $1 today and invest at a zero rate, you still have just $1 at the end of one year. In this case, you are indifferent about the two choices. At any interest rate other than zero (positive or negative), however, there will always be a clear preference.

Two apparently different choices can actually be equivalent across time. For example, suppose you were offered your choice of $1 today or $1.05 at the end of one year. If you knew the interest rate on invested funds to be 5 percent, the two choices would be equivalent—at the end of a year, both choices are worth $1.05. The absolute values of the choices, however, $1 now or $1.05 a year from now, are different because they fall in different times.

Compounding versus Noncompounding

Calculating the time value of money takes into consideration the compounding effect of interest. **Compounding**, in plain language, simply means that you get interest on your interest—in addition to the interest earned on the original principal.

Without Compounding

To illustrate, suppose that you invest $100 for two years at 5 percent, compounding annually. Further assume that you earn interest only on the principal amount invested. The total amount you have at the end of year 2 is calculated by the following formula:

Principal amount + Interest year 1 + Interest year 2

Note that in this case, interest year 1 is interest only on the principal amount and interest year 2 is only on the principal amount. No interest is earned on interest.

If i stands for the interest rate, we can write the formula for the total amount at the end of year 2 as:

$$\text{Principal amount} + i_1\,(\text{Principal}) + i_2\,(\text{Principal})$$

or

$$\text{Principal}\,(1 + i_1 + i_2)$$

Assuming that the interest earned the first year is the same as the interest earned the second year, written $i_1 = i_2$, then we can write the equation as follows:

$$\text{Principal}\,(1 + 2i) \qquad (5.1)$$

Thus the \$100 investment at 5 percent for two years without compounding yields \$110:

$$\$100[1 + 2(0.05)] = \$100(1 + 0.10) = \$100(1.10) = \$110$$

With Compounding

With compounding, the investor earns interest on principal and on reinvested interest. The total amount accumulated now is:

Principal + Interest year 1 + Interest year 2

This formula looks like the previous formula, but there is a major difference. In this example, interest year 2 consists of interest on both the original principal and on the reinvested interest year 1. See the following formula:

$$\text{Principal} + i_1\,(\text{Principal}) + i_2\,(\text{Principal} + \text{Interest year 1})$$

Substituting i_1 (Principal) in the above formula for interest year 1, the formula becomes:

$$\text{Principal} + i_1\,(\text{Principal}) + i_2\,(\text{Principal}) + i_2\,[i_1\,(\text{Principal})]$$

$$\text{Principal}\,(1 + i_1 + i_2 + i_1 i_2)$$

Remember that i is the interest rate. Since the interest rate is the same for each of the two years, $i_1 = i_2$. Now we can simplify the formula as follows:

$$\text{Principal}\,(1 + 2i + i^2)$$

or

$$\text{Principal}\,(1 + i)^2 \qquad (5.2)$$

This compounding effect is present in the different time value of money calculations presented in this chapter.

Compounding and Discounting (Coming and Going)

The terms *compounding* and *discounting* both refer to calculating the value of an investment over time. Compounding refers to calculating what an investment will be worth after a given period of time, including the interest it will earn. A "compounding" question might be "How much will an investment of $6,000 at 9 percent interest be worth at the end of three years?"

Discounting refers to calculating what an investment will cost now, in the present, if it is to be worth a certain amount of money in the future. A "discounting" question might be "For an investment to be worth $10,000 at the end of five years, if the interest rate is 8 percent, how much money do I need to invest now?" or "What is the present value of an investment that will be worth $10,000 at the end of five years if the interest rate is 8 percent?"

Compounding: Finding the Future Value of an Investment

To set the stage for what follows, consider this compounding situation. Someone offers you an "investment": If you will give him $10,000 now, he will return to you a sum of $16,000 at the end of five years. To keep the example simple, assume that there is no default risk whatsoever. That is, you are certain to receive the $16,000 at the end of five years. Also, assume that interest rates will not change in the next five years and that you are content to tie up your investment for the entire period. By making these assumptions, we can concentrate on the value of this investment without considering risk.

In this example, you are the lender; and the seller of the investment is the borrower. You lend money to the borrower in return for the promise to return a greater sum to you in the future. The "interest" that you will earn over the five-year period is the difference between the amount you lend today and the amount returned at the end of the term.

Now, we want to determine if this is a "good" investment. To do this, we compare the return of this investment with alternatives available in the "market." If there are investments with the same risk characteristics that offer better returns—in this case, returns greater than $16,000—you will not want to make this loan.

Here is one possibility. Assume that your local banker will give you 10 percent interest at the end of each and any year on funds in your account at the beginning of that year. This is termed **compounding annually**. Furthermore, assume that the banker will guarantee this 10 percent rate for the next five years.

Now you can compare the two alternatives—loan the money to your friend or place your funds in the local bank. If you put the $10,000 in the bank, how much will the account be worth at the end of the fifth year?

Start by calculating the amount at the end of the first year, which will equal the initial amount plus 10 percent, as shown below:

$$\begin{aligned}\text{Year 1 balance} &= \$10{,}000 + (0.10 \times \$10{,}000)\\ &= \$10{,}000 \times (1 + 0.10)\\ &= \$10{,}000 \times (1.10)\\ &= \$11{,}000\end{aligned}$$

Since the year-end balance for year 1 is the beginning balance for the second year, the year-end balance for year 2 will be:

$$\begin{aligned}\text{Year 2 balance} &= \$11{,}000 \times (1.10)\\ &= \$10{,}000 \times (1.10) \times (1.10)\\ &= \$10{,}000 \times (1.10)^2\\ &= \$12{,}100\end{aligned}$$

Similarly, the year-end balance for year 3 will be:

$$\begin{aligned}\text{Year 3 balance} &= \$12{,}100 \times (1.10)\\ &= \$10{,}000 \times (1.10) \text{ x } (1.10) \times (1.10)\\ &= \$10{,}000 \times (1.10)^3\\ &= \$13{,}310\end{aligned}$$

As you might guess, continuing this process will produce an end-of-year balance for Year 5 equal to:

$$\text{Year 5 balance} = \$10{,}000 \times (1.10)^5$$

To generalize for any present value amount compounded at a given interest rate over a given time period, the equation can be written as:

$$FV_n = PV\,(1 + i)^n \qquad (5.3)$$

where

FV_n = the future value at time n,
PV = the present value amount (initial investment),
i = the periodic interest rate, and
n = the number of compounding periods.

The $(1 + i)^n$ portion of the equation is called the future value interest factor (FVIF).

Two ways to compute this value are fairly easy: use a table or use a financial calculator. A table provides a factor for the future value of each dollar invested in the present. (This and other time-value-of-money tables are included in Appendix 5.) Table 5A-1 in Appendix 5 includes the future value interest factors (FVIF) of one dollar for various combinations of years and interest rates. The value of one dollar in Table 5A-1 with 10 percent interest for five years is 1.611. This means that each dollar invested now at 10 percent annual compounding will return $1.611 at the end of five years. So, $10,000 invested now will return $16,110 at the end of five years.

Check your understanding of the tables by using Table 5A-1 to confirm that $10,000 invested today for six years and compounded annually at 12 percent will result in a future value of $19,740.

A second way to find the future value is to use a financial calculator. An equation such as 5.3 involves four elements:

the present value amount of the investment ($10,000);
the interest rate (10 percent);
the term of the investment (five years); and
the amount to be returned at the end of the term (the future value).

Given any three of the four elements, the fourth can be determined with the use of a financial calculator. Most financial calculators will have (at least) four buttons representing the elements of an equation such as Equation 5.3. Generally, the buttons will be marked as follows:

Beginning amount (present value)	PV
Interest Rate	% or I/YR
Term	N
Future Value	FV
Payment (or Cash Flow)	PMT

By entering values for any of three elements in the equation, the fourth can be determined. For a Hewlett-Packard 10-B financial calculator, the keystroke entries would appear as shown here. Financial calculators also have a payment key. The usefulness of this key is discussed later. Enter the following numbers after each number, then press the key indicated to the right of each number:

10000	+/– PV
10	I/YR
5	N

Press the FV key. The calculator will display the answer of $16,105.10. Any difference from the answer obtained using financial tables is due to rounding. Other types of financial calculators may use somewhat different notation or require different keystroke entries. However, they will come with a manual that includes typical examples. Note that the HP 10-B should be set for one payment per year to account for annual compounding.

Because you can accumulate $16,105.10 at the end of five years by placing your funds in the bank, but only $16,000 by purchasing an investment from your friend, it would make sense to place your money in the bank. When investments are identical in all respects except the future value, it makes sense to select the one with the largest future value.

Discounting: Finding the Present Value of a Future Sum

How much is it worth? How much should I pay? Now that you have rejected the investment, the seller of this investment may turn to you and say, "Well, if you will not give me $10,000 for the promise to return $16,000 at the end of five years, how much will you give me for it?"

You know that the investment is not worth $10,000, but it must be worth something. The question is how much? This is asking the present value of the investment. How can you find out what it is worth? Since the investment is similar to placing your funds in the bank, you simply ask, "How much would I have to put in the bank to have $16,000 at the end of five years?" or "What amount at 10 percent interest for five years will give me $16,000?" Calculating the answer involves discounting, or counting back from the future value. Stated this way, you can see the equation form of the question:

$$x(1.10)^5 = \$16,000 \tag{5.4}$$

We want to know the amount, or the value, of x. Rearranging Equation (5.4) we find the value of x to be:

$$\begin{aligned} x &= \$16,000/(1.10)^5 \\ &= \$9,934.74 \end{aligned} \tag{5.5}$$

That is, if you were to put $9,934.74 in the bank and it earned 10 percent annually, it would grow to $16,000 at the end of the fifth year. Whereas $16,000 is the future value of the investment, $9,934.74 is the present value of the investment opportunity.

The present value of an investment opportunity can be determined in two ways: by using tables or using a financial calculator. A table of factors shows the present value of $1 for various interest rates and terms. The appendix at the end of this chapter provides numerous financial tables of factors that can be used to find future values, present values, and other mortgage calculations. For instance, Table 5A-3 shows the present-value interest factor of $1 to be invested at 10 percent and to be received in five years is 0.621. Therefore, 0.621 × $16,000 = $9,936. (The difference compared to our previous calculation of $9,934.74 is due, again, to rounding.)

Can you show that the present value of the $16,000 payment to be received at the end of the fifth year is worth only $9,072 if the rate is 12 percent? Can you explain why?

Alternatively, the present value can be determined by using a financial calculator. The following entries would accomplish this. Enter the following numbers. After each number, press the key indicated:

16000	FV
10	I/YR
5	N

Then press the PV key. The answer should be $9,934.74.

The general equation for the *present value* of a future lump sum is

$$PV = FV_n \left[\frac{1}{(1+i)^n} \right]$$

where the terms are as described above. The portion of the equation in brackets is the present value interest factor (PVIF).

Discounting and Compounding Annuities

The same discounting principles can be applied to a series of payments rather than just one. A series of equal payments is called an **annuity**. With identical payments, calculating factors and placing them in tables, just as in the above examples, is not difficult.

Discounting Annuities

First, let's work backward. Assume that someone offers you the following investment opportunity. In return for you giving him $10,000 now, he would return to you $2,500 at the end of each of the next five years. The cash flows look like this:

	End of				
	Year 1	**Year 2**	**Year 3**	**Year 4**	**Year 5**
Cash flow	$2,500	$2,500	$2,500	$2,500	$2,500

To find out if this is a good deal, proceed as follows. Envision putting a sum of money in the bank (again at 10 percent annual interest) that would provide you with these exact cash flows. What sum would accomplish this goal? To make the calculation simple, consider opening five different accounts in the bank. The entire contents of account 1 will be removed at the end of the first year. The entire contents of account 2 will be removed at the end of the second year. The entire contents of account 3 will be removed at the end of the third year, and so forth.

The amount that must be deposited in account 1 is $2,272.73:

$$\$2{,}500/(1.10) = \$2{,}272.73 \tag{5.6}$$

The amount to be deposited in account 2 is $2,066.11:

$$\$2{,}500/(1.10)^2 = \$2{,}066.11 \tag{5.7}$$

This amount also can be determined by applying the present value interest factor for 10 percent for year 2 from Table 5A-3, 0.826. That is, 0.826 × $2,500 = $2,065. Continuing, the amount needed for deposit to the remaining accounts would be:

$$\$2{,}500/(1.10)^3 = \$1{,}878.28$$
$$\$2{,}500/(1.10)^4 = \$1{,}707.53$$
$$\$2{,}500/(1.10)^5 = \$1{,}552.30$$

Thus, the total to be deposited will be:

$$\$2{,}272.73 + \$2{,}066.11 + \$1{,}878.28 + \$1{,}707.53 + \$1{,}552.30 = \$9{,}476.95$$

Depositing $9,476.95 at the outset will allow you to withdraw $2,500 at the end of each of the next five years and have no money remaining in the bank. This is equivalent to:

$$\$9{,}476.95 = \$2{,}500/(1.10) + \$2{,}500/(1.10)^2 + \$2{,}500/(1.10)^3 + \ldots + \$2{,}500/(1.10)^5 \tag{5.8}$$

By factoring out the $2,500, this formula can be rewritten as:

$$\$9{,}476.95 = \$2{,}500 \times [1/(1.10) + 1/(1.10)^2 + 1/(1.10)^3 \ldots + 1/(1.10)^5]$$

This can be generalized to:

$$PV_a = PMT\left[\frac{(1+i)^n - 1}{i(1+i)^n}\right] \tag{5.9}$$

where PV_a is the present value of an annuity, and PMT is the annuity payment. The term in brackets is called the present value interest factor of an annuity (PVIFA). Again, tables are constructed that show the factors for a large array of discount rates and times. Table 5A-4 is an example. Note the entry under the 10 percent column and row five: 3.791. If one multiplies this factor times the amount of the annuity payment, the result will be the present value of the annuity. That is,

$$3.791 \times \$2{,}500 = \$9{,}477 \tag{5.10}$$

Can you demonstrate that the present value of an annuity of $4,400 for six years at 9 percent is $19,738.40?

Another way to determine the present value of an annuity is by using the financial calculator. For our example the entries would appear as follows. As before, enter the following numbers. After each number, press the key indicated:

2500	PMT
5	N
10	I/YR

Then press PV. The display should show $9,476.95.

You should pay no more than \$9,476.95 for this investment since you can replicate its cash flows by placing this sum in the bank. (Of course, you need not set up five different accounts; one will do. We only set the problem up in this fashion to draw a clear picture of the cash flows.)

To verify the answer, we can set up an amortization schedule of the funds placed in and withdrawn from the bank, as follows:

Year	Beginning Balance	+	Interest Earned	−	End of Year Withdrawal	=	Ending Balance
1	\$9,476.95		\$947.70		\$2,500		\$7,924.67
2	\$7,924.67		\$792.47		\$2,500		\$6,217.13
3	\$6,217.13		\$621.71		\$2,500		\$4,338.85
4	\$4,338.85		\$433.88		\$2,500		\$2,272.73
5	\$2,272.73		\$227.27		\$2,500		\$ 0.00

Compounding Annuities

Now let's consider the future value of an annuity. For example, "If I place \$2,500 in a bank account at the end of each of five years, beginning with a deposit one year from today, how much will I have in the account at the end of the fifth year?"

The answer to such questions, called the **future value of an annuity**, can be determined by considering the amount that will accumulate on each of the deposits. In other words, view the annuity as a series of deposits and solve the problem by considering the future value of each of the payments. For example, the first cash flow will be deposited one year from the present and will, thus, accumulate interest for four years by the time of the end of the fifth year. The future value will be:

$$\$2{,}500 \times (1.10)^4 = \$3{,}660.25 \tag{5.11}$$

(The future value interest factor from Table 5A-1 for 10 percent for four years is 1.464 and 1.464 × \$2,500 = \$3,660.)

Likewise, the future value of the second payment at the end of the fifth year will be \$3,327.27:

$$\$2{,}500 \times (110)^3 = \$3{,}327.27 \tag{5.12}$$

Continuing, the future values of the remaining three payments will be \$3,024.79, \$2,749.81, and \$2,500, respectively:

$$\begin{aligned} \$2{,}500 \times (1.10)^2 &= \$3{,}024.79 \\ \$2{,}500 \times (1.10)^1 &= \$2{,}749.81 \\ \$2{,}500 \times 1 &= \$2{,}500.00 \end{aligned}$$

The sum of these five values is \$15,262.12. This sum is equivalent to:

$$2{,}500 \times [(1.10)^4 + (1.10)^3 + (1.10)^2 + (1.10)^1 + 1\,] \tag{5.13}$$

This equation will simply be:

$$\$2{,}500 \times (6.105) = \$15{,}262.50$$

The portion in parentheses (6.105) is called the future value interest factor of an annuity (FVIFA) and the equation for finding the future value of the annuity is:

$$FV_a = \text{Payment} \times (\text{FVIFA}_{i,n})$$

where FV_a is the future value of an annuity and $\text{FVIFA}_{i,n}$ is the future value of an annuity factor for a given interest rate (i) and number of payments (n). The equation can also be written as:

$$FV_a = \text{Payment}\left[\frac{(1+i)^n - 1}{i}\right]$$

As you might expect by now, future value interest factor of an annuity can be determined for various combinations of interest rates and number of payments. The FVIFA for this case is included in Table 5A-2 under the 10 percent column, in the fifth row: 6.105. So, 6.105 × \$2,500 is equal to \$15,262.

Now use Table 5A-2 to confirm that the future value of a \$1,000 annuity deposited at the end of each of the next 11 years will be worth \$17,560 if the funds earn 9 percent interest.

The financial calculator can be used to solve these types of problems as well. For our present example, the entries would be as follows:

\$2,500	PMT
5	N
10	I/YR

Then press FV. The display should show \$15,262.75.

Discounting and Compounding at Intervals Other Than One Year

In the examples so far, the relevant interval for compounding and discounting was one year. The intervals can, however, be of other lengths.

For example, how do the calculations change if the relevant interval is six months? Assume that the bank in the above examples credits the account with interest at the end of six months based on the amount in the account at the beginning of the six months. Consider an initial deposit of \$10,000. At the end of the first six months, the bank will credit the account with six months' (or one-half year's) worth of interest at the 10 percent annual rate, or 5 percent. The amount in the account at the end of the first six months will be \$10,500.

$$\$10{,}000 \times (1.05) = \$10{,}500 \tag{5.14}$$

This is the beginning balance for the next six-month period. At the end of the second six-month period, the amount in the account will be \$11,025.

$$\$10{,}500 \times 1.05 = \$10{,}000 \times 1.05 \times 1.05 = \$10{,}000 \times (1.05)^2 = \$11{,}025 \tag{5.15}$$

Note that when the bank credited the account with interest only at the end of the year, the amount (from the first example) in the account at the end of the first year was \$11,000. The extra \$25 in this example results from interest being paid in the second six months on the interest earned in the first six months. That is, it compounded:

$$0.05 \times \$500 = \$25$$

The amount in the account at the end of five years will be:

$$\$10,000 \times (1.05)^{10} = \$16,288.94$$

Note that this amount is greater than the amount that resulted with annual compounding ($16,105).

When interest is compounded semi-annually (twice a year), the investment accumulates earnings twice a year at half the interest rate. The formula is adjusted by halving the interest rate and doubling the number of payments.

To find the future value interest factor for this example in Table 5A-1, find the factor in the column for 5 percent and the row for 10 periods. There you will see that the factor is 1.629. Alternatively, the financial calculator can be used as follows:

10,000	PV
5	%
10	N

Then press FV. *Note:* Using an HP 10-B, the calculator should be set to one payment per year.

More frequent compounding leads to a larger future value. If the compounding is monthly, the future value of our example will be $16,453.09:

$$\$10,000 \times (1 + 0.1/12)^{60} = \$16,453.09 \qquad (5.16)$$

Compounding more often than monthly will lead to even higher future values. The future value at the end of five years will not increase without limit, however. If the compounding is accomplished every day, minute, or second, the future value will reach a limit. Indeed, if the compounding is accomplished over an infinitesimal interval, called continuous compounding, the future value will be given by the following:

$$\$10,000 \times e^{it} = \$16,487.21 \qquad (5.17)$$

Here e is the base of the natural logarithm and is equal to 2.7182818, i is the rate of interest, and t is the term of the investment.

When we reverse the process and find the present value of a future cash flow, more frequent compounding leads to a smaller present value. The present value of $10,000 to be received at the end of the second year when discounted at 10 percent annually is $8,264.46:

$$\$10,000/(1.10)^2 = \$8,264.46$$

When discounted semiannually, the present value is $8,227.03:

$$\$10,000/(1.05)^4 = \$8,227.03$$

When discounted continuously, the present value is $8,187.31:

$$\$10,000/e^{it} = \$8,187.31 \qquad (5.18)$$

Annuity Due

When an annuity is received at the end of each period, it is known as an **ordinary annuity**. When the payment falls at the beginning of each period, it is known as an **annuity due**. To account for this, the PVAFD and the FVAFD can be revised in the following manner:

$$\text{PVAFD} = \left[\frac{(1+i)^n - 1}{i(1+i)^n}\right](1+i) \tag{5.19}$$

$$\text{FVAFD} = \left[\frac{(1+i)^n - 1}{i}\right](1+i) \tag{5.20}$$

Multiplying the payment by the adjusted annuity factor gives the value of the annuity due. For our earlier example, the present value of an annuity due is $10,245, and the future value of an annuity due is $16,789.

Note: The equations that show the present value of a future stream of cash flow(s) can be referred to as basic valuation equations. Such equations capitalize future cash flows into a present value. These equations all consist of four elements: the present value, the amount of the cash flows(s), the interest or discount rate, and the term over which the cash flows are to be received. Given any three of these elements, the fourth can be determined. Furthermore, different situations in real estate finance will require determining different elements in the equation.

Summary

The time value of money refers to financial relationships over time. It is clear that money earning a positive (negative) interest rate will increase (decrease) in value with the passage of time. The final, or future, amount that the investment will grow to depends on the rate of interest earned on the investment and how long the money is invested. It will also depend on how frequently the interest is credited to the investment (compounding). Invested money will grow to a higher value when the interest rate is higher, the term of investment is longer, and it is compounded more frequently.

Since money invested now, in the present, will grow to a larger value in the future, we can say that the two values (present and future) are "equivalent." Thus, a large sum to be received in the future is equivalent to a smaller sum to be received in the present. For any given sum of money to be received in the future, its present value will be smaller if the rate of interest is large and the future sum is received far in the future. Finding the present value of a future sum to be received is called discounting.

Time value of money concepts explained in this chapter are crucial to understanding real estate finance. This is so because real estate finance deals with these concepts at all times. A mortgage, for example, is a loan made at present (present value) in return for a promise of future payments (an annuity). The elements of a mortgage (amount, payments, term, etc.) are determined with reference to the time value of money concepts learned in this chapter. These concepts involve present value, annuities, compounding, discounting, and interest rates.

Key Terms and Definitions

annuity—A series of equal payments.

annuity due—An annuity where the payments are made at the beginning of each payment period.

compounding—The process where interest is added to the principal amount periodically so that subsequent interest is earned not only on the original principal but on the added interest as well.

compounding annually—The process of compounding on an annual basis—that is, interest is added at one-year intervals.

discounting—The process of establishing an amount of money at present, that, with added interest, will equal a given amount of money in the future or a future value.

future value of an annuity—An amount of money to be received at a future date.

ordinary annuity—An annuity where the payments are made at the end of each payment period.

Problems to Solve (Answers may be checked against the Answer section)

1. Old Bank offers to pay 6 percent interest, compounded annually. New Bank, to be competitive, offers 6 percent interest, compounded monthly. If you buy from each bank a five year, $1,000 certificate of deposit, with all interest compounded, what is the difference in values at the end of five years?
2. Mr. Ace Investor has $10,000 to invest for one year. He has three investment alternatives: (1) earn 8 percent, compounded annually, (2) earn interest compounded quarterly, and (3) earn interest compounded monthly. What must the nominal interest rates be on the second and third options to make all the investments earn the same yield?
3. An apartment house has a projected net income of $15,000 per year, and its projected net sales price after five years is $150,000. Considering its risk, you require a 14 annual percent return on this investment. How much would you be willing to pay for it?
4. Jane Ire is offered a real estate investment that promises to pay $80,000 after 5 years. She feels, based on the investment's riskiness, that the annual rate of return should be 15 percent, compounded quarterly. What price should she pay for the property?
5. Peter Piper is offered an investment that will pay $5,000 at the end of each year for the next 10 years. He wants to earn an annual rate of return of 16 percent. How much is he willing to pay for the investment today?
6. Jim Douglas pays $10,000 for a mortgage contract that will pay $3,000 at the end of each of the next 5 years.
   a. What rate of return will he earn?
   b. Suppose that the annuity is paid as an annuity due. What is the return in this case?
7. The value of a house today is $98,000. If it has increased in value at 6 percent per year, what was the value eight years ago?
8. Doctor John purchased 50 acres of land ten years ago for $800 per acre.
   a. If he could have alternatively invested the money at 8 percent per year, what price must he receive today to break even with his opportunity rate?

b. If Doctor John sold the land for $1,400 per acre today, what is his actual rate of return?

9. Suppose you are interested in buying 25 acres of land to start a blueberry farm. The owner is willing to finance 70 percent of the $100,000 purchase price at 10 percent interest over 8 years.
   a. What will be the payment assuming annual amortization?
   b. What would the payment be if monthly payments are required?
10. The Smiths desire to purchase a house and they open a savings account that pays 5.75 percent interest, with monthly compounding. If they put $120 per month beginning one month from now and they must have 20 percent of the price of a house as a down payment, what price can they pay for a house after saving for five years?
11. Mr. Wrinter purchases 10 duplexes (20 rentable units) and he expects to have to replace the air conditioning equipment in each rentable unit 10 years from now at a cost of $5,000 per unit. The bank that loaned Mr. Wrinter the money to purchase the duplexes requires that he deposit a part of the monthly rents into an account earning 6 percent interest to ensure that the money will be available to replace the air conditioning units. How much money must Mr. Wrinter deposit at the end of each month?
12. You are considering the purchase of 75 acres of land that you believe will be developed as a shopping center. You estimate that you can sell the land three years from now at $25,000 per acre. How much should you pay now for the land if the required rate of return is 25 percent?
13. What is the current value of a leasehold interest where lease payments are $1,500 per month (annuity due) for five years? Assume a 10 percent discount rate.
14. Suppose that, as a lessee, you just signed a lease to pay $1,000 per month (annuity due) for five years. Simultaneously, you can sublease the property for $1,800 per month (annuity due) for five years. What is the value of your leasehold interest at a discount rate of 12 percent?
15. What is the present worth of an income-producing property which receives an after-tax cash flow of $20,000 in year one, $22,000 in year two, $25,000 in year three, $30,000 in year four, and $32,000 in year five. Assume the discount rate is 15 percent.
16. Tom makes a deposit of $5,000 in a bank account that earns interest annually at the rate of 8 percent.
    a. How much will Tom have in the account at the end of five years?
    b. Assuming the account earns 8 percent compounded quarterly, how much will he have at the end of five years?
    c. In comparing *a* and *b*, how much additional interest do you earn with quarterly compounding?
    d. What are the effective annual yields for each alternative?

Appendix 5: Financial Tables

These tables can be used when a financial calculator is unavailable.

Table 5A-1 Future Value Interest Factor for One Dollar Compounded at *i* Percent for *n* Periods: $FVIF_{i,n} = (1 + i)^n$

Period	1%	2%	3%	4%	5%	6%	7%	8%	9%	10%
1	1.010	1.020	1.030	1.040	1.050	1.060	1.070	1.080	1.090	1.100
2	1.020	1.040	1.061	1.082	1.102	1.124	1.145	1.166	1.188	1.210
3	1.030	1.061	1.093	1.125	1.158	1.191	1.225	1.260	1.295	1.331
4	1.041	1.082	1.126	1.170	1.216	1.262	1.311	1.360	1.412	1.464
5	1.051	1.104	1.159	1.217	1.276	1.338	1.403	1.469	1.539	1.611
6	1.062	1.126	1.194	1.265	1.340	1.419	1.501	1.587	1.677	1.772
7	1.072	1.149	1.230	1.316	1.407	1.504	1.606	1.714	1.828	1.949
8	1.083	1.172	1.267	1.369	1.477	1.594	1.718	1.851	1.993	2.144
9	1.094	1.195	1.305	1.423	1.551	1.689	1.838	1.999	2.172	2.358
10	1.105	1.219	1.344	1.480	1.629	1.791	1.967	2.159	2.367	2.594
11	1.116	1.243	1.384	1.539	1.710	1.898	2.105	2.332	2.580	2.853
12	1.127	1.268	1.426	1.601	1.796	2.012	2.252	2.518	2.813	3.138
13	1.138	1.294	1.469	1.665	1.886	2.133	2.410	2.720	3.066	3.452
14	1.149	1.319	1.513	1.732	1.980	2.261	2.579	2.937	3.342	3.797
15	1.161	1.346	1.558	1.801	2.079	2.397	2.759	3.172	3.642	4.177
16	1.173	1.373	1.605	1.873	2.183	2.540	2.952	3.426	3.970	4.595
17	1.184	1.400	1.653	1.948	2.292	2.693	3.159	3.700	4.328	5.054
18	1.196	1.428	1.702	2.026	2.407	2.854	3.380	3.996	4.717	5.560
19	1.208	1.457	1.753	2.107	2.527	3.026	3.616	4.316	5.142	6.116
20	1.220	1.486	1.806	2.191	2.653	3.207	3.870	4.661	5.604	6.727
21	1.232	1.516	1.860	2.279	2.786	3.399	4.140	5.034	6.109	7.400
22	1.245	1.546	1.916	2.370	2.925	3.603	4.430	5.436	6.658	8.140
23	1.257	1.577	1.974	2.465	3.071	3.820	4.740	5.871	7.258	8.954
24	1.270	1.608	2.033	2.563	3.225	4.049	5.072	6.341	7.911	9.850
25	1.282	1.641	2.094	2.666	3.386	4.292	5.427	6.848	8.623	10.834
30	1.348	1.811	2.427	3.243	4.322	5.743	7.612	10.062	13.267	17.449
35	1.417	2.000	2.814	3.946	5.516	7.686	10.676	14.785	20.413	28.102
40	1.489	2.208	3.262	4.801	7.040	10.285	14.974	21.724	31.408	45.258
45	1.565	2.438	3.781	5.841	8.985	13.764	21.002	31.920	48.325	72.888
50	1.645	2.691	4.384	7.106	11.467	18.419	29.456	46.900	74.354	117.386

Table 5A-1 (Continued)

Period	11%	12%	13%	14%	15%	16%	17%	18%	19%	20%
1	1.110	1.120	1.130	1.140	1.150	1.160	1.170	1.180	1.190	1.200
2	1.232	1.254	1.277	1.300	1.322	1.346	1.369	1.392	1.416	1.440
3	1.368	1.405	1.443	1.482	1.521	1.561	1.802	1.643	1.685	1.728
4	1.518	1.574	1.630	1.689	1.749	1.811	1.874	1.939	2.005	2.074
5	1.685	1.762	1.842	1.925	2.011	2.100	2.192	2.288	2.386	2.488
6	1.870	1.974	2.082	2.195	2.313	2.436	2.565	2.700	2.840	2.986
7	2.076	2.211	2.353	2.502	2.660	2.826	3.001	3.185	3.379	3.583
8	2.305	2.476	2.658	2.853	3.059	3.278	3.511	3.759	4.021	4.300
9	2.558	2.773	3.004	3.252	3.518	3.803	4.108	4.435	4.785	5.160
10	2.839	3.106	3.395	3.707	4.046	4.411	4.807	5.234	5.695	6.192
11	3.152	3.479	3.836	4.226	4.652	5.117	5.624	6.176	6.777	7.430
12	3.498	3.896	4.334	4.818	5.350	5.936	6.580	7.288	8.064	8.916
13	3.883	4.363	4.898	5.492	6.153	6.886	7.699	8.599	9.596	10.699
14	4.310	4.887	5.535	6.261	7.076	7.987	9.007	10.147	11.420	12.839
15	4.785	5.474	6.254	7.138	8.137	9.265	10.539	11.974	13.589	15.407
16	5.311	6.130	7.067	8.137	9.358	10.748	12.330	14.129	16.171	18.488
17	5.895	6.866	7.986	9.276	10.761	12.468	14.426	16.672	19.244	22.186
18	6.543	7.690	9.024	10.575	12.375	14.462	16.879	19.673	22.900	26.623
19	7.263	8.613	10.197	12.055	14.232	16.776	19.748	23.214	27.251	31.948
20	8.062	9.646	11.523	13.743	16.366	19.461	23.105	27.393	32.429	38.337
21	8.949	10.804	13.021	15.667	18.821	22.574	27.033	32.323	38.591	46.005
22	9.933	12.100	14.713	17.861	21.644	26.186	31.629	38.141	45.923	55.205
23	11.026	13.552	16.626	20.361	24.891	30.376	37.005	45.007	54.648	66.247
24	12.239	15.178	18.788	23.212	28.625	35.236	43.296	53.108	65.031	79.496
25	13.585	17.000	21.230	26.461	32.918	40.874	50.656	62.667	77.387	95.395
30	22.892	29.960	39.115	50.949	66.210	85.849	111.061	143.367	184.672	237.373
35	38.574	52.799	72.066	98.097	133.172	180.311	243.495	327.988	440.691	590.657
40	64.999	93.049	132.776	188.876	267.856	378.715	533.846	750.353	1051.642	1469.740
45	109.527	163.985	244.629	363.662	538.752	795.429	1170.425	1716.619	2509.583	3657.176
50	184.559	288.996	450.711	700.197	1083.619	1670.669	2566.080	3927.189	5988.730	9100.191

Table 5A-1 (Continued)

Period	21%	22%	23%	24%	25%	26%	27%	28%	29%	30%
1	1.210	1.220	1.230	1.240	1.250	1.260	1.270	1.280	1.290	1.300
2	1.464	1.488	1.513	1.538	1.562	1.588	1.613	1.638	1.664	1.690
3	1.772	1.816	1.861	1.907	1.953	2.000	2.048	2.097	2.147	2.197
4	2.144	2.215	2.289	2.364	2.441	2.520	2.601	2.684	2.769	2.856
5	2.594	2.703	2.815	2.932	3.052	3.176	3.304	3.436	3.572	3.713
6	3.138	3.297	3.463	3.635	3.815	4.001	4.196	4.398	4.608	4.827
7	3.797	4.023	4.259	4.508	4.768	5.042	5.329	5.629	5.945	6.275
8	4.595	4.908	5.239	5.589	5.960	6.353	6.767	7.206	7.669	8.157
9	5.560	5.987	6.444	6.931	7.451	8.004	8.595	9.223	9.893	10.604
10	6.727	7.305	7.926	8.594	9.313	10.086	10.915	11.806	12.761	13.786
11	8.140	8.912	9.749	10.657	11.642	12.708	13.862	15.112	16.462	17.921
12	9.850	10.872	11.991	13.215	14.552	16.012	17.605	19.343	21.236	23.298
13	11.918	13.264	14.749	16.386	18.190	20.175	22.359	24.759	27.395	30.287
14	14.421	16.182	18.141	20.319	22.737	25.420	28.395	31.691	35.339	39.373
15	17.449	19.742	22.314	25.195	28.422	32.030	36.062	40.565	45.587	51.185
16	21.113	24.085	27.446	31.242	35.527	40.357	45.799	51.923	58.808	66.541
17	25.547	29.384	33.758	38.740	44.409	50.850	58.165	66.461	75.862	86.503
18	30.912	35.848	41.523	48.038	55.511	64.071	73.869	85.070	97.862	112.454
19	37.404	43.735	51.073	59.567	69.389	80.730	93.813	108.890	126.242	146.190
20	45.258	53.357	62.820	73.863	86.736	101.720	119.143	139.379	162.852	190.047
21	54.762	65.095	77.268	91.591	108.420	128.167	151.312	178.405	210.079	247.061
22	66.262	79.416	95.040	113.572	135.525	161.490	192.165	228.358	271.002	321.178
23	80.178	96.887	116.899	140.829	169.407	203.477	244.050	292.298	349.592	417.531
24	97.015	118.203	143.786	174.628	211.758	256.381	309.943	374.141	450.974	542.791
25	117.388	144.207	176.857	216.539	264.698	323.040	393.628	478.901	581.756	705.627
30	304.471	389.748	497.904	634.810	807.793	1025.904	1300.477	1645.488	2078.208	2619.936
35	789.716	1053.370	1401.749	1861.020	2465.189	3258.053	4296.547	5653.840	7423.988	9727.598
40	2048.309	2846.941	3946.340	5455.797	7523.156	10346.879	14195.051	19426.418	26520.723	36117.754
45	5312.758	7694.418	11110.121	15994.316	22958.844	32859.457	46897.973	66748.500	94739.937	134102.187
50	13779.844	20795.680	31278.301	46889.207	70064.812	104354.562	154942.687	229345.875	338440.000	497910.125

Table 5A-2 Future Value Interest Factor for a One Dollar Annuity Compounded at *i* Percent for *n* Periods:

$$FVIFA_{i,n} = \frac{(1+i)^n - 1}{i}$$

Period	1%	2%	3%	4%	5%	6%	7%	8%	9%	10%
1	1.000	1.000	1.000	1.000	1.000	1.000	1.000	1.000	1.000	1.000
2	2.010	2.020	2.030	2.040	2.050	2.060	2.070	2.080	2.090	2.100
3	3.030	3.060	3.091	3.122	3.052	3.184	3.215	3.246	3.278	3.310
4	4.060	4.122	4.184	4.246	4.310	4.375	4.440	4.506	4.573	4.641
5	5.101	5.204	5.309	5.416	5.526	5.637	5.751	5.867	5.985	6.105
6	6.152	6.308	6.468	6.633	6.802	6.975	7.153	7.336	7.523	7.716
7	7.214	7.434	7.662	7.898	8.142	8.394	8.654	8.923	9.200	9.487
8	8.286	8.583	8.892	9.214	9.549	9.897	10.260	10.637	11.028	11.436
9	9.368	9.755	10.159	10.583	11.027	11.491	11.978	12.488	13.021	13.579
10	10.462	10.950	11.464	12.006	12.578	13.181	13.816	14.487	15.193	15.937
11	11.567	12.169	12.808	13.486	14.207	14.972	15.784	16.645	17.560	18.531
12	12.682	13.412	14.192	15.026	15.917	16.870	17.888	18.977	20.141	21.384
13	13.809	14.680	15.618	16.627	17.713	18.882	20.141	21.495	22.953	24.523
14	14.947	15.974	17.086	18.292	19.598	21.015	22.550	24.215	26.019	27.975
15	16.097	17.293	18.599	20.023	21.578	23.276	25.129	27.152	29.361	31.772
16	17.258	18.639	20.157	21.824	23.657	25.672	27.888	30.324	33.003	35.949
17	18.430	20.012	21.761	23.697	25.840	28.213	30.840	33.750	36.973	40.544
18	19.614	21.412	23.414	25.645	28.132	30.905	33.999	37.450	41.301	45.599
19	20.811	22.840	25.117	27.671	30.539	33.760	37.379	41.446	46.018	51.158
20	22.019	24.297	26.870	29.778	33.066	36.785	40.995	45.762	51.159	57.274
21	23.239	25.783	28.676	31.969	35.719	39.992	44.865	50.422	56.764	64.002
22	24.471	27.299	30.536	34.248	38.505	43.392	49.005	55.456	62.872	71.402
23	25.716	28.845	32.452	36.618	41.430	46.995	53.435	60.893	69.531	79.542
24	26.973	30.421	34.426	39.082	44.504	50.815	58.176	66.764	76.789	88.496
25	28.243	32.030	36.459	41.645	47.726	54.864	63.248	73.105	84.699	98.346
30	36.784	40.567	47.575	56.084	66.438	79.057	94.459	113.282	136.305	164.491
35	41.659	49.994	60.461	73.651	90.318	111.432	138.234	172.314	215.705	271.018
40	48.885	60.401	75.400	95.024	120.797	154.758	199.630	259.052	337.872	442.580
45	56.479	71.891	92.718	121.027	159.695	212.737	285.741	386.497	525.840	718.881
50	64.461	84.577	112.794	152.664	209.341	290.325	406.516	573.756	815.051	1163.865

Table 5A-2 (Continued)

Period	11%	12%	13%	14%	15%	16%	17%	18%	19%	20%
1	1.000	1.000	1.000	1.000	1.000	1.000	1.000	1.000	1.000	1.000
2	2.110	2.120	2.130	2.140	2.150	2.160	2.170	2.180	2.190	2.200
3	3.342	3.374	3.407	3.440	3.472	3.506	3.539	3.572	3.606	3.640
4	4.710	4.779	4.850	4.921	4.993	5.066	5.141	5.215	5.291	5.368
5	6.228	6.353	6.480	6.610	6.742	6.877	7.014	7.154	7.297	7.442
6	7.913	8.115	8.323	8.535	8.754	8.977	9.207	9.442	9.683	9.930
7	9.783	10.089	10.405	10.730	11.067	11.414	11.772	12.141	12.523	12.916
8	11.859	12.300	12.757	13.233	13.727	14.240	14.773	15.327	15.902	16.499
9	14.164	14.776	15.416	16.085	16.786	17.518	18.285	19.086	19.923	20.799
10	16.722	17.549	18.420	19.337	20.304	21.321	22.393	23.521	24.709	25.959
11	19.561	20.655	21.814	23.044	24.349	25.733	27.200	28.755	30.403	32.150
12	22.713	24.133	25.650	27.271	29.001	30.850	32.824	34.931	37.180	39.580
13	26.211	28.029	29.984	32.088	34.352	36.786	39.404	42.218	45.244	48.496
14	30.095	32.392	34.882	37.581	40.504	43.672	47.102	50.818	54.871	59.196
15	34.405	37.280	40.417	43.842	47.580	51.659	56.109	60.965	66.260	72.035
16	39.190	42.753	46.671	50.980	55.717	60.925	66.648	72.938	79.850	87.442
17	44.500	48.883	53.738	59.117	65.075	71.673	78.978	87.067	96.021	105.930
18	50.396	55.749	61.724	68.393	75.836	84.140	93.404	103.739	115.265	128.116
19	56.939	63.439	70.748	78.968	88.211	98.603	110.283	123.412	138.165	154.739
20	64.202	72.052	80.946	91.024	102.443	115.379	130.031	146.626	165.417	186.687
21	72.264	81.698	92.468	104.767	118.809	134.840	153.136	174.019	197.846	225.024
22	81.213	92.502	105.489	120.434	137.630	157.414	180.169	206.342	236.436	271.028
23	91.147	104.602	120.203	138.295	159.274	183.600	211.798	244.483	282.359	326.234
24	102.173	118.154	136.829	158.656	184.166	213.976	248.803	289.490	337.007	392.480
25	114.412	133.333	155.616	181.867	212.790	249.212	292.099	342.598	402.038	471.976
30	199.018	241.330	293.192	356.778	434.738	530.306	647.423	790.932	966.698	1181.865
35	341.583	431.658	546.663	693.552	881.152	1120.699	1426.448	1816.607	2314.173	2948.294
40	581.812	767.080	1013.667	1341.979	1779.048	2360.724	3134.412	4163.094	5529.711	7343.715
45	986.613	1358.208	1874.086	2590.464	3585.031	4965.191	6879.008	9531.258	13203.105	18280.914
50	1668.723	2399.975	3459.344	4994.301	7217.488	10435.449	15088.8705	21812.273	31514.492	45496.094

Table 5A-2 (Continued)

Period	21%	22%	23%	24%	25%	26%	27%	28%	29%	30%
1	1.000	1.000	1.000	1.000	1.000	1.000	1.000	1.000	1.000	1.000
2	2.210	2.220	2.230	2.240	2.250	2.260	2.270	2.280	2.290	2.300
3	3.674	3.708	3.743	3.778	3.813	3.848	3.883	3.918	3.954	3.990
4	5.446	5.524	5.604	5.684	5.766	5.848	5.931	6.016	6.101	6.187
5	7.589	7.740	7.893	8.048	8.207	8.368	8.533	8.700	8.870	9.043
6	10.183	10.442	10.708	10.980	11.259	11.544	11.837	12.136	12.442	12.756
7	13.321	13.740	14.171	14.615	15.073	15.546	16.032	16.534	17.051	17.583
8	17.119	17.762	18.430	19.123	19.842	20.588	21.361	22.163	22.995	23.858
9	21.714	22.670	23.669	24.712	25.802	26.940	28.129	29.369	30.664	32.015
10	27.274	28.657	30.113	31.643	33.253	34.945	36.723	38.592	40.556	42.619
11	34.001	35.962	38.039	40.238	42.566	45.030	47.639	50.398	53.318	56.405
12	42.141	44.873	47.787	50.895	54.208	57.738	61.501	65.510	69.780	74.326
13	51.991	55.745	59.778	64.109	68.760	73.750	79.106	84.853	91.016	97.624
14	63.909	69.009	74.528	80.496	86.949	93.925	101.465	109.611	118.411	127.912
15	78.330	85.191	92.669	100.815	109.687	119.346	129.860	141.302	153.750	167.285
16	95.779	104.933	114.983	126.010	138.109	151.375	165.922	181.867	199.337	218.470
17	116.892	129.019	142.428	157.252	173.636	191.733	211.721	233.790	258.145	285.011
18	142.439	158.403	176.187	195.993	218.045	242.583	269.885	300.250	334.006	371.514
19	173.351	194.251	217.710	244.031	273.556	306.654	343.754	385.321	431.868	483.968
20	210.755	237.986	268.783	303.598	342.945	387.384	437.568	494.210	558.110	630.157
21	256.013	291.343	331.603	377.461	429.681	489.104	556.710	633.589	720.962	820.204
22	310.775	356.438	408.871	469.052	538.101	617.270	708.022	811.993	931.040	1067.265
23	377.038	435.854	503.911	582.624	673.626	778.760	990.187	1040.351	1202.042	1388.443
24	457.215	532.741	620.810	723.453	843.032	982.237	1144.237	1332.649	1551.634	1805.975
25	554.230	650.944	765.596	898.082	1054.791	1238.617	1454.180	1706.790	2002.608	2348.765
30	1445.111	1767.044	2160.459	2640.881	3227.172	3941.953	4812.891	5873.172	7162.785	8729.805
35	3755.814	4783.520	6090.227	7750.094	9856.746	12527.160	15909.480	20188.742	25596.512	32422.090
40	9749.141	12936.141	17153.691	22728.367	30088.621	39791.957	52570.707	69376.562	91447.375	120389.375
45	25294.223	34970.230	48300.660	66638.937	91831.312	126378.937	173692.875	238384.312	326686.375	447005.062
50	65617.200	94525.280	135992.150	195372.640	280255.690	401374.470	573877.870	819103.070	1167041.000	1659760.000

Table 5A-3 Present Value Interest Factor for One Dollar Discounted at *i* Percent for *n* Periods:

$$PVIF_{i,n} = \frac{1}{(1+i)^n}$$

Period	1%	2%	3%	4%	5%	6%	7%	8%	9%	10%
1	.990	.980	.971	.962	.952	.943	.935	.926	.917	.909
2	.980	.961	.943	.925	.907	.890	.873	.857	.842	.826
3	.971	.942	.915	.889	.864	.840	.816	.794	.772	.751
4	.961	.924	.888	.855	.823	.792	.763	.735	.708	.683
5	.951	.906	.863	.822	.784	.747	.713	.681	.650	.621
6	.942	.888	.837	.790	.746	.705	.666	.630	.596	.564
7	.933	.871	.813	.760	.711	.665	.623	.583	.547	.513
8	.923	.853	.789	.731	.677	.627	.582	.540	.502	.467
9	.914	.837	.766	.703	.645	.592	.544	.500	.460	.424
10	.905	.820	.744	.676	.614	.558	.508	.463	.422	.386
11	.896	.804	.722	.650	.585	.527	.475	.429	.388	.350
12	.887	.789	.701	.625	.557	.497	.444	.397	.356	.319
13	.879	.773	.681	.601	.530	.469	.415	.368	.326	.290
14	.870	.758	.661	.577	.505	.442	.388	.340	.299	.263
15	.861	.743	.642	.555	.481	.417	.362	.315	.275	.239
16	.853	.728	.623	.534	.458	.394	.339	.292	.252	.218
17	.844	.714	.605	.513	.436	.371	.317	.270	.231	.198
18	.836	.700	.587	.494	.416	.350	.296	.250	.212	.180
19	.828	.686	.570	.475	.396	.331	.277	.232	.194	.164
20	.820	.673	.554	.456	.377	.312	.258	.215	.178	.149
21	.811	.660	.538	.439	.359	.294	.242	.199	.164	.135
22	.803	.647	.522	.422	.342	.278	.226	.184	.150	.123
23	.795	.634	.507	.406	.326	.262	.211	.170	.138	.112
24	.788	.622	.492	.390	.310	.247	.197	.158	.126	.102
25	.780	.610	.478	.375	.295	.233	.184	.146	.116	.092
30	.742	.552	.412	.308	.231	.174	.131	.099	.075	.057
35	.706	.500	.355	.253	.181	.130	.094	.068	.049	.036
40	.672	.453	.307	.208	.142	.097	.067	.046	.032	.022
45	.639	.410	.264	.171	.111	.073	.048	.031	.021	.014
50	.608	.372	.228	.141	.087	.054	.034	.021	.013	.009

Table 5A-3 (Continued)

Period	11%	12%	13%	14%	15%	16%	17%	18%	19%	20%
1	.901	.893	.885	.877	.870	.862	.855	.847	.840	.833
2	.812	.797	.783	.769	.756	.743	.731	.718	.706	.694
3	.731	.712	.693	.675	.658	.641	.624	.609	.593	.579
4	.659	.636	.613	.592	.572	.552	.534	.516	.499	.482
5	.593	.567	.543	.519	.497	.476	.456	.437	.419	.402
6	.535	.507	.480	.456	.432	.410	.390	.370	.352	.335
7	.482	.452	.425	.400	.376	.354	.333	.314	.296	.279
8	.434	.404	.376	.351	.327	.305	.285	.266	.249	.233
9	.391	.361	.333	.308	.284	.263	.243	.225	.209	.194
10	.352	.322	.295	.270	.247	.227	.208	.191	.176	.162
11	.317	.287	.261	.237	.215	.195	.178	.162	.148	.135
12	.286	.257	.231	.208	.187	.168	.152	.137	.124	.112
13	.258	.229	.204	.182	.163	.145	.130	.116	.104	.093
14	.232	.205	.181	.160	.141	.125	.111	.099	.088	.078
15	.209	.183	.160	.140	.123	.108	.095	.084	.074	.065
16	.188	.163	.141	.123	.107	.093	.081	.071	.062	.054
17	.170	.146	.125	.108	.093	.080	.069	.060	.052	.045
18	.153	.130	.111	.095	.081	.069	.059	.051	.044	.038
19	.138	.116	.098	.083	.070	.060	.051	.043	.037	.031
20	.124	.104	.087	.073	.061	.051	.043	.037	.031	.026
21	.112	.093	.077	.064	.053	.044	.037	.031	.026	.022
22	.101	.083	.068	.056	.046	.038	.032	.026	.022	.018
23	.091	.074	.060	.049	.040	.033	.027	.022	.018	.015
24	.082	.066	.053	.043	.035	.028	.023	.019	.015	.013
25	.074	.059	.047	.038	.030	.024	.020	.016	.013	.010
30	.044	.033	.026	.020	.015	.012	.009	.007	.005	.004
35	.026	.019	.014	.010	.008	.006	.004	.003	.002	.002
40	.015	.011	.008	.005	.004	.003	.002	.001	.001	.001
45	.009	.006	.004	.003	.002	.001	.001	.001	*	*
50	.005	.003	.002	.001	.001	.001	*	*	*	*

*PVIF is zero to three decimal places.

Table 5A-3 (Continued)

Period	21%	22%	23%	24%	25%	26%	27%	28%	29%	30%
1	.826	.820	.813	.806	.800	.794	.787	.781	.775	.769
2	.683	.672	.661	.650	.640	.630	.620	.610	.601	.592
3	.564	.551	.537	.524	.512	.500	.488	.477	.466	.455
4	.467	.451	.437	.423	.410	.397	.384	.373	.361	.350
5	.386	.370	.355	.341	.328	.315	.303	.291	.280	.269
6	.319	.303	.289	.275	.262	.250	.238	.227	.217	.207
7	.263	.249	.235	.222	.210	.198	.188	.178	.168	.159
8	.218	.204	.191	.179	.168	.157	.148	.139	.130	.123
9	.180	.167	.155	.144	.134	.125	.116	.108	.101	.094
10	.149	.137	.126	.116	.107	.099	.092	.085	.078	.073
11	.123	.112	.103	.094	.086	.079	.072	.066	.061	.056
12	.102	.092	.083	.076	.069	.062	.057	.052	.047	.043
13	.084	.075	.068	.061	.055	.050	.045	.040	.037	.033
14	.069	.062	.055	.049	.044	.039	.035	.032	.028	.025
15	.057	.051	.045	.040	.035	.031	.028	.025	.022	.020
16	.047	.042	.036	.032	.028	.025	.022	.019	.017	.015
17	.039	.034	.030	.026	.023	.020	.017	.015	.013	.012
18	.032	.028	.024	.021	.018	.016	.014	.012	.010	.009
19	.027	.023	.020	.017	.014	.012	.011	.009	.008	.007
20	.022	.019	.016	.014	.012	.010	.008	.007	.006	.005
21	.018	.015	.013	.011	.009	.008	.007	.006	.005	.004
22	.015	.013	.011	.009	.007	.006	.005	.004	.004	.003
23	.012	.010	.009	.007	.006	.005	.004	.003	.003	.002
24	.010	.008	.007	.006	.005	.004	.003	.003	.002	.002
25	.009	.007	.006	.005	.004	.003	.003	.002	.002	.001
30	.003	.003	.002	.002	.001	.001	.001	.001	*	*
35	.001	.001	.001	.001	*	*	*	*	*	*
40	*	*	*	*	*	*	*	*	*	*
45	*	*	*	*	*	*	*	*	*	*
50	*	*	*	*	*	*	*	*	*	*

*PVIF is zero to three decimal places.

Table 5A-4 Present Value Interest Factor for a One Dollar Annuity Discounted at *i* Percent for *n* Periods:

$$PVIFA_{i,n} = \frac{(1+i)^n - 1}{i(1+i)^n}$$

Period	1%	2%	3%	4%	5%	6%	7%	8%	9%	10%
1	.990	.980	.971	.962	.952	.943	.935	.926	.917	.909
2	1.970	1.942	1.913	1.886	1.859	1.833	1.808	1.783	1.759	1.736
3	2.941	2.884	2.829	2.775	2.723	2.673	2.624	2.577	2.531	2.487
4	3.902	3.808	3.717	3.630	3.546	3.465	3.387	3.312	3.240	3.170
5	4.853	4.713	4.580	4.452	4.329	4.212	4.100	3.993	3.890	3.791
6	5.795	5.601	5.417	5.242	5.076	4.917	4.767	4.623	4.486	4.355
7	6.728	6.472	6.230	6.002	5.786	5.582	5.389	5.206	5.033	4.868
8	7.652	7.326	7.020	6.733	6.463	6.210	5.971	5.747	5.535	5.335
9	8.566	8.162	7.786	7.435	7.108	6.802	6.515	6.247	5.995	5.759
10	9.471	8.983	8.530	8.111	7.722	7.360	7.024	6.710	6.418	6.145
11	10.368	9.787	9.253	8.760	8.306	7.887	7.499	7.139	6.805	6.495
12	11.255	10.575	9.954	9.385	8.863	8.384	7.943	7.536	7.161	6.814
13	12.134	11.348	10.635	9.986	9.394	8.853	8.358	7.904	7.487	7.013
14	13.004	12.106	11.296	10.563	9.899	9.295	8.745	8.244	7.786	7.367
15	13.865	12.849	11.938	11.118	10.380	9.712	9.108	8.560	8.061	7.606
16	14.718	13.578	12.561	11.652	10.838	10.106	9.447	8.851	8.313	7.824
17	15.562	14.292	13.166	12.166	11.274	10.477	9.763	9.122	8.544	8.022
18	16.398	14.992	13.754	12.659	11.690	10.828	10.059	9.372	8.756	8.201
19	17.226	15.679	14.324	13.134	12.085	11.158	10.336	9.604	8.950	8.365
20	18.046	16.352	14.878	13.590	12.462	11.470	10.594	9.818	9.129	8.514
21	18.857	17.011	15.415	14.029	12.821	11.764	10.836	10.017	9.292	8.649
22	19.661	17.658	15.937	14.451	13.163	12.042	11.061	10.201	9.442	8.772
23	20.456	18.292	16.444	14.857	13.489	12.303	11.272	10.371	9.580	8.883
24	21.244	18.914	16.936	15.247	13.799	12.550	11.469	10.529	9.707	8.985
25	22.023	19.524	17.413	15.622	14.094	12.783	11.654	10.675	9.823	9.077
30	25.808	22.396	19.601	17.292	15.373	13.765	12.409	11.258	10.274	9.427
35	29.409	24.999	21.487	18.665	16.374	14.498	12.948	11.655	10.567	9.644
40	32.835	27.356	23.155	19.793	17.159	15.046	13.332	11.925	10.757	9.779
45	36.095	29.490	24.519	20.720	17.774	15.456	13.606	12.108	10.881	9.863
50	39.196	31.424	25.730	21.482	18.256	15.762	13.801	12.233	10.962	9.915

Table 5A-4 (Continued)

Period	11%	12%	13%	14%	15%	16%	17%	18%	19%	20%
1	.901	.893	.885	.877	.870	.862	.855	.847	.840	.833
2	1.713	1.690	1.668	1.647	1.626	1.605	1.585	1.566	1.547	1.528
3	2.444	2.402	2.361	2.322	2.283	2.246	2.210	2.174	2.140	2.106
4	3.102	3.037	2.974	2.914	2.855	2.798	2.743	2.690	2.639	2.589
5	3.696	3.605	3.517	3.433	3.352	3.274	3.199	3.127	3.058	2.991
6	4.231	4.111	3.998	3.889	3.784	3.685	3.589	3.498	3.410	3.326
7	4.712	4.564	4.423	4.288	4.160	4.039	3.922	3.812	3.706	3.605
8	5.146	4.968	4.799	4.639	4.487	4.344	4.207	4.078	3.954	3.837
9	5.537	5.328	5.132	4.946	4.772	4.607	4.451	4.303	4.163	4.031
10	5.889	5.650	5.426	5.216	5.019	4.833	4.659	4.494	4.339	4.192
11	6.207	5.938	5.687	5.453	5.234	5.029	4.836	4.656	4.486	4.327
12	6.492	6.194	5.918	5.660	5.421	5.197	4.988	4.793	4.611	4.439
13	6.750	6.424	6.122	5.842	5.583	5.342	5.118	4.910	4.715	4.533
14	6.982	6.628	6.302	6.002	5.724	5.468	5.229	5.008	4.802	4.611
15	7.191	6.811	6.462	6.142	5.847	5.575	5.324	5.092	4.876	4.675
16	7.379	6.974	6.604	6.265	5.954	5.668	5.405	5.162	4.938	4.730
17	7.549	7.120	6.729	6.373	6.047	5.749	5.475	5.222	4.990	4.775
18	7.702	7.250	6.840	6.467	6.128	5.818	5.534	5.273	5.033	4.812
19	7.839	7.366	6.938	6.550	6.198	5.877	5.584	5.316	5.070	4.843
20	7.963	7.469	7.025	6.623	6.259	5.929	5.628	5.353	5.101	4.870
21	8.075	7.562	7.102	6.687	6.312	5.973	5.665	5.384	5.127	4.891
22	8.176	7.645	7.170	6.743	6.359	6.001	5.696	5.410	5.149	4.909
23	8.266	7.718	7.230	6.792	6.399	6.044	5.723	5.432	5.167	4.925
24	8.348	7.784	7.283	6.835	6.434	6.073	5.746	5.451	5.182	4.937
25	8.422	7.843	7.330	6.873	6.464	6.097	5.766	5.467	5.195	4.948
30	8.694	8.055	7.496	7.003	6.566	6.177	5.829	5.517	5.235	4.979
35	8.885	8.176	7.586	7.070	6.617	6.215	5.858	5.539	5.251	4.992
40	8.951	8.244	7.634	7.105	6.642	6.233	5.871	5.548	5.258	4.997
45	9.008	8.283	7.661	7.123	6.654	6.242	5.877	5.552	5.261	4.999
50	9.042	8.304	7.675	7.133	6.661	6.246	5.880	5.554	5.262	4.999

Table 5A-4 (Continued)

Period	21%	22%	23%	24%	25%	26%	27%	28%	29%	30%
1	.826	.820	.813	.806	.800	.794	.787	.781	.775	.769
2	1.509	1.492	1.474	1.457	1.440	1.424	1.407	1.392	1.376	1.361
3	2.074	2.042	2.011	1.981	1.952	1.923	1.896	1.868	1.842	1.816
4	2.540	2.494	2.448	2.404	2.362	2.320	2.280	2.241	2.203	2.166
5	2.926	2.864	2.803	2.745	2.689	2.635	2.583	2.532	2.483	2.436
6	3.245	3.167	3.092	3.020	2.951	2.885	2.821	2.759	2.700	2.643
7	3.508	3.416	3.327	3.242	3.161	3.083	3.009	2.937	2.868	2.802
8	3.726	3.619	3.518	3.421	3.329	3.241	3.156	3.076	2.999	2.925
9	3.905	3.786	3.673	3.566	3.463	3.366	3.273	3.184	3.100	3.019
10	4.054	3.923	3.799	3.682	3.570	3.465	3.364	3.269	3.178	3.092
11	4.177	4.035	3.902	3.776	3.656	3.544	3.437	3.335	3.239	3.147
12	4.278	4.127	3.985	3.851	3.725	3.606	3.493	3.387	3.286	3.190
13	4.362	4.203	4.053	3.912	3.780	3.656	3.538	3.427	3.322	3.223
14	4.432	4.265	4.108	3.962	3.824	3.695	3.573	3.459	3.351	3.249
15	4.489	4.315	4.153	4.001	3.859	3.726	3.601	3.483	3.373	3.268
16	4.536	4.357	4.189	4.033	3.887	3.751	3.623	3.503	3.390	3.283
17	4.576	4.391	4.219	4.059	3.910	3.771	3.640	3.518	3.403	3.295
18	4.608	4.419	4.243	4.080	3.928	3.786	3.654	3.529	3.413	3.304
19	4.635	4.442	4.263	4.097	3.942	3.799	3.664	3.539	3.421	3.311
20	4.657	4.460	4.279	4.110	3.954	3.808	3.673	3.546	3.427	3.316
21	4.675	4.476	4.292	4.121	3.963	3.816	3.679	3.551	3.432	3.320
22	4.690	4.488	4.302	4.130	3.970	3.822	3.684	3.556	3.436	3.323
23	4.703	4.499	4.311	4.137	3.976	3.827	3.689	3.559	3.438	3.325
24	4.713	4.507	4.318	4.143	3.981	3.831	3.692	3.562	3.441	3.327
25	4.721	4.514	4.323	4.147	3.985	3.834	3.694	3.564	3.442	3.329
30	4.746	4.534	4.339	4.160	3.995	3.842	3.701	3.569	3.447	3.332
35	4.756	4.541	4.345	4.164	3.998	3.845	3.703	3.571	3.448	3.333
40	4.760	4.544	4.347	4.166	3.999	3.846	3.703	3.571	3.448	3.333
45	4.761	4.545	4.347	4.166	4.000	3.846	3.704	3.571	3.448	3.333
50	4.762	4.545	4.348	4.167	4.000	3.846	3.704	3.571	3.448	3.333

Table 5A-5 Monthly Mortgage Constants (Monthly Payment = Loan Amount × Monthly Mortgage Constant)

	Annual Contract Interest Rate							
Year	9.00	9.25	9.50	9.75	10.00	10.25	10.50	10.75
1	0.08745	0.08757	0.08768	0.08780	0.08792	0.08803	0.08815	0.08827
2	0.04568	0.04580	0.04591	0.04603	0.04614	0.04626	0.04638	0.04649
3	0.03180	0.03192	0.03203	0.03215	0.03227	0.03238	0.03250	0.03262
4	0.02489	0.02500	0.02512	0.02524	0.02536	0.02548	0.02560	0.02572
5	0.02076	0.02088	0.02100	0.02112	0.02125	0.02137	0.02149	0.02162
6	0.01803	0.01815	0.01827	0.01840	0.01853	0.01865	0.01878	0.01891
7	0.01609	0.01622	0.01634	0.01647	0.01660	0.01673	0.01686	0.01699
8	0.01465	0.01478	0.01491	0.01504	0.01517	0.01531	0.01544	0.01557
9	0.01354	0.01368	0.01381	0.01394	0.01408	0.01421	0.01435	0.01449
10	0.01267	0.01280	0.01294	0.01308	0.01322	0.01335	0.01349	0.01363
11	0.01196	0.01210	0.01224	0.01238	0.01252	0.01266	0.01280	0.01295
12	0.01138	0.01152	0.01166	0.01181	0.01195	0.01210	0.01224	0.01239
13	0.01090	0.01104	0.01119	0.01133	0.01148	0.01163	0.01178	0.01192
14	0.01049	0.01064	0.01078	0.01093	0.01108	0.01123	0.01138	0.01154
15	0.01014	0.01029	0.01044	0.01059	0.01075	0.01090	0.01105	0.01121
16	0.00985	0.01000	0.01015	0.01030	0.01046	0.01062	0.01077	0.01093
17	0.00959	0.00974	0.00990	0.01005	0.01021	0.01037	0.01053	0.01069
18	0.00936	0.00952	0.00968	0.00984	0.01000	0.01016	0.01032	0.01049
19	0.00917	0.00933	0.00949	0.00965	0.00981	0.00998	0.01014	0.01031
20	0.00900	0.00916	0.00932	0.00949	0.00965	0.00982	0.00998	0.01015
21	0.00885	0.00901	0.00917	0.00934	0.00951	0.00968	0.00985	0.01002
22	0.00871	0.00888	0.00904	0.00921	0.00938	0.00955	0.00973	0.00990
23	0.00859	0.00876	0.00893	0.00910	0.00927	0.00944	0.00962	0.00979
24	0.00849	0.00866	0.00883	0.00900	0.00917	0.00935	0.00952	0.00970
25	0.00839	0.00856	0.00874	0.00891	0.00909	0.00926	0.00944	0.00962
26	0.00831	0.00848	0.00866	0.00883	0.00901	0.00919	0.00937	0.00955
27	0.00823	0.00841	0.00858	0.00876	0.00894	0.00912	0.00930	0.00949
28	0.00816	0.00834	0.00852	0.00870	0.00888	0.00906	0.00925	0.00943
29	0.00810	0.00828	0.00846	0.00864	0.00882	0.00901	0.00919	0.00938
30	0.00805	0.00823	0.00841	0.00859	0.00878	0.00896	0.00915	0.00933
31	0.00800	0.00818	0.00836	0.00855	0.00873	0.00892	0.00911	0.00930
32	0.00795	0.00813	0.00832	0.00851	0.00869	0.00888	0.00907	0.00926
33	0.00791	0.00810	0.00828	0.00847	0.00866	0.00885	0.00904	0.00923
34	0.00787	0.00806	0.00825	0.00844	0.00863	0.00882	0.00901	0.00920
35	0.00784	0.00803	0.00822	0.00841	0.00860	0.00879	0.00898	0.00918

Table 5A-5 (Continued)

Year	11.00	11.25	11.50	11.75	12.00	12.25	12.50	12.75
	Annual Contract Interest Rate							
1	0.08838	0.08850	0.08862	0.08873	0.08885	0.08897	0.08908	0.08920
2	0.04661	0.04672	0.04684	0.04696	0.04707	0.04719	0.04731	0.04742
3	0.03274	0.03286	0.03298	0.03310	0.03321	0.03333	0.03345	0.03357
4	0.02585	0.02597	0.02609	0.02621	0.02633	0.02646	0.02658	0.02670
5	0.02174	0.02187	0.02199	0.02212	0.02224	0.02237	0.02250	0.02263
6	0.01903	0.01916	0.01929	0.01942	0.01955	0.01968	0.01981	0.01994
7	0.01712	0.01725	0.01739	0.01752	0.01765	0.01779	0.01792	0.01806
8	0.01571	0.01584	0.01598	0.01612	0.01625	0.01639	0.01653	0.01667
9	0.01463	0.01476	0.01490	0.01504	0.01518	0.01533	0.01547	0.01561
10	0.01378	0.01392	0.01406	0.01420	0.01435	0.01449	0.01464	0.01478
11	0.01309	0.01324	0.01338	0.01353	0.01368	0.01383	0.01398	0.01413
12	0.01254	0.01268	0.01283	0.01298	0.01313	0.01329	0.01344	0.01359
13	0.01208	0.01223	0.01238	0.01253	0.01269	0.01284	0.01300	0.01315
14	0.01169	0.01185	0.01200	0.01216	0.01231	0.01247	0.01263	0.01279
15	0.01137	0.01152	0.01168	0.01184	0.01200	0.01216	0.01233	0.01249
16	0.01109	0.01125	0.01141	0.01157	0.01174	0.01190	0.01207	0.01223
17	0.01085	0.01102	0.01118	0.01135	0.01151	0.01168	0.01185	0.01202
18	0.01065	0.01082	0.01098	0.01115	0.01132	0.01149	0.01166	0.01183
19	0.01047	0.01064	0.01081	0.01098	0.01115	0.01133	0.01150	0.01167
20	0.01032	0.01049	0.01066	0.01084	0.01101	0.01119	0.01136	0.01154
21	0.01019	0.01036	0.01054	0.01071	0.01089	0.01106	0.01124	0.01142
22	0.01007	0.01025	0.01042	0.01060	0.01078	0.01096	0.01114	0.01132
23	0.00997	0.01015	0.01033	0.01051	0.01069	0.01087	0.01105	0.01123
24	0.00988	0.01006	0.01024	0.01042	0.01060	0.01079	0.01097	0.01116
25	0.00980	0.00998	0.01016	0.01035	0.01053	0.01072	0.01090	0.01109
26	0.00973	0.00991	0.01010	0.01028	0.01047	0.01066	0.01084	0.01103
27	0.00967	0.00985	0.01004	0.01023	0.01041	0.01060	0.01079	0.01098
28	0.00961	0.00980	0.00999	0.01018	0.01037	0.01056	0.01075	0.01094
29	0.00957	0.00975	0.00994	0.01013	0.01032	0.01052	0.01071	0.01090
30	0.00952	0.00971	0.00990	0.01009	0.01029	0.01048	0.01067	0.01087
31	0.00948	0.00968	0.00987	0.01006	0.01025	0.01045	0.01064	0.01084
32	0.00945	0.00964	0.00984	0.01003	0.01022	0.01042	0.01062	0.01081
33	0.00942	0.00961	0.00981	0.01000	0.01020	0.01039	0.01059	0.01079
34	0.00939	0.00959	0.00978	0.00998	0.01018	0.01037	0.01057	0.01077
35	0.00937	0.00956	0.00976	0.00996	0.01016	0.01035	0.01055	0.01075

Table 5A-5 (Continued)

Year	Annual Contract Interest Rate 13.00	13.25	13.50	13.75	14.00	14.25	14.50	14.75
1	0.08932	0.08943	0.08955	0.08967	0.08979	0.08990	0.90020	0.09014
2	0.04754	0.04766	0.04778	0.04789	0.04801	0.04813	0.04825	0.04837
3	0.03369	0.03381	0.03394	0.03406	0.02418	0.03430	0.03442	0.03454
4	0.02683	0.02695	0.02708	0.02720	0.02733	0.02745	0.02758	0.02770
5	0.02275	0.02288	0.02301	0.02314	0.02327	0.02340	0.02353	0.02366
6	0.02007	0.02021	0.02034	0.02047	0.02061	0.02074	0.02087	0.02101
7	0.01819	0.01833	0.01846	0.01860	0.01874	0.01888	0.01902	0.01916
8	0.01681	0.01695	0.01709	0.01723	0.01737	0.01751	0.01766	0.01780
9	0.01575	0.01590	0.01604	0.01619	0.01633	0.01648	0.01663	0.01678
10	0.01493	0.01508	0.01523	0.01538	0.01553	0.01568	0.01583	0.01598
11	0.01428	0.01443	0.01458	0.01473	0.01489	0.01504	0.01520	0.01535
12	0.01375	0.01390	0.01406	0.01421	0.01437	0.01453	0.01469	0.01485
13	0.01331	0.01347	0.01363	0.01379	0.01395	0.01411	0.01428	0.01444
14	0.01295	0.01300	0.01328	0.01344	0.01360	0.01377	0.01394	0.01410
15	0.01265	0.01282	0.01298	0.01315	0.01332	0.01349	0.01366	0.01383
16	0.01240	0.01257	0.01274	0.01291	0.01308	0.01325	0.01342	0.01359
17	0.01219	0.01236	0.01253	0.01270	0.01287	0.01305	0.01322	0.01340
18	0.01200	0.01218	0.01235	0.01253	0.01270	0.01288	0.01306	0.01324
19	0.01185	0.01203	0.01220	0.01238	0.01256	0.01274	0.01292	0.01310
20	0.01172	0.01189	0.01207	0.01225	0.01244	0.01262	0.01280	0.01298
21	0.01160	0.01178	0.01196	0.01215	0.01233	0.01251	0.01270	0.01288
22	0.01150	0.01169	0.01187	0.01205	0.01224	0.01243	0.01261	0.01280
23	0.01142	0.01160	0.01179	0.01197	0.01216	0.01235	0.01254	0.01273
24	0.01134	0.01153	0.01172	0.01191	0.01210	0.01229	0.01248	0.01267
25	0.01128	0.01147	0.01166	0.01185	0.01204	0.01223	0.01242	0.01261
26	0.01122	0.01141	0.01160	0.01180	0.01199	0.01218	0.01238	0.01257
27	0.01117	0.01137	0.01156	0.01175	0.01195	0.01214	0.01234	0.01253
28	0.01113	0.01132	0.01152	0.01171	0.01191	0.01210	0.01230	0.01250
29	0.01109	0.01129	0.01148	0.01168	0.01188	0.01207	0.01227	0.01247
30	0.01106	0.01126	0.01145	0.01165	0.01185	0.01205	0.01225	0.01244
31	0.01103	0.01123	0.01143	0.01163	0.01182	0.01202	0.01222	0.01242
32	0.01101	0.01121	0.01141	0.01160	0.01180	0.01200	0.01220	0.01241
33	0.01099	0.01119	0.01139	0.01159	0.01179	0.01199	0.01219	0.01239
34	0.01097	0.01117	0.01137	0.01157	0.01177	0.01197	0.01217	0.01238
35	0.01095	0.01115	0.01135	0.01155	0.01176	0.01196	0.01216	0.01236

Table 5A-5 (Continued)

	Annual Contract Interest Rate							
Year	15.00	15.25	15.50	15.75	16.00	16.25	16.50	16.75
1	0.09026	0.09038	0.09049	0.09061	0.09073	0.09085	0.09097	0.09109
2	0.04849	0.04861	0.04872	0.04884	0.04896	0.04908	0.04920	0.04932
3	0.03467	0.03479	0.03491	0.03503	0.03516	0.03528	0.03540	0.03553
4	0.02783	0.02796	0.02808	0.02821	0.02834	0.02847	0.02860	0.02873
5	0.02379	0.02392	0.02405	0.02419	0.02432	0.02445	0.02458	0.02472
6	0.02115	0.02128	0.02142	0.02155	0.02169	0.02183	0.02197	0.02211
7	0.01930	0.01944	0.01958	0.01972	0.01986	0.02000	0.02015	0.02029
8	0.01795	0.01809	0.01824	0.01838	0.01853	0.01868	0.01882	0.01897
9	0.01692	0.01707	0.01722	0.01737	0.01753	0.01768	0.01783	0.01798
10	0.01613	0.01629	0.01644	0.01660	0.01675	0.01691	0.01706	0.01722
11	0.01551	0.01567	0.01582	0.01598	0.01614	0.01630	0.01646	0.01663
12	0.01501	0.01517	0.01533	0.01549	0.01566	0.01582	0.01599	0.01615
13	0.01460	0.01477	0.01493	0.01510	0.01527	0.01543	0.01560	0.01577
14	0.01427	0.01444	0.01461	0.01478	0.01495	0.01512	0.01529	0.01546
15	0.01400	0.01417	0.01434	0.01451	0.01469	0.01486	0.01504	0.01521
16	0.01377	0.01394	0.01412	0.01429	0.01447	0.01465	0.01483	0.01501
17	0.01358	0.01375	0.01393	0.01411	0.01429	0.01447	0.01465	0.01484
18	0.01342	0.01360	0.01378	0.01396	0.01414	0.01433	0.01451	0.01469
19	0.01328	0.01346	0.01365	0.01383	0.01402	0.01420	0.01439	0.01458
20	0.01317	0.01335	0.01354	0.01373	0.01391	0.01410	0.01429	0.01448
21	0.01307	0.01326	0.01345	0.01364	0.01382	0.01401	0.01420	0.01440
22	0.01299	0.01318	0.01337	0.01356	0.01375	0.01394	0.01413	0.01433
23	0.01292	0.01311	0.01330	0.01349	0.01369	0.01388	0.01407	0.01427
24	0.01286	0.01305	0.01325	0.01344	0.01363	0.01383	0.01402	0.01422
25	0.01281	0.01300	0.01320	0.01339	0.01359	0.01379	0.01398	0.01418
26	0.01276	0.01296	0.01316	0.01335	0.01355	0.01375	0.01395	0.01415
27	0.01273	0.01292	0.01312	0.01332	0.01352	0.01372	0.01392	0.01412
28	0.01270	0.01289	0.01309	0.01329	0.01349	0.01369	0.01389	0.01409
29	0.01267	0.01287	0.01307	0.01327	0.01347	0.01367	0.01387	0.01407
30	0.01264	0.01284	0.01305	0.01325	0.01345	0.01365	0.01385	0.01405
31	0.01262	0.01283	0.01303	0.01323	0.01343	0.01363	0.01384	0.01404
32	0.01261	0.01281	0.01301	0.01321	0.01342	0.01362	0.01382	0.01403
33	0.01259	0.01279	0.01300	0.01320	0.01340	0.01361	0.01381	0.01402
34	0.01258	0.01278	0.01299	0.01319	0.01339	0.01360	0.01380	0.01401
35	0.01257	0.01277	0.01298	0.01318	0.01338	0.01359	0.01379	0.01400

Table 5A-6 Annual Percentage Rate (APR), Terms of Loan: 20 years

	Percentage Points Charged							
Contract Rate	0.50	1.00	1.50	2.00	2.50	3.00	3.50	4.00
7.00	7.0648	7.1301	7.1960	7.2623	7.3291	7.3965	7.4644	7.5329
7.25	7.3155	7.3814	7.4479	7.5149	7.5824	7.6505	7.7191	7.7882
7.50	7.5661	7.6328	7.6999	7.7676	7.8358	7.9045	7.9738	8.0437
7.75	7.8168	7.8841	7.9519	8.0203	8.0892	8.1586	8.2286	8.2992
8.00	8.0675	8.1354	8.2040	8.2730	8.3426	8.4128	8.4835	8.5548
8.25	8.3181	8.3868	8.4560	8.5258	8.5961	8.6669	8.7384	8.8104
8.50	8.5688	8.6382	8.7081	8.7786	8.8496	8.9212	8.9934	9.0661
8.75	8.8195	8.8896	8.9602	9.0314	9.1031	9.1755	9.2484	9.3219
9.00	9.0702	9.1410	9.2123	9.2842	9.3567	9.4298	9.5035	9.5778
9.25	9.3209	9.3924	9.4645	9.5371	9.6104	9.6842	9.7586	9.8337
9.50	9.5717	9.6439	9.7167	9.7901	9.8641	9.9386	10.0138	10.0897
9.75	9.8224	9.8953	9.9689	10.0430	10.1178	10.1931	10.2691	10.3457
10.00	10.0731	10.1468	10.2211	10.2960	10.3715	10.4477	10.5244	10.6019
10.25	10.3239	10.3983	10.4734	10.5491	10.6253	10.7023	10.7798	10.8580
10.50	10.5746	10.6498	10.7257	10.8021	10.8792	10.9569	11.0353	11.1143
10.75	10.8254	10.9014	10.9780	11.0552	11.1331	11.2116	11.2908	11.3706
11.00	11.0761	11.1529	11.2303	11.3083	11.3870	11.4663	11.5464	11.6270
11.25	11.3269	11.4045	11.4827	11.5615	11.6410	11.7211	11.8020	11.8835
11.50	11.5777	11.6560	11.7350	11.8147	11.8950	11.9760	12.0577	12.1400
11.75	11.8285	11.9076	11.9874	12.0679	12.1490	12.2309	12.3134	12.3966
12.00	12.0793	12.1592	12.2399	12.3212	12.4031	12.4858	12.5692	12.6533
12.25	12.3301	12.4109	12.4923	12.5744	12.6573	12.7408	12.8250	12.9100
12.50	12.5809	12.6625	12.7448	12.8278	12.9114	12.9958	13.0810	13.1668
12.75	12.8317	12.9142	12.9973	13.0811	13.1657	13.2509	13.3369	13.4237
13.00	13.0826	13.1658	13.2498	13.3345	13.4199	13.5061	13.5929	13.6806
13.25	13.3334	13.4175	13.5024	13.5879	13.6742	13.7612	13.8470	13.9376
13.50	13.5843	13.6692	13.7549	13.8413	13.9285	14.0165	14.1052	14.1946
13.75	13.8351	13.9209	14.0075	14.0948	14.1829	14.2717	14.3613	14.4518
14.00	14.0860	14.1727	14.2601	14.3483	14.4373	14.5270	14.6176	14.7089
14.25	14.3368	14.4244	14.5128	14.6019	14.6917	14.7824	14.8739	14.9662
14.50	14.5877	14.6762	14.7654	14.8554	14.9462	15.0378	15.1302	15.2235
14.75	14.8386	14.9280	15.0181	15.1090	15.2007	15.2933	15.3866	15.4808
15.00	15.0895	15.1798	15.2708	15.3626	15.4553	15.5488	15.6431	15.7383
15.25	15.3404	15.4316	15.5235	15.6163	15.7099	15.8043	15.8996	15.9957
15.50	15.5913	15.6834	15.7763	15.8700	15.9645	16.0599	16.1562	16.2533
15.75	15.8422	15.9352	16.0290	16.1237	16.2192	16.3156	16.4128	16.5109
16.00	16.0931	16.1871	16.2818	16.3774	16.4739	16.5712	16.6694	16.7685
16.25	16.3441	16.4389	16.5346	16.6312	16.7286	16.8269	16.9261	17.0263
16.50	16.5950	16.6908	16.7875	16.8850	16.9834	17.0827	17.1829	17.2840
16.75	16.8459	16.9427	17.0403	17.1388	17.2382	17.3385	17.4397	17.5419

Table 5A-6 (Continued)

Contract Rate	Percentage Points Charged 4.50	5.00	5.50	6.00	6.50	7.00	7.50	8.00
7.00	7.6018	7.6714	7.7415	7.8121	7.8834	7.9552	8.0276	8.1007
7.25	7.8579	7.9282	7.9990	8.0704	8.1424	8.2149	8.2881	8.3619
7.50	8.1141	8.1850	8.2566	8.3287	8.4015	8.4748	8.5488	8.6233
7.75	8.3703	8.4420	8.5143	8.5872	8.6607	8.7348	8.8095	8.8849
8.00	8.6266	8.6991	8.7721	8.8458	8.9200	8.9949	9.0704	9.1466
8.25	8.8830	8.9562	9.0300	9.1044	9.1795	9.2551	9.3314	9.4084
8.50	9.1395	9.2134	9.2880	9.3632	9.4390	9.5155	9.5926	9.6704
8.75	9.3960	9.4707	9.5461	9.6221	9.6987	9.7760	9.8539	9.9325
9.00	9.6526	9.7281	9.8043	9.8811	9.9858	10.0366	10.1154	10.1948
9.25	9.9093	9.9856	10.0626	10.1402	10.2184	10.2973	10.3769	10.4572
9.50	10.1661	10.2432	10.3210	10.3994	10.4784	10.5582	10.6386	10.7198
9.75	10.4230	10.5009	10.5794	10.6587	10.7386	10.8192	10.9005	10.9825
10.00	10.6799	10.7586	10.8380	10.9181	10.9988	11.0803	11.1624	11.2453
10.25	10.9369	11.0165	11.0967	11.1776	11.2592	11.3415	11.4246	11.5083
10.50	11.1940	11.2744	11.3554	11.4372	11.5197	11.6029	11.6868	11.7715
10.75	11.4512	11.5324	11.6143	11.6969	11.7803	11.8644	11.9492	12.0347
11.00	11.7084	11.7905	11.8733	11.9568	12.0410	12.1260	12.2117	12.2982
11.25	11.9657	12.0487	12.1323	12.2167	12.3018	12.3877	12.4743	12.5617
11.50	12.2231	12.3069	12.3914	12.4767	12.5627	12.6495	12.7371	12.8254
11.75	12.4806	12.5653	12.6507	12.7369	12.8238	12.9115	13.0000	13.0893
12.00	12.7381	12.8237	12.9100	12.9971	13.0849	13.1736	13.2630	13.3533
12.25	12.9957	13.0822	13.1694	13.2574	13.3462	13.4358	13.5262	13.6174
12.50	13.2534	13.3408	13.4289	13.5179	13.6076	13.6981	13.7895	13.8817
12.75	13.5112	13.5995	13.6885	13.7784	13.8691	13.9606	14.0529	14.1461
13.00	13.7690	13.8582	13.9482	14.0390	14.1307	14.2231	14.3164	14.4106
13.25	14.0269	14.1171	14.2080	14.2998	14.3924	14.4858	14.5801	14.6783
13.50	14.2849	14.3760	14.1679	14.5606	14.6542	14.7486	14.8439	14.9401
13.75	14.5430	14.6350	14.7278	14.8215	14.9161	15.0115	15.1078	15.2050
14.00	14.8011	14.8941	14.9879	15.0826	15.1781	15.2745	15.3719	15.4701
14.25	15.0593	15.1532	15.2480	15.3437	15.4402	15.5377	15.6360	15.7353
14.50	15.3175	15.4125	15.5082	15.6049	15.7025	15.8009	15.9003	16.0006
14.75	15.5759	15.6718	15.7686	15.8662	15.9648	16.0643	16.1647	16.2661
15.00	15.8343	15.9312	16.0289	16.1276	16.2272	16.3278	16.4292	16.5317
15.25	16.0927	16.1906	16.2894	16.3891	16.4898	16.5913	16.6939	16.7974
15.50	16.3513	16.4502	16.5500	16.6507	16.7524	16.8550	16.9586	17.0632
15.75	16.6099	16.7098	16.8106	16.9124	17.0151	17.1188	17.2235	17.3292
16.00	16.8685	16.9695	17.0713	17.1742	17.2779	17.2827	17.4885	17.5953
16.25	17.1273	17.2292	17.3321	17.4360	17.5409	17.6467	17.7536	17.8615
16.50	17.3861	17.4891	17.5930	17.6980	17.8039	17.9108	18.0188	18.1278
16.75	17.6449	17.7490	17.8540	17.9600	18.0670	18.1750	18.2841	18.3942

Table 5A-6 (Continued)

	Percentage Points Charged							
Contract Rate	**8.50**	**9.00**	**9.50**	**10.00**	**10.50**	**11.00**	**11.50**	**12.00**
7.00	8.1743	8.2486	8.3235	8.3990	8.4752	8.5521	8.6296	8.7078
7.25	8.4363	8.5114	8.5871	8.6634	8.7405	8.8181	8.8965	8.9756
7.50	8.6985	8.7744	8.8509	8.9280	9.0059	9.0844	9.1636	9.2435
7.75	8.9609	9.0375	9.1148	9.1928	9.2715	9.3509	9.4309	9.5117
8.00	9.2234	9.3008	9.3790	9.4578	9.5373	9.6175	9.6985	9.7801
8.25	9.4860	9.5643	9.6433	9.7230	9.8033	9.8844	9.9662	10.0488
8.50	9.7488	9.8280	9.9078	9.9883	10.0696	10.1515	10.2342	10.3177
8.75	10.0118	10.0918	10.1725	10.2539	10.3360	10.4188	10.5024	10.5868
9.00	10.2749	10.3558	10.4373	10.5195	10.6026	10.6863	10.7709	10.8561
9.25	10.5382	10.6199	10.7023	10.7855	10.8694	10.9541	11.0395	11.1257
9.50	10.8016	10.8842	10.9675	11.0516	11.1364	11.2220	11.3084	11.3955
9.75	11.0652	11.1487	11.2329	11.3179	11.4036	11.4901	11.5774	11.6656
10.00	11.3290	11.4133	11.4984	11.5843	11.6710	11.7585	11.8467	11.9358
10.25	11.5928	11.6781	11.7642	11.8510	11.9386	12.0270	12.1163	12.2063
10.50	11.8569	11.9431	12.0301	12.1178	12.2064	12.2958	12.3860	12.4770
10.75	12.1211	12.2082	12.2961	12.3848	12.4774	12.5647	12.6559	12.7480
11.00	12.3854	12.4735	12.5624	12.6520	12.7425	12.8339	12.9261	13.0192
11.25	12.6499	12.7390	12.8288	12.9194	13.0109	13.1033	13.1965	13.2906
11.50	12.9146	13.0046	13.0954	13.1870	13.2795	13.3728	13.4671	13.5622
11.75	13.1794	13.2703	13.3621	13.4547	13.5482	13.6426	13.7379	13.8340
12.00	13.4444	13.5363	13.6290	13.7227	13.8172	13.9126	14.0089	14.1061
12.25	13.7095	13.8024	13.8961	13.9908	14.0863	14.1827	14.2801	14.3784
12.50	13.9747	14.0686	14.1634	14.2590	14.3556	14.4531	14.5515	14.6509
12.75	14.2401	14.3350	14.4308	14.5275	14.6251	14.7237	14.8232	14.9236
13.00	14.5056	14.6016	14.6984	14.7961	14.8948	14.9944	15.0950	15.1966
13.25	14.7713	14.8683	14.9661	15.0649	15.1647	15.2654	15.3670	15.4697
13.50	15.0371	15.1351	15.2341	15.3339	15.4347	15.5365	15.6393	15.7431
13.75	15.3031	15.4022	15.5021	15.6031	15.7050	15.8079	15.9117	16.0167
14.00	15.5692	15.6693	15.7704	15.8724	15.9754	16.0794	16.1844	16.2905
14.25	15.8355	15.9366	16.0388	16.1419	16.2460	16.3511	16.4572	16.5644
14.50	16.1019	16.2041	16.3073	16.4115	16.5167	16.6230	16.7303	16.8386
14.75	16.3684	16.4717	16.5760	16.6813	16.7877	16.8951	17.0035	17.1131
15.00	16.6351	16.7395	16.8449	16.9513	17.0588	17.1673	17.2769	17.3877
15.25	16.9019	17.0074	17.1139	17.2215	17.3301	17.4398	17.5506	17.6625
15.50	17.1688	17.2754	17.3831	17.4918	17.6015	17.7124	17.8244	17.9375
15.75	17.4359	17.5436	17.6524	17.7622	17.8732	17.9852	18.0984	18.2127
16.00	17.7031	17.8119	17.9218	18.0328	18.1450	18.2582	18.3725	18.4881
16.25	17.9704	18.0804	18.1915	18.3036	18.4169	18.5313	18.6469	18.7636
16.50	18.2378	18.3490	18.4612	18.5746	18.6890	18.8046	18.9214	19.0394
16.75	18.5054	18.6177	18.7311	18.8456	18.9613	19.0781	19.1961	19.3154

Table 5A-6 (Continued) Term of Loan: 25 Years

	Percentage Points Charged							
Contract Rate	0.50	1.00	1.50	2.00	2.50	3.00	3.50	4.00
7.00	7.0556	7.1117	7.1682	7.2251	7.2825	7.3404	7.3987	7.4575
7.25	7.3063	7.3631	7.4203	7.4780	7.5361	7.5947	7.6538	7.7133
7.50	7.5570	7.6145	7.6725	7.7309	7.7897	7.8491	7.9089	7.9693
7.75	7.8078	7.8660	7.9246	7.9838	8.0434	8.1036	8.1642	8.2253
8.00	8.0585	8.1174	8.1769	8.2368	8.2972	8.3581	8.4195	8.4814
8.25	8.3092	8.3689	8.4291	8.4898	8.5510	8.6127	8.6749	8.7376
8.50	8.5600	8.6205	8.6814	8.7429	8.8049	8.8673	8.9304	8.9939
8.75	8.8107	8.8720	8.9337	8.9960	9.0588	9.1221	9.1859	9.2503
9.00	9.0615	9.1236	9.1861	9.2491	9.3127	9.3768	9.4415	9.5067
9.25	9.3123	9.3751	9.4385	9.5023	9.5667	9.6317	9.6972	9.7632
9.50	9.5631	9.6267	9.6909	9.7556	9.8208	9.8866	9.9529	10.0199
9.75	9.8139	9.8783	9.9433	10.0088	10.0749	10.1416	10.2088	10.2766
10.00	10.0647	10.1300	10.1958	10.2622	10.3291	10.3966	10.4647	10.5333
10.25	10.3155	10.3816	10.4483	10.5155	10.5833	10.6517	10.7206	10.7902
10.50	10.5664	10.6333	10.7008	10.7689	10.8376	10.9068	10.9767	11.0471
10.75	10.8172	10.8850	10.9534	11.0223	11.0919	11.1620	11.2328	11.3042
11.00	11.0681	11.1367	11.2060	11.2758	11.3462	11.4173	11.4890	11.5613
11.25	11.3189	11.3885	11.4586	11.5293	11.6006	11.6726	11.7452	11.8184
11.50	11.5698	11.6402	11.7112	11.7828	11.8551	11.9280	12.0015	12.0757
11.75	11.8207	11.8920	11.9639	12.0364	12.1096	12.1834	12.2579	12.3330
12.00	12.0716	12.1438	12.2166	12.2900	12.3641	12.4389	12.5143	12.5904
12.25	12.3225	12.3956	12.4693	12.5437	12.6187	12.6945	12.7708	12.8479
12.50	12.5734	12.6474	12.7221	12.7974	12.8734	12.9501	13.0274	13.1055
12.75	12.8243	12.8992	12.9748	13.0511	13.1281	13.2057	13.2841	13.3631
13.00	13.0752	13.1511	13.2276	13.3049	13.3828	13.4614	13.5408	13.6208
13.25	13.3262	13.4030	13.4805	13.5587	13.6376	13.7172	13.7975	13.8786
13.50	13.5771	13.6549	13.7333	13.8125	13.8924	13.9730	14.0544	14.1365
13.75	13.8280	13.9068	13.9862	14.0664	14.1473	14.2289	14.3112	14.3944
14.00	14.0790	14.1587	14.2391	14.3203	14.4022	14.4848	14.5682	14.6524
14.25	14.3300	14.4106	14.4921	14.5742	14.6571	14.7408	14.8252	14.9104
14.50	14.5809	14.6626	14.7450	14.8282	14.9121	14.9968	15.0822	15.1658
14.75	14.8319	14.9146	14.9980	15.0822	15.1671	15.2528	15.3394	15.4267
15.00	15.0829	15.1666	15.2510	15.3362	15.4222	15.5090	15.5965	15.6849
15.25	15.3339	15.4186	15.5040	15.5902	15.6773	15.7651	15.8538	15.9433
15.50	15.5849	15.6706	15.7571	15.8443	15.9324	16.0213	16.1110	16.2016
15.75	15.8359	15.9226	16.0101	16.0985	16.1876	16.2776	16.3684	16.4601
16.00	16.0869	16.1747	16.2632	16.3526	16.4428	16.5339	16.6258	16.7185
16.25	16.3380	16.4267	16.5163	16.6068	16.6980	16.7902	16.8832	16.9771
16.50	16.5890	16.6788	16.7695	16.8610	16.9533	17.0466	17.1407	17.2357
16.75	16.8400	16.9309	17.0226	17.1152	17.2086	17.3030	17.3982	17.4944

Table 5A-6 (Continued)

Contract Rate	Percentage Points Charged 4.50	5.00	5.50	6.00	6.50	7.00	7.50	8.00
7.00	7.5168	7.5766	7.6368	7.6976	7.7589	7.8207	7.8831	7.9459
7.25	7.7734	7.8340	7.8950	7.9566	8.0187	8.0813	8.1445	8.2082
7.50	8.0301	8.0915	8.1533	8.2157	8.2786	8.3421	8.4061	8.4707
7.75	8.2869	8.3491	8.4118	8.4750	8.5387	8.6030	8.6679	8.7333
8.00	8.5439	8.6068	8.6703	8.7344	8.7989	8.8641	8.9298	8.9961
8.25	8.8009	8.8647	8.9290	8.9939	9.0593	9.1253	9.1919	9.2591
8.50	9.0580	9.1226	9.1878	9.2535	9.3198	9.3867	9.4542	9.5223
8.75	9.3152	9.3806	9.4467	9.5133	9.5805	9.6483	9.7167	9.7856
9.00	9.5725	9.6388	9.7057	9.7732	9.8413	9.9100	9.9793	10.0492
9.25	9.8299	9.8971	9.9649	10.0332	10.1022	10.1718	10.2420	10.3129
9.50	10.0873	10.1554	10.2241	10.2934	10.3633	10.4338	10.5050	10.5768
9.75	10.3449	10.4139	10.4835	10.5537	10.6245	10.6960	10.7681	10.8408
10.00	10.6026	10.6725	10.7430	10.8141	10.8859	10.9583	11.0313	11.1051
10.25	10.8604	10.9312	11.0026	11.0746	11.1474	11.2207	11.2948	11.3695
10.50	11.1182	11.1899	11.2623	11.3353	11.4090	11.4833	11.5583	11.6340
10.75	11.3762	11.4488	11.5221	11.5961	11.6707	11.7461	11.8221	11.8988
11.00	11.6342	11.7078	11.7821	11.8570	11.9326	12.0089	12.0860	12.1637
11.25	11.8923	11.9669	12.0421	12.1180	12.1947	12.2720	12.3500	12.4288
11.50	12.1505	12.2261	12.3023	12.3792	12.4568	12.5351	12.6142	12.6940
11.75	12.4088	12.4854	12.5626	12.6405	12.7191	12.7985	12.8786	12.9594
12.00	12.6672	12.7447	12.8229	12.9019	12.9815	13.0619	13.1431	13.2250
12.25	12.9257	13.0042	13.0834	13.1634	13.2440	13.3255	13.4077	13.4907
12.50	13.1843	13.2638	13.3440	13.4250	13.5067	13.5892	13.6725	13.7566
12.75	13.4429	13.5234	13.6047	13.6867	13.7695	13.8531	13.9374	14.0226
13.00	13.7016	13.7832	13.8655	13.9485	14.0324	14.1171	14.2025	14.2888
13.25	13.9604	14.0430	14.1264	14.2105	14.2954	14.3812	14.4677	14.5551
13.50	14.2193	14.3029	14.3873	14.4726	14.5586	14.6454	14.7331	14.8216
13.75	14.4783	14.5629	14.6484	14.7347	14.8218	14.9098	14.9986	15.0882
14.00	14.7373	14.8230	14.9096	14.9970	15.0852	15.1743	15.2642	15.3550
14.25	14.9964	15.0832	15.1709	15.2594	15.3487	15.4389	15.5300	15.6219
14.50	15.2556	15.3435	15.4322	15.5218	15.6123	15.7036	15.7958	15.8890
14.75	15.5149	15.6039	15.6937	15.7844	15.8760	15.9685	16.0618	16.1561
15.00	15.7742	15.8643	15.9552	16.0471	16.1398	16.2334	16.3280	16.4235
15.25	16.0336	16.1248	16.2169	16.3098	16.4037	16.4985	16.5942	16.6909
15.50	16.2931	16.3854	16.4786	16.5727	16.6677	16.7437	16.8606	16.9585
15.75	16.5526	16.6461	16.7404	16.8357	16.9319	17.0290	17.1271	17.2262
16.00	16.8122	16.9068	17.0023	17.0987	17.1961	17.2944	17.3937	17.4940
16.25	17.0719	17.1676	17.2642	17.3618	17.4604	17.5599	17.6604	17.7620
16.50	17.3316	17.4285	17.5263	17.6251	17.7248	17.8255	17.9273	18.0300
16.75	17.5914	17.6894	17.7884	17.8884	17.9893	18.0912	18.1942	18.2982

Table 5A-6 (Continued)

	Percentage Points Charged							
Contract Rate	**8.50**	**9.00**	**9.50**	**10.00**	**10.50**	**11.00**	**11.50**	**12.00**
7.00	8.0094	8.0733	8.1379	8.2030	8.2687	8.3349	8.4018	8.4693
7.25	8.2725	8.3373	8.4027	8.4687	8.5353	8.6024	8.6702	8.7386
7.50	8.5358	8.6015	8.6678	8.7347	8.8021	8.8702	8.9389	9.0083
7.75	8.7993	8.8659	8.9331	9.0008	9.0692	9.1383	9.2079	9.2782
8.00	9.0630	9.1305	9.1986	9.2673	9.3366	9.4065	9.4771	9.5484
8.25	9.3269	9.3953	9.4643	9.5339	9.6042	9.6751	9.7467	9.8189
8.50	9.5910	9.6603	9.7302	9.8008	9.8720	9.9439	10.0165	10.0897
8.75	9.8553	9.9255	9.9964	10.0679	10.1401	10.2130	10.2865	10.3608
9.00	10.1197	10.1909	10.2628	10.3353	10.4084	10.4823	10.5568	10.6321
9.25	10.3844	10.4565	10.5293	10.6028	10.6770	10.7519	10.8274	10.9037
9.50	10.6492	10.7223	10.7961	10.8706	10.9458	11.0217	11.0983	11.1756
9.75	10.9143	10.9884	11.0632	11.1386	11.2148	11.2918	11.3694	11.4478
10.00	11.1795	11.2546	11.3304	11.4069	11.4841	11.5621	11.6408	11.7203
10.25	11.4449	11.5210	11.5978	11.6753	11.7536	11.8327	11.9125	11.9930
10.50	11.7105	11.7876	11.8654	11.9440	12.0234	12.1035	12.1844	12.2660
10.75	11.9762	12.0544	12.1333	12.2129	12.2933	12.3745	12.4565	12.5393
11.00	12.2422	12.3214	12.4013	12.4820	12.5635	12.6458	12.7289	12.8128
11.25	12.5083	12.5885	12.6696	12.7514	12.8340	12.9174	13.0016	13.0866
11.50	12.7746	12.8559	12.9380	13.0209	13.1046	13.1891	13.2745	13.3607
11.75	13.0410	13.1235	13.2066	13.2907	13.3755	13.4611	13.5476	13.6350
12.00	13.3077	13.3912	13.4755	13.5606	13.6466	13.7334	13.8210	13.9096
12.25	13.5745	13.6591	13.7445	13.8308	13.9179	14.0058	14.0947	14.1844
12.50	13.8415	13.9272	14.0137	14.1011	14.1894	14.2785	14.3685	14.4595
12.75	14.1086	14.1954	14.2831	14.3717	14.4611	14.5514	14.6426	14.7348
13.00	14.3759	14.4639	14.5527	14.6424	14.7330	14.8245	17.9169	15.0103
13.25	14.6434	14.7325	14.8225	17.9134	15.0051	15.0979	15.1915	15.2861
13.50	14.9110	15.0013	15.0924	15.1845	15.2775	15.3714	15.4663	15.5621
13.75	15.1788	15.2702	15.3625	15.4558	15.5500	15.6451	15.7413	15.8384
14.00	15.4467	15.5393	15.6328	15.7273	15.8227	15.9191	16.0165	16.1148
14.25	15.7148	15.8086	15.9033	15.9990	16.0956	16.1933	16.2919	16.3915
14.50	15.9830	16.0780	16.1739	16.2708	16.3687	16.4676	16.5675	16.6685
14.75	16.2514	16.3476	16.4447	16.5429	16.6420	16.7421	16.8433	16.9456
15.00	16.5199	16.6173	16.7157	16.8151	16.9155	17.0169	17.1194	17.2229
15.25	16.7886	16.8872	16.9868	17.0874	17.1891	17.2918	17.3956	17.5005
15.50	17.0573	17.1572	17.2581	17.3600	17.4629	17.5669	17.6720	17.7782
15.75	17.3263	17.4274	17.5295	17.6327	17.7369	17.8422	17.9486	18.0561
16.00	17.5953	17.6977	17.8011	17.9055	18.0110	18.1177	18.2254	18.3343
16.25	17.8645	17.9681	18.0728	18.1785	18.2853	18.3933	18.5024	18.6126
16.50	18.1338	18.2387	18.3446	18.4517	18.5598	18.6691	18.7795	18.8911
16.75	18.4033	18.5094	18.6166	18.7250	18.8344	18.9450	19.0568	19.1698

Table 5A-6 Term of Loan: 30 Years (Continued)

	Percentage Points Charged							
Contract Rate	0.50	1.00	1.50	2.00	2.50	3.00	3.50	4.00
7.00	7.0497	7.0999	7.1504	7.2014	7.2527	7.3045	7.3568	7.4094
7.25	7.3005	7.3514	7.4027	7.4545	7.5066	7.5592	7.6123	7.6658
7.50	7.5513	7.6029	7.6551	7.7076	7.7606	7.8140	7.8679	7.9222
7.75	7.8020	7.8545	7.9074	7.9608	8.0146	8.0688	8.1236	8.1787
8.00	8.0528	8.1061	8.1599	8.2140	8.2687	8.3238	8.3793	8.4354
8.25	8.3037	8.3578	8.4123	8.4673	8.5228	8.5788	8.6352	8.6921
8.50	8.5545	8.6094	8.6648	8.7207	8.7770	8.8338	8.8911	8.9489
8.75	8.8053	8.8611	8.9173	8.9740	9.0313	9.0890	9.1472	9.2059
9.00	9.0561	9.1128	9.1699	9.2275	9.2856	9.3442	9.4033	9.4629
9.25	9.3070	9.3645	9.4225	9.4810	9.5399	9.5994	9.6595	9.7200
9.50	9.5579	9.6162	9.6751	9.7345	9.7944	9.8548	9.9157	9.9772
9.75	9.8087	9.8680	9.9278	9.9880	10.0489	10.1102	10.1721	10.2345
10.00	10.0596	10.1198	10.1805	10.2417	10.3034	10.3657	10.4285	10.4919
10.25	10.3105	10.3716	10.4332	10.4953	10.5580	10.6212	10.6850	10.7494
10.50	10.5614	10.6234	10.6859	10.7490	10.8127	10.8769	10.9416	11.0070
10.75	10.8124	10.8753	10.9387	11.0028	11.0674	11.1325	11.1983	11.2647
11.00	11.0633	11.1271	11.1916	11.2565	11.3221	11.3883	11.4551	11.5224
11.25	11.3142	11.3790	11.4444	11.5104	11.5769	11.6441	11.7119	11.7803
11.50	11.5652	11.6309	11.6973	11.7642	11.8318	11.9000	11.9688	12.0382
11.75	11.8161	11.8829	11.9502	12.0182	12.0867	12.1559	12.2257	12.2962
12.00	12.0671	12.1348	12.2032	12.2721	12.3417	12.4119	12.4828	12.5543
12.25	12.3181	12.3868	12.4561	12.5261	12.5967	12.6679	12.7399	12.8124
12.50	12.5691	12.6388	12.7091	12.7801	12.8517	12.9240	12.9970	13.0707
12.75	12.8201	12.8908	12.9622	13.0342	13.1068	13.1802	13.2543	13.3290
13.00	13.0711	13.1428	13.2152	13.2883	13.3620	13.4364	13.5115	13.5874
13.25	13.3221	13.3949	13.4683	13.5424	13.6172	13.6927	13.7689	13.8458
13.50	13.5731	13.6469	13.7214	13.7966	13.8724	13.9490	14.0263	14.1044
13.75	13.8242	13.8990	13.9745	14.0508	14.1277	14.2054	14.2838	14.3630
14.00	14.0752	14.1511	14.2277	14.3050	14.3830	14.4618	14.5413	14.6216
14.25	14.3262	14.4032	14.4809	14.5593	14.6384	14.7183	14.7989	14.8804
14.50	14.5773	14.6553	14.7341	14.8135	14.8938	14.9748	15.0566	15.1392
14.75	14.8284	14.9075	14.9873	15.0679	15.1492	15.2314	15.3143	15.3980
15.00	15.0794	15.1596	15.2405	15.3222	15.4047	15.4880	15.5720	15.6569
15.25	15.3305	15.4118	15.4938	15.5766	15.6602	15.7446	15.8298	15.9159
15.50	15.5816	15.6639	15.7471	15.8310	15.9158	16.0013	16.0877	16.1749
15.75	15.8327	15.9161	16.0004	16.0855	16.1713	16.2580	16.3456	16.4340
16.00	16.0838	16.1683	16.2537	16.3399	16.4269	16.5148	16.6036	16.6932
16.25	16.3349	16.4206	16.5071	16.5944	16.6826	16.7716	16.8615	16.9523
16.50	16.5860	16.6728	16.7604	16.8489	16.9383	17.0285	17.1196	17.2116
16.75	16.8371	16.9250	17.0138	17.1035	17.1940	17.2854	17.3777	17.4709

Table 5A-6 (Continued)

Contract Rate	Percentage Points Charged 4.50	5.00	5.50	6.00	6.50	7.00	7.50	8.00
7.00	7.4625	7.5161	7.5701	7.6246	7.6796	7.7350	7.7910	7.8474
7.25	7.7197	7.7741	7.8290	7.8844	7.9402	7.9965	8.0534	8.1107
7.50	7.9770	8.0323	8.0880	8.1442	8.2010	8.2582	8.3159	8.3742
7.75	8.2344	8.2905	8.3472	8.4043	8.4619	8.5201	8.5787	8.6379
8.00	8.4919	8.5489	8.6065	8.6645	8.7230	8.7821	8.8417	8.9018
8.25	8.7495	8.8074	8.8659	8.9248	8.9843	9.0443	9.1049	9.1660
8.50	9.0073	9.0661	9.1254	9.1853	9.2457	9.3067	9.3682	9.4303
8.75	9.2651	9.3249	9.3851	9.4460	9.5074	9.5693	9.6318	9.6949
9.00	9.5231	9.5837	9.6450	9.7068	9.7691	9.8320	9.8955	9.9596
9.25	9.7811	9.8428	9.9050	9.9677	10.0310	10.0950	10.1595	10.2246
9.50	10.0393	10.1019	10.1651	10.2288	10.2931	10.3581	10.4236	10.4897
9.75	10.2976	10.3611	10.4253	10.4900	10.5554	10.6213	10.6879	10.7551
10.00	10.5559	10.6205	10.6856	10.7514	10.8178	10.8848	10.9524	11.0206
10.25	10.8144	10.8800	10.9461	11.0129	11.0803	11.1483	11.2170	11.2864
10.50	11.0730	11.1396	11.2067	11.2746	11.3430	11.4121	11.4819	11.5523
10.75	11.3317	11.3993	11.4675	11.5363	11.6059	11.6760	11.7469	11.8184
11.00	11.5904	11.6591	11.7283	11.7983	11.8688	11.9401	12.0120	12.0847
11.25	11.8493	11.9190	11.9893	12.0603	12.1320	12.2043	12.2774	12.3511
11.50	12.1083	12.1790	12.2504	12.3225	12.3952	12.4687	12.5429	12.6178
11.75	12.3673	12.4391	12.5116	12.5848	12.6586	12.7332	12.8085	12.8846
12.00	12.6265	12.6994	12.7729	12.8472	12.9222	12.9979	13.0743	13.1515
12.25	12.8857	12.9597	13.0344	13.1097	13.1859	13.2627	13.3403	13.4187
12.50	13.1450	13.2201	13.2959	13.3724	13.4497	13.5277	13.6064	13.6860
12.75	13.4044	13.4806	13.5575	13.6352	13.7136	13.7928	13.8727	13.9535
13.00	13.6639	13.7412	13.8193	13.8981	13.9776	14.0580	14.1391	14.2211
13.25	13.9235	14.0019	14.0811	14.1611	14.2418	14.3233	14.4057	14.4888
13.50	14.1832	14.2627	14.3431	14.4242	14.5061	14.5888	14.6724	14.7567
13.75	14.4429	14.5236	14.6051	14.6874	14.7705	14.8544	14.9392	15.0248
14.00	14.7027	14.7846	14.8672	14.9507	15.0350	15.1201	15.2061	15.2930
14.25	14.9626	15.0456	15.1294	15.2141	15.2996	15.3860	15.4732	15.5613
14.50	15.2225	15.3067	15.3917	15.4776	15.5643	15.6519	15.7404	15.8298
14.75	15.4826	15.5679	15.6541	15.7412	15.8292	15.9180	16.0077	16.0984
15.00	15.7426	15.8292	15.9166	16.0049	16.0941	16.1842	16.2752	16.3671
15.25	16.0028	16.0906	16.1792	16.2687	16.3591	16.4504	16.5427	16.6359
15.50	16.2630	16.3520	16.4418	16.5326	16.6242	16.7168	16.8104	16.9049
15.75	16.5233	16.6135	16.7045	16.7965	16.8894	16.9833	17.0781	17.1739
16.00	16.7836	16.8750	16.9673	17.0606	17.1547	17.2499	17.3460	17.4431
16.25	17.0440	17.1366	17.2302	17.3247	17.4201	17.5165	17.6139	17.7124
16.50	17.3045	17.3983	17.4931	17.5889	17.6856	17.7833	17.8820	17.9817
16.75	17.5650	17.6601	17.7561	17.8531	17.9511	18.0501	18.1502	18.2512

Table 5A-6 (Continued)

Contract Rate	8.50	9.00	9.50	10.00	10.50	11.00	11.50	12.00
	Percentage Points Charged							
7.00	7.9043	7.9618	8.0197	8.0782	8.1372	8.1968	8.2569	8.3176
7.25	8.1685	8.2269	8.2858	8.3453	8.4052	8.4658	8.5269	8.5886
7.50	8.4330	8.4923	8.5522	8.6126	8.6735	8.7351	8.7972	8.8599
7.75	8.6976	8.7579	8.8188	8.8801	8.9421	9.0047	9.0678	9.1315
8.00	8.9625	9.0238	9.0856	9.1480	9.2110	9.2745	9.3387	9.4035
8.25	9.2277	9.2899	9.3527	9.4161	9.4801	9.5447	9.6100	9.6758
8.50	9.4930	9.5562	9.6201	9.6845	9.7495	9.8152	9.8815	9.9485
8.75	9.7585	9.8228	9.8877	9.9532	10.0193	10.0860	10.1534	10.2214
9.00	10.0243	10.0896	10.1555	10.2221	10.2892	10.3571	10.4256	10.4947
9.25	10.2903	10.3566	10.4236	10.4912	10.5595	10.6284	10.6980	10.7683
9.50	10.5565	10.6239	10.6920	10.7607	10.8300	10.9001	10.9708	11.0422
9.75	10.8229	10.8914	10.9605	11.0303	11.1008	11.1720	11.2439	11.3165
10.00	11.0895	11.1591	11.2293	11.3003	11.3719	11.4442	11.5172	11.5910
10.25	11.3563	11.4270	11.4984	11.5704	11.6432	11.7167	11.7909	11.8658
10.50	11.6234	11.6952	11.7676	11.8408	11.9147	11.9894	12.0648	12.1410
10.75	11.8906	11.9635	12.0371	12.1115	12.1866	12.2624	12.3390	12.4164
11.00	12.1580	12.2320	12.3068	12.3824	12.4586	12.5357	12.6135	12.6921
11.25	12.4256	12.5008	12.5768	12.6535	12.7309	12.8092	12.8882	12.9681
11.50	12.6934	12.7698	12.8469	12.9248	13.0035	13.0830	13.1632	13.2444
11.75	12.9614	13.0389	13.1172	13.1963	13.2762	13.3570	13.4385	13.5209
12.00	13.2295	13.3082	13.3878	13.4681	13.5492	13.6312	13.7140	13.7977
12.25	13.4978	13.5778	13.6585	13.7401	13.8225	13.9057	13.9898	14.0748
12.50	13.7663	13.8475	13.9295	14.0123	14.0959	14.1804	14.2658	14.3521
12.75	14.0350	14.1174	14.2006	14.2846	14.3696	14.4554	14.5420	14.6296
13.00	14.3038	14.3874	14.4719	14.5572	14.6434	14.7305	14.8185	14.9074
13.25	14.5728	14.6577	14.7434	14.8300	14.9175	15.0059	15.0952	15.1855
13.50	14.8420	14.9281	15.0151	15.1029	15.1917	15.2815	15.3721	15.4637
13.75	15.1113	15.1986	15.2869	15.3761	15.4662	15.5572	15.6492	15.7422
14.00	15.3807	15.4694	15.5589	15.6494	15.7408	15.8332	15.9266	16.0209
14.25	15.6503	15.7402	15.8311	15.9229	16.0156	16.1094	16.2041	16.2999
14.50	15.9201	16.0113	16.1034	16.1966	16.2906	16.3857	16.4818	16.5790
14.75	16.1899	16.2824	16.3759	16.4704	16.5658	16.6623	16.7598	16.8583
15.00	16.4599	16.5538	16.6486	16.7444	16.8412	16.9390	17.0379	17.1378
15.25	16.7301	16.8252	16.9213	17.0185	17.1167	17.2159	17.3162	17.4175
15.50	17.0003	17.0968	17.1943	17.2928	17.3923	17.4929	17.5946	17.6974
15.75	17.2707	17.3685	17.4673	17.5672	17.6681	17.7701	17.8732	17.9775
16.00	17.5412	17.6403	17.7405	17.8418	17.9441	18.0475	18.1520	18.2577
16.25	17.8118	17.9123	18.0138	18.1165	18.2202	18.3250	18.4310	18.5381
16.50	18.0825	18.1844	18.2873	18.3913	18.4964	18.6027	18.7101	18.8187
16.75	18.3534	18.4566	18.5608	18.6663	18.7728	18.8805	18.9893	19.0994

Table 5A-7 Mortgage Pricing as a Percent of Loan Amount, 30-Year Term and 12 Year Prepayment

Required Percentage Yield	Net Percentage Contract Rate							
	9.00	9.25	9.50	9.75	10.00	10.25	10.50	10.75
7.00	1.15426	1.17390	1.19360	1.21337	1.23319	1.25307	1.27300	1.29298
7.25	1.13329	1.15264	1.17206	1.19154	1.21108	1.23067	1.25031	1.27001
7.50	1.11283	1.13190	1.15104	1.17024	1.18949	1.20881	1.22817	1.24758
7.75	1.09286	1.11166	1.13052	1.14944	1.16843	1.18747	1.20656	1.22569
8.00	1.07338	1.09190	1.11050	1.12915	1.14787	1.16664	1.18546	1.20433
8.25	1.05436	1.07262	1.09095	1.10934	1.12780	1.14630	1.16486	1.18347
8.50	1.03580	1.05381	1.07188	1.09001	1.10820	1.12645	1.14475	1.16310
8.75	1.01768	1.03544	1.05325	1.07114	1.08908	1.10707	1.12512	1.14322
9.00	1.00000	1.01751	1.03508	1.05271	1.07040	1.08815	1.10595	1.12380
9.25	0.98274	1.00000	1.01733	1.03472	1.05217	1.06967	1.08723	1.10484
9.50	0.96588	0.98291	1.00000	1.01715	1.03436	1.05163	1.06895	1.08632
9.75	0.94943	0.96622	0.98308	1.00000	1.01698	1.03401	1.05110	1.06824
10.00	0.93337	0.94993	0.96656	0.98325	1.00000	1.01681	1.03366	1.05057
10.25	0.91768	0.93402	0.95042	0.96689	0.98342	1.00000	1.01663	1.03332
10.50	0.90236	0.91848	0.93467	0.95091	0.96722	0.98358	1.00000	1.01647
10.75	0.88740	0.90331	0.91928	0.93531	0.95140	0.96755	0.98375	1.00000
11.00	0.87279	0.88848	0.90424	0.92007	0.93595	0.95188	0.96787	0.98391
11.25	0.85852	0.87401	0.88956	0.90518	0.92085	0.93658	0.95236	0.96820
11.50	0.84458	0.85986	0.87521	0.89063	0.90610	0.92163	0.93721	0.95284
11.75	0.83096	0.84605	0.86120	0.87641	0.89169	0.90702	0.92240	0.93783
12.00	0.81765	0.83255	0.84751	0.86253	0.87760	0.89274	0.90792	0.92316
12.25	0.80466	0.81936	0.83413	0.84896	0.86384	0.87878	0.89378	0.90882
12.50	0.79195	0.80647	0.82105	0.83569	0.85039	0.86515	0.87996	0.89481
12.75	0.77954	0.79388	0.80827	0.82273	0.83725	0.85182	0.86644	0.88112
13.00	0.76742	0.78157	0.79579	0.81006	0.82440	0.83879	0.85323	0.86773
13.25	0.75556	0.76954	0.78358	0.79768	0.81184	0.82605	0.84032	0.85464
13.50	0.74398	0.75778	0.77165	0.78558	0.79956	0.81360	0.82770	0.84184
13.75	0.73266	0.74629	0.75999	0.77374	0.78756	0.80143	0.81535	0.82932
14.00	0.72159	0.73505	0.74858	0.76218	0.77582	0.78953	0.80328	0.81708
14.25	0.71076	0.72407	0.73744	0.75086	0.76435	0.77789	0.79148	0.80512
14.50	0.70018	0.71333	0.72654	0.73980	0.75313	0.76650	0.77993	0.79341
14.75	0.68984	0.70283	0.71588	0.72899	0.74215	0.75537	0.76864	0.78196
15.00	0.67973	0.69256	0.70545	0.71841	0.73142	0.74448	0.75760	0.77076
15.25	0.66983	0.68252	0.69526	0.70806	0.72092	0.73383	0.74679	0.75981
15.50	0.66016	0.67269	0.68529	0.69794	0.71065	0.72341	0.73623	0.74909
15.75	0.65070	0.66308	0.67553	0.68804	0.70060	0.71322	0.72589	0.73860
16.00	0.64144	0.65369	0.66599	0.67836	0.69077	0.70325	0.71577	0.72834
16.25	0.63239	0.64449	0.65666	0.66888	0.68116	0.69349	0.70587	0.71830
16.50	0.62353	0.63550	0.64752	0.65961	0.67175	0.68394	0.69618	0.70847
16.75	0.61487	0.62670	0.63859	0.65054	0.66254	0.67459	0.68670	0.69885

Table 5A-7 (Continued)

Required Percentage Yield	Net Percentage Contract Rate 11.00	11.25	11.50	11.75	12.00	12.25	12.50	12.75
7.00	1.31300	1.33307	1.35317	1.37331	1.39348	1.41369	1.43392	1.45418
7.25	1.28974	1.30952	1.32934	1.34920	1.36909	1.38901	1.40896	1.42893
7.50	1.26704	1.28654	1.30608	1.32566	1.34527	1.36491	1.38458	1.40429
7.75	1.24488	1.26410	1.28337	1.30268	1.32201	1.34139	1.36079	1.38022
8.00	1.22324	1.24220	1.26120	1.28024	1.29931	1.31841	1.33755	1.35671
8.25	1.20212	1.22082	1.23955	1.25833	1.27714	1.29598	1.31485	1.33376
8.50	1.18150	1.19994	1.21842	1.23693	1.25549	1.27407	1.29269	1.31134
8.75	1.16136	1.17955	1.19777	1.21604	1.23434	1.25268	1.27105	1.28944
9.00	1.14170	1.15964	1.17762	1.19564	1.21369	1.23178	1.24990	1.26805
9.25	1.12249	1.14019	1.15793	1.17571	1.19352	1.21137	1.22925	1.24716
9.50	1.10374	1.12120	1.13870	1.15624	1.17382	1.19143	1.20907	1.22675
9.75	1.08542	1.10265	1.11992	1.13723	1.15457	1.17195	1.18936	1.20681
10.00	1.06753	1.08453	1.10157	1.11865	1.13577	1.15292	1.17011	1.18732
10.25	1.05005	1.06683	1.08365	1.10050	1.11740	1.13433	1.15129	1.16828
10.50	1.03298	1.04954	1.06613	1.08277	1.09945	1.11616	1.13290	1.14968
10.75	1.01630	1.03264	1.04902	1.06545	1.08191	1.09840	1.11493	1.13149
11.00	1.00000	1.01613	1.03230	1.04852	1.06477	1.08105	1.09737	1.11372
11.25	0.98408	1.00000	1.01597	1.03197	1.04802	1.06410	1.08021	1.09635
11.50	0.96851	0.98424	1.00000	1.01580	1.03165	1.04752	1.06343	1.07937
11.75	0.95331	0.96883	0.98439	1.00000	1.01564	1.03132	1.04703	1.06277
12.00	0.93844	0.95377	0.96914	0.98455	1.00000	1.01548	1.03100	1.04655
12.25	0.92392	0.93905	0.95423	0.96945	0.98471	1.00000	1.01533	1.03068
12.50	0.90972	0.92467	0.93966	0.95469	0.96976	0.98486	1.00000	1.01517
12.75	0.89584	0.91060	0.92541	0.94026	0.95514	0.97006	0.98501	1.00000
13.00	0.88227	0.89685	0.91148	0.92614	0.94085	0.95559	0.97036	0.98517
13.25	0.86900	0.88340	0.89785	0.91234	0.92687	0.94143	0.95603	0.97066
13.50	0.85603	0.87026	0.88453	0.89885	0.91320	0.92759	0.94201	0.95647
13.75	0.84334	0.85740	0.87151	0.88565	0.89983	0.91405	0.92830	0.94259
14.00	0.83093	0.84483	0.85877	0.87274	0.88676	0.90081	0.91489	0.92901
14.25	0.81880	0.83253	0.84630	0.86012	0.87397	0.88785	0.90177	0.91572
14.50	0.80694	0.82050	0.83411	0.84777	0.86145	0.87518	0.88894	0.90272
14.75	0.79533	0.80874	0.82219	0.83568	0.84921	0.86278	0.87638	0.89001
15.00	0.78397	0.79723	0.81052	0.82386	0.83723	0.85064	0.86409	0.87756
15.25	0.77286	0.78597	0.79911	0.81229	0.82552	0.83877	0.85206	0.86538
15.50	0.76200	0.77495	0.78794	0.80098	0.81405	0.82715	0.84029	0.85346
15.75	0.75136	0.76417	0.77701	0.78990	0.80282	0.81578	0.82877	0.84180
16.00	0.74096	0.75362	0.76632	0.77906	0.79184	0.80465	0.81750	0.83038
16.25	0.73077	0.74329	0.75585	0.76845	0.78109	0.79376	0.80646	0.81920
16.50	0.72081	0.73318	0.74560	0.75806	0.77056	0.78309	0.79566	0.80825
16.75	0.71105	0.72329	0.73558	0.74790	0.76026	0.77265	0.78508	0.79754

Table 5A-7 (Continued)

Required Percentage Yield	Net Percentage Contract Rate 13.00	13.25	13.50	13.75	14.00	14.25	14.50	14.75
7.00	1.47446	1.49477	1.51510	1.53544	1.55581	1.57619	1.59658	1.61698
7.25	1.44894	1.46896	1.48901	1.50907	1.52916	1.54925	1.56937	1.58949
7.50	1.42401	1.44376	1.46353	1.48332	1.50313	1.52295	1.54276	1.56264
7.75	1.39967	1.41915	1.43865	1.45817	1.47771	1.49726	1.51683	1.53641
8.00	1.37590	1.39511	1.41435	1.43360	1.45288	1.47217	1.49147	1.51080
8.25	1.35269	1.37164	1.39061	1.40961	1.42862	1.44766	1.46670	1.48577
8.50	1.33001	1.34871	1.36743	1.38617	1.40493	1.42371	1.44251	1.46132
8.75	1.30786	1.32631	1.34478	1.36328	1.38179	1.40032	1.41886	1.43743
9.00	1.28623	1.30443	1.32266	1.34091	1.35918	1.37746	1.39577	1.41408
9.25	1.26510	1.28306	1.30105	1.31905	1.33708	1.35513	1.37319	1.39127
9.50	1.24445	1.26218	1.27993	1.29770	1.31549	1.33331	1.35114	1.36898
9.75	1.22428	1.24177	1.25929	1.27683	1.29440	1.31198	1.32958	1.34720
10.00	1.20456	1.22183	1.23913	1.25644	1.27378	1.29114	1.30851	1.32590
10.25	1.18530	1.20235	1.21942	1.23651	1.25363	1.27077	1.28792	1.30509
10.50	1.16648	1.18331	1.20016	1.21704	1.23394	1.25085	1.26779	1.28475
10.75	1.14808	1.16470	1.18134	1.19800	1.21468	1.23139	1.24811	1.26486
11.00	1.13010	1.14651	1.16294	1.17939	1.19587	1.21236	1.22888	1.24541
11.25	1.11252	1.12872	1.14495	1.16120	1.17747	1.19376	1.21007	1.22640
11.50	1.09534	1.11134	1.12736	1.14341	1.15948	1.17557	1.19168	1.20781
11.75	1.07855	1.09435	1.11017	1.12602	1.14189	1.15778	1.17370	1.18963
12.00	1.06213	1.07773	1.09336	1.10902	1.12469	1.14039	1.15611	1.17185
12.25	1.04607	1.06148	1.07692	1.09239	1.10788	1.12338	1.13891	1.15446
12.50	1.03037	1.04560	1.06085	1.07613	1.09143	1.10675	1.12209	1.13745
12.75	1.01502	1.03006	1.04513	1.06022	1.07534	1.09048	1.10564	1.12081
13.00	1.00000	1.01486	1.02975	1.04467	1.05960	1.07456	1.08954	1.10454
13.25	0.98531	1.00000	1.01471	1.02945	1.04421	1.05899	1.07379	1.08861
13.50	0.97095	0.98546	1.00000	1.01456	1.02915	1.04376	1.05839	1.07303
13.75	0.95690	0.97124	0.98561	1.00000	1.01442	1.02885	1.04331	1.05779
14.00	0.94315	0.95733	0.97153	0.98575	1.00000	1.01427	1.02856	1.04287
14.25	0.92970	0.94371	0.95775	0.97181	0.98589	1.00000	1.01413	1.02827
14.50	0.91654	0.93039	0.94427	0.95817	0.97209	0.98603	1.00000	1.01399
14.75	0.90367	0.91736	0.93107	0.94481	0.95858	0.97237	0.98617	1.00000
15.00	0.89107	0.90460	0.91816	0.93175	0.94536	0.95899	0.97264	0.98631
15.25	0.87874	0.89212	0.90552	0.91896	0.93241	0.94589	0.95939	0.97291
15.50	0.86667	0.87990	0.89315	0.90644	0.91974	0.93307	0.94642	0.95979
15.75	0.85485	0.86793	0.88104	0.89418	0.90734	0.92052	0.93372	0.94694
16.00	0.84329	0.85623	0.86919	0.88218	0.89519	0.90823	0.92128	0.93436
16.25	0.83197	0.84476	0.85758	0.87043	0.88330	0.89619	0.90911	0.92204
16.50	0.82088	0.83354	0.84622	0.85893	0.87166	0.88441	0.89718	0.90998
16.75	0.81003	0.82255	0.83509	0.84766	0.86025	0.87287	0.88550	0.89816

Table 5A-7 (Continued)

Required Percentage Yield	Net Percentage Contract Rate 15.00	15.25	15.50	15.75	16.00	16.25	16.50	16.75
7.00	1.63740	1.65782	1.67826	1.69870	1.71915	1.73960	1.76006	1.78052
7.25	1.60963	1.62978	1.64993	1.67010	1.69027	1.71044	1.73063	1.75081
7.50	1.58250	1.60238	1.62226	1.64216	1.66205	1.68196	1.70187	1.72179
7.75	1.55601	1.57562	1.59523	1.61486	1.63449	1.65413	1.67378	1.69343
8.00	1.53013	1.54947	1.56883	1.58819	1.60757	1.62694	1.64633	1.66572
8.25	1.50484	1.52393	1.54303	1.56214	1.58125	1.60038	1.61951	1.63865
8.50	1.48014	1.49898	1.51782	1.53668	1.55554	1.57442	1.59330	1.61218
8.75	1.45600	1.47459	1.49319	1.51180	1.53042	1.54905	1.56768	1.58632
9.00	1.43242	1.45076	0.46912	1.48749	1.50587	1.52425	1.54265	1.56105
9.25	1.40937	1.42748	1.44560	1.46373	1.48187	1.50002	1.51818	1.53634
9.50	1.38684	1.40472	1.42261	1.44050	1.45841	1.47633	1.49425	1.51219
9.75	1.36483	1.38247	1.40013	1.41780	1.43548	1.45317	1.47087	1.48858
10.00	1.34331	1.36073	1.37817	1.39561	1.41307	1.43053	1.44801	1.46549
10.25	1.32228	1.33948	1.35669	1.37392	1.39116	1.40840	1.42566	1.44292
10.50	1.30172	1.31870	1.33570	1.35271	1.36973	1.38676	1.40380	1.42085
10.75	1.28161	1.29839	1.31517	1.33197	1.34878	1.36560	1.38243	1.39927
11.00	1.26196	1.27852	1.29510	1.31169	1.32830	1.34491	1.36153	1.37816
11.25	1.24274	1.25910	1.27548	1.29186	1.30826	1.32467	1.34109	1.35752
11.50	1.22395	1.24011	1.25628	1.27247	1.28867	1.30488	1.32110	1.33733
11.75	1.20557	1.22154	1.23751	1.25350	1.26951	1.28552	1.30155	1.31758
12.00	1.18760	1.20337	1.21916	1.23495	1.25076	1.26658	1.28242	1.29826
12.25	1.17002	1.18560	1.20120	1.21681	1.23243	1.24806	1.26370	1.27936
12.50	1.15283	1.16822	1.18363	1.19905	1.21449	1.22994	1.24539	1.26086
12.75	1.13601	1.15122	1.16644	1.18168	1.19694	1.21220	1.22748	1.24277
13.00	1.11955	1.13458	1.14963	1.16469	1.17977	1.19485	1.20995	1.22506
13.25	1.10345	1.11831	1.13318	1.14806	1.16296	1.17787	1.19280	1.20773
13.50	1.08770	1.10238	1.11708	1.13179	1.14652	1.16126	1.17601	1.19077
13.75	1.07229	1.08680	1.10133	1.11587	1.13043	1.14499	1.15957	1.17417
14.00	1.05720	1.07155	1.08591	1.10028	1.11467	1.12908	1.14349	1.15792
14.25	1.04244	1.05662	1.07082	1.08503	1.09926	1.11349	1.12775	1.14201
14.50	1.02799	1.04201	1.05605	1.07010	1.08416	1.09824	1.11233	1.12643
14.75	1.01385	1.02771	1.04159	1.05548	1.06939	1.08331	1.09724	1.11118
15.00	1.00000	1.01371	1.02743	1.04117	1.05492	1.06869	1.08246	1.09625
15.25	0.98645	1.00000	1.01357	1.02716	1.04076	1.05437	1.06800	1.08163
15.50	0.97317	0.98658	1.00000	1.01344	1.02689	1.04035	1.05383	1.06731
15.75	0.96018	0.97344	0.98671	1.00000	1.01330	1.02662	1.03995	1.05329
16.00	0.94746	0.96057	0.97370	0.98684	1.00000	1.01317	1.02636	1.03955
16.25	0.93499	0.94797	0.96095	0.97395	0.98697	1.00000	1.01304	1.02610
16.50	0.92279	0.93562	0.94847	0.96133	0.97421	0.98710	1.00000	1.01291
16.75	0.91084	0.92353	0.93624	0.94896	0.96170	0.97446	0.98722	1.00000

PART II

The Instruments of Residential Real Estate Finance

Part II focuses on residential real estate finance, primarily the one- to four-family (but typically one-family) residential mortgage. Included in this part is a discussion of federal policies and laws related to residential finance, financing terms and their effects on property prices, the structure of the secondary mortgage market, and the pricing of mortgage-related securities. Risk management also is discussed. Here we talk about borrower and property qualification and mortgage insurance—both private and government (FHA/VA).

Chapter 6

The Early History of Residential Finance and Creation of the Fixed-Rate Mortgage

Chapter Outline

Learning Objectives

After reading this chapter you will be able to:

- Describe how residential lending developed from its earliest instances through World War II.
- List causes of the high number of mortgage defaults during the 1930s Depression.
- Describe how federal programs supported the mortgage and housing market during the 1930s Depression.
- Describe the important characteristics of mortgages in the latter half of the 19th century.

Key Terms

building and loan associations
equitable right of redemption
Federal Housing Administration
fiducia
gage
Home Owners Loan Corporation
hypotheca
mortgagors
pigus
reconveyance
statutory right of redemption

Introduction

Real estate finance involves the advancing of funds from a lender to a borrower, usually for buying or improving real property. As with any contract freely entered into by two parties, the arrangement provides benefits to both parties. Because the transaction involves moving funds from one party to another over time, the agreement also involves risk to one or both parties. Lenders minimize their risks when loans are made to creditworthy individuals, when the amount is much less than the value of the property, and when they can secure possession of the property quickly.

Rules and laws define the rights and duties of the parties to a loan contract. These developed over the course of history and sometimes in response to specific historical circumstances. Understanding the development of residential finance will help you appreciate the structure of our present system. This chapter gives a brief history of the evolution of real estate lending.

Historical Foundations of Modern Residential Finance

Roman Law

Many aspects of U.S. law can be traced to the real property law of the Roman Empire, which went through several stages. Initially the instrument used for real estate loans was called the ***fiducia***, from the Latin word for "trust" or "confidence." A *fiducia* transferred legal title and possession of a property to the lender. According to *fiducia*, if the borrower paid the obligation under the terms of the loan, the lender returned the title and possession of the property to the borrower. The return of title is called **reconveyance**. You may note the similarity of the word *fiducia* to today's use of the word *fiduciary*. The Latin word *fides* means trust so that a person who has a fiduciary relationship has one of trust.

Later, under ***pigus***, the borrower retained title and possession. The rights of the lender, however, were still well protected. Under *pigus*, the lender had the right to take title and possession of the property for "suspicion of the probability of default" by the borrower.

A later development was the ***hypotheca***, or "pledge." This instrument was similar to *pigus* except that the lender could take possession of the property only in case of an actual default, not for mere suspicion that the borrower might default.

German Influence

As the Roman Empire began to weaken, German customs became more influential in Europe. German law recognized the concept of a **gage**, which was a deposit made to ensure fulfillment of an agreement. Often a borrower would physically deliver portable property as a gage, as is done today at pawnshops. Such a circumstance was called a *live gage*. When the collateral for a loan was real property, the gage stipulated that the lender could take possession of the property in case of default. The lender could not, however, look beyond that gage or deposit to obtain payment.

English Developments

The French introduced the Germanic gage system to medieval England after William the Conqueror's invasion in 1066. A loan involving real property was now called a *dead gage*. The French word for "dead" is *mort*, so a loan for real property came to be called a *mort gage*, which led to our modern term *mortgage*.

In the Middle Ages, lending in England was complicated by a Church prohibition against charging interest. Charging interest for a loan was considered "usury" and thought to be sinful. The basis of the prohibition, as indicated by the writings of Thomas Aquinas and other Church scholars, was "natural law." Thomas Aquinas relied heavily on Aristotelian philosophy, which sought guidance in natural law—or what seemed natural. It was natural in an agrarian economy for land to produce food, for animals to produce offspring, and so forth. But it was not natural for money to reproduce.

Lenders sought ways to gain some benefit from making loans without breaking the Church's prohibition. The solution was to loan funds not for interest but for the right to possess and reap the benefits of a portion of the land securing the loan. If the borrower defaulted on the loan, the lender had the right to take possession of the entire land and had no obligation to give the borrower anything in return.

As English common law developed during the reign of Queen Elizabeth I (1558–1603), the Chancery Court ruled that forfeiture of the entire land was unduly harsh, especially when the debt was small and the borrower's financial difficulties were temporary. Borrowers could petition the court, stating how they intended to pay the debt. The court began to allow borrowers to recover their property on payment of the delinquent amounts. This borrower's right was called the **equitable right of redemption**.

In practice, borrowers could redeem their property long after the actual default by paying the delinquent amount. Lenders, of course, objected to the unlimited period during which borrowers could regain the property. They sought and received a provision that limited the period for borrowers' redemption of their property.

Remnants of this system are apparent in today's real estate finance. In all states, borrowers (**mortgagors**) can redeem their property by paying delinquent amounts, plus any legal and other expenses, up to the time of actual foreclosure. This is the equitable right of redemption. Some states have also enacted statutes that grant an additional period during which a mortgagor can redeem a property. This additional period is called a **statutory right of redemption**.

American Residential Finance: Early American History through the Depression Years

The years following the American Revolution saw little need for real estate lending. In rural areas, most families lived on small farms that were kept in the family and passed down from generation to generation. The need to finance a purchase of these small properties was rare or nonexistent.

Occasionally, a "building society" would form in an urban area to gather funds for its members to purchase their residences. Once it acquired sufficient funds, the society would discontinue its fund raising. The first such building society was the Oxford Provident Building Association, formed in Philadelphia in 1831. The "dices" (or "dues") that were collected from the members were not considered deposits or liabilities, but rather shares of equity. At first the shareholders were not entitled to a fixed dividend, nor even to redeem their shares on demand. Later, building societies began to provide for liquidation of shares at face value. This change moved the societies away from being stock-ownership corporations toward being "thrifts" as we know them today. By the time of the Civil War, only a handful of such societies remained.

Post–Civil War westward expansion created the need for real estate financing. For the most part, large institutional investors in the East controlled the funds needed to finance the purchase of small farms. Mortgage banking increased, and mortgage bankers originated mortgages in the expanding West for their investors in the East. The typical farm mortgage was a short-term loan (usually five years) with only the interest paid semi-annually. A loan that has interest-only payments is called a nonamortizing loan, which means that none of the original amount borrowed, the principal, is included in the payments. Because the principal balance of these loans was never reduced, the loans usually covered only 40 to 50 percent of the property's value. Upon maturity, the loan would often be refinanced at a new rate of interest for a small origination fee, say, 1 percent of the loan's balance.

Until the latter part of the 1800s, few savings and loans or commercial banks were active, and mortgage bankers dominated the small-farm mortgage market. Under the National Banking System (1863–1913), federally chartered banks were prohibited from making real estate loans. In 1913, however, the establishment of the Federal Reserve System authorized banks to originate five-year loans with a maximum 50 percent loan-to-value ratio. State banks that were allowed to issue real estate loans also originated short-term, nonamortizing loans.

The type of loan originated in this era was similar to today's five-year adjustable-rate mortgage. By keeping the term short, lenders minimized their interest rate risk. If market rates rose after the loan origination, the lender would experience, at most, only a few years of below-market returns. Some default risk was associated with this type of loan, however. Because they were nonamortizing, there was a greater likelihood that the value of the property might slip below the balance of the loan. This was particularly true for properties with second and third mortgages. The default risk associated with such loans became painfully apparent in the late 1920s and early 1930s during America's pre-Depression and Depression years: Huge numbers of borrowers were forced to default on their loans.

During the early 1920s, **building and loan associations** experienced their most rapid growth. Associations grew from 5,356 with $571 million in total assets in 1900 to 11,777 with $8.8 billion in assets in 1930. During this time the associations gradually changed the rules on dividends and retirement of shares to compete with commercial banks; this represented essentially a circumvention of the laws that restricted entry into banking. For example, some associations issued "shares" with a definite "interest" (dividend) rate maturing at specific dates. They were analogous to certificates of deposit. Other shares could be redeemed on short notice at par and without a penalty. The growth of associations at this time also was aided by federal income tax regulations that exempted the associations from taxes as long as they loaned their funds to members for home building.

During the early 1920s property values rose rapidly as the money supply grew at a historically rapid rate. Lenders were not restrained in advancing funds to purchase high-priced properties. Then, with the collapse of the banking system in the early 1930s, the money supply plummeted, property prices declined, and the number of defaults skyrocketed. All of these conditions eroded the financial position of lenders.

The default risk of the short-term, nonamortizing loan can be seen in their performance during the 1920s and 1930s. Saulnier discusses the loan histories of the 24 largest insurance companies during this period.[1] From 1920 through 1924, only 24.4 percent of the loans originated by this group of lenders were fully amortized, meaning that by the end of the payments the debt would be zero. During this time the foreclosure rate was 5.3 percent of all loans—15 percent on the nonamortizing loans and 2.8 percent on the amortizing loans. From 1930 through 1934, the worst years of the Great Depression, foreclosure rates rose to 21.1 percent overall—28.1 percent on nonamortizing loans and 17.8 percent on amortizing loans. During the entire decade of the 1920s, the foreclosure rate was 21 percent on loans of 4 years or less maturity and 13.5 percent on 10- to 14-year maturity loans. For this particular set of loans, the shorter, nonamortizing mortgages clearly experienced greater foreclosure rates.

The lessons of the Depression led to changes in the mortgages originated by all lenders, with the proportion of fully amortized loans increasing and, conversely, the proportion of short-term, nonamortizing loans decreasing. The changes made by the life insurance companies used in the Saulnier study provide examples. For the period from 1920 through 1924, 24 percent of the loans originated were fully amortized and 79 percent had maturity of less than nine years. By comparison, for the period from 1930 to 1934, 31.5 percent of loans were fully amortized, and loans with a maturity of less than nine years dropped to 66 percent. For 1940 through 1946, 94 percent of all loans originated by life insurance companies were fully amortized, and only 3 percent had a maturity of less than nine years. The dramatic drop in the proportion of short-term, nonamortizing loans in the latter period also reflects the effects of the laws and agencies established by the federal government during the Depression to support the mortgage market.

---

[1] Saulnier, R.J., *Urban Mortgage Lending by Life Insurance Companies*. New York: National Bureau of Economic Research, 1950. During this time, insurance companies held about one-sixth of all outstanding residential mortgage debt.

The collapse of the nation's economy from 1929 through 1933 created upheaval in the real estate lending market. After the Crash of 1929, property values fell to about half their 1928 levels. Dramatic drops in personal income led to large-scale delinquencies on mortgage loans. Lenders, particularly depository institutions such as thrifts, were not receiving their periodic payments on the loans, and foreclosures on properties whose values had sunk offered little remedy. Depositors withdrew large sums of cash to meet their living expenses. Between 1931 and 1934, net withdrawals from savings and loan institutions amounted to $1.84 billion, about one-third of the 1930 deposit level. By 1935, one-fifth of all mortgage loans resulted in real estate owned (REO) properties for the thrifts. Real estate owned properties are those that the lender has ownership of by virtue of having to foreclose on the property. When the payment on the mortgage wasn't paid, the lender would foreclose on the loan and receive ownership of the property. Many states passed legislation to stop or delay foreclosures. Following Iowa's lead in passing legislation in February 1933, 26 other states passed such "moratoria" legislation. Generally intended to last for only two years or so, some moratoria lasted well into the 1940s.

The chaotic situation led the federal government to create six programs or agencies to aid the real estate lending market. The programs were intended to provide liquidity to lenders through direct loans and insuring of deposits and to promote a long-term, amortizing type of loan through default insurance and a secondary market for such loans. These were the Reconstruction Finance Corporation, the Federal Home Loan Bank System, the Home Owners Loan Corporation, the Federal Savings and Loan Insurance Corporation, the Federal Housing Administration, and the Federal National Mortgage Association.

The Reconstruction Finance Corporation (RFC) was established in early 1932. From its start through October 1937, the RFC used government credit to lend $114 million to savings and loan associations and $290 million to mortgage loan companies. The loans helped the thrifts survive.

The Federal Home Loan Bank Act created the Federal Home Loan Bank System in July 1932. The act established 12 Federal Home Loan Banks, which in turn chartered federal institutions and accepted qualified state institutions as members. Through the sale of bonds and a line of credit to the Treasury, the system loaned more than $200 million to thrifts from 1932 through 1937.

In June 1933, the Home Owners Loan Act established the **Home Owners Loan Corporation (HOLC)**. The U.S. Treasury provided an initial capitalization of $200 million. The HOLC was authorized to issue up to $4.75 billion in 4 percent notes guaranteed by the government. Through the end of 1936, it loaned more than $3 billion to homeowners with mortgages held by thrifts, commercial banks, and mortgage companies. It also loaned money directly to mortgagors for up to 80 percent of a property's value. The homeowner could then negotiate a new mortgage with better terms. The HOLC ended its lending in 1936.

The Federal Savings and Loan Insurance Corporation (FSLIC) was established by the National Housing Act in 1934. FSLIC, similar to the Federal Deposit Insurance Corporation (FDIC) for commercial banks, worked to insure the deposits at thrifts. The agency charged thrifts a small premium for the insurance. It used these funds to pay claims of depositors of failed institutions. Government backing gave the agency credibility. When the FSLIC was abolished in 1989 by a thrift reform act, the FDIC assumed its duties.

In 1934, the National Housing Act established the **Federal Housing Administration (FHA)**, which insured mortgages against default. The FHA charged an insurance premium to mortgagors to cover the cost of expected claims. Again, government backing established credibility for this insurance provider. The FHA would insure loans up to 80 percent of the value of one- to four-family properties as long as the loans were long term and amortizing. At first the term was 15 years, but later 20-, 25-, and 30-year loans became common. Lenders, hurt by the high default rates on short-term loans during the Depression, were quick to make loans with the new insurance provisions. In addition, conventional (non-government-insured) loans took on the characteristics of the long-term FHA loan. By making the term longer, lenders traded default risk for interest rate risk. The interest rate risk became apparent a few decades later when it caused thrifts great problems. Remember that in a volatile interest rate environment, the interest rate risk on a long-term mortgage with a prepayment option is very great.

The Federal National Mortgage Association (FNMA) was established in 1938. Originally called the National Mortgage Association of Washington, FNMA stood ready to purchase and sell FHA-insured mortgages. It raised funds by borrowing from the Treasury and selling shares in the association to the financial institutions with which it did business. Its main purpose was to facilitate the acceptance of FHA-insured loans by establishing a market for them. As interest rates rose, the value of some FHA loans fell. The FNMA would purchase the loans at face value, which provided lenders with additional funds to originate mortgages. FNMA would sell the loans later, when interest rates dropped. Temporary losses were covered by a line of credit from the U.S. Treasury. FNMA gained private-company status late in the 1960s. By the 1990s, FNMA was a major secondary mortgage market agency. (Chapter 3 discusses current FNMA operations.)

Were the programs successful? Did they achieve the goals they had set out to accomplish? Through its programs and the establishment of insurance guaranteed by the Veterans Administration in 1947, the postwar residential finance system was in place. America entered this new era with a well-established system of thrifts, insured by the government and able to provide the services of intermediaries; a long-term, fixed-rate, amortizing mortgage as the main (virtually only) type of loan; and an economy characterized by stable inflation and interest rates.

Summary

Rules and laws defining the rights and duties of the parties to a loan contract developed over the course of history and sometimes in response to specific historical circumstances. Many of today's rules and practices have their origins in the law of the Roman Empire with later German and other European as well as English influences.

The need for real estate financing in the United States became significant at the time of post–Civil War westward expansion, toward the end of the 19th century. Real estate finance in the 20th century was in many ways shaped by the collapse of the nation's economy during the Great Depression from 1929 through 1933. Property values fell to about half their 1928 levels, and dramatic drops in personal income led to large-scale delinquencies on mortgage loans.

The government mortgage market programs of the Depression years were established for two purposes: (1) to provide liquidity to lenders through direct loans and insuring of deposits and (2) to promote a long-term, amortizing type of loan through default insurance and a secondary market for such loans. The government was successful. Through its programs and the establishment of insurance guaranteed by the Veterans Administration in 1947, the postwar residential finance system was in place. America entered this new era with the following:

1. A well-established system of thrifts, insured by the government and able to provide services of intermediaries.
2. A long-term, fixed-rate, amortizing mortgage as the main (virtually only) type of loan.
3. An economy characterized by stable inflation and interest rates.

Key Terms and Definitions

building and loan association—Early financial intermediary established to provide financing for neighborhood home loans.

equitable right of redemption—The common law right to redeem property during the foreclosure period by paying past due amounts. In some states the mortgagor has a statutory right to redeem property after a foreclosure sale. This is limited to several months or a year.

Federal Housing Administration (FHA)—Its main activity is the insuring of residential mortgage loans made by private lenders. FHA is a division of HUD, which sets standards for construction and underwriting and charges a fee, generally 3.8 percent of the loan amount.

fiducia—In Roman times acted as a deed-of-trust.

gage—A deposit or pledge to ensure fulfillment of an agreement.

Home Owners Loan Corporation (HOLC)—An agency formed in 1933 to help stabilize the economy. HOLC issued government-guaranteed bonds to lenders for delinquent mortgages and then refinanced homeowner indebtedness.

hypotheca—An instrument allowing lenders, in Roman times, to take possession of property in the event of actual default.

mortgagor—A borrower who pledges property through a mortgage to secure a loan.

pigus—The same as *hypotheca*, except the lender could take possession in the event of anticipated default.

reconveyance—The transfer of the title of real estate from one person to the immediately preceding owner. It is used when the performance of debt is satisfied under the terms of a deed of trust.

statutory right of redemption—The right of a borrower after a foreclosure sale to reclaim her property by repaying her defaulted loan.

Review Questions

1. Summarize the historical use of property as collateral for a loan to finance its purchase.
2. What was the major difference between the *fiducia*, the *pigus*, and the *hypotheca* in Roman law?
3. Define an equitable right of redemption.
4. What is the origin of the equitable right of redemption?
5. Why were mortgage bankers popular in the post–Civil War era?
6. What were the important characteristics of mortgages in the latter half of the nineteenth century?
7. How did mortgages minimize interest rate risk for lenders?
8. List causes of the high mortgage default rate during the 1930s Depression.
9. How did federal programs support the mortgage and housing market in the 1930s Depression?
10. What was the purpose of the following agencies: (a) FSLIC, (b) FHA, and (c) FNMA?
11. Explain how the mortgage market of the 1940s differed from that of the 1920s.
12. How does knowing a little of the history of residential finance help you understand or remember how today's real estate finance works?

Suggested Readings

Chandler, L. V. *America's Great Depression 1929–1941*. New York: Harper and Row, 1970.

Colean, M. L. *The Impact of Government on Real Estate in the United States*. New York: National Bureau of Economic Research, 1950.

Goldsmith, R. *Financial Intermediaries in the American Economy since 1900*. New York: National Bureau of Economic Research, 1950.

Peterson, P. T. "History of Mortgages." *Secondary Mortgage Markets* 7(3) (Fall 1990).

Schwartz, E. "The Problems of Savings and Loans." In E. Schwartz and G. Vasconcellos, Eds., *Restructuring the Thrift Industry*. Bethlehem, PA: Lehigh University Press.

Sirmans, C. F. *Real Estate Finance*, 2nd ed. New York: McGraw-Hill, 1989.

Chapter 7

Instruments of Real Estate Finance

Chapter Outline

Introduction
Promissory Notes
  Types of Promissory Notes
  Provisions of Promissory Notes
  Sale, Transfer, or Assignment of a Note
Deed of Trust or Trust Deeds
  Provisions of a Trust Deed
Summary
Key Terms and Definitions
Review Questions
Suggested Readings

Learning Objectives

After reading this chapter you will be able to:

- Explain the basic characteristics of real estate financial instruments.
- List and define the basic provisions of a promissory note.
- List and define the basic provisions of a trust deed.

Key Terms

deed-of-trust (trust deed)
guarantor
mortgage
nonrecourse
promissory note
recourse

Introduction

This chapter describes the legal instruments of residential real estate finance. Although the characteristics of such instruments vary from state to state, an understanding of their basics is essential to a working knowledge of real estate finance.

Some provisions are subject to negotiation between the borrower and the lender, although this seldom occurs. Some of the provisions may be modified or obviated by law in some states. State legislatures often pass laws (or state courts make decisions) to protect the borrower in a financial transaction. For example, many state laws allow a prepayment of the mortgage without penalty, thus preserving the value of the prepayment option for the borrower.

In general, an instrument of real estate finance is intended to protect the rights of the parties involved, both borrower and lender. Some rules apply to these instruments or contractual agreements in order for them to be valid. These include the following: (1) The terms of the contract must be in writing, (2) the terms must clearly delineate the property involved, (3) the terms must clearly delineate the details of the loan payment, (4) the parties to the contract must be competent and of legal age, (5) the parties must sign the contract, (6) the signatures must be properly witnessed, and (7) the amount being paid must be sufficient.

Promissory Notes

In a residential finance arrangement, the borrower's promise to repay the lender is outlined in a **promissory note**. Another instrument—either a **mortgage** or a **deed of trust** (also called a trust deed or security deed)—secures the loan itself, with the residence as security. Together, these instruments contain the contractual provisions that state the rights and obligations of the borrower and the lender.

The reason there are two types of instruments (mortgage and deed of trust) that secure the property for the note is that various states have different laws with regard to this instrument. States that allow a deed of trust establish a trustee to hold the deed. In cases where the borrower defaults on the loan, the lender can request the trustee to simply sell the property and hand over the amount due to the lender. In states that require a mortgage, generally, in the case where the borrower defaults a court procedure is required whereby the lender must "prove" the case of default and request the court to order the property sold. In essence, mortgages and deeds of trust accomplish the same purpose but under different procedure as allowed under various state laws.

The lender can sell a promissory note to another investor. When this occurs, the mortgage or trust deed is also transferred. A sale or assignment of the latter without the sale of the promissory note is meaningless.

Types of Promissory Notes

A promissory note can be a **recourse** note or a **nonrecourse** note. A recourse note is one in which the lender has the right to pursue the borrower's other assets in the event that, through a default and foreclosure, the liquidation value of the residence is not sufficient to satisfy the debt. The lender may obtain a court-ordered judgment for the amount of the deficiency, called a *deficiency judgment*. A nonrecourse note limits the lender's remedy for default and foreclosure to the value of the residence that is serving as collateral. This is done through its *exculpatory clause*, which literally means "to hold blameless."

Although the terms of a note may determine its status, state legislation could prohibit certain loans from being recourse notes. Seller carryback loans and home improvement loans often are required to be nonrecourse. A seller carryback exists when the owner-seller of the residence agrees to grant a loan to the buyer instead of receiving cash. Some states have enacted antideficiency judgment legislation to require first mortgages to be nonrecourse. Most states allow *deficiency judgments* on first mortgages so that the lender can proceed against the borrower's remaining assets. However, the borrower's ability to declare personal bankruptcy may discourage a lender from incurring the legal expenses required to pursue a deficiency judgment.

Provisions of Promissory Notes

Amount, Consideration, and Payer

Because a note has value, the lender must give consideration to make it enforceable. Usually that consideration is the amount of the loan (cash), but it can also be personal property, or in the case of seller carrybacks, real estate. The note must specify the amount to be repaid and the person or entity to be repaid (see Figure 7-1). The phrase "or other" appearing after the identification of the lender as payee allows the lender to sell the note or designate another to collect the payments. Virtually all notes have this provision.

Interest and Payment

A promissory note indicates the annual rate of interest and the date from which interest begins to accrue. For adjustable-rate mortgages, the note will indicate the date that the interest rate may change (anniversary date), the basis on which the new rate will be calculated (index), and any limitations (caps) on the interest change or the payment change. (See Chapter 9 for more on adjustable-rate mortgages.) For the standard fixed-rate, amortizing loan, the amount of the installment payment (principal and interest) and due dates are noted.

Interest is commonly charged on an "accrual" (versus an "add-on") method when the installment payment covers both interest and principal reduction. Interest is charged only on the unpaid balance.

Assignment Provision

Many notes have a provision that if the borrower defaults, he or she assigns the right to receive rents or other income from the property to the lender. This prevents the borrower from obtaining benefits from ownership while not making the payments to the lender.

Prepayment

Mortgage notes contain a phrase similar to "and the borrower promises to pay the installment amounts or more." The "or more" portion of the clause allows the borrower to prepay any portion or all of the debt at any time prior to the term of the loan. The lender may impose a prepayment fee or penalty to discourage

Figure 7-1 Promissory Note

Multistate **NOTE** FHA Case No.

[Property Address]

1. PARTIES

"Borrower" means each person signing at the end of this Note, and the person's successors and assigns. "Lender" means ____

and its successors and assigns.

2. BORROWER'S PROMISE TO PAY; INTEREST

In return for a loan received from Lender, Borrower promises to pay the principal sum of

Dollars (U.S. $________________________), plus interest, to the order of Lender. Interest will be charged on unpaid principal, from the date of disbursement of the loan proceeds by Lender, at the rate of (______%) per year until the full amount of principal has been paid.

3. PROMISE TO PAY SECURED

Borrower's promise to pay is secured by a mortgage, deed of trust or similar security instrument that is dated the same date as this Note and called the "Security Instrument." That Security Instrument protects the Lender from losses which might

4. MANNER OF PAYMENT

(A) Time

Borrower shall make a payment of principal and interest to Lender on the first day of each month beginning on ________________________ __________. Any principal and interest remaining on the first day of ________________________ __________, will be due on that date, which is called the maturity date.

(B) Place

Payment shall be made at ____

or at such other place as Lender may designate in writing by notice to Borrower.

(C) Amount

Each monthly payment of principal and interest will be in the amount of $____________________. This amount will be part of a larger monthly payment required by the Security Instrument, that shall be applied to principal, interest and other items in the order described in the Security Instrument.

(D) Allonge to this note for payment adjustments

If an allonge providing for payment adjustments is executed by Borrower together with this Note, the covenants of the allonge shall be incorporated into and shall amend and supplement the covenants of this Note as if the allonge were a part of this Note.

[Check applicable box]

☐ Growing Equity Allonge ☐ Graduated Payment Allonge

☐ Other [Specify]

5. BORROWER'S RIGHT TO PREPAY

Borrower has the right to pay the debt evidenced by this Note, in whole or in part, without charge or penalty, on the first day of any month.

6. BORROWER'S FAILURE TO PAY

(A) Late Charge for Overdue Payments

If Lender has not received the full monthly payment required by the Security Instrument, as described in Paragraph 4(C) of this Note by the end of fifteen calendar days after the payment is due, Lender may collect a late charge in the amount of four percent (4.0%) of the overdue amount of each payment.

(B) Default

If Borrower defaults by failing to pay in full any monthly payment, then Lender may, except as limited by regulations of the Secretary in the case of payment defaults, require immediate payment in full of the principal balance remaining due and all accrued interest. Lender may choose not to exercise this option without waiving its rights in the event of any subsequent default. In many circumstances regulations issued by the Secretary will limit Lender's rights to require immediate payment in full in the case of payment defaults. This Note does not authorize acceleration when not permitted by HUD regulations. As used in this Note, "Secretary" means the Secretary of Housing and Urban Development or his or her designee.

(C) Payment of Costs and Expenses

If Lender has required immediate payment in full, as described above, Lender may require Borrower to pay costs and expenses including reasonable and customary attorneys' fees for enforcing this Note. Such fees and costs shall bear interest from the date of disbursement at the same rate as the principal of this Note.

Page 1 of 2 L80/12-93

Figure 7-1 Promissory Note (continued)

7. WAIVERS

Borrower and any other person who has obligations under this Note waive the rights of presentment and notice of dishonor. "Presentment" means the right to require Lender to demand payment of amounts due. "Notice of dishonor" means the right to require Lender to give notice to other persons that amounts due have not been paid.

8. GIVING OF NOTICES

Unless applicable law requires a different method, any notice that must be given to borrower under this Note will be given by delivering it or by mailing it by first class mail to Borrower at the property address above or at a different address if Borrower has given Lender a notice of Borrower's different address.

Any notice that must be given to Lender under this Note will be given by first class mail to Lender at the address stated in Paragraph 4(B) or at a different address if Borrower is given a notice of that different address.

9. OBLIGATIONS OF PERSONS UNDER THIS NOTE

If more than one person signs this Note, each person is fully and personally obligated to keep all of the promises made in this Note, including the promise to pay the full amount owed. Any person who is a guarantor, surety or endorser of this Note is also obligated to do these things. Any person who takes over these obligatioins, including the obligations of a guarantor, surety or endorser of this Note, is also obligated to keep all of the promises made in this Note. Lender may enforce its rights under this Note against each person individually or against all signatories together. Any one person signing this Note may be required to pay all of the amounts owed under this Note.

BY SIGNING BELOW, Borrower accepts and agrees to the terms and covenants contained in this Note.

_______________________________ (Seal)
Borrower

_______________________________ (Seal)
Borrower

_______________________________ (Seal)
Borrower

_______________________________ (Seal)
Borrower

L80-1/12-93

Page 2 of 2

prepayment. Competition, state legislation, and federal regulations have limited the use of prepayment penalties. The penalty may be limited in amount (say, the next six months' interest) or in time (for example, within only the first three years of the loan). Prepayment penalties are not allowed in cases where a loan is accelerated because of a transfer of the property and the lender's exercise of the due-on-sale provision (see below). The general disuse of prepayment penalties on residential mortgages means that the majority of borrowers are free to exercise prepayments.

Default, Late Performance, and Acceleration

Often a promissory note will stipulate that a fee may be charged if the borrower is late in paying the installment amount. The note will indicate the number of days that the payment can be late before the loan is considered to be in default. It may also stipulate that, in the event of default, the borrower will be required to pay attorneys' and other legal fees necessary to cure the default.

When a default occurs, the *acceleration clause* requires that the entire debt be repaid. The *equitable right of redemption*, available in all states, allows the borrower to cure the default up to several days before a trustee's sale of the property by making the payments up to date, so the loan is current, along with any legal and other foreclosure fees.

Escrow (Impound) Accounts

Because the security for a note is the residence, lenders want to be certain that insurance and taxes are paid properly. The lender needs to ensure that the hazard insurance is paid, because a loss of value due to a fire, for example, would reduce or eliminate the security for the note. Property tax payments also must be made, because any lien placed on the property for failure to pay taxes is superior to the lien of the lender. Therefore, lenders often require that payments for hazard insurance and property taxes be made as part of the regular installment payment. These payment amounts are placed in an account for later disbursement to pay the insurance and taxes. Lenders may not charge a fee for handling the account, and the borrower has the right to an end-of-year accounting and to have any excess accumulated funds returned. Lenders may require a cushion of one-sixth of the total amounts paid out of the account (approximately two months' worth).

Guarantor

Sometimes an individual other than the borrower, called a **guarantor**, may guarantee the payment of a note. When the borrower is a corporation or a limited partnership, for example, lenders will require a *personal* guarantee.

Due-on-Sale Clause

When a property is sold, a due-on-sale provision of the note makes the entire balance due and payable. This eliminates the sometimes-valuable option of mortgage assumption when the current rate of interest is high relative to that on a mortgage that was originated during a time of low interest rates.

Rather than sell a property financed with a due-on-sale note, the owner may attempt to take advantage of the low rate on the note by leasing the property. A lease with an option to purchase the property would also trigger the due-on-sale provision, even if less than three years. In addition, a foreclosure on the junior trust deed can activate the due-on-sale clause for all residential properties.

Residential properties often are transferred from one party to another upon death, divorce, or simply through a voluntary transfer (parents to children). In such situations, the transfer of the property will not activate the due-on-sale clause unless the new owner does not occupy the residence or the property is not a single-family residence. Likewise, a transfer of the property to a trust will not activate the due-on-sale clause if the owner remains the beneficiary and no change in occupancy occurs. Also, a lender that accepts payments on the original note from the new owners of the property may have waived the right to enforce the due-on-sale clause.

In an involuntary conversion such as a fire that destroys a residence, the lender has the right to require that the proceeds from insurance be applied to paying off the note rather than to rebuilding the property. The borrower could be forced to rebuild the residence by obtaining a loan, which could have a higher interest rate. In some states, however, the courts have required the lender to extend the terms of the original note.

Lenders may allow a loan to be assumed even if there is a due-on-sale clause. In such cases, the lender is allowed to, and may, charge an assumption fee. However, the fee cannot consist of "points" ordinarily associated with new loans. To be reasonable, the fee should reflect the expenses incurred by the lender in transferring the note to the new owner (credit evaluation, for example).

Sale, Transfer, or Assignment of a Note

The sale of notes and transfer of mortgages and trust deeds are two independent events. The sale (transfer) of the note can occur by several means. One is by *absolute assignment*, in which the seller retains no property rights or liabilities. The buyer of the note will not have recourse to the seller in the event of a default.

A second type of transfer is by *endorsement*. This leaves the seller personally liable to the buyer.

Finally, a transfer by *guarantee* occurs when a third party, not a party to the transaction, guarantees to the buyer that the note will be paid in full. The guarantee is really a separate transaction between the note buyer and the guarantor.

Deed of Trust or Trust Deeds

A *trust deed* is an instrument that serves as security for the note (see Figure 7-2). A third party (in addition to the lender and borrower) is added to hold the deed in trust. The trustee is usually a bank, attorney, title company, or other individual. There is generally no prohibition of the lender also serving as trustee, but this is unusual. The borrower is the trustor and the lender is the beneficiary.

Provisions of a Trust Deed

The provisions of the trust deed outline the rights and obligations of the lender/beneficiary and the borrower/trustor. In addition, the trust deed may include many of the same provisions that are in the promissory note, such as those related to payments, escrow accounts, the due-on-sale clause, actions in the event of default, and so forth.

Figure 7-2 Sample Deed of Trust

[Space Above This Line For Recording Data]

State of Nevada

DEED OF TRUST

FHA Case No.

THIS DEED OF TRUST ("Security Instrument") is made on
The grantor is

("Borrower"). The trustee is
("Trustee"). The beneficiary is

which is organized and existing under the laws of THE UNITED STATES, and whose address is

("Lender"). Borrower owes Lender the principal sum of

Dollars (U.S. $). This debt is evidenced by Borrower's note dated the same date as this Security Instrument ("Note"), which provides for monthly payments, with the full debt, if not paid earlier, due and payable on . This Security Instrument secures to Lender: (a) the repayment of the debt evidenced by the Note, with interest, and all renewals, extensions and modifications; (b) the payment of all other sums, with interest, advanced under paragraph 6 to protect the security of this Security Instrument; and (c) the performance of Borrower's covenants and agreements under this Security Instrument and the Note. For this purpose, Borrower irrevocably grants and conveys to Trustee, in trust, with power of sale, the following described property located in

County, Nevada:

which has the address of [Street, City],
Nevada [ZIP Code]. ("Property Address");

TOGETHER WITH all the improvements now or hereafter erected on the property, and all easements, rights, appurtenances, rents, royalties, mineral, oil and gas rights and profits, water rights and stock and all fixtures now or hereafter a part of the property. All replacements and additions shall also be covered by this Security Instrument. All of the foregoing is referred to in this Security Instrument as the "Property."

BORROWER COVENANTS that Borrower is lawfully seised of the estate hereby conveyed and has the right to mortgage, grant and convey the Property and that the Property is unemcumbered, except for encumbrances of record. Borrower warrants and will defend generally the title to the Property against all claims and demands, subject to any encumbrances of record.

1. **Payment of Principal, Interest and Late Charge.** Borrower shall pay when due the principal of, and interest on, the debt evidenced by the Note and late charges due under the Note.

2. **Monthly Payments of Taxes, Insurance and Other Charges.** Borrower shall include in each monthly payment, together with the principal and interest as set forth in the Note and any late charges, an installment of any (a) taxes and special assessments levied or to be levied against the Property, (b) leasehold payments or ground rents on the Property, and (c) premiums for insurance required by paragraph 4.

FHA Nevada Deed of Trust - 7/91 Page 1 of 4 L76N / 11-93

Figure 7-2 Sample Deed of Trust (continued)

Each monthly installment for items (a), (b), and (c) shall equal one-twelfth of the annual amounts, as reasonably estimated by Lender, plus an amount sufficient to maintain an additional balance of not more than one-sixth of the estimated amounts. The full annual amount for each item shall be accumulated by Lender within a period ending one month before an item would become delinquent. Lender shall hold the amounts collected in trust to pay items (a), (b), and (c) before they become delinquent.

If at any time the total of the payments held by Lender for items (a), (b), and (c), together with the future monthly payments for such items payable to Lender prior to the due dates of such items, exceeds by more than one-sixth the estimated amount of payments required to pay such items when due, and if payments on the Note are current, then Lender shall either refund the excess over one-sixth of the estimated payments or credit the excess over one-sixth of the estimated payments to subsequent payments by Borrower, at the option of Borrower. If the total of the payments made by Borrower for item (a), (b), or (c) is insufficient to pay the item when due, then Borrower shall pay to Lender any amount necessary to make up the deficiency on or before the date the item becomes due.

As used in this Security Instrument, "Secretary" means the Secretary of Housing and Urban Development or his or her designee. In any year in which the Lender must pay a mortgage insurance premium to the Secretary, each monthly payment shall also include either: (i) an installment of the annual mortgage insurance premium to be paid by Lender to the Secretary, or (ii) a monthly charge instead of a mortgage insurance premium if this Security Instrument is held by the Secretary. Each monthly installment of the mortgage insurance premium shall be in an amount sufficient to accumulate the full annual mortgage insurance premium with Lender one month prior to the date the full annual mortgage insurance premium is due to the Secretary, or if this Security Instrument is held by the Secretary, each monthly charge shall be in an amount equal to one-twelfth of one-half percent of the outstanding principal balance due on the Note.

If Borrower tenders to Lender the full payment of all sums secured by this Security Instrument, Borrower's account shall be credited with the balance remaining for all installments for items (a), (b), and (c) and any mortgage insurance premium installment that Lender has not become obligated to pay to the Secretary, and Lender shall promptly refund any excess funds to Borrower. Immediately prior to a foreclosure sale of the Property or its acquisition by Lender, Borrower's account shall be credited with any balance remaining for all installments for items (a), (b), and (c).

3. **Application of Payments.** All payments under paragraphs 1 and 2 shall be applied by Lender as follows:

First, to the mortgage insurance premium to be paid by Lender to the Secretary or to the monthly charge by the Secretary instead of the monthly mortgage insurance premium;

Second, to any taxes, special assessments, leasehold payments or ground rents, and fire, flood and other hazard insurance premiums, as required;

Third, to interest due under the Note;

Fourth, to amortization of the principal of the Note;

Fifth, to late charges due under the Note.

4. **Fire, Flood and Other Hazard Insurance.** Borrower shall insure all improvements on the Property, whether now in existence or subsequently erected, against any hazards, casualties, and contingencies, including fire, for which Lender requires insurance. This insurance shall be maintained in the amounts and for the periods that Lender requires. Borrower shall also insure all improvements on the Property, whether now in existence or subsequently erected, against loss by floods to the extent required by the Secretary. All insurance shall be carried with companies approved by Lender. The insurance policies and any renewals shall be held by Lender and shall include loss payable clauses in favor of, and in a form acceptable to, Lender.

In the event of loss, Borrower shall give Lender immediate notice by mail. Lender may make proof of loss if not made promptly by Borrower. Each insurance company concerned is hereby authorized and directed to make payment for such loss directly to Lender, instead of to Borrower and to Lender jointly. All or any part of the insurance proceeds may be applied by Lender, at its option, either (a) to the reduction of the indebtedness under the Note and this Security Instrument, first to any delinquent amounts applied in the order in Paragraph 3, and then to prepayment of principal, or (b) to the restoration or repair of the damaged Property. Any application of the proceeds to the principal shall not extend or postpone the due date of the monthly payments which are referred to in Paragraph 2, or change the amount of such payments. Any excess insurance proceeds over an amount required to pay all outstanding indebtedness under the Note and this Security Instrument shall be paid to the entity legally entitled thereto.

In the event of foreclosure of this Security Instrument or other transfer of title to the Property that extinguishes the indebtedness, all right, title and interest of Borrower in and to insurance policies in force shall pass to the purchaser.

5. **Occupancy, Preservation, Maintenance and Protection of the Property; Borrower's Loan Application; Leaseholds.** Borrower shall occupy, establish, and use the Property as Borrower's principal residence within sixty days after the execution of this Security Instrument and shall continue to occupy the Property as Borrower's principal residence for at least one year after the date of occupancy, unless the Secretary determines this requirement will cause undue hardship for Borrower, or unless extenuating circumstances exist which are beyond Borrower's control. Borrower shall notify Lender of any extenuating circumstances. Borrower shall not commit waste or destroy, damage or substantially change the Property or allow the Property to deteriorate, reasonable wear and tear excepted. Lender may inspect the Property if the Property is vacant or abandoned or the loan is in default. Lender may take reasonable action to protect and preserve such vacant or abandoned Property. Borrower shall also be in default if Borrower, during the loan application process, gave materially false or inaccurate information or statements to Lender (or failed to provide Lender with any material information) in connection with the loan evidenced by the Note including, but not limited to, representations concerning Borrower's occupancy of the Property as a principal residence. If this Security Instrument is on a leasehold, Borrower shall comply with the provisions of the lease. If Borrower acquires fee title to the Property, the leasehold and fee title shall not be merged unless Lender agrees to the merger in writing.

6. **Charges to Borrower and Protection of Lender's Rights in the Property.** Borrower shall pay all governmental or municipal charges, fines and impositions that are not included in Paragraph 2. Borrower shall pay these obligations on time directly to the entity which is owed the payment. If failure to pay would adversely affect Lender's interest in the Property, upon Lender's request Borrower shall promptly furnish to Lender receipts evidencing these payments.

If Borrower fails to make these payments or the payments required by Paragraph 2, or fails to perform any other covenants and agreements contained in this Security Instrument, or there is a legal proceeding that may significantly affect Lender's rights in the Property (such as a proceeding in bankruptcy, for condemnation or to enforce laws or regulations), then Lender may do and pay whatever is necessary to protect the value of the Property and Lender's rights in the Property, including payment of taxes, hazard insurance and other items mentioned in Paragraph 2.

Any amounts disbursed by Lender under this Paragraph shall become an additional debt of Borrower and be secured by this Security Instrument. These amounts shall bear interest from the date of disbursement, at the Note rate, and at the option of Lender, shall be immediately due and payable.

7. **Condemnation.** The proceeds of any award or claim for damages, direct or consequential, in connection with any condemnation or other taking of any part of the Property, or for conveyance in place of condemnation, are hereby assigned and shall be paid to Lender to the extent of the full amount of the indebtedness that remains unpaid under the Note and this Security Instrument. Lender shall apply such proceeds to the reduction of the indebtedness under the Note and this Security Instrument, first to any delinquent amounts applied in the order provided in Paragraph 3, and then to prepayment of principal. Any application of the proceeds to the principal shall not extend or postpone the due date of

Page 2 of 4

L76N-1 / 11-93

Figure 7-2 Sample Deed of Trust (continued)

the monthly payments, which are referred to in Paragraph 2, or change the amount of such payments. Any excess proceeds over an amount required to pay all outstanding indebtedness under the Note and this Security Instrument shall be paid to the entity legally entitled thereto.

8. Fees. Lender may collect fees and charges authorized by the Secretary.

9. Grounds for Acceleration of Debt.

(a) Default. Lender may, except as limited by regulations issued by the Secretary in the case of payment defaults, require immediate payment in full of all sums secured by this Security Instrument if:
(i) Borrower defaults by failing to pay in full any monthly payment required by this Security Instrument prior to or on the due date of the next monthly payment, or
(ii) Borrower defaults by failing, for a period of thirty days, to perform any other obligations contained in this Security Instrument.

(b) Sale Without Credit Approval. Lender shall, if permitted by applicable law and with the prior approval of the Secretary, require immediate payment in full of all the sums secured by this Security Instrument if:
(i) All or part of the Property, or a beneficial interest in a trust owning all or part of the Property, is sold or otherwise transferred (other than by devise or descent) by the Borrower, and
(ii) The Property is not occupied by the purchaser or grantee as his or her principal residence, or the purchaser or grantee does so occupy the Property but his or her credit has not been approved in accordance with the requirements of the Secretary.

(c) No Waiver. If circumstances occur that would permit Lender to require immediate payment in full, but Lender does not require such payments, Lender does not waive its rights with respect to subsequent events.

(d) Regulations of HUD Secretary. In many circumstances regulations issued by the Secretary will limit Lender's rights in the case of payment defaults to require immediate payment in full and foreclose if not paid. This Security Instrument does not authorize acceleration or foreclosure if not permitted by regulations of the Secretary.

(e) Acceleration Clause. Borrower agrees that should this Security Instrument and the note secured thereby not be eligible for insurance under the National Housing Act within 60 DAYS from the date hereof, Lender may, at its option and notwithstanding anything in Paragraph 9, require immediate payment in full of all sums secured by this Security Instrument. A written statement of any authorized agent of the Secretary dated subsequent to 120 DAYS from the date hereof, declining to insure this Security Instrument and the note secured thereby, shall be deemed conclusive proof of such ineligibility. Notwithstanding the foregoing, this option may not be exercised by Lender when the unavailability of insurance is solely due to Lender's failure to remit a mortgage insurance premium to the Secretary.

10. Reinstatement. Borrower has a right to be reinstated if Lender has required immediate payment in full because of Borrower's failure to pay an amount due under the Note or this Security Instrument. This right applies even after foreclosure proceedings are instituted. To reinstate the Security Instrument, Borrower shall tender in a lump sum all amounts required to bring Borrower's account current including, to the extent they are obligations of Borrower under this Security Instrument, foreclosure costs and reasonable and customary attorneys' fees and expenses properly associated with the foreclosure proceeding. Upon reinstatement by Borrower, this Security Instrument and the obligations that it secures shall remain in effect as if Lender had not required immediate payment in full. However, Lender is not required to permit reinstatement if: (i) Lender has accepted reinstatement after the commencement of foreclosure proceedings within two years immediately preceding the commencement of a current foreclosure proceeding, (ii) reinstatement will preclude foreclosure on different grounds in the future, or (iii) reinstatement will adversely affect the priority of the lien created by this Security Instrument.

11. Borrower Not Released; Forbearance By Lender Not a Waiver. Extension of the time of payment or modification of amortization of the sums secured by this Security Instrument granted by Lender to any successor in interest of Borrower shall not operate to release the liability of the original Borrower or Borrower's successor in interest. Lender shall not be required to commence proceedings against any successor in interest or refuse to extend time for payment or otherwise modify amortization of the sums secured by this Security Instrument be reason of any demand made by the original Borrower or Borrower's successors in interest. Any forbearance by Lender in exercising any right or remedy shall not be a waiver of or preclude the exercise of any right or remedy.

12. Successors and Assigns Bound; Joint and Several Liability; Co-Signers. The covenants and agreements of this Security Instrument shall bind and benefit the successors and assigns of Lender and Borrower, subject to the provisions of paragraph 9.b. Borrower's covenants and agreements shall be joint and several. Any Borrower who co-signs this Security Instrument but does not execute the Note: (a) is co-signing this Security Instrument only to mortgage, grant and convey that Borrower's interest in the Property under the terms of this Security Instrument; (b) is not personally obligated to pay the sums secured by this Security Instrument; and (c) agrees that Lender and any other Borrower may agree to extend, modify, forbear or make any accommodations with regard to the terms of this Security Instrument or the Note without that Borrower's consent.

13. Notices. Any notice to Borrower provided for in this Security Instrument shall be given by delivering it or by mailing it by first class mail unless applicable law requires use of another method. The notice shall be directed to the Property Address or any other address Borrower designates by notice to Lender. Any notice to Lender shall be given by first class mail to Lender's address stated herein or any address Lender designates by notice to Borrower. Any notice provided for in this Security Instrument shall be deemed to have been given to Borrower or Lender when given as provided in this paragraph.

14. Governing Law; Severability. This Security Instrument shall be governed by Federal law and the law of the jurisdiction in which the Property is located. In the event that any provision or clause of this Security Instrument or the Note conflicts with applicable law, such conflict shall not affect other provisions of this Security Instrument or the Note which can be given effect without the conflicting provision. To this end the provisions of this Security Instrument and the Note are declared to be severable.

15. Borrower's Copy. Borrower shall be given one conformed copy of this Security Instrument.

16. Assignment of Rents. Borrower unconditionally assigns and transfers to Lender all the rents and revenues of the Property. Borrower authorizes Lender or Lender's agents to collect the rents and revenues and hereby directs each tenant of the Property to pay the rents to Lender or Lender's agents. However, prior to Lender's notice to Borrower of Borrower's breach of any covenant or agreement in the Security Instrument, Borrower shall collect and receive all rents and revenues of the Property as trustee for the benefit of Lender and Borrower. This assignment of rents constitutes an absolute assignment and not an assignment for additional security only.

If Lender gives notice of breach to Borrower: (a) all rents received by Borrower shall be held by Borrower as trustee for benefit of Lender only, to be applied to the sums secured by the Security Instrument; (b) Lender shall be entitled to collect and receive all of the rents of the Property; and (c) each tenant of the Property shall pay all rents due and unpaid to Lender or Lender's agent on Lender's written demand to the tenant.

Borrower has not executed any prior assignment of the rents and has not and will not perform any act that would prevent Lender from exercising its right under this paragraph 16.

Page 3 of 4

L76N-2 / 11-93

Figure 7-2 Sample Deed of Trust (continued)

Lender shall not be required to enter upon, take control of or maintain the Property before or after giving notice of breach to Borrower. However, Lender or a judicially appointed receiver may do so at any time there is a breach. Any application of rents shall not cure or waive any default or invalidate any other right or remedy of Lender. This assignment of rents of the Property shall terminate when the debt secured by the Security Instrument is paid in full.

NON-UNIFORM COVENANTS. Borrower and Lender further covenant and agree as follows:

17. Foreclosure Procedure. If Lender requires immediate payment in full under paragraph 9, Lender may invoke the power of sale and any other remedies permitted by applicable law. Lender shall be entitled to collect all expenses incurred in pursuing the remedies provided in this paragraph 17, including, but not limited to, reasonable attorneys' fees and costs of title evidence.

If Lender invokes the power of sale, Lender shall execute or cause Trustee to execute written notice of the occurrence of an event of default and of Lender's election to cause the Property to be sold, and shall cause such notice to be recorded in each county in which any part of the Property is located. Lender shall mail copies of the notice as prescribed by applicable law to Borrower and to the persons prescribed by applicable law. Trustee shall give public notice of sale to the persons and in the manner prescribed by applicable law. After the time required by applicable law, Trustee, without demand on Borrower, shall sell the Property at public auction to the highest bidder at the time and place and under the terms designated in the notice of sale in one or more parcels and in any order Trustee determines. Trustee may postpone sale of all or any parcel of the Property by public announcement at the time and place of any previously scheduled sale. Lender or its designee may purchase the Property at any sale.

Trustee shall deliver to the purchaser Trustee's deed conveying the Property without any covenant or warranty, expressed or implied. The recitals in the Trustee's deed shall be prima facie evidence of the truth of the statements made therein. Trustee shall apply the proceeds of the sale in the following order: (a) to all expenses of the sale, including, but not limited to, reasonable Trustee and attorney fees; (b) to all sums secured by this Security Instrument; and (c) any excess to the person or persons legally entitled to it.

18. Reconveyance. Upon payment of all sums secured by this Security Instrument, Lender shall request Trustee to reconvey the Property and shall surrender this Security Instrument and all notes evidencing debt secured by this Security Instrument to Trustee. Trustee shall reconvey the Property without warranty and without charge to the person or persons legally entitled to it. Such person or persons shall pay any recordation costs.

19. Substitute Trustee. Lender at its option, may from time to time remove Trustee and appoint a successor trustee to any Trustee appointed hereunder. Without conveyance of the Property, the successor trustee shall succeed to all the title, power and duties conferred upon Trustee herein and by applicable law.

20. Waiver of Homestead. Borrower waives all right of homestead exemption in the Property.

21. Assumption Fee. If there is an assumption of this loan, Lender may charge an assumption fee of U.S. $ NOT LESS THAN $45.00 AND NOT MORE THAN $500.00.

Riders to this Security Instrument. If one or more riders are executed by Borrower and recorded together with this Security Instrument, the covenants and agreements of each such rider shall be incorporated into and shall amend and supplement the covenants and agreements of this Security Instrument as if the rider(s) were a part of this Security Instrument. [Check applicable box(es)]

☐ Condominium Rider ☐ Graduated Payment Rider ☐ Growing Equity Rider
☐ Planned Unit Development Rider ☐ Other [Specify]

BY SIGNING BELOW, Borrower accepts and agrees to the terms contained in this Security Instrument and in any rider(s) executed by Borrower and recorded with it.

Witnesses:

______________________ ______________________ (Seal)
-Borrower

______________________ ______________________ (Seal)
-Borrower

______________________ (Seal) ______________________ (Seal)
-Borrower -Borrower

STATE OF NEVADA)
)
County of)

On (date) personally appeared before me, a notary public (or judge or other authorized person, as the case may be), , personally known (or proved) to me to be the person whose name is subscribed to the above instrument who acknowledged that he executed the instrument.

____

REQUEST FOR RECONVEYANCE

TO TRUSTEE:

The undersigned is the holder of the note or notes secured by this Deed of Trust. Said note or notes, together with all other indebtedness secured by this Deed of Trust, have been paid in full. You are hereby directed to cancel said note or notes and this Deed of Trust, which are delivered hereby, and to reconvey, without warranty, all the estate now held by you under this Deed of Trust to the person or persons legally entitled thereto.

Date: ______________________ ______________________

Page 4 of 4

L76N-3 / 11-93

Assignment of Rents

In the event of a default, this provision allows the lender to collect any rents from the property and apply them to the debt. In the event that the rents are substantial, they may be sufficient to cure the default.

Waste

The waste provision indicates that the borrower agrees to keep the property in good condition so that it will not lose value. In this way, the value of the collateral is not impaired.

Nonwaiver

The nonwaiver provision indicates that a lender's failure to exercise a right given in the trust deed does not mean that the lender cannot the exercise the right at some time in the future.

Security Protection

According to the security protection provision, the borrower must reimburse the lender for costs of protecting the property from adversary interests in the event that the borrower fails to do so.

Successors and Assigns

This provision assures that any person or entity that receives an interest in the property must adhere to the same provisions as the borrower.

Substitution of Trustee

This provision allows the lender to replace the trustee by filing the proper papers with the county recorder.

Reconveyance

Upon complete payment of the indebtedness, this provision directs the lender to give the note and trust deed to the trustee, who in turn delivers the title to the borrower.

Release Clause

This provision is typical for large residential real estate developments, where the land is used as collateral for a development loan. It permits the borrower to have some portion of the collateral (land) released from the provisions of the note and trust deed in return for a partial payment of the debt. This allows the borrower/developer to sell off parcels of the development without having to pay the entire debt.

Owner Occupancy

By this provision, the owner promises to occupy the property. This prevents borrowers from purchasing the property as an investment.

Award from Eminent Domain

In the event that a governmental authority expropriates the property, the lender can claim the proceeds from the action to satisfy the debt. (If the borrower received the proceeds, he or she could default on the debt and the lender would have no collateral.)

Covenants and Restrictions

These appear in the trust deed and can limit the use of the property by the borrowers in many ways. They may be as substantial as a prohibition of the use of the property as a business or as minor as a limitation on the number of pets.

Summary

This chapter presented the provisions in the instruments of real estate finance, the promissory note and the mortgage and/or trust deed. Most of these provisions protect the lender in case of default. The lender can step in and collect any rents or proceeds from insurance claims or eminent domain awards. The lender also can foreclose on the property and sell it to recover the amount of the indebtedness. The lender can require the owner to maintain the property in good condition. Although the deed of trust may give the borrower some rights, state law sets out most of those rights. These include the right to cure a deficiency and reinstate the loan by making required payments. In some states, the right extends for a period beyond the foreclosure and liquidation of the property.

Key Terms and Definitions

deed of trust (trust deed)—A type of security instrument conveying title (in trust) to a third party (trustee). It is used to secure the payment of a note. A conveyance of the title land to a trustee as collateral security for the payment of a debt with the condition that the trustee shall reconvey the title to the borrower (trustor) upon the payment of the debt. The trustee has the power to sell the real estate and pay the debt in the event of a default on the part of the debtor.

guarantor—A person or entity that guarantees the performance of a loan taken out by another party.

mortgage—A conveyance of an interest in real property given as security for the payment of a debt.

nonrecourse—In the event of a default by the borrower this is a provision that prevents a lender from pursuing any assets of the borrower other than the property that serves as collateral for the loan.

promissory note—A written instrument that is evidence of a loan and contains provisions for the repayment of the loan.

recourse—The right of the holder of a note secured by a mortgage or deed of trust to look personally to the borrower or endorser for payment, not just to the property.

Review Questions

1. Farnum's Mortgage Company loaned Bob Batchelder the money to buy his house. By signing the promissory note, Bob has promised to pay back the money. Bob defaulted on the loan, and the value of the home was not sufficient to pay Farnum's in full. According to the note, Farnum's could pursue other assets that Bob might have. What type of promissory note did Bob sign?
2. How does equitable right of redemption protect a borrower?
3. Why are the majority of borrowers free to pay off their loan early?
4. What is an escrow (impound) account? Explain why lenders want to set up such accounts.
5. Name three ways in which a note can be transferred. How do these differ?
6. List four important provisions of promissory notes.
7. Answer the following questions about a trust deed:
   a. What is a trust deed?
   b. Who are the parties to a trust deed?
   c. What are the duties of the trustee?
8. What is the purpose of each of the following provisions of a trust deed?
   a. security protection
   b. successors and assigns
   c. reconveyance
   d. rebase clause

Suggested Readings

Clauretie, T. M., and T. Herzog. "The Effect of State Foreclosure Laws on Loan Losses: Evidence from the Mortgage Insurance Industry." *Journal of Money, Credit and Banking* 22(2) (1990), pp. 221–233.

Clauretie, T. M., and M. Jameson. "Residential Loan Renegotiation: Theory and Evidence." *Journal of Real Estate Research* 10 (1995), pp. 153–161.

Dennis, M. W. *Residential Mortgage Lending*, Upper Saddle River, NJ: Prentice Hall, 1989.

Melicher, R. W., and M. Unger. *Real Estate Finance*, Chap. 1. Cincinnati, OH: South-Western Publishing, 1989.

Sirmans, C. F. *Real Estate Finance*, 2nd ed. Chap. 3. New York: McGraw-Hill, 1989.

Wiedemer, J. P. *Real Estate Finance*, 7th ed., Chap. 5. Upper Saddle River, NJ: Prentice Hall, 1995.

Chapter 8

The Fixed-Rate Mortgage

Chapter Outline

Learning Objectives

After reading this chapter you will be able to:

- Describe the features of a fixed-rate mortgage.
- Calculate payments, amortization, outstanding balance, and the effective cost of a fixed-rate mortgage.
- Determine if refinancing a loan is profitable.

Key Terms

amortization schedule
annual percentage rate (APR)
discount point
effective cost (yield)
fixed-rate mortgage
fully amortized mortgage

mortgage constant
mortgage payment
prepayment fee (penalty)
prepayment protection mortgage (PPM)
refinance

Introduction

One of the most enduring products to emerge from the Depression era was the fixed-rate, fixed-payment, 30-year, amortizing mortgage. This mortgage dominated the mortgage market during the last half of the 20th century. Currently, mortgage lenders also offer a 15-year fixed-rate mortgage and adjustable-rate mortgages.

Less common are growing-equity mortgages (GEMs) and graduated-payment mortgages (GPMs). In a GEM, the borrower pays additional funds toward the principal each month. In this way, the mortgage is "paid off" earlier. In a GPM, the loan is set up as a negative amortization loan. The traditional and most common loan, however, continues to be the fixed-rate mortgage, whose fixed payments include principal and interest.

This chapter demonstrates the mechanics of fixed-rate mortgages by showing how to calculate payments, amortization, outstanding balances, and effective cost of fixed-rate mortgages. This background on how mortgages work will be valuable for understanding real estate finance concepts presented later in this text.

Hint: Review this chapter with a calculator at hand. Confirming the values given in the math section will provide you with a brief review of the time value of money presented in Chapter 5.

Characteristics of Fixed-Rate Mortgages

Fixed-rate mortgages are most often paid in equal monthly payments that include principal and interest. However, they may also be set up so that the borrower pays only on the interest each month (or other period) and then makes a "balloon" payment at some date in the future.

Mortgage Math: Payments

The payment on a fixed-rate mortgage is an annuity. Chapter 5 demonstrated a time value of money analysis showing the formula for the present value of an annuity as:

$$\text{Present value of an annuity} = \frac{(1 + i)^n - 1}{i(1 + i)^n}$$

Using this equation we can calculate the present value of the annuity when the payment, the interest or discount rate (i), and the number of payments (n) are known.

Because the payment on a fixed-rate mortgage is an annuity, and when the present value of the annuity (the initial amount borrowed) is known, the present value of an annuity equation can be rearranged to form a **mortgage constant**. This is written as follows:

$$\text{Mortgage constant } (MC_{i,n}) = \frac{i(1+i)^n}{(1+i)^n - 1} \qquad (8.1)$$

The mortgage constant calculates the payment amount required to amortize one dollar at a certain interest rate and a given number of payments. The mortgage constant multiplied by the amount borrowed gives us the **mortgage payment** amount. Note that mortgage payments are structured as ordinary annuities, which means that the payments fall at the end of each period. For example, suppose that you borrow \$100,000 at 10 percent for 30 years with annual payments. The yearly payment required to repay principal and interest would be:

$$\text{Annual payment} = \$100{,}000\,(MC_{10,30}) = \$100{,}000\left[\frac{0.10(1.10)^{30}}{(1.10)^{30} - 1}\right]$$

Mortgages are commonly repaid monthly, so the payment must be adjusted to reflect monthly amortization. The mortgage constant would be written as follows:

$$\text{Mortgage constant } (MC_{i,n}) = \frac{i/12(1+i/12)^{12n}}{(1+i/12)^{12n} - 1}$$

Using the monthly mortgage constant, the monthly payment to satisfy principal and interest is \$877.57. This is calculated as follows:

$$\text{Monthly payment} = \$100{,}000\,(MC_{10,30})$$

$$= \$100{,}000\left[\frac{0.008333(1.008333)^{360}}{(1.008333)^{360} - 1}\right]$$

Note that although the mortgage constant is expressed on an annual basis, the interest rate and term are adjusted to reflect monthly amortization. That is, the interest rate is divided by 12 and the term is multiplied by 12. The interest rate and term must always be measured in the same units (yearly, monthly, etc.).

A financial calculator can be used to solve for the payment. For example, using the HP 10B, the keystrokes would be

Enter 100000 as a negative PV (–100000)
Enter 10 I/YR
Enter 360 N
Solve for PMT

This solution assumes that the calculator is set to 12 payments per year. With the calculator set to one payment per year, the steps are the same except the interest rate (10%) must be manually divided by twelve.

Amortization of the Fixed-Rate Mortgage

When the entire payback of a mortgage is included in the monthly payments, we say that the mortgage is fully *amortized* over its specified term. Each consecutive payment reduces the balance of the mortgage so that when all the payments have been made, the mortgage balance is zero.

Each payment in a **fully amortized mortgage** is the sum of two components—interest and principal. Although the total payment remains the same for each month, the amount applied to interest decreases each month while the amount applied to the principal repayment increases each month. In fact, the early payments consist *primarily* of interest. With each payment, the interest portion decreases (because the principal balance is decreasing) and the principal repayment portion increases. Over the total payments, the sum of the principal repayment amounts equals the original amount borrowed.

Table 8-1 shows an **amortization schedule** for a $100,000 loan made at 10 percent for 30 years. It details how much of each payment goes toward interest and how much goes toward principal for the first six months and the last six months of the sample loan. Notice that the interest portion is greatest in the first month and declines each month thereafter. The principal repayment portion is just the opposite—the smallest amount of principal repayment is found in the payment for month 1. The amortization of the mortgage is a form of forced saving because the borrower is gradually building up equity in the property. Figure 8-1 shows the change in allocation of payment to interest and principal over time.

Table 8-1 Monthly Amortization Schedule for $100,000 Loan at 10% for 30 Years

Payment Number	Payment Amount	Beginning Balance	Amt. Paid on Interest	Amt. Paid on Principal	Ending Balance
01	$877.57	$100,000	$833.33	$44.24	$99,956
02	877.57	99,956	832.96	44.61	99,911
03	877.57	99,911	832.59	44.98	99,866
04	877.57	99,866	832.22	45.35	99,821
05	877.57	99,821	831.84	45.73	99,775
06	877.57	99,775	831.46	46.11	99,729
–	–	–	–	–	–
–	–	–	–	–	–
–	–	–	–	–	–
355	877.57	5,115	42.63	834.94	4,80
356	877.57	4,280	35.67	841.90	3,438
357	877.57	3,438	28.65	848.92	2,589
358	877.57	2,589	21.58	855.99	1,733
359	877.57	1,733	14.44	863.13	870
360	877.57	870	7.25	870.32	0

Note: Balances are rounded to the nearest dollar.

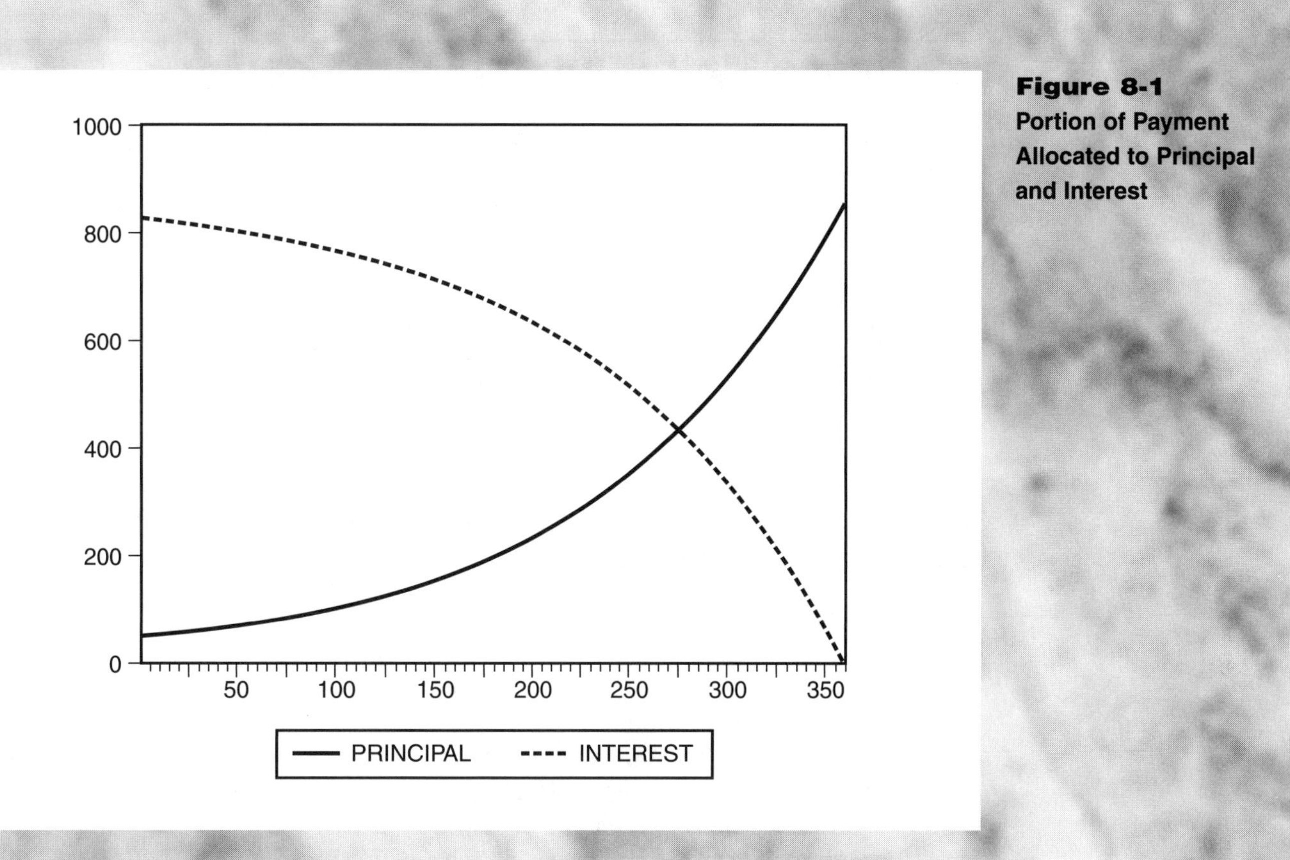

Figure 8-1
Portion of Payment Allocated to Principal and Interest

Outstanding Balance

As Table 8-1 and Figure 8-1 show, the balance owed on the principal of a mortgage decreases with each payment. After each payment, the mortgage will have some outstanding balance. The balance remaining at any point in time is the *present value of the remaining stream of payments discounted at the contract interest rate.* In other words, the outstanding balance is the sum of the principal portion of the remaining payments.

> **SIDEBAR**
>
> **Tax Note**
> Because only the interest portion of the mortgage payment is tax deductible and because interest is a declining portion of the monthly payment, the after-tax cost of the mortgage increases over time. For example, note from Table 8-1 that interest in month 1 is \$833.33 and the principal repayment amount is \$44.24. For a borrower in a 28 percent marginal tax bracket, the after-tax cost of the payment is \$644.24 (44.24 + [833.33(1 – 0.28)]). However the after-tax cost of 360th payment is much higher at \$875.54 (870.32 + [7.25(1 – 0.28)]).

The Effective Cost of the Mortgage

The **effective cost** of the mortgage is the borrower's actual percentage cost. This is also the **effective yield** earned by the lender. Loan fees charged by the lender are included in determining the effective cost of the loan. Higher loan fees result in higher actual percentage cost (effective cost). In the absence of loan fees, the effective cost of the loan is equal to the contract interest rate. Any closing costs classified as additional finance charges are loan fees and affect the cost of the loan. Loan

Mortgage Math: Outstanding Balance

For the example used previously, the outstanding balance at the end of six months is:

$$\text{Outstanding Balance} = \frac{\$877.57}{MC_{10,\,29.5}} = \$99{,}729$$

where the monthly mortgage constant is

$$MC_{10,\,29.5} = \frac{0.008333(1.008333)^{354}}{(1.008333)^{354} - 1}$$

Recall that the mortgage constant factor is the reciprocal of the present value of an annuity factor. Also, note that the interest rate and number of payments are adjusted to reflect the monthly amortization.

fees are charged by the lender to cover expenses incurred in processing the loan and preparing the loan documents. It is common for a loan origination fee to appear on the closing statement. Other items typically classified as finance charges that can affect the cost of a loan include (1) lender inspection fee, (2) assumption fee, (3) underwriting fee, (4) VA funding fee/FHA MIP, (5) tax service fee, (6) document preparation fee, (7) flood certification fee, (8) prepaid interest, and (9) mortgage insurance premium (first year).

The lender may also "discount" the mortgage, that is, charge the borrower **discount points**. A point is equal to 1 percent of the loan amount. The borrower pays the points as a cash fee to the lender at the time of loan origination. In effect, lenders allow borrowers to "buy down" their contract interest rate by paying points at the outset. Remember that the contract rate is the rate on which the mortgage payment is based. Thus a borrower can trade an initial cash charge for a lower monthly payment. The payment of points has the effect of raising the effective cost of the loan.

When loan fees and/or points are charged, the lender must disclose to the borrower the effect on the cost of the loan. Along with other items, truth-in-lending laws require the lender to disclose the **annual percentage rate (APR)** of the loan. The APR is the effective cost of a loan that is held to maturity.

Discount points increase the cost of a loan by reducing the amount of funds actually acquired by the borrower. Here's an example. If a borrower pays two points on a loan of $100,000, or $2,000, the borrower is then really borrowing only $98,000. But the borrower has to pay back the whole $100,000 (the face amount of the loan) plus the interest that is calculated on the $100,000.

Consider our previous example with a loan amount of $100,000 at 10 percent for 30 years and a monthly payment of $877.57. If no points or loan fees are charged, the APR on the loan will be the contract rate of 10 percent. However, with points or fees, the APR increases to more than 10 percent.

Mortgage Math: Calculating the APR

The changing rate for an APR can be illustrated by considering an equation that shows the amount of funds effectively received by the borrower (face amount minus the points/fees) on the left and the amount that the borrower repays on the right. If the loan is held to maturity, the amount repaid is the total of the series of monthly payments. Review the following examples using your calculator to recreate the calculations yourself.

APR with No Points or Fees

$$\$100{,}000 - 0 = \$877.57\ (\text{PVAIF}_{i,\,360})$$

Solving for i (an internal rate of return calculation) yields an interest rate of 0.8333 percent monthly, which annualizes to 10 percent (0.8333% × 12). The left side of the equation is the face amount of the loan minus the points or fees. PVAIF is the present value interest factor for an annuity.

The keystrokes on the HP 10B are as follows:

Enter 100000 minus 0 as a negative PV
Enter 877.57 as PMT
Enter 360 N
Solve for I/YR

APR with Two Discount Points

$$\$100{,}000 - 2000 = \$877.57\ (\text{PVAIF}_{i,\,360})$$

This equation shows that the amount of funds actually acquired by the borrower is \$98,000. However, the payment stream is based on the face value of the loan; the borrower repays 360 payments of \$877.57. Solving for i yields an APR of 10.24 percent. A rough rule of thumb is that one point will increase the APR by about one-eighth of 1 percent (or 12.5 basis points). The calculator keystrokes to solve this problem are the same as above.

Effective Cost and Early Repayment

Because the typical mortgage is not held for its entire term, borrowers also must consider the effective cost of a loan (in percentage terms) that is held for a shorter period. If a loan does not have any financing fees (such as discount points), the effective cost under any holding period is equal to the contract rate. When financing costs are introduced, however, the holding period becomes critical. As we illustrate below, when financing costs are present, the effective cost of the loan is sensitive to the holding period. For example, a loan with two points will have a different effective cost for different holding periods. Holding other factors constant, the shorter the holding period, the higher the effective cost of the loan.

An understanding of this raises questions about how mortgages are priced, that is, how lenders set the trade-off between contract rates and discount points. Avery, Beeson, and Sniderman[1] looked at the relationship between the mortgage rates advertised by lenders and the behavior of borrowers. Specifically, they examined how the quality and number of applicants vary in response to short-run fluctuations in lender rates. They found that lower advertised rates attract more and better qualified applicants. They also found that the low-rate lenders tend to be mortgage banks and mortgage subsidiaries of commercial banks and savings and loans that sell a larger portion of the loans they originate.

Mortgage Math: Effect of Early Repayment on Effective Cost

Because most mortgages are not held to maturity, how a shortened holding period will affect the interest cost is an important consideration. For now, we assume there is no prepayment penalty on the mortgage. Using our previous example, suppose that the 30-year loan is prepaid at the end of 5 years. This means that the payment stream for the borrower is the monthly payment for 60 periods plus the outstanding balance at the end of the fifth year. The effective cost would be calculated as follows:

$$\$100{,}000 - 0 = \$877.57\ (\text{PVAIF}_{i,\,60}) + \$96{,}574\ (\text{PVIF}_{i,\,60})$$

where the balance of the mortgage at the end of year 5 is

$$\text{Bal} = \$877.57/\text{MC}_{10,\,25} = \$96{,}574$$

PVIF is the present value interest factor of one dollar. Note that in deriving the outstanding balance the mortgage constant reflects an interest rate and term adjusted to monthly compounding.

Solving the above equation for the internal rate of return yields an i of 10 percent. This shows that with no discount points or loan fees, the holding period does not affect the effective cost (yield) of the loan.

The keystrokes on the HP 10B to solve this equation are as follows:

Enter 100000 minus 0 as a negative PV
Enter 877.57 as PMT
Enter 96574 as FV
Enter 60 N
Solve for I/YR

If points and/or loan fees are present, the effective cost over the holding period will be a function of the time the mortgage is held. Using the example

[1] Avery, R.B., P.E. Beeson, and M.S. Sniderman. "Posted Rates and Mortgage Lending Activity," *Journal of Real Estate Finance and Economics* 13 (1996), pp. 11–26.

of two points, and assuming that the mortgage is held for five years, the effective cost (yield) is calculated as follows:

$$\$100{,}000 - \$2000 = \$877.57\ (\text{PVAIF}_{i,\,60}) + \$96{,}574\ (\text{PVIF}_{i,\,60})$$

The effective cost is 10.52 percent. Remember that, with other factors held constant, *the shorter the holding period, the higher the effective cost of the loan.*

Effective Cost and Prepayment Penalties

Some mortgages (a minority) charge a penalty to the borrower for repaying a mortgage before maturity. The penalty may be a percentage of the outstanding balance at the time of prepayment. The mortgage may also have a specified period during which the penalty can apply. For example, a mortgage may specify a required prepayment penalty if the loan is repaid within the first 10 years. The prepayment penalty has the effect of increasing the cost (yield) of the loan.

Mortgage Math: Effect of Prepayment Penalties on Effective Cost

Using our previous example, suppose the mortgage has no points or fees, but it does have a prepayment penalty of 5 percent of the outstanding balance if the loan is repaid within the first 10 years. The effect on the cost of the loan if it is repaid at the end of year 5 would be:

$$\$100{,}000 = \$877.57\ (\text{PVAIF}_{i,\,60}) + \$96{,}574\ (1.05)\ (\text{PVIF}_{i,\,60})$$

The prepayment penalty increases the effective cost (yield) from 10 percent to 10.74 percent.

Prepayment Protection Mortgage

Some lenders offer a **prepayment protection mortgage (PPM)**. This type of mortgage, prominent in the 1940s, faded in the 1970s when high market rates made refinancing unattractive. The mortgage market became more standardized with the emergence of the secondary mortgage market. The use of PPMs continued to fade into the early 1980s. However, the decreasing interest rates of the late 1980s and 1990s renewed borrower interest in refinancing—and raised the interest of lenders and/or investors in prepayment protection. Lenders and investors were seeing their returns eroded by borrowers' replacing older, higher interest rate loans with new, lower rate mortgages.

The PPM differs from the standard mortgage in that the borrower gives up the right to prepay the mortgage without penalty in exchange for a lower interest rate. This provision does not prevent prepayment; it simply attaches a cost to it. The cost may be assessed in different ways. For example, Freddie Mac has two PPM structures that apply to both fixed-rate and adjustable-rate mortgages. One method restricts prepayment for the first three years and charges a penalty of 2 percent of the outstanding loan balance. The other provision has a five-year restriction and charges a penalty of six months' interest on the remaining balance. The penalty applies only to refinancing; it is not triggered by loan repayment resulting from sale of the property.

Countrywide Home Funding Corporation, the largest independent mortgage banker in the United States, offers a program whereby borrowers can reduce their contract rate by accepting a prepayment penalty. The rate is generally reduced by about one-fourth of a percent (from 8 percent to 7.75 percent, for example). The homeowner may sell the property or pay down the mortgage by as much as 20 percent during the first five years without a penalty. After that, however, the borrower must pay a penalty equal to six months' interest on the outstanding balance minus 20 percent of principal.

Refinancing a Mortgage

Many borrowers are inquisitive about the benefits and optimal time to refinance their existing loan. It may benefit the borrower to **refinance** an existing loan if market interest rates have fallen subsequent to the origination of the loan in question. This means that a borrower may substitute a loan with a lower rate of interest for the one he or she currently has. This results in a monthly payment savings for the remainder of the loan. Often, some expenses or charges are associated with a refinancing. So the borrower must be sure that the value of the payment savings exceeds the cost of the refinancing. Costs or charges associated with refinancing include an appraisal on the house and origination fees for the new loan.

For example, assume a borrower has a current loan that was taken out 5 years ago and has 25 years remaining. The original loan amount was $100,000 and carried a 9 percent rate. Using a calculator, you can find the monthly payment:

PV	100,000
N	360
I/YR	9

Solve for payment:

PMT = $804.62

Current balance can be solved for as follows:

PMT	804.62
N	300
I/YR	9

Solve for PV:

PV = $95,880

Now, assume interest rates are currently 7 percent. What will be the new payment on a 25-year loan for $95,880 at 7 percent?

PV	95,880
N	300
I/YR	7

Solve for payment:

PMT	$677.66

The payment savings is thus 804.62 – 677.66 = 126.96.

Now, let's find the present value of the payment savings. We will find the present value using the current interest rate:

PMT	126.96
N	300
I/YR	7

Solve for present value:

PV = $17,963

As long as the costs of refinancing (appraisal and origination fees) are less than $17,963 then refinancing makes sense. This is likely to be the case because an appraisal is likely to be only a few hundred dollars and the origination points are often around 2 percent of the loan amount.

Summary

The mechanics of the fixed-rate, fixed-payment mortgage include calculation of the payment, the outstanding balance, the amortization schedule, and the effective cost. The annual percentage rate is the effective cost of the loan if it is held to maturity. A holding period influences the effective cost of a loan that is discounted or has a prepayment penalty.

Key Terms and Definitions

amortization schedule—A schedule showing the amount of each payment and the portion that is interest and the portion that is principal.

annual percentage rate (APR)—The annual rate of interest on a loan after consideration for additional loan charges such as origination points, discount points, and mortgage insurance.

discount point—A fee charged by a lender at closing or settlement that results in increasing the lender's effective yield on the money borrowed. An amount equal to 1 percent of a loan's principal.

effective cost (yield)—The rate of interest actually incurred when the mortgage is paid off before its scheduled maturity.

fixed-rate mortgage—A mortgage for which the interest rate does not change.

fully amortized mortgage—A mortgage that has a portion of the principal paid so that there is no remaining balance with the last payment.

mortgage constant—A value that when multiplied by the initial loan amount will produce the amount of the payment.

mortgage payment—The amount due on each payment date.

prepayment fee (penalty)—The dollar amount levied against a borrower by a lender for paying off a loan before its maturity date. Also known as a prepayment penalty.

prepayment protection mortgage (PPM)—A mortgage with a prepayment penalty.

refinance—To repay one or more existing mortgage loans by simultaneously borrowing funds through another mortgage loan.

Problems to Solve (Answers may be checked against the Answer section)

1. John Corbitt takes a fully amortizing mortgage for $80,000 at 10 percent interest for 30 years, monthly payments. What will be his monthly payment?
2. Dave Burns wants to buy a house. To do so, he must take out a mortgage. A local lender has determined that Dave can afford a monthly payment of $600, principal and interest. If the current interest rate on 30-year, fixed-rate mortgages is 9.50 percent, what is the maximum amount of mortgage that Dave could qualify for?
3. Mary Long qualifies to borrow $120,000 on a mortgage at 9 percent for 30 years, monthly payments.
   a. What is her monthly payment?
   b. How much interest does Mary pay in the first month of the loan?
   c. How much interest does she pay in the first year of the mortgage?
   d. If she decides to repay the mortgage at the end of year 3, what is the outstanding balance at that time?
   e. How much total interest does she pay over this three-year period?
4. You borrow $75,000 for 30 years with monthly amortization, and your payment is $590.03. What interest rate is being charged?
5. You want to purchase a house that has an asking price of $125,000. You can get a loan for 80 percent of the bank's appraised value at 9.50 percent for 30 years, monthly payments. The appraiser values the house at 95 percent of the asking price.
   a. What will be your monthly payment if you take the loan?
   b. What would be the balance of the mortgage after five years?
   c. Set up a five-year amortization schedule showing total annual mortgage payments, total interest and principal paid annually and the balance at the end of each year. (Do not set up a monthly amortization schedule to answer this problem.)
6. Local lenders are offering the following terms for 30-year, fixed-rate mortgages. If your objective is to minimize the cost of borrowing, which alternative do you prefer?

Contract Interest Rate	Discount Points
8.25%	2.75
8.50%	2.00
8.75%	1.00

a. Assume monthly payments and that the mortgage is held to its maturity. What is the effective cost (APR) of each alternative?
b. Assume monthly payments and a holding period of five years. What is the effective cost of each alternative?
c. Assume that each mortgage has a 3 percent prepayment penalty. What is the effective cost of each alternative?

7. Determine the monthly payment for the following mortgages of $90,000 each.

Mortgage	Interest Rate	Maturity (in Months)	Payment
A	10%	360	______
B	11%	300	______
C	09%	300	______
D	08%	260	______

8. Determine the yield-to-maturity at origination for the following mortgages.

Mortgage	Monthly Payment	Maturity (in Months)	Amount at Origination	Yield to Maturity
A	$500	360	$50,000	______
B	$600	360	$65,000	______
C	$550	260	$62,000	______
D	$550	300	$60,000	______

9. How long would it take to pay off the following mortgages? (*Hint:* "Never" is a possible answer.)

Mortgage	Monthly Payment	Coupon Rate	Initial Loan	Maturity
A	$400	10.0%	$45,000	______
B	$800	10.5%	$75,000	______
C	$600	11.0%	$62,000	______
D	$550	11.0%	$60,000	______

10. Determine the discount points necessary to provide a yield to maturity of 10 percent for the following mortgages with 30-year maturities.

Mortgage	Monthly Payment	Coupon Rate	Amount at Origination	Discount Points (in dollars)
A	$800	N/A	$100,000	______
B	$900	N/A	$110,000	______
C	$950	N/A	$125,000	______
D	$700	N/A	$110,000	______

11. Determine the balance of the following 30-year mortgages at the end of the fifth year. (*Hint*: The balance of a standard fixed-rate mortgage at any time is equal to the present value of the remaining payments discounted by the rate on the mortgage.)

Mortgage	Original Amount	Contract Rate	Balance
A	$100,000	10%	______
B	$ 90,000	8%	______
C	$ 80,000	12%	______

Related Web Sites

Time value of money calculator:
http://www.Timevalue.com/cgi-bin/tvscalc.exe

Current mortgage information, rates, ARM indexes, etc.:
http://www.hsh.com and http://www.bankrate.com

Countrywide mortgages:
http://www.countrywide.com

Chapter 9

Alternative Mortgage Instruments

Chapter Outline

Learning Objectives

After reading this chapter you will be able to:

- List the basic characteristics of several types of alternative mortgage instruments.
- Define standard mortgage elements such as interest rate, payment, discount points, and term.
- Describe how the elements are determined and how they are interrelated.
- State how characteristics of various alternative mortgage instruments solve the problems of a fixed-rate mortgage in an inflationary environment.

Key Terms

adjustable-rate mortgage (ARM)
adjustment rate cap
biweekly mortgage
cost of funds index (COFI)
fully indexed rate
graduated-payment mortgage (GPM)
home equity loan
index
initial period discount
life-of-loan rate cap
margin
negative amortization
price level adjusted mortgage (PLAM)
reverse annuity mortgage (RAM)
teaser rate
tilt effect

Introduction

In previous chapters, we discussed inflation and other risk factors associated with lending in general and with the standard fixed-rate mortgage (FRM) in particular. What can be done to reduce risk? What lower risk alternatives to the standard fixed-rate mortgage are available? This chapter presents information on alternative mortgage instruments (AMIs), which are mortgages *other* than the standard, fixed-rate, 30-year, amortizing loan.

Interest Rate Risk

Thrifts hold *short-term* liabilities (deposits) and originate *long-term* assets (mortgages). Inflation creates expectations of continued inflation, which in turn cause the interest rates on thrift deposits to rise. Mortgage prepayments slow with rising rates, leaving the thrifts holding relatively low-rate mortgages and paying higher rates on their short-term deposits. This scenario, which exemplifies the interest rate risk of fixed-rate mortgages, turns profits to losses.[1]

---

[1] In today's mortgage market, lenders commonly offer the 15-year fixed-rate mortgage as an alternative to the standard 30-year fixed-rate loan. The shorter term loan, by nature, will repay faster, which can be an advantage to the mortgage lender in periods of slow prepayment (such as when interest rates are rising). The borrower would have to weigh the advantages of the shorter term loan (such as faster equity buildup) with the disadvantages (such as a higher monthly payment). For an analysis of choosing between 15- and 30-year mortgages, see Richard A. Phillips, Eric Rosenblatt, and James H. Vanderhoff, "The Effect of Relative Pricing on the Fixed-Rate Mortgage Term Decision," *Journal of Real Estate Research* 7 (Spring 1992), pp. 187–194.

Affordability

Rising interest rates on mortgages cause the payment to increase beyond the affordability range of many potential homeowners. The "tilt" problem causes the "real" payment to be extraordinarily high at the beginning of the FRM and very low at the end.

We now take a look at the various alternative mortgage instruments available to borrowers.

Adjustable-Rate Mortgages

When interest rates go up, lenders of fixed-rate mortgages cannot increase the interest rate they are charging on existing loans. They have to pay more to borrow money, but they cannot get more money from their existing loans. Also, when interest rates go up, borrowers tend to keep their existing mortgages rather than prepay them. This means that the lenders need to look elsewhere for funds, and that elsewhere is usually more costly.

One solution for the lenders is a loan whose interest rate can go up when the market interest rates go up. This type of mortgage is called an **adjustable-rate mortgage (ARM)**. The ARM lowers the lender's risk of interest rate changes by allowing the loan's rate to move up or down along with the market rate. This shifts some of the risk to the borrower. Because the lender has less interest rate risk with an ARM, these loans are generally originated at lower rates than fixed-rate mortgages.

ARMs usually have provisions that protect borrowers from extreme adjustments. Nearly all of these mortgages limit how much a rate can increase in a given period or over the term of the mortgage.

ARMs share a number of characteristics:

1. A lower initial interest rate than FRMs
2. A rate that in some fashion is tied to the market (an index)
3. Provisions for limiting the amount by which the rate or payments can change.

Adjustable-rate mortgages have several salient features. These include frequency of rate changes, index, margin, interest rate caps, payment caps, caps on negative amortization, initial period discount (teaser rate), and convertibility. We discuss each of these in turn.

Frequency of Rate Change

The *frequency of rate change* refers to how often a lender can adjust the contract rate on a loan. An ARM that makes continuous adjustments would expose the lender to no interest rate risk at all. This, however, is not practical. Typical adjustment periods include six months, one year, three years, or five years. Greater time between adjustments means greater interest rate risk for the lender. Longer adjustment periods increase the probability that the market rate will move above the rate being paid by the borrower.

The 1-year adjustable ARM has become the standard. This means that the contract rate is adjusted once a year, and the monthly payment usually reflects this adjustment. However, Freddie Mac surveys have shown that about two-thirds of responding lenders offer a 7/1 ARM. This loan locks in an initial interest rate for 7 years and adjusts each year thereafter. Some lenders also offer a 10/1 ARM (initial interest rate holds for 10 years and adjusts each year thereafter).

Index

The **index** is the market rate that provides the basis for adjustment to the interest rate on the ARM. When the index goes up or down, so does the ARM rate. In general, the index must be (1) beyond manipulation by the lender, (2) not excessively volatile, (3) an established, recognized index, and (4) acceptable to the borrower.

The rate on a Treasury bill or bond or some measure of the cost of funds to the lender is usually used as the index. If the index is the yield on a Treasury security; the maturity on the Treasury will be matched to the frequency of the ARM adjustment. For example, if the ARM adjusts once a year, the index will be the yield on the one-year Treasury bill. If the rate on the ARM changes only every three years, the index will be a three-year Treasury note yield.

If the index is the lender's cost of funds (**cost of fund index** or **COFI**), it will be equal to some recent (regional) rate paid on savings deposits as determined by a federal regulatory agency. Because thrifts do not make frequent changes in the rate they offer on deposits, COFIs tend to be less volatile than Treasury bill indices.

Margin

The **margin** is the amount, in "basis points," added to the index to arrive at the contract rate for the loan. One hundred basis points equals one percentage point. If the index value is 5 percent and the margin is 150 basis points, the rate on the loan will be 6.5 percent (until the next adjustment). If a COFI is used as the index, the margin is the amount the lender will have available to cover non-interest costs, such as operating expenses and a return to capital. In simple terms, the margin is the difference between the index and the contract rate of the loan. Once stated in the mortgage contract, the margin cannot change for that loan. Changes in the contract rate are a result of movements in the index (over which the lender has no control) and not changes in the margin. Most margins range from 150 to 275 basis points.

Interest Rate Caps

The two types of *interest rate caps* are **adjustment rate caps** (also called rate caps) and **life-of-loan rate caps** (also called life caps). The former places a limit on how much the contract rate on the loan can change at each adjustment anniversary date. The latter establishes a ceiling that the rate on the loan can never exceed. The life-of-loan cap is usually stated as a number of percentage points over the initial rate. If the initial rate on an ARM is 6 percent and the life cap is 6 percentage points, the maximum contract rate over the life of the loan is 12 percent.

Adjustment rate caps are usually 1 or 2 percent. The smaller (or "tighter") the adjustment cap, the greater the interest rate risk to the lender. A 2 percent adjustment cap on a one-year ARM means that the rate can increase by, at most, 2 percent (200 basis points) in one year. If the market rate has increased by 3 percentage points, the lender will not receive the market return. Adjustment caps also establish a floor of the same size. A 2 percent adjustment cap means that the rate on the loan cannot increase *or decrease* by more than 2 percent on the adjustment date.

The interest rate caps establish the worst case scenario for the contract rate. In general, the lender cannot charge a contract rate greater than the index plus the margin. The adjustment caps mean that the lender cannot charge this amount if the cap is lower than this. The contract rate for any given period will be either (1) the index plus the margin or (2) the previous period's contract rate plus the adjustment cap. (An exception would be if the index plus the margin were less than some established floor rate. These circumstances are rare.)

Negative Amortization Caps

Negative amortization is an increase in the loan balance from one period to the next. This happens when payments are less than the interest charged for that period. Because negative amortization increases the loan balance, the default risk also increases. To control that risk, lenders may limit the amount of negative amortization an ARM may have. ARMs with rate caps and no optional payment cap generally will not have negative amortization. The usual limit is 125 percent of the original loan amount. The balance on a $100,000 loan, for example, will not be allowed to exceed $125,000 through negative amortization.

To attract borrowers, lenders often give an **initial period discount**, or **teaser rate**. This is an initial contract rate that is less than the index plus the margin. If, for example, the index is 5 percent and the margin is 250 basis points, the **fully indexed rate** on the loan would be 7.5 percent. The lender may offer a rate, for the initial period only, of 5 percent.

Convertibility

Some adjustable-rate mortgages are *convertible*. This means that, within a given period of time, the loan can be converted to a fixed-rate mortgage, usually with an interest rate slightly above market rates. The lender charges a nominal conversion fee for the change.

An ARM also may have some other features that are common to other types of loans. They can be assumable or not, have a prepayment penalty (rare), or have up-front discount points or origination fees.

Mortgage Math: Adjustable Rate Mortgage

This example illustrates the features and pricing of ARMs. Assume that the future indexes (Treasury rates) to which the rate on the example ARMs are tied will behave as indicated in Table 9-1.

Table 9-1
Future Interest Indexes and Contract Interest Rates for Adjustable-Rate Mortgage Example

End of Month	Six-Month TB Yield	Six-Month ARM Rate	One-Year TB yield	One-Year ARM Rate
0	4.50	5.00	4.75	5.25
6	5.00	7.00	—	—
12	5.50	7.50	5.75	7.25
18	6.00	8.00	—	—
24	6.25	8.25	6.37	8.87
30	6.50	8.50	—	—
36	6.75	8.75	7.00	9.50
42	7.25	9.25	—	—
48	7.75	9.75	7.87	10.37
54	8.00	10.00	—	—
60	8.25	—	8.50	—

TB = Treasury bill.

They are shown to be increasing over a five-year period.

Table 9-2
Information for Adjustable-Rate Mortgage Example

	ARM 1	ARM 2
Loan amount	$100,000	$100,000
Months amortized	360	360
Rate change interval	6 months	1 year
Margin over index	200.00	250.00
Teaser rate	5.00	5.25
Discount points	2.00	2.00
Periodic interest rate cap	2.00	2.00
Floor rate cap	2.00	2.00
Payment cap	None	None
Lifetime interest rate cap	6.00	6.00

Next, Table 9-2 describes the characteristics of two different ARMs. The terms reflect a trade-off that is representative of modern ARMs. For example, the first ARM (ARM 1), which adjusts every six months, has a lower beginning rate and a smaller margin applied to the index.

Because the examples assume that interest rates will rise, the less restrictive ARMs will be most beneficial to the lender. ARM 1 has the smallest margin but also provides for more frequent rate changes than the other ARM.

For illustration, see the initial payment and subsequent adjustment for the one-year ARM (ARM 2). The initial payment is calculated as:

$$\text{PMT}_1 = \textit{Loan amount}\left[\frac{i(1+i)^n}{(1+i)^n - 1}\right]$$
$$= \$100{,}000\,(\text{MC}_{5.25/12,360})$$
$$= \$100{,}000\,(0.0055220)$$
$$= \$552.20$$

One year later at the first adjustment, the index has a value of 5.75 percent; thus, the fully indexed rate (index plus the margin) is 8.25 percent (5.75 + 2.50). With the ceiling rate cap, the lender must compare this new rate to the sum of the previous period's rate plus the cap (5.25 + 2.00 = 7.25 percent) to determine which is smaller. In this case, the lender cannot charge the fully indexed rate since the contract rate is constrained to 7.25 percent by the interest rate cap.

To determine the payment for year 2, one must first know the amount to be financed, that is, the outstanding balance of the loan at the end of the first year. This is calculated as:

$$\text{Outstanding balance} = \text{Payment}\,(\text{PVAIF}_{5.25/12,\,348})$$
$$= \$840.85\,(178.54038)$$
$$= \$98{,}590$$

The information needed to determine the new payment is now known: the new contract rate (7.25 percent) and the amount to be financed ($98,590). The new payment is thus:

$$\text{PMT}_2 = \$98{,}590\,(\text{MC}_{7.25/12,\,348})$$
$$= \$679.13$$

This process is repeated for each adjustment. Remember that, regardless of adjustments where the payment may increase in some periods and decrease in others, the loan will fully amortize over the contract period of 30 years.

The payments associated with each of the ARMs in our example are shown in Table 9-3. The loan balances for each ARM are shown in Table 9-4. Because of the calculations involved, many lenders have made mistakes in deriving the new payments on ARMs.[2]

Table 9-3
Payment Summary for ARM Example

Month	**ARM 1**	**ARM 2**
1–6	$536.82	$552.20
7–12	663.77	552.20
13–18	696.94	679.13
19–24	730.41	679.13
25–30	747.21	787.39
31–36	763.98	787.39
37–42	780.73	830.25
43–48	814.29	830.25
49–54	848.02	889.59
55–60	864.90	889.59

[2] Elledge, B., S. Fletcher, and G. Norris. "Fumbles, Oversights, and Omissions: Bank ARM Calculations." *Real Estate Review* 25 (Fall 1995), pp. 48–54.

Table 9-4
Loan Balance for ARM Example

Month	ARM 1	ARM 2
0	$100,000	$100,000
12	98,756	98,590
24	97,811	97,554
36	96,900	96,725
48	96,013	95,917
60	95,180	95,152

FRM-ARM Spread

The rate of interest on an ARM is typically 1 to 3 percentage points below that on a fixed-rate loan. The reason is simple. Lenders accept a lower rate when they can shift part of the interest rate risk to borrowers. Loose (high) rate caps and frequent adjustment periods, therefore, usually result in lower rates, relative to that of a fixed-rate loan.

At any particular time the difference between the rates of a FRM and an ARM will depend on several factors. Two of the most important factors are the market's expectation of rate trends and the volatility in interest rates. If interest rates are expected to rise, for example, the lenders will desire to originate ARMs and will, accordingly, offer a better initial interest rate on the ARMs relative to that on the FRM. So, when interest rates are expected to rise the spread between the rate on the FRM and the ARM will widen. Now, if interest rates have been, and are expected to be, volatile then this means that the chances of an increase in rates are also greater than otherwise. So a volatile interest rate environment will cause the spread to also widen. You should see that the spread will widen when interest rates are volatile and expected to rise. The spread will narrow when interest rates are stable and not expected to rise.

The demand for ARMs is affected by two factors: (1) the level of market interest rates in general and (2) the spread between the prices of FRMs and ARMs. Higher general market rates reduce the affordability of FRMs and make ARMs more appealing. Likewise, as the difference between the rate on FRMs and the rate on ARMs increases, so does the demand for ARMs.

The APR on an ARM

The annual percentage rate on a fixed-rate loan can easily be calculated because the future payments are known with certainty. However, the future payments on an ARM are not known with certainty. For this reason lenders must calculate the APR as if interest rates will not change. In this case the payments will not change once the ARM is fully indexed.

Calculating the Effective Cost of an ARM

Suppose that an ARM2 is repaid at the end of Year 3. Using information from Tables 9-3 and 9-4, what is the effective cost of borrowing? Assume that the borrower pays no discount points or other financing costs. The effective cost would be calculated as:

$$\$100{,}000 = 552.20(\text{PVAIF}_{i/12,\,12}) + 679.13\,(\text{PVAIF}_{i/12,\,12})(\text{PVIF}_{i/12,\,12}) + 787.39\,(\text{PVAIF}_{i/12,\,12})(\text{PVIF}_{i/12,\,24}) + 96{,}725(\text{PVIF}_{i/12,\,36})$$

The unknown variable in this equation is i. Solving for i yields 7.03%. Thus the effective cost of this loan if it is held for three years is 7.03%.

If financing costs were present, they would be subtracted from the left-hand side. Suppose, for example, that $2,000 in financing costs were charged. The left-hand side would now equal $98,000 while the right-hand side remains the same. This would result in a higher effective cost.

The keystrokes to solve the above equation on the HP 10B are:

1. Enter 100,000 negative CF,
2. Enter 552.20 CF_1,
3. Enter 12 shift key n,
4. Enter 679.13 CF_2,
5. Enter 12 shift key n,
6. Enter 787.39 CF_3,
7. Enter 11 shift key n,
8. Enter 787.39 plus 96,725 CF_4.

Solve for IRR.

Graduated-Payment Mortgage

When expectations of future inflation cause interest rates to rise, lenders charge a higher rate on new loans to compensate for expected inflation and preserve the real rate of return. The higher rate causes payments on a standard, fixed-rate loan to increase relative to the borrower's income. This is known as the **tilt effect**. Because the FRM is an annuity, all payments are raised uniformly. The real (inflation-adjusted) amount of the initial payment can be substantially greater than later payments as inflation increases over time. That is, in terms of buying power, a $1,000 monthly payment today is greater than a $1,000 payment 10, 20, or 30 years from today.

Although the income of a borrower is expected to increase over the term of a loan, the borrower must make the early payments out of current income, not future income. High inflation results in the payment becoming a greater proportion of the borrower's income, especially early in the loan's life. This can result in burdensome payments at the start of the loan.

The principal alternative mortgage instrument designed to offset the tilt effect is the **graduated-payment mortgage (GPM)**. The concept of the GPM is simple: The payments on a fixed-rate loan are rearranged to be lower at the beginning of the loan and higher at the end. The payment pattern is designed to track the income of the borrower. The rate on the loan is not changed, just the pattern of payments. Usually, the payments are constant for a year, increase for several (about six) years, and then level off for the remainder of the mortgage term. Because the interest rate on a GPM is approximately the same as that on a level-payment FRM, the initial smaller payment may be insufficient to meet the entire interest obligation. Any residual is added to the balance of the loan, resulting in negative amortization.

Mortgage Math: Graduated-Payment Mortgage

Let's say that the rate on a level-payment FRM is 12 percent and that, for simplicity, payments are made monthly. With no discount points, the equation for a standard FRM of $100,000 appears as follows:

$$\$100{,}000 = 1{,}028.61/(1.01) + 1{,}028.61/(1.01)^2 + \ldots + 1{,}028.61/(1.01)^{360} \quad (9.1)$$

To convert this loan to a GPM with payments rising by 7.5 percent for the first 5 years and fixed thereafter, the payments must be restructured. The initial payment must be chosen such that each of the five succeeding payments is 7.5 percent greater than the preceding, the remaining payments for 24 years are equal to that of the sixth year, and the above equation is maintained. The following payment schedule is the result:

$$\begin{aligned}\$100{,}000 = {} & 791.40/(1.01) + \ldots + 850.72/(1.01)^{13} + \ldots + 914.53/(1.01)^{25} \\ & + \ldots + 983.12/(1.01)^{37} + \ldots + 1{,}056.85/(1.01)^{49} \\ & + \ldots + 1{,}136.11/(1.01)^{61} + \ldots + 1{,}136.11/(1.01)^{360}\end{aligned}$$

The amortization schedule for this loan appears in Table 9-5. Note that negative amortization occurs through the first five years. The payment on the GPM is insufficient to meet the interest charges during this period. The payment does not equal that for the standard FRM until approximately the fifth year of the loan. For example, the interest charge on a $100,000 loan at 12 percent is approximately $12,000 for the first year. Yet the 12 payments of $791.40 add up to only $9,496. The difference, $2,504, is added to the loan balance. Payments exceed the interest charge only at the end of the fifth year.

Table 9-5
Amortization Schedule of GPM Loan for $100,000, 12%, Initial Monthly Payment = $791.37

Year	Beginning Balance	Interest	Payment	Ending Balance[a]
1	$100,000	$12,142[b]	$ 9,496[c]	$102,646
2	102,646	12,439	10,209	104,875
3	104,874	12,677	10,974	106,577
4	106,577	12,845	11,797	107,625
5	107,625	12,928	12,682	107,871
6	107,871	12,905	13,633	107,143
7	107,143	12,813	13,633	106,323
–	–	–	–	–
–	–	–	–	–
–	–	–	–	–
30	13,812	179	13,633	0

[a]Ending balance = Beginning balance + Interest – Payment.

[b]Although the interest rate is 12% per annum, the interest cost is slightly higher than $12,000 because of the negative amortization in the initial months.

[c]12 × $791.37.

The mathematical method for solving for the initial monthly payment is involved and complicated. For this reason, standard tables have been developed to ease the problem of determining the initial payment. Table 9-6 is an example of such a table. The factors in the table are multiplied by the amount of the loan balance to arrive at the initial payment. Note that the entry for a 12 percent loan with a 7.5 percent growth in payments for five years is 0.007914, or $791.40, for a $100,000 loan.

Table 9-6

Factors to Compute Monthly Payment in First Year of GPM[a]

Growth Rate for	**Interest Rate**						
First Five Years	**9**	**9.5**	**10**	**10.5**	**11**	**11.5**	**12**
0.050	0.006671	0.006986	0.007305	0.007631	0.007961	0.008296	0.008635
0.075	0.006079	0.006372	0.006670	0.006971	0.007283	0.007596	0.007914
0.010	0.005543	0.005816	0.006094	0.006377	0.000666	0.006958	0.007255

[a]First payment = factor × loan balance.

The benefits of the graduated-payment mortgage are simple. By reducing the tilt effect, borrowers can qualify for a larger loan than they could otherwise, that is, with a level-payment mortgage. Housing becomes more affordable. Also, the increase in payments each year corresponds with the expected increase in the borrower's income. Graduated-payment mortgages have three main problems, however: negative amortization, interest rate risk, and inflexible payment schedules.

The most popular GPMs are insured by the FHA. At one time, the FHA had two GPM programs, 245a and 245b. The 245a program set the initial loan-to-value ratio such that the negative amortization would not exceed 97 percent of the initial appraised value of the property. The 245b program was more liberal; under this program negative amortization could bring the loan balance to 113 percent of the property value. The 245b program was terminated in October 1987 because of its default risk.

Price Level Adjusted Mortgage

One alternative mortgage instrument, the **price level adjusted mortgage (PLAM)**, solves both the tilt and the interest rate risk problems of an FRM.[3]

The price level adjusted mortgage solves these problems by separating the return to the lender into two components: the real return and compensation for inflation. With the PLAM, the inflation component is determined *after* the inflation has occurred and is equal to the exact amount of the inflation. The contract rate on the PLAM is the real rate. The balance of the loan is adjusted

[3]Scott, Houston, and Do show that a hybrid PLAM that permits inflation risk sharing and also accommodates a wide range of amortization-graduation schemes for loan repayment may be the optimal mortgage. See William H. Scott, Jr., Arthur L. Houston, Jr., and A. Quang Do, "Inflation Risk, Payment Tilt, and the Design of Partially Indexed Affordable Mortgages," *Journal of the American Real Estate and Urban Economics Association* 21 (Spring 1993), pp. 1–26.

annually for the amount of the previous year's rate of inflation. For instance, a lender makes a $100,000 loan, and the rate of inflation in the first year is 6 percent. Under the PLAM, the lender would receive a 9 percent return in the first year—3 percent as the contract rate of interest and a 6 percent increase in the balance of the loan. If there were no inflation at all in the first year, there would be no upward adjustment of the loan balance. The lender would receive only the real rate of return, which would be sufficient in the absence of inflation.

The low contract rate makes the loan more affordable for the borrower. Because inflation need not be anticipated with the PLAM, there is no tilt effect. The borrower only pays the inflation premium through an upward adjustment of the balance after the inflation has occurred. Presumably, the increase in the borrower's income will have approximated the rate of inflation.

Mortgage Math: Price Level Adjusted Mortgage

To understand how a PLAM works, consider Table 9-7. For purposes of illustration, we assume that the inflation rate is 4 percent for the first three years, 6 percent for years 4 through 6, and 5 percent for the remainder of the loan. The contract rate is the real rate, 3 percent. Each year the beginning balance is amortized over the remaining life of the loan at the real rate.

Table 9-7
Price Level Adjusted Mortgage Examples[a]

Year	Beginning Balance	Interest (3%)	Payments	Ending Balance Before Adjustment	Ending Balance After Adjustment
1	100,000	3,000	5,102	97,898	101,814
2	101,814	3,054	5,306	99,562	103,545
3	103,545	3,106	5,518	101,133	105,178
4	105,178	3,155	5,739	102,595	108,750
5	108,750	3,263	6,083	105,930	112,285
6	112,285	3,369	6,448	109,206	115,758
7	115,758	3,473	6,835	112,395	118,015
–	–	–	–	–	–
–	–	–	–	–	–
14	126,629	3,799	9,618	120,810	126,851
–	–	–	–	–	–
–	–	–	–	–	–
28	53,864	1,616	19,043	36,438	38,259
29	38,259	1,148	19,995	19,412	20,383
30	20,383	611	20,994	0	0

Inflation rate: 4%, years 1–3; 6%, years 4–6; 5%, years 7–30.

[a]Loan amount = $100,000; real rate = 3%.

The PLAM behaves as follows:

Year 1: In the first year, the annual payment is established by amortizing the $100,000 loan over 30 years at 3 percent. The payment is substantially less than that on a standard loan amortized at 9 percent: $5,102 versus $9,734. In the absence of inflation, the ending balance would be $97,898. The actual ending balance is adjusted upward by 4 percent ($101,814 = $97,898 × 1.04).

Year 2: This payment is set by amortizing the adjusted balance ($101,814) over 29 years at 3 percent. Because the ending balance from year 1 was adjusted upward by 4 percent, the payment in year 2 will be 4 percent greater than in year 1: $5,306 versus $5,102. Recall that it is amortized at the same rate, 3 percent. If the borrower's income has kept pace with inflation, the real payment will not increase. The ending balance in the absence of inflation would be $99,562. This is adjusted upward by the year 2 inflation, 4 percent, so that the adjusted ending balance is $103,545.

Year 5: Skipping to year 5, the beginning balance is $108,750. Amortized at 3 percent the payment rises to $6,083. This is a 6 percent increase from the previous year, reflecting the 6 percent inflation in year 4. Negative amortization continues.

Remaining years: Continued inflation causes the loan balance to increase for several years. In this example it reaches a peak in year 14. The reason the balance does not continue to grow beyond year 14 is that with each successive year the balance is amortized over a shorter remaining term. For short terms, a large proportion of the payment represents amortization. In year 14, only $3,799 of the $9,618 payment is interest; the rest is principal reduction. Eventually, this large amount of amortization exceeds the adjustment of the balance for inflation. The payments in the last few years of the loan appear very high. The last payment, nearly $21,000, is four times greater than the first. This will not be a burden if the borrower's income has kept up with inflation. The last payment is greater than the first by a compounded growth factor of about 5 percent annually over the 30 years.

Mortgage Math: Effective Cost of a PLAM

Calculating the effective cost of the PLAM is an internal rate of return (IRR) process similar to that shown earlier for the ARM. Using our example from Table 9-7, let's calculate the effective cost for a five-year holding period. The equation would be:

$$\$100{,}000 = \$5{,}102/(1 + \text{IRR}) + \$5{,}306/(1 + \text{IRR})^2 + \$5{,}518/(1 + \text{IRR})^3 + \$5{,}739/(1 + \text{IRR})^4 + \$6{,}083/(1 + \text{IRR})^5 + 112{,}285/(1 + \text{IRR})^5 \quad (9.2)$$

Solving for the IRR shows the effective cost to be 7.62 percent. The steps on the financial calculator would be:

1. Enter 100,000 as a negative CF_0.
2. Enter 5,102 as CF_1.
3. Enter 5,306 as CF_2.
4. Enter 5,518 as CF_3.
5. Enter 5,739 as CF_4.
6. Enter the sum of 6,083 plus 112,285 as CF_5.
7. Solve for IRR.

The PLAM has several drawbacks that explain its lack of use in the mortgage market. First, it is complex and difficult to explain to borrowers. Second, even with moderate inflation, the upward adjustment in the loan balance in the early years creates negative amortization. The PLAM's negative amortization is greater and occurs for a longer time than that of a typical GPM. With negative amortization, default risk becomes a concern if equity in the property is eroded. Also, payments increase as a result of inflation, and if a borrower's income fails to keep up with inflation, unacceptable payment-to-income ratios can result.

Another problem with the PLAM is that it does not quite solve the maturity mismatch problem. At the beginning of the year a lender may offer 8 percent on one-year deposits. If inflation that year turns out to be only 2 percent, then the rate of return on PLAM mortgages will only be 5 percent, less than the interest expense. That is, although the PLAM eliminates the need to accurately predict inflation from the standpoint of the lender's assets, it does not do the same from the standpoint of deposit liabilities. Lenders that originate substantial numbers of PLAMs may have to issue deposits for which the rate is also tied to inflation after the fact. Such price level adjusted deposits (PLADs) would allow the lender to originate mortgages without any risk of predicting future inflation. Whether depositors of thrifts could be persuaded to accept PLADs is another question. Later, we indicate that the PLAM also suffers from an unfavorable income tax treatment of the borrower's interest expense.

Reverse Annuity Mortgage

A **reverse annuity mortgage** or **RAM** is, essentially, a "backward" mortgage. Instead of the homeowner borrowing a large sum of money and repaying the loan over many years the homeowner receives a series of payments over several years and at the end owes a sum to the lender. This type of loan is ideal for persons with a large amount of equity built up in their home who also have a need for a steady income stream. This is the case with many retired persons.

If, for example, a retired person had a $100,000 house with no debt he or she could contract with a lender to receive about $481 dollars per month for 10 years if the interest rate were 8 percent. Note that 120 payments of $481 is approximately $57,700. However, with interest accumulating at 8 percent the balance due at the end of the tenth year would be $100,000. Now, if the home appreciates in value the homeowner can extend the RAM loan if he or she needs additional payments after the tenth year. If the homeowner dies before the end of the tenth year, the house can be sold and the balance on the RAM at the time can be paid off.

Home Equity Loan

A **home equity loan** is simply a loan that is taken out, usually, after the original mortgage on the property. Because the original mortgage is paid down and property values typically increase, the amount of equity in the house grows over time. At some point the amount of equity may be sufficient to justify additional borrowing on the property. This additional loan is termed a home equity loan. The terms of the home equity loan can be similar to those of an ordinary fixed-rate loan. Often they have an open line of credit so that the homeowner can borrow from the line of credit periodically as he or she needs the funds. Because the loan is secured by a residence the interest payments are tax deductible.

Biweekly Mortgage

Many lenders offer the homeowner the opportunity to make a mortgage payment on a biweekly basis rather than monthly. At first one might suspect that the payment would be half the monthly payment and there would be twice as many payments. This is not the case, however, because there are more than four weeks in the typical month. So, rather than there being 24 payments there will actually be 26 payments (one-half of 52 weeks). Because there are more than twice the payments the amount will be less than one-half the monthly payment. For example, at 8 percent the monthly payment on a typical 30-year mortgage for $100,000 will be $733.36. The payment on a **biweekly mortgage** will be $338.52 or 46 percent of the larger payment.

Fifteen- versus Thirty-Year Loan

Many homeowners choose to amortize their loan over a 15-year period rather than the typical 30-year span. The payments are not that much larger on the shorter loan but the homeowner builds up equity more rapidly and is, of course, out of debt in half the time. The payment on a $100,000, 8 percent, 30-year loan is $733.76. The payment on a 15 year loan of the same amount is $955.65, about 30 percent greater. That is, a payment that is 30 percent greater reduces the payoff time by 50 percent.

Alternative Mortgage Instruments and the Tax Deductibility of Interest Payments

The relative attractiveness to lenders and borrowers of alternative mortgage instruments is affected by the tax treatment of the interest deduction on these loans. The amount and timing of the deduction depends on the type of mortgage instrument, whether a standard loan or an AMI. With a standard home loan, all interest payments are taxed as income to the lender and deductions by the borrower. With some AMIs, however, this symmetry may not hold because borrowers, being cash-basis taxpayers, may not fully use interest deductions, while lenders, being accrual-basis taxpayers, must include all interest charges in income.

Consider the graduated-payment mortgage as an example. In the initial years the interest expense will be greater than the payment, leading to negative amortization. The borrower cannot deduct the excess of the interest charge over the amount of the payment. The deduction is deferred until positive amortization begins.[4] Thus, although the initial payments are less on a GPM, so are the interest deductions. The lender, on the other hand, must include all of the interest charge in income even though the cash inflow is less.

Mortgage Refinancing

Rising interest rates motivate borrowers to retain their loans and not pay them off early. However, falling rates motivate borrowers to refinance their loans at the lower rate. Although borrowers may not be planning to sell the property that is mortgaged, they may well have an incentive to trade an existing mortgage for a new one. Two common reasons that homeowners refinance when rates are falling are (1) to obtain a lower monthly payment or (2) to increase the amount of the loan, using the cash to remodel or send a child to college. Likewise, an owner of an income-producing property might refinance to lower financing costs and thereby improve cash flow.

[4] Revenue Ruling 77–135.

Mortgage Math: Refinancing a Residential Property

Suppose a borrower took a 30-year fixed-rate mortgage for $100,000 at a 10 percent contract rate with monthly payments. Five years later the contract rate on 25-year, fixed-rate mortgages is 7.5 percent. The attraction of the lower rate would cause the borrower to consider refinancing. A quick analysis shows the borrower's current position:

Current payment = $877.57
Outstanding balance = $96,574
Prepayment penalty = 3 percent of outstanding balance if repaid within the first eight years

Obtaining a new 25-year, fixed-rate mortgage will cost the borrower 4 percent in financing costs. This includes 1 point origination fee, 2 discount points, and 1 percent other costs (such as an appraisal, survey, etc.). Thus, the total cost to get out of the existing mortgage and into the new one is a prepayment penalty on the existing loan of $2,897 ($96,574 × 0.03) and financing cost on the new loan of $3,863 ($96,574 × 0.04). This totals to $6,760.

Refinancing the outstanding balance for 25 years at the lower 7.5 percent rate results in a payment of $713.67. By refinancing the borrower has a monthly payment savings of $163.90. Because the refinancing decision is essentially an investment decision, all values would be set to present value terms using the borrower's opportunity cost of capital, which is 7.5 percent. Assuming that the borrower plans to hold the mortgage for its full term, the present value of the payment savings is $22,179. Comparing this with the cost to refinance of $6,760 produces a positive net present value of $15,419. Thus, the borrower would refinance. This calculation can be shown as:

$$\text{NPV} = \$163.90\,(\text{PVAIF}_{7.5/12,\,300}) - \$6{,}760 = \$22{,}179 - \$6{,}760 = \$15{,}419$$

One important consideration is the length of time the borrower plans to hold the mortgage. The above calculations assumed that the borrower planned either to hold the existing mortgage for its remaining life of 25 years or to hold the new mortgage for its entire 25 years. The analysis would be revised somewhat if the borrower has a planned holding period less than 25 years. Suppose that, when considering refinancing, the borrower knows that the mortgage will be held for 8 more years. Thus if no refinancing takes place, the existing loan will be 13 years old (out of its 30-year life) when it is repaid. If refinancing takes place, the new loan will be 8 years old (out of its 25-year life) when it is repaid. Note that at that future point in time, both mortgages will have the same remaining term (17 years).

This becomes an important consideration since the outstanding balances of the two loans will not be equal at that time. Other things being constant, the lower the contract rate the faster a loan will amortize.[5] Thus, the refinanced loan will have a lower balance at that time than the existing loan. This is viewed as a savings to the borrower and would be considered a cash inflow. After the additional eight years, the outstanding balance on the existing mortgage if refinancing did not take place would be $85,934. With refinancing, the balance on the new loan would be $82,153. Note that the prepayment penalty on the existing loan has expired. This produces a savings at that time of $3,781. The net present value equation now would be:

$$\begin{aligned}\text{NPV} &= \$163.90\,(\text{PVAIF}_{8/12,\,96}) + \$3{,}781\,(\text{PVIF}_{8/12,\,96}) - \$6{,}760\\ &= \$11{,}805 + \$2{,}079 - \$6{,}760\\ &= \$13{,}884 - \$6{,}760\\ &= \$7{,}124\end{aligned}$$

The net present value, although lower than before, is positive, and the borrower would refinance.

[5]This means that given two loans with everything equal except the contract rates, the loan with the lower contract rate will amortize faster and will have a lower outstanding balance at any point in time between inception and maturity. Only at the beginning and the end (when the balance is zero) will the balances on the loans be equal.

The refinancing decision is essentially a net present value (NPV) decision. If refinancing were costless, borrowers would refinance if any decrease in the interest rate occurred. Because transactions costs can be substantial, however, borrowers will refinance when they are confident that the benefits will outweigh the costs.

Refinancing Owner-Occupied Residential Property

To make an effective refinancing decision, homeowners compare the terms on their existing mortgage with the terms on possible new financing. The terms they compare include the amount owed, the contract interest rate, the maturity, discount points, etc. They also examine the costs of ending the existing mortgage (maybe a prepayment penalty) and of acquiring the new mortgage (origination fee, discount points, etc.). If the benefit outweighs the cost, the borrower would refinance.

Summary

Table 9-8 summarizes the advantages and disadvantages of various AMI loans. Default risk is considered from the standpoint of both the provision for negative amortization and for increases in the payment-to-income ratio. The GPM and the PLAM have the greatest risk of default through negative amortization, while the ARM loan joins these two in terms of the likelihood that the payment-to-income ratio can increase. The standard, fixed-rate (SFR) loan is the only loan for which the payment cannot increase. In terms of interest rate risk, the ARM is superior to all other loans. Although both the GPM and the PLAM have provisions for negative amortization, that on the PLAM compensates for changes in the rate of inflation. Thus, the risk is less with the PLAM than with the GPM, which has a rather long duration.

Loans that do not allow the borrower to deduct all of the interest charges when they occur (GPM, PLAM) are inferior to those that do. ARMs have a moderate level of complexity because of the various cap, margin, and index choices. The GPM is the only AMI for which the payment schedule is predetermined at origination and is, therefore, not complex. When interest rates are high, the GPM

Table 9-8
Characteristics of Various Mortgages

	SFR	ARM	GPM	PLAM
Default risk from negative amortization	Moderate	Moderate	Large	Large
Default risk from payment/income ratio	Moderate	Large	Large	Large
Interest rate risk	Moderate	None	Substantial	Little
Tax savings	Standard	Standard	Poor	Poor
Level of complexity	Low	Moderate	Low	High
Affordability at high interest rates	Poor	Moderate	Good	Excellent

lowers the initial payments and solves the tilt problem. The loans that rank highest in overall characteristics are the FRM and the ARM. This explains their dominance in the mortgage market. This is true whether a borrower is seeking funds to purchase real property or to refinance property currently owned.

Key Terms and Definitions

adjustable-rate mortgage (ARM)—A type of mortgage in which the interest rate adjusts periodically according to a preselected index, such as Treasury bill rates, and a margin. This adjustment results in the mortgage payment either increasing or decreasing. Limits can be set on the amount by which interest rates or payments can change.

adjustment rate cap—A limit on the contract rate of interest (for a particular adjustment period) on an adjustable-rate mortgage. Commonly referred to as *rate cap*.

biweekly mortgage—A mortgage with payments due every two weeks, totaling 26 payments per year.

cost of funds index (COFI)—Index for an adjustable-rate mortgage based on the average of interest rates paid by thrifts to their depositors (their cost of funds).

fully indexed rate—The rate of interest on an adjustable-rate mortgage when no discount or teaser rate applies.

graduated payment mortgage (GPM)—A residential mortgage designed to overcome the tilt effect. The monthly mortgage payments start at a level below that on an FRM and increase at a predetermined rate with later payments above that on an FRM. They may level off at some predetermined point.

home equity loan—A second loan on a house based on existing equity.

index—A rate of interest, such as a Treasury-bill rate, used to measure periodic interest rate adjustments for an adjustable-rate mortgage.

initial period discount—See teaser rate.

life-of-loan rate cap—The maximum rate of interest allowed under the terms of an adjustable rate-mortgage. Commonly referred to as *life cap*.

margin—The number of basis points a lender adds to an index to determine the interest rate of an adjustable-rate mortgage.

negative amortization—A loan payment schedule in which the outstanding principal balance goes up, rather than down, because the payments do not cover the full amount of interest due. The unpaid interest is added to the principal.

price level adjusted mortgage (PLAM)—A loan that adjusts the outstanding balance by the actual inflation rate.

reverse annuity mortgage (RAM)—A financing arrangement whereby a lender pays the borrower a fixed annuity or periodic payment based on a percentage of the property's value.

teaser rate—A below market rate of interest for an initial period of time only on an adjustable-rate mortgage.

tilt effect—The effect of a rise in interest rates whereby the real payments on a standard fixed-rate mortgage are much greater at the beginning of the loan than at the end.

Review Questions

1. Name two AMIs that solve the maturity mismatch problem of thrifts and explain how they do so.
2. Identify seven common terms that characterize an ARM.
3. What is meant by "pricing" ARM terms?
4. How would a lender change the margin on an ARM (increase or decrease) in response to (a) imposing a 1 percent rate cap on a previously uncapped ARM, (b) granting an initial period discount, and (c) removing a life-of-loan cap? Explain each of your answers.
5. What factors affect the share of newly originated mortgages that are ARMs?
6. What are the major shortcomings of the graduated-payment mortgage?
7. Explain how the price level adjusted mortgage compensates the lender for both the real rate of return and the rate of inflation.
8. What are the major shortcomings of the price level adjusted mortgage?
9. Why are GPMs and PLAMs poor AMIs from the standpoint of income tax regulations?
10. Name two reasons why homeowners refinance their property when interest rates fall.

Problems to Solve (Answers may be checked against the Answer section)

1. You are given the following data: Determine the first monthly payment for the following types of mortgages:

Market rate	10%
Real rate	3%
Mortgage amount	$100,000
Maturity	30 years

   a. Standard, fixed-rate mortgage
   b. GPM, growth rate first five years, 7.5%
   c. Price level adjusted mortgage
   d. ARM, special first-year rate 8%

2. Determine the first payment in the second year of the one-year adjustable ARMs shown in the following table (mortgage amount at origination, $100,000; maturity, 30 years)

ARM	Contract Rate	Teaser Rate	Rate Cap	Margin	Year 1 Index	Year 2 Index
A	9%	8%	1%	100	8%	8%
B	10	8	2	200	8	10
C	11	8	2	300	8	11

3. Suppose you are considering an ARM with the following characteristics:

Mortgage amount	$100,000
Index	One-year treasury bill yield
Margin	2.50
Maximum annual adjustment	2%
Lifetime interest cap	6%
Discount points	2.00
Loan maturity	30 years

Answer the following:

a. If the Treasury bill yield is currently 6 percent, what is the monthly payment for the first year? (Assume the loan is fully indexed at the outset.)

b. If the index moves to 7.5 percent at the end of the first year, what is the monthly payment for year 2?

c. If the loan is paid off at the end of year 2, what is the effective cost (yield)?

4. Consider a PLAM with the following features:

Mortgage amount	$90,000
Mortgage term	30 years
Current real rate	5%
Inflation for the next three years, respectively	2%, 3%, 5%
Mortgage payments adjusted annually	

Answer the following:

a. What are the monthly payments for each of the first three years?

b. What is the effective cost if the loan is repaid at the end of year 3?

c. What is the effective cost if the loan is repaid at the end of year 3 and the lender charges two discount points up front?

5. Compare the following mortgages and determine which has the lower cost:

	FRM	ARM
Mortgage amount	$100,000	$100,000
Term	30 years	30 years
Discount points	2.00	3.25
Initial contract interest rate	9.75%	7.75%
Margin	—	2.75
Caps	—	2% annual, 6% lifetime
Index value at outset	—	7.75%
Prepayment	End of year 3	End of year 3

Assume that the ARM rate adjusts from the initial beginning rate and the index has the following values:

Beginning of Year	Index Value
1	7.75%
2	9.00%
3	10.75%

6. A widow wishes to take out a reverse annuity mortgage on her house. What annual payment can she get if she decides on a $100,000 debt at the end of 10 years and the current rate is 9 percent?
7. Five years ago a borrower incurred a mortgage for $80,000 at 10 percent for 30 years with monthly payments. Currently the market rate is 8 percent on 25-year mortgages. The existing mortgage has a prepayment penalty of 5 percent of the outstanding balance at prepayment for the first 10 years of the mortgage and the lender will charge 4 percent financing cost on a new loan. The borrower's opportunity investment rate is 8 percent. The borrower is considering refinancing the remaining balance.
   a. If the borrower plans to hold either mortgage (the existing mortgage or the new mortgage) for the next 25 years, should she refinance?
   b. If the borrower plans to hold the mortgage financing for eight more years, should she refinance at the present time?
   c. Assume everything in part *a* except that, instead of refinancing the outstanding balance, the borrower borrows $100,000. Should she refinance?

Suggested Reading

Gordon, J. D., J. Lugtjes, and J. Feid. *Thrifts' Pricing of Adjustable Rate Mortgages*, Research Paper No. 90-02. Washington, DC: Office of Thrift Supervision, 1990.

Jaffee, D., and J. Kearl. "Macroeconomics Simulations of Alternative Mortgage Instruments." Paper presented at New Mortgage Designs for Stable Housing in an Inflationary Environment Conference, Series 14. Boston: Federal Reserve Bank of Boston, 1975.

Lessard, D., and F. Modligliani. "Inflation and the Housing Market: Problems and Potential Solutions." Paper presented at New Mortgage Designs for Stable Housing in an Inflationary Environment Conference, Series 14. Boston: Federal Reserve Bank of Boston, 1975.

Mettling, S. R. *Modern Residential Financing Methods*. Chicago: Real Estate Education Company, 1984, Chaps. 6, 7, and 8.

Ryding, J. "Housing Finance and the Transmission of Monetary Policy." *Federal Reserve Bank of New York Quarterly Review* (Summer 1990): 42–55.

Related Web Sites

Board of Governors of the Federal Reserve System; provides various interest rate data.
http://www.bog.frb.fed.us

Provides tips on buying and financing a home. Online mortgage calculations are also available.
http://www.coldwellbanker.com

Provides online applications for mortgages, loan information and services, and information for real estate professionals.
http://www.countrywide.com

The Loan Process

Part III reviews the residential loan transaction process, which, in most cases, is a detailed step-by-step procedure. After origination of the loan, the processing involves analysis of the application (borrower information collection and verification), submission for credit approval, property appraisal, and closing the loan. Some of the steps are uniform and some are standardized by the government agency involved in the loan.

Government-insured loans allow little variation in the process or in the documents used. The forms and procedures used in loan processing change frequently, however, and you should always refer to the latest guidelines and practices.

The chapters in Part III address the loan process as it relates to the borrower, the collateral (the property), and the closing, including mortgage insurance and title insurance. In addition, Chapter 13 presents information on what we have called "modern finance," though just how modern it really is may be open to debate. Chapter 13 includes discussions on property exchanges and installment sales.

Chapter 10

The Borrower

Chapter Outline

Introduction
Borrower Qualification and Loan Underwriting
Theories of Default
  Ability-to-Pay Theory of Default
  Equity Theory of Default
Loan Application and Financial Statement
Income Ratios
  HUD/FHA Borrower Guidelines
  Definition of Housing Expenses
  Definition of Income
  VA Borrower Qualification
Conforming Conventional Loan Qualification
  Credit Scoring
  Prime and Subprime Loans
Summary
Key Terms and Definitions
Review Questions
Problem to Solve

Learning Objectives

After reading this chapter you will be able to:

- Describe the borrower characteristics that are important to loan qualification.
- Describe the steps involved in borrower qualification and loan underwriting.
- List the data that must be collected and analyzed and the guidelines that must be observed in loan qualification and loan underwriting.

Key Terms

ability-to-pay default theory
borrower qualification and loan underwriting
conforming conventional loan
deficiency judgment
equity default theory
payment-to-income ratios
prime loan
subprime loan

Introduction

A major aspect of the residential loan process is the qualifying of the borrower. Lenders want assurance that a borrower is likely to make timely payments or repay the principal amount of the loan when it is due. The risk that a borrower will fail to do so is the lender's default risk. Lenders use several precautionary measures to reduce default risk, including close scrutiny of the financial position of the borrower, accurate estimates of the value of the property that serves as collateral, and use of legal instruments (deeds of trust and mortgages) with provisions that protect their interests. The focus of the present chapter is the first of these measures—the financial position of the borrower.

Borrower Qualification and Loan Underwriting

Borrower qualification and loan underwriting refers to the process of determining and controlling a lender's risk on a residential loan. In general, the following steps are part of the qualification and underwriting process:

1. Determining the maximum loan amount,
2. Estimating settlement requirements and costs,
3. Analyzing the borrower's credit history,
4. Calculating the borrower's effective income,
5. Estimating the borrower's monthly housing expense, and
6. Assessing the borrower's ability to repay mortgage and other liabilities in a timely fashion.

Taken together, these six evaluations are called a *mortgage credit analysis.*

When a borrower defaults on a loan obligation, the lender must take legal action (foreclosure) to obtain title to the property. The lender will then sell the property. If the loan was insured—and virtually all of them are—the lender will submit a claim to the insurer. (See the next chapter for more on mortgage insurance.)

The foreclosure process can be time consuming and expensive. The lender must pay legal fees, property taxes, maintenance expenses, hazard insurance, repairs, homeowners association assessments, and so forth. A loss for the lender equal to 40 or 50 percent of the loan amount is not uncommon for lengthy foreclosure procedures. Careful borrower qualification can minimize this risk, so both the lender and the mortgage insurer are serious about the process.

When the mortgage credit analysis indicates that the risk is too high, a loan application is rejected. Some reasons for loan rejection are (1) the borrower cannot support the payments, (2) the borrower has a bad credit history (especially pertaining to mortgage repayment), and (3) the borrower is currently delinquent. Also, loans may be rejected if the value of the property, according to the lender-ordered appraisal, is below the selling price or the loan amount.

Theories of Default

Borrower qualification addresses two theories of default risk: the *ability-to-pay theory* and the *equity theory*.

Ability-to-Pay Theory of Default

The **ability-to-pay default theory** states that default and default risk occur when the borrower cannot make the monthly payments on the loan. Loss of employment, disputes that emerge from a divorce proceeding, and an unexpected addition to the family are typical reasons why borrowers may fail to make their loan payments. After several payments are missed, the expensive foreclosure procedure begins. To reduce ability-to-pay default risk, borrower qualification includes an analysis of borrower characteristics and circumstances, such as the number of dependents and the amount and stability of family earnings, that have a direct bearing on a borrower's ability to make the payments on the loan.

Equity Theory of Default

The **equity default theory** focuses on the value of the equity in the property. This theory states that no borrower with substantial positive equity would default, even if unable to make the monthly payment. Instead, the borrower would sell the property and pay off the loan. The amount that does not go toward paying off the loan is the equity that the borrower can now retain. If, for example, John Evans sells his home for $200,000 and uses $150,000 to pay the loan and costs of the sale of the house, he still has $50,000 to retain—a much better position for John than if the lender foreclosed on the property.

The other part of the equity theory of default is that if the value of the property is less than the amount of the loan, a situation called *negative equity*, the borrower may default on the loan even if he or she is able to is able to make the monthly payment. For example, if Susan Evans owes $180,000 on a home that now is worth only $150,000 for some reason, she has negative equity and she may decide to default on the loan. Why? Because if she sells the house, the proceeds from the sale will not pay off her debt on the house. She may be better off with nothing (losing the home to foreclosure) than with (eventually) selling the house and still owing the $30,000 negative equity. Note that this is not always the case. Tax implications and the type of loan (original or refinance, for example) must also be considered.

Depending on the jurisdiction and the type of loan, a lender who forecloses on a property when the house is worth less than the money owed on it can seek a judgment in court for the difference—a **deficiency judgment**. In practice, this may be difficult. The cost of pursuing the judgment in court and the ability of defaulters to declare personal bankruptcy to avoid the consequences of the judgment mitigate the power of the deficiency judgment. Also, a few states prohibit deficiency judgments.

Loan Application and Financial Statement

Procedures for borrower qualification involve a determination of the ability of the borrower to make mortgage payments from earnings and assets. The borrower's loan application provides information on the type and stability of income, supplemental sources of income, nonmortgage debt obligations, and living expenses. Personal information is also included, such as family size and ages of dependents.

As shown in Figure 10-1, a standard loan application includes a financial statement showing the applicant's *assets* and *liabilities*. Assets are those things of value belonging to the applicant, including cash. Cash includes money in checking and savings accounts. Borrowers who demonstrate good money management skills as evidenced by their cash assets inspire more confidence in potential lenders. Assets also include any real estate the applicant owns, automobiles, stocks, bonds, and other valuables.

Liabilities are the debts of the borrower. Lenders examine any notes the borrower may owe very carefully because notes can have a priority position against cash assets. Liabilities also include payments on automobiles, appliances, credit card debt, insurance premiums, unpaid taxes, child support or alimony payments, and so forth.

Lenders examine the ratio of assets to liabilities. An applicant whose assets are twice the amount of the liabilities is more likely to be a good credit risk. Lenders also look at an applicant's *net worth*, that is, the difference between the applicant's assets and liabilities. A positive net worth means the applicant has more assets than liabilities; a negative net worth means the opposite. Applicants with a negative net worth may find obtaining a loan to be difficult.

A lender who decides to proceed with the loan processing after reviewing the application next begins a process of verifying the information. The applicant gives the lender permission to verify the balances in his or her accounts and to check employment status, wages, and length of employment. The applicant signs permission forms for these purposes. The lender also orders a formal credit report on the applicant.

Figure 10-1 Sample Loan Application

Uniform Residential Loan Application

This application is designed to be completed by the applicant(s) with the lender's assistance. Applicants should complete this form as "Borrower" or "Co-Borrower", as applicable. Co-Borrower information must also be provided (and the appropriate box checked) when ☐ the income or assets of a person other than the "Borrower" (including the Borrower's spouse) will be used as a basis for loan qualification or ☐ the income or assets of the Borrower's spouse will not be used as a basis for loan qualification, but his or her liabilities must be considered because the Borrower resides in a community property state, the security property is located in a community property state, or the Borrower is relying on other property located in a community property state as a basis for repayment of the loan.

I. TYPE OF MORTGAGE AND TERMS OF LOAN

Mortgage Applied for: ☐ VA ☐ Conventional ☐ Other: ☐ FHA ☐ FmHA | Agency Case Number | Lender Case No.

Amount $ | Interest Rate % | No. of Months | Amortization Type: ☐ Fixed Rate ☐ GPM ☐ Other (explain): ☐ ARM (type):

II. PROPERTY INFORMATION AND PURPOSE OF LOAN

Subject Property Address (street, city, state & ZIP) | No. of Units

Legal Description of Subject Property (attach description if necessary) | Year Built

Purpose of Loan ☐ Purchase ☐ Refinance ☐ Construction ☐ Construction-Permanent ☐ Other (explain): | Property will be: ☐ Primary Residence ☐ Secondary Residence ☐ Investment

Complete this line if construction or construction-permanent loan.

Year Lot Acquired | Original Cost $ | Amount Existing Liens $ | (a) Present Value of Lot $ | (b) Cost of Improvements $ | Total (a + b) $

Complete this line if this is a refinance loan.

Year Acquired | Original Cost $ | Amount Existing Liens $ | Purpose of Refinance | Describe Improvements ☐ made ☐ to be made Cost: $

Title will be held in what Name(s) | Manner in which Title will be held | Estate will be held in: ☐ Fee Simple ☐ Leasehold (show expiration date)

Source of Down Payment, Settlement Charges and/or Subordinate Financing (explain)

III. BORROWER INFORMATION

Borrower	Co-Borrower
Borrower's Name (include Jr. or Sr. if applicable)	Co-Borrower's Name (include Jr. or Sr. if applicable)
Social Security Number / Home Phone (incl. area code) / Age / Yrs. School	Social Security Number / Home Phone (incl. area code) / Age / Yrs. School
☐ Married ☐ Unmarried (include single, divorced, widowed) ☐ Separated / Dependents (not listed by Co-Borrower) no. ages	☐ Married ☐ Unmarried (include single, divorced, widowed) ☐ Separated / Dependents (not listed by Borrower) no. ages
Present Address (street, city, state, ZIP) ☐ Own ☐ Rent ____ No. Yrs.	Present Address (street, city, state, ZIP) ☐ Own ☐ Rent ____ No. Yrs.

If residing at present address for less than two years, complete the following:

Borrower	Co-Borrower
Former Address (street, city, state, ZIP) ☐ Own ☐ Rent ____ No. Yrs.	Former Address (street, city, state, ZIP) ☐ Own ☐ Rent ____ No. Yrs.
Former Address (street, city, state, ZIP) ☐ Own ☐ Rent ____ No. Yrs.	Former Address (street, city, state, ZIP) ☐ Own ☐ Rent ____ No. Yrs.

IV. EMPLOYMENT INFORMATION

Borrower	Co-Borrower
Name & Address of Employer ☐ Self Employed / Yrs. on this job / Yrs. employed in this line of work/profession	Name & Address of Employer ☐ Self Employed / Yrs. on this job / Yrs. employed in this line of work/profession
Position/Title/Type of Business / Business Phone (incl. area code)	Position/Title/Type of Business / Business Phone (incl. area code)

If employed in current position for less than two years or if currently employed in more than one position, complete the following:

Borrower	Co-Borrower
Name & Address of Employer ☐ Self Employed / Dates (from - to) / Monthly Income $	Name & Address of Employer ☐ Self Employed / Dates (from - to) / Monthly Income $
Position/Title/Type of Business / Business Phone (incl. area code)	Position/Title/Type of Business / Business Phone (incl. area code)
Name & Address of Employer ☐ Self Employed / Dates (from - to) / Monthly Income $	Name & Address of Employer ☐ Self Employed / Dates (from - to) / Monthly Income $
Position/Title/Type of Business / Business Phone (incl. area code)	Position/Title/Type of Business / Business Phone (incl. area code)

Freddie Mac Form 65 10/92 | Page 1 of 4 | Fannie Mae Form 1003 10/92

UNI-FORM (R) / MLM / 1003P1 / 10-92/11-93

INTIALS ________ ________

Figure 10-1 Sample Loan Application (Continued)

V. MONTHLY INCOME AND COMBINED HOUSING EXPENSE INFORMATION

Gross Monthly Income	Borrower	Co-Borrower	Total	Combined Monthly Housing Expense	Present	Proposed
Base Empl. Income*	$	$	$	Rent	$	
Overtime				First Mortgage (P&I)		$
Bonuses				Other Financing (P&I)		
Commissions				Hazard Insurance		
Dividends/Interest				Real Estate Taxes		
Net Rental Income				Mortgage Insurance		
Other (before completing, see the notice in "describe other income," below)				Homeowner Assn. Dues		
				Other:		
Total	$	$	$	Total	$	$

***Self Employed Borrower(s) may be required to provide additional documentation such as tax returns and financial statements.**

Describe Other Income Notice: Alimony, child support, or separate maintenance income need not be revealed if the Borrower (B) or Co-Borrower (C) does not choose to have it considered for repaying this loan.

B/C		Monthly Amount
		$

VI. ASSETS AND LIABILITIES

This Statement and any applicable supporting schedules may be completed jointly by both married and unmarried Co-Borrowers if their assets and liabilities are sufficiently joined so that the Statement can be meaningfully and fairly presented on a combined basis; otherwise separate Statements and Schedules are required. If the Co-Borrower section was completed about a spouse, this Statement and supporting schedules must be completed about that spouse also.

Completed ☐ Jointly ☐ Not Jointly

ASSETS Description	Cash or Market Value
Cash deposit toward purchase held by:	$
List checking and savings accounts below	
Name and address of Bank, S&L, or Credit Union	
Acct. no.	$
Name and address of Bank, S&L, or Credit Union	
Acct. no.	$
Name and address of Bank, S&L, or Credit Union	
Acct. no.	$
Name and address of Bank, S&L, or Credit Union	
Acct. no.	$
Stocks & Bonds (Company name/number & description)	$
Life insurance net cash value Face amount: $	$
Subtotal Liquid Assets	$
Real estate owned (enter market value from schedule of real estate owned)	$
Vested interest in retirement fund	$
Net worth of business(es) owned (attach financial statement)	$
Automobiles owned (make and year)	$
Other Assets (itemize)	$
Total Assets a.	$

Liabilities and Pledged Assets. List the creditor's name, address and account number for all outstanding debts, including automobile loans, revolving charge accounts, real estate loans, alimony, child support, stock pledges, etc. Use continuation sheet, if necessary. Indicate by (*) those liabilities which will be satisfied upon sale of real estate owned or upon refinancing of the subject property.

LIABILITIES	Monthly Payt. & Mos. Left to Pay	Unpaid Balance
Name and address of Company	$ Payt./Mos.	$
Acct. no.	/	
Name and address of Company	$ Payt./Mos.	$
Acct. no.	/	
Name and address of Company	$ Payt./Mos.	$
Acct. no.	/	
Name and address of Company	$ Payt./Mos.	$
Acct. no.	/	
Name and address of Company	$ Payt./Mos.	$
Acct. no.	/	
Name and address of Company	$ Payt./Mos.	$
Acct. no.	/	
Name and address of Company	$ Payt./Mos.	$
Acct. no.	/	
Alimony/Child Support/Separate Maintenance Payments Owed to:	$ /	
Job Related Expense (child care, union dues, etc.)	$	
Total Monthly Payments	$	
Net Worth (a minus b) $	**Total Liabilities b.**	$

Figure 10-1 Sample Loan Application (Continued)

VI. ASSETS AND LIABILITIES (cont.)

Schedule of Real Estate Owned (If additional properties are owned, use continuation sheet.)

Property Address (enter S if sold, PS if pending sale or R if rental being held for income)		Type of Property	Present Market Value	Amount of Mortgages & Liens	Gross Rental Income	Mortgage Payments	Insurance, Maintenance, Taxes & Misc.	Net Rental Income
			$	$	$	$	$	$
		Totals	$	$	$	$	$	$

List any additional names under which credit has previously been received and indicate appropriate creditor name(s) and account number(s):

Alternate Name	Creditor Name	Account Number

VII. DETAILS OF TRANSACTION

a. Purchase price	$
b. Alterations, improvements, repairs	
c. Land (if acquired separately)	
d. Refinance (incl. debts to be paid off)	
e. Estimated prepaid items	
f. Estimated closing costs	
g. PMI, MIP, Funding Fee	
h. Discount (if Borrower will pay)	
i. Total costs (add items a through h)	
j. Subordinate financing	
k. Borrower's closing costs paid by Seller	
l. Other Credits (explain)	
m. Loan amount (exclude PMI, MIP, Funding Fee financed)	
n. PMI, MIP, Funding Fee financed	
o. Loan amount (add m & n)	
p. Cash from/to Borrower (subtract j, k, l & o from i)	

VIII. DECLARATIONS

If you answer "yes" to any questions a through i, please use continuation sheet for explanation.

	Borrower Yes	Borrower No	Co-Borrower Yes	Co-Borrower No
a. Are there any outstanding judgments against you?	☐	☐	☐	☐
b. Have you been declared bankrupt within the past 7 years?	☐	☐	☐	☐
c. Have you had property foreclosed upon or given title or deed in lieu thereof in the last 7 years?	☐	☐	☐	☐
d. Are you a party to a lawsuit?	☐	☐	☐	☐
e. Have you directly or indirectly been obligated on any loan which resulted in foreclosure, transfer of title in lieu of foreclosure, or judgment? (This would include such loans as home mortgage loans, SBA loans, home improvement loans, educational loans, manufactured (mobile) home loans, any mortgage, financial obligation, bond, or loan guarantee. If "Yes," provide details, including date, name and address of Lender, FHA or VA case number, if any, and reasons for the action.)	☐	☐	☐	☐
f. Are you presently delinquent or in default on any Federal debt or any other loan, mortgage, financial obligation, bond, or loan guarantee? If "Yes," give details as described in the preceding question.	☐	☐	☐	☐
g. Are you obligated to pay alimony, child support, or separate maintenance?	☐	☐	☐	☐
h. Is any part of the down payment borrowed?	☐	☐	☐	☐
i. Are you a co-maker or endorser on a note?	☐	☐	☐	☐
j. Are you a U.S. citizen?	☐	☐	☐	☐
k. Are you a permanent resident alien?	☐	☐	☐	☐
l. Do you intend to occupy the property as your primary residence? If "Yes," complete question m below.	☐	☐	☐	☐
m. Have you had an ownership interest in a property in the last three years?	☐	☐	☐	☐
(1) What type of property did you own--principal residence (PR), second home (SH), or investment property (IP)?				
(2) How did you hold title to the home--solely by yourself (S), jointly with your spouse (SP), or jointly with another person (O)?				

IX. ACKNOWLEDGMENT AND AGREEMENT

The undersigned specifically acknowledge(s) and agree(s) that: (1) the loan requested by this application will be secured by a first mortgage or deed of trust on the property described herein; (2) the property will not be used for any illegal or prohibited purpose or use; (3) all statements made in this application are made for the purpose of obtaining the loan indicated herein; (4) occupation of the property will be as indicated above; (5) verification or reverification of any information contained in the application may be made at any time by the Lender, its agents, successors and assigns, either directly or through a credit reporting agency, from any source named in this application, and the original copy of this application will be retained by the Lender, even if the loan is not approved; (6) the Lender, its agents, successors and assigns will rely on the information contained in the application and I/we have a continuing obligation to amend and/or supplement the information provided in this application if any of the material facts which I/we have represented herein should change prior to closing; (7) in the event my/our payments on the loan indicated in this application become delinquent, the Lender, its agents, successors and assigns, may, in addition to all their other rights and remedies, report my/our name(s) and account information to a credit reporting agency; (8) ownership of the loan may be transferred to successor or assign of the Lender without notice to me and/or the administration of the loan account may be transferred to an agent, successor or assign of the Lender with prior notice to me; (9) the Lender, its agents, successors and assigns make no representations or warranties, express or implied, to the Borrower(s) regarding the property, the condition of the property, or the value of the property.

Certification: I/We certify that the information provided in this application is true and correct as of the date set forth opposite my/our signature(s) on this application and acknowledge my/our understanding that any intentional or negligent misrepresentation(s) of the information contained in this application may result in civil liability and/or criminal penalties including, but not limited to, fine or imprisonment or both under the provisions of Title 18, United States Code, Section 1001, et seq. and liability for monetary damages to the Lender, its agents, successors and assigns, insurers and any other person who may suffer any loss due to reliance upon any misrepresentation which I/we have made on this application.

Borrower's Signature	Date	Co-Borrower's Signature	Date
X		X	

The following information is requested by the Federal Government for certain types of loans related to a dwelling, in order to monitor the Lender's compliance with equal credit opportunity, fair housing and home mortgage disclosure laws. You are not required to furnish this information, but are encouraged to do so. The law provides that a Lender may neither discriminate on the basis of this information, nor on whether you choose to furnish it. However, if you choose not to furnish it, under Federal regulations this Lender is required to note race and sex on the basis of visual observation or surname. If you do not wish to furnish the above information, please check the box below. (Lender must review the above material to assure that the disclosures satisfy all requirements to which the Lender is subject under applicable state law for the particular type of loan applied for.)

BORROWER

☐ I do not wish to furnish this information

Race/National Origin: ☐ American Indian or Alaskan Native ☐ Asian or Pacific Islander ☐ White, not of Hispanic Origin ☐ Black, not of Hispanic origin ☐ Hispanic ☐ Other (specify) ______

Sex: ☐ Female ☐ Male

CO-BORROWER

☐ I do not wish to furnish this information

Race/National Origin: ☐ American Indian or Alaskan Native ☐ Asian or Pacific Islander ☐ White, not of Hispanic Origin ☐ Black, not of Hispanic origin ☐ Hispanic ☐ Other (specify) ______

Sex: ☐ Female ☐ Male

To be Completed by Interviewer

This application was taken by:

☐ face-to-face interview
☐ by mail
☐ by telephone

Interviewer's Name (print or type)	Name and Address of Interviewer's Employer
Interviewer's Signature Date	
Interviewer's Phone Number (incl. area code)	

Freddie Mac Form 65 10/92
UNI-FORM (R) / MLM / 1003P3 / 10-92/11-93

Page 3 of 4

Fannie Mae Form 1003 10/92

Figure 10-1 Sample Loan Application (Continued)

Continuation Sheet/Residential Loan Application

Use this continuation sheet if you need more space to complete the Residential Loan Application. Mark **B** for Borrower or **C** for Co-Borrower.	Borrower:	Agency Case Number:
	Co-Borrower:	Lender Case Number:

Prior Employment Information Continued

Name & Address of Employer	☐ Self Employed	Dates (from - to)	Name & Address of Employer	☐ Self Employed	Dates (from - to)
		Monthly Income $			Monthly Income $
Position/Title/Type of Business	Business Phone (incl. area code)		Position/Title/Type of Business	Business Phone (incl. area code)	

I/We fully understand that it is a Federal crime punishable by fine or imprisonment, or both, to knowingly make any false statements concerning any of the above facts as applicable under the provisions of Title 18, United States Code, Section 1001, et seq.

Borrower's Signature:	Date	Co-Borrower's Signature:	Date
X		X	

Freddie Mac Form 65 10/92
UNI-FORM (R) / MLM / 1003P4 / 10-92/11-93

Page 4 of 4

Fannie Mae Form 1003 10/92

Income Ratios

Borrower qualification evaluations for conforming conventional, Federal Housing Administration (FHA), and Veterans Administration (VA) loans all compare maximum ratios of *housing-related expenses* to either gross or after-tax *income*. Table 10-1 compares the definitions and ratios. Ratios for nonconforming conventional loans will vary by lender but will approximate those given in the table.

HUD/FHA Borrower Guidelines

The Department of Housing and Urban Development (HUD) requires that FHA-approved lenders use a percentage calculation to help determine an applicant's eligibility for a loan. Lenders follow a mortgage credit analysis worksheet in which two **payment-to-income ratios** are utilized: (1) the ratio of the monthly *total mortgage payment* (TMP) to the *gross monthly effective income* and (2) the ratio of the sum of TMP plus other monthly expenses to the gross monthly effective income. *Gross effective income* is the borrower and co-borrower's regular plus supplemental gross income. For example, if a borrower's mortgage payment is $1,000 and her gross monthly income is $4,000, the first ratio is 1:4 or 25 percent. If her total monthly expenses, including

Table 10-1 Comparison of Borrower Qualification Guidelines

	Conforming		VA	
	Conventional	FHA	Residual Method	Income Ratios
(1) Monthly income	Gross income	Gross income	Net effective income (gross less federal taxes)	Gross income
(2) Monthly housing expense	Principal, interest, taxes, insurance (PITI)	Principal, interest, taxes, insurance, association fees (TMP)	Principal, interest, taxes, insurance, utilities, maintenance	Principal, interest, taxes, insurance, association fees
(3) Other monthly expense	State and local taxes, car payment	Installment debt, loan payments, child support	State and local taxes, Social Security taxes, installment debt, retirement contributions, life insurance premiums, loan payments	Installment debt, loan payments, child support
(4) Minimum residual			Food, clothing, transportation, medical care, personal items; by region and family size	
Maximum ratio 2/1	Generally 28% 25% (95% L/V)	29%		
Maximum ratio (2 + 3)/1	Generally 36% 33% (95% L/V)	41%		41%
Minimum excess residual ratio [(1) – (2) – (3) – (4)]/(4)			20%	

L/V = Loan-to-value ratio.

mortgage payment, equal $1,500, then the second ratio is 1.5:4 or 37.5 percent. Payment-to-income ratios that exceed 29 and 41 percent, respectively, generally will lead to a denial of the loan application. However, HUD will permit the qualifying ratios to be increased by two percentage points (to 31 and 43 percent, respectively) on newly constructed homes that are identified as being "energy- efficient homes." In fact, the FHA has an "energy-efficient mortgage" in which the borrower can buy or refinance and incorporate into the loan the cost of energy-efficient improvements.

Definition of Housing Expenses

Borrower qualification for conventional loans may consider only the principal, interest, insurance, and taxes (PITI) as "housing expenses." The FHA, however, includes the *monthly mortgage insurance premium* (MIP) and any homeowner association or condominium fees.

The total fixed expense is determined by adding the total mortgage payment installment debt, child support, and other debt payments (as on an automobile loan, for example). Any installment payment scheduled to be paid off within six months can be excluded from this calculation. The goal is to estimate the borrower's total monthly obligation over an extended period of time.

Definition of Income

HUD determines gross monthly effective income as the gross income from all sources that can be expected to continue for the first five years of the mortgage. A borrower whose two qualifying payment-to-income ratios exceed the guidelines can still qualify for the loan if there are significant compensating factors. These factors include borrower characteristics such as the following:

1. The borrower has a conservative attitude toward the use of credit and has accumulated liquid assets (other than by gift).
2. The borrower has at least a 10 percent investment in the property.
3. The borrower's housing expenses are increased only slightly as a result of the purchase.
4. The borrower has other compensation not reflected in the effective income figure.
5. A considerable amount of the borrower's effective income is from nontaxable sources.

Self-employed borrowers can pose some difficult problems for estimating effective income. A borrower is considered self-employed if he or she has a 25 percent or greater ownership in a business. For such borrowers, the lender must verify at least two years of income. An average income figure must be used for the purpose of qualification. Furthermore, the self-employed borrower must have been self-employed for a minimum of two years. A person who has been self-employed between one and two years must have at least two years' previous employment in order to qualify. No person self-employed for less than a year can qualify for an FHA-insured loan.

HUD/FHA bases an accept/reject decision on the following four credit rating factors:

1. Credit characteristics,
2. Stability of effective income,
3. Adequacy of effective income, and
4. Adequacy of wealth or assets.

A failure to meet the guidelines in any of these categories will lead to denial of the loan application.

VA Borrower Qualification

The main purpose of the VA mortgage loan program is to help veterans finance the purchase of homes with favorable loan terms and at competitive interest rates. VA mortgages are available to buy homes, townhomes, condominiums, and mobile homes, to repair or improve a home, and to refinance. Basic characteristics of VA loans include the following:

1. No down payment,
2. Limits on closing costs paid by the buyer, and
3. No prepayment penalty.

Typical requirements are:

(a) Eligibility with loan entitlement,
(b) The home must be owner occupied,
(c) The borrower must meet income requirements, and
(d) The borrower must have good credit.

Most VA loans are made by local lenders and guaranteed by the VA. Loans to Native Americans on trust land and some cases of veteran disability, however, are made directly by the VA.

The VA offers loans with a maximum term of 30 years and 32 days. A VA loan can be a fixed-rate loan, an adjustable-rate mortgage, a graduated-payment loan, or a growing-equity mortgage. The growing-equity mortgage allows for gradual annual increases in payments with all extra applied to the mortgage principal. The increases for the non-fixed-payment loans may be fixed (3 percent per year, for example) or tied to some index. VA loans require no down payment if the value of the property exceeds the purchase price. However, a down payment is required on the graduated-payment mortgage because of the negative amortization. The interest rate is negotiated and only reasonable closing costs can be charged. These costs might include the cost of the VA appraisal, credit report, and survey, as well as title insurance, recording and origination fees, and discount points.

Wartime veterans are eligible for a VA loan if they have served 90 days of active duty during a "hot war." This would include (1) World War II (1940–1947), (2) the Korean conflict (1950–1955), (3) the Vietnam War (1964–1975), and (4) the Persian Gulf War (1990–1991). Peacetime service requires a minimum of 181 days of continuous active duty. For reservists and national guardsmen, six years of service is required for eligibility.

The VA employs a two-step method using ratios similar to those employed in FHA qualification. The ratios are displayed in Table 10-1 (see earlier section). The residual method has been used for many years; the income ratio method was added in October 1986.

Conforming Conventional Loan Qualification

Loan qualification for conventional loan underwriting does not have uniform guidelines to follow. However, the Federal National Mortgage Association (FNMA) and the Federal Home Loan Mortgage Corporation (FHLMC), both of whom purchase conventional loans from lender/originators, have established qualification guidelines to which the loan application must conform—hence, the term **conforming conventional loan**. Most conventional loans are originated under these guidelines. These agencies will not purchase loans that do not meet these guidelines, and, consequently, lenders are not likely to offer such loans. Due to the efficiencies of the secondary mortgage market, conforming loans often carry interest rates 10 to 50 basis points lower than nonconforming loans.

For 95 percent loan-to-value loans, FNMA requires that the mortgage payment not exceed 25 percent of gross income and that the total of the payment and other obligations not exceed 33 percent of gross income. For less than 95 percent loan-to-value loans, the limits are 28 and 36 percent, respectively.

Table 10-2 indicates that federal agencies have additional guidelines that pertain to loans other than the standard fixed-rate type. For example, FNMA will not purchase adjustable-rate mortgages (ARMs) with negative amortization. The FHLMC will purchase such loans, but requires a 10 percent down payment. The same is true for graduated-payment mortgages.

Freddie Mac and Fannie Mae determine a loan limit subject to an annual survey of home purchase prices conducted by the Federal Housing Finance Board (FHFB). As of January 1, 1995, that limit has been set at $203,150. By

Table 10-2 Federal Agency Guidelines for Purchased Conventional Mortgages

	Investor Loans Allowed?	Minimum Down Payment	Minimum Down Payment for Regular ARMS	Minimum Down Payment for Reg. Am. ARMS
Fannie Mae	Yes, maximum 80% loan-to-value ratio	10% (with tougher income-standards if less)	10%	Not acceptable
Freddie Mac	Yes	5%	5%	10% Max 125% neg. amortization

	Graduated Payment ARM	Builder Buydowns	Refinanced Loans	PMI Mortgage Insurance Required	Title Insurance Required
Fannie Mae	Not acceptable	Fixed rate, less than 10% down limited to 3%; 10% down limited to 6%. ARM, no contributions	10%	Yes, if loan-to-value ratio more than 80%	Yes
Freddie Mac	10% down 5%, 7.5% adjustment for first five years	Value of buydown less than 10% of loan amount; annual increase in payment 7.5% or less	10%	Yes, if loan-to-value ratio more than 80%	Yes

law, as of 1981, the Fannie Mae and Freddie Mac loan purchase limit is adjusted annually on the basis of the October-to-October percent change in the average home price reported in the FHFB's monthly survey of terms on conventional home mortgages.

Credit Scoring

In the 1990s there was a shift from the traditional manual mortgage underwriting process to more sophisticated credit scoring models and automated underwriting procedures. Automated underwriting measures the overall expected mortgage default risk of the borrower. Of the traditional three "Cs" of mortgage underwriting (collateral, capacity, and credit), credit has been the most difficult to assess. Automated underwriting was introduced on a massive scale in 1994 by Freddie Mac. Freddie Mac and Fannie Mae have both endorsed the use of credit scoring in assessing credit quality. Today, most mortgage applications are scored in some way.

Recently, lenders have been assigning letter grades to loans based on the credit history of the applicant. Lenders commonly refer to loans as "A," "B," "C," "D," or "F" loans. Under the A rating, the borrower has no more than 38 percent of income allocated to pay debt, has no late mortgage payments in the last two years, no bankruptcy in the previous 10 years, no more than one 30-days-late installment payment or 60-days-late credit card payment. The A borrower has a low default rate. For a B loan, no more than 50 percent of the borrower's income may be allocated to debt payments, no more than three 30-days late mortgage payments in the last year (no 60-days-late payments at all), no more than four 30-days late installment loan payments or two 30-days-late credit card payments. Also, the borrower cannot have declared bankruptcy in the last two to four years. The B borrower may be self-employed and have trouble documenting income. A C loan limits debt payments to 55 percent of income, allows no more than four 30-days-late installment loan payments or four 60-days-late credit card payments. The borrower cannot have declared bankruptcy in the last two years. This borrower has only fair credit and high debt ratios. A D borrower has poor credit and high debt ratios. An F borrower is currently in foreclosure or bankruptcy.

Mortgage Math: Calculating an Income Ratio

The Johnsons have just applied for a 30-year conventional loan of $120,000 at 9 percent interest. The property taxes on the home they are purchasing amount to $2,400 per year. They will be required to pay a hazard insurance premium of $360 and homeowner association fees of $100/month. The Johnsons make two car payments of $420/month each, and have 3 years remaining to pay them off. The previous residents of the home told the Johnsons that their utilities average $200/month and that they spend about $1,800/year on maintenance and repairs. How much income must the Johnsons have in order to qualify for a conventional loan? For an FHA loan? The answer can be calculated using the payment-to-income or expense-to-income ratios that meet the lenders' guidelines (see Table 10-3.)

Table 10-3
Lender Income Ratio Guidelines

	Conventional	FHA	VA
Loan payment	900		
Property tax	200		
HOA fee	100		
Hazard insurance	30		
Total monthly payment	1230		
Loan ratio	1230/0.28 = 4392.86	1230/0.29 = 4231.38	1230/0.41 = 3000
Loan payment	900		
Property tax	200		
HOA fee	100		
Hazard insurance	30		
Car payment	840		
Utilities	200		
Maintenance	150		
Total monthly payment	2420		
Loan Ratio	2420/0.36=6722.22	2420/0.41=5902.44	2420/0.41=5902.44

So the Johnsons would need to have $6,722 or $5,902 per month to qualify for a conventional or an FHA loan, respectively, under the stricter lender guidelines.

Prime and Subprime Loans

When lenders review the characteristics and qualities of the loan applicant they will often divide loan applicants according to their credit risk. When borrowers have good financial characteristics (good credit history, no history of bankruptcy, steady income, large income relative to mortgage payments, adequate wealth, and so forth) they will be categorized as prime and offered a **prime loan**. The opposite is true when borrowers have a spotty credit history or less than adequate current financial strength. In this case the borrower will be classified as subprime and offered a **subprime loan**. The rate of interest on the subprime loan is generally higher to reflect the added risk. In addition, some lenders specialize in offering one or the other of the two categories of loans.

Summary

Lenders and mortgage insurers follow guidelines that help minimize default risk. They perform careful evaluations of borrower and property characteristics to make sure that (1) the borrower can make the loan payments, and (2) in the event of foreclosure, the value of the property is worth the investment.

One guideline that lenders and insurers use to gauge a borrower's ability to pay is the payment-to-income ratio. These ratios should not exceed 29 and 41 percent, respectively.

Key Terms and Definitions

ability-to-pay default theory—The theory that mortgage defaults occur because the mortgagor is unable to meet the monthly payment.

borrower qualification and loan underwriting—The process of assessing the riskiness of a loan according to the financial position of the borrower.

conforming conventional loan—a loan whose terms, such as the loan-to-value, comply with the requirements of the GSE's.

deficiency judgment—A judgment levied against the borrower personally (personal assets) for the difference between the mortgage debt (including payments in arrears) and the liquidation value of the property.

equity default theory—A theory that states that mortgage defaults only occur if there is negative equity in the property.

payment-to-income ratios—The borrower's monthly payment on a mortgage divided by his or her monthly income.

prime loan—Prime loans are those made to well-qualified borrowers.

subprime loans—Subprime loans are those made to borrowers with some past credit problems such as frequent delinquent payments and/or previous foreclosures and bankruptcies.

Review Questions

1. State and explain the two theories of default. Which theory makes more "intuitive" sense?
2. What is a deficiency judgment?
3. How useful are deficiency judgments in mitigating losses through borrower default?
4. Define borrower qualification.
5. Contrast borrower qualification under VA and FHA procedures.
6. Henry Marsh owes $115,000 on a home that now is worth only $82,000. Why might Henry decide to let the mortgage company foreclose on his home?
7. When (under what conditions) do VA loans not require a down payment?
8. What borrower characteristics are important for loan qualification?
9. List the main steps of borrower qualification and loan underwriting.
10. List the data that must be collected for borrower qualification and loan underwriting.
11. What does a conforming conventional loan conform to?
12. What is a payment-to-income ratio?

Problem to Solve (Answer may be checked against the Answer section)

1. The Marshalls have just applied for a 30-year conventional loan of $280,000 at 8 percent interest. The property taxes on the home they are purchasing amount to $3,600 per year. They will be required to pay a hazard insurance premium of $480 and homeowners association fees of $100/month. The Marshalls make two car payments of $620/month each, and have 3 years remaining to pay them off. The previous residents of the home told the Marshalls that their utilities average $400/month and that they spend about $3,600/year on maintenance and repairs. How much income must the Marshalls have in order to qualify for a conventional loan? For an FHA loan? Use the payment-to-income or expense-to-income ratios that meet the lenders' guidelines.

Chapter 11

The Collateral

Chapter Outline

Introduction
Property Appraisal
  Ordering the Appraisal
  Monitoring the Appraisal
  Evaluating the Appraisal
Valuation
  Cost Approach
  Market Approach
  Income Approach
  Reconciliation
Summary
Key Terms and Definitions
Review Questions
Problems to Solve

Learning Objectives

After reading this chapter you will be able to:

- Describe the appraisal process.
- List the data that must be collected and analyzed to appraise a property.
- List the forms needed to process a loan and explain the purpose of each.
- List the guidelines that must be observed in processing a loan.
- Describe the FHA direct endorsement program.

Key Terms

appraisal
cost approach
gross rent multiplier
income approach
market approach
market value

Introduction

Does a property have sufficient value to warrant its use as collateral for the loan to purchase it? Put another way, if a lender finds it necessary to foreclose on a property, will he or she be able to recover the money invested in the loan? To ensure that a property is worth the investment, lenders require an **appraisal** of the property as part of the loan qualification procedure. Someone on the lender's staff or an independent person may do the appraisal, but the lender orders it. The appraiser will note the physical characteristics of the property, such as the square footage, number of bedrooms, structure (frame, masonry, concrete), description (split level, bilevel), and condition of the electrical, plumbing, and heating systems. The appraiser also will indicate the property's location, such as urban, rural, or in a floodplain. Next, the appraiser will determine the recent selling price of at least three nearby and comparable properties in forming an opinion of value. Finally, the value of the residence as a rental property will be estimated. Even though the intended use is for owner occupancy, its value—as reflected by what rent it could bring (the economic market rent)—is considered. All of this information is taken into consideration by the potential lender and potential insurer of the mortgage.

Property Appraisal

Property appraisal is one of the first steps in the loan process. Lenders want assurance that the property being used as collateral has sufficient *value* to reduce the risk of making the loan. In other words, if the borrower should default on the loan for whatever reason, does the lender have a reasonable expectation of recovering the investment by foreclosing and selling the property? The value of property can be defined in various ways and from various points of view, for example, from the seller's or the government's view. The lender, however, is interested in the property's **market value**. This is the price for which a property could probably be sold if it were placed on the open market for a reasonable length of time. To determine this value, the lender orders an appraisal.

The appraisal process happens in three stages: ordering the appraisal, monitoring the appraisal, and evaluating (reviewing) the appraisal.

Ordering the Appraisal

The procedures for ordering appraisals vary from lender to lender and from investor to investor. Most lenders are free to use an appraiser of their own choosing. Since 1994, lenders have been able to choose the appraiser in Federal Housing Administration/Veterans Administration (FHA/VA) loan applications, whereas previously these agencies assigned appraisers to the property. The

Financial Institutions Reform, Recovery, and Enforcement Act of 1989 (FIRREA) mandated that state-certified or licensed appraisers must be used for the appraisal of properties involving federally related mortgage transactions after July 1, 1991. In banking legislation by Congress, the deadline was extended to January 1993. Since January 1995, a *Uniform Residential Appraisal Report* has been used for nearly all loans (see Figure 11-1), including those intended for sale to Fannie Mae or Freddie Mac and those insured by the FHA or VA. Separate forms are used for condominiums and for small (generally, up to four families) residential income properties.

Under FIRREA, each federal regulatory agency [Federal Reserve Board, Federal Deposit Insurance Corporation, Office of the Comptroller of the Currency, Office of Thrift Supervision (formally the FHLBB), and the National Credit Union Administration] establishes appraisal guidelines for federally related transactions. Virtually all mortgages are federally related, because they are either insured by the FHA, guaranteed by the VA, originated by federally insured institutions, or originated for sale to federal secondary mortgage market agencies.

Monitoring the Appraisal

In monitoring an appraisal, the loan processor makes sure that the appraisal is performed within the time specified by Department of Housing and Urban Development (HUD) if an FHA loan, or by a private investor or secondary market agency. The loan processor makes certain that the appraiser gains access to the property and is paid on submission of the report.

Evaluating the Appraisal

For government-insured loans, the lender receives a conditional commitment (for HUD/FHA loans) or a certificate of reasonable value (for a VA loan) rather than a copy of the appraisal itself. Because lenders are not at risk in cases of government-insured loans, they are somewhat less concerned about the appraisal.

HUD/FHA appraisals may require that repairs be made if the health and safety of the occupants are endangered by a defect. In some cases, lenders can request that HUD/FHA waive repairs if they feel that the defects do not materially affect the value of the property. For VA-guaranteed loans, on the other hand, the value established is an "as is" value. These loans require that the veteran acknowledge the condition of the property prior to the close of the sale.

The lender will receive a complete appraisal report for conventional loans. An *underwriter* or *review appraiser* will review the report for acceptability. The review appraiser will consider several important elements of the appraisal, including the physical characteristics of the subject property, the neighborhood, present and alternative land uses, predominant occupancy (owner-occupied versus rental units), price range of single-family properties, and range in age of properties. The appraisal report must indicate if the property is located in a HUD-identified flood hazard area, in which case, flood insurance is required.

Lenders do not need to have an appraisal performed if the loan is for an amount less than $200,000 and the lender will retain the loan in its own portfolio instead of selling it in the secondary market. However, because most lenders like to reserve the option to sell the loan, they generally have an appraisal done, even when not required.

Figure 11-1 Uniform Residential Appraisal Report

COMPLETE SUMMARY REPORT

Property Description **UNIFORM RESIDENTIAL APPRAISAL REPORT** **File No.**

SUBJECT

Property Address City State Zip Code

Legal Description County

Assessor's Parcel No. Tax Year R.E. Taxes $ Special Assessments $

Borrower Current Owner Occupant: ☐ Owner ☐ Tenant ☐ Vacant

Property rights appraised ☐ Fee Simple ☐ Leasehold Project Type ☐ PUD ☐ Condominium (HUD/VA only) HOA$ /Mo.

Neighborhood/Project Name Map Reference Census Tract

Sale Price $ Date of Sale Description and $ amount of loan charges/concessions to be paid by seller

Lender/Client Address

Appraiser Address

NEIGHBORHOOD

				Predominant occupancy	**Single family housing** PRICE $(000) AGE (yrs)	**Present land use %**	**Land use change**
Location	☐ Urban	☐ Suburban	☐ Rural			One family ____	☐ Not likely ☐ Likely
Built up	☐ Over 75%	☐ 25-75%	☐ Under 25%			2-4 family ____	☐ In process
Growth rate	☐ Rapid	☐ Stable	☐ Slow	☐ Owner	____ Low ____	Multi-family ____	To: ____
Property values	☐ Increasing	☐ Stable	☐ Declining	☐ Tenant	____ High ____	Commercial ____	
Demand/supply	☐ Shortage	☐ In balance	☐ Over supply	☐ Vacant (0-5%)	Predominant	( )	
Marketing time	☐ Under 3 mos.	☐ 3-6 mos.	☐ Over 6 mos.	☐ Vacant (over 5%)			

Note: Race and the racial composition of the neighborhood are not appraisal factors.

Neighborhood boundaries & characteristics: ____

Factors that affect the marketability of the properties in the neighborhood (proximity to employment and amenities, employment stability, appeal to market, etc.):

Market conditions in the subject neighborhood (including support for the above conclusions related to the trend of property values, demand/supply, and marketing time - - such as data on competitive properties for sale in the neighborhood, description of the prevalence of sales and financing concessions, etc.):

PUD

Project Information for PUDs (if applicable) - - Is the developer/builder in control of the Home Owners' Association (HOA)? ☐ Yes ☐ No

Approximate total number of units in the subject project ____. Approximate total number of units for sale in the subject project ____

Describe common elements and recreational facilities:

SITE

Dimensions ____ Topography ____

Site area ____ Corner Lot ☐ Yes ☐ No Size ____

Specific zoning classification and description ____ Shape ____

Zoning compliance ☐ Legal ☐ Legal nonconforming (Grandfathered use) ☐ Illegal ☐ No Zoning Drainage ____

Highest & best use as improved: ☐ Present use ☐ Other use (explain) View ____

Utilities	Public	Other	**Off-site Improvements**	Type	Public	Private
Electricity	☐		Street		☐	☐
Gas	☐		Curb/gutter		☐	☐
Water	☐		Sidewalk		☐	☐
Sanitary sewer	☐		Street lights		☐	☐
Storm Sewer	☐		Alley		☐	☐

Landscaping ____

Driveway Surface ____

Apparent easements ____

FEMA Special Flood Hazard Area ☐ Yes ☐ No

FEMA Zone ____ Map Date ____

FEMA Map No.

Comments (apparent adverse easements, encroachments, special assessments, slide areas, illegal or legal nonconforming zoning, use, etc.): ____

IMPROVEMENTS

GENERAL DESCRIPTION	EXTERIOR DESCRIPTION	FOUNDATION	BASEMENT	INSULATION
No. of Units	Foundation	Slab	Area Sq. Ft.	Roof ☐
No. of Stories	Exterior Walls	Crawl Space	% Finished	Ceiling ☐
Type (Det./Att.)	Roof Surface	Basement	Ceiling	Walls ☐
Design (Style)	Gutters & Dwnspts.	Sump Pump	Walls	Floor ☐
Existing/Proposed	Window Type	Dampness	Floor	None ☐
Age (Yrs.)	Storm/Screens	Settlement	Outside Entry	Unknown ☐
Effective Age (Yrs.)	Manufactured House	Infestation		

ROOM LIST

ROOMS	Foyer	Living	Dining	Kitchen	Den	Family Rm.	Rec. Rm.	Bedrooms	# Baths	Laundry	Other	Area Sq. Ft.
Basement												
Level 1												
Level 2												

Finished area above grade contains: Rooms; Bedroom(s); Bath(s); Square Feet of Gross Living Area

DESCRIPTION

INTERIOR	Materials/Condition	HEATING	KITCHEN EQUIP.	ATTIC	AMENITIES	CAR STORAGE:
Floors		Type	Refrigerator ☐	None ☐	Fireplace(s)# ____ ☐	None ☐
Walls		Fuel	Range/Oven ☐	Stairs ☐	Patio ____ ☐	Garage # of cars
Trim/Finish		Condition	Disposal ☐	Drop Stair ☐	Deck ____ ☐	Attached ____
Bath Floor		COOLING	Dishwasher ☐	Scuttle ☐	Porch ____ ☐	Detached ____
Bath Wainscot		Central	Fan/Hood ☐	Floor ☐	Fence ____ ☐	Built-In ____
Doors		Other	Microwave ☐	Heated ☐	Pool ____ ☐	Carport ____
		Condition	Washer/Dryer ☐	Finished ☐	☐	Driveway

COMMENTS

Additional features (special energy efficient items, etc.): ____

Condition of the improvements, depreciation (physical, functional, and external), repairs needed, quality of construction, remodeling/additions, etc.:

Adverse environmental conditions (such as, but not limited to, hazardous wastes, toxic substances, etc.) present in the improvements, on the site, or in the immediate vicinity of the subject property: ____

Figure 11-1 Uniform Residential Appraisal Report (Continued)

Valuation Section — UNIFORM RESIDENTIAL APPRAISAL REPORT — File No.

COST APPROACH

ESTIMATED SITE VALUE .... = $ ________

ESTIMATED REPRODUCTION COST-NEW-OF IMPROVEMENTS:

Dwelling ________ Sq. Ft @ $ ________ = $ ________

________ Sq. Ft @ $ ________ = ________

Garage/Carport ________ Sq. Ft @ $ ________ = ________

Total Estimated Cost New .... = $ ________

Less Depreciation — Physical | Functional | External ________ = $ ________

Depreciated Value of Improvements .... = $ ________

"As-is" Value of Site Improvements .... = $ ________

INDICATED VALUE BY COST APPROACH .... = $

Comments on Cost Approach (such as, source of cost estimate, site value, square foot calculation and, for HUD, VA, and FmHA, the estimated remaining economic life of the property): ________

SALES COMPARISON ANALYSIS

ITEM	SUBJECT	COMPARABLE NO. 1		COMPARABLE NO. 2		COMPARABLE NO. 3	
Address							
Proximity to Subject							
Sales Price	$	$		$		$	
Price/Gross Liv. Area	$ ☐	$ ☐		$ ☐		$ ☐	
Data and/or Verification Sources							
VALUE ADJUSTMENTS	DESCRIPTION	DESCRIPTION	+(-)$Adjustment	DESCRIPTION	+(-)$Adjustment	DESCRIPTION	+(-)$Adjustment
Sales or Financing Concessions							
Date of Sale/Time							
Location							
Leasehold/Fee Simple							
Site							
View							
Design and Appeal							
Quality of Construction							
Age							
Condition							
Above Grade Room Count	Total | Bdrms | Baths	Total | Bdrms | Baths		Total | Bdrms | Baths		Total | Bdrms | Baths	
Gross Living Area	Sq. Ft.	Sq. Ft.		Sq. Ft.		Sq. Ft.	
Basement & Finished Rooms Below Grade							
Functional Utility							
Heating/Cooling							
Energy Efficient Items							
Garage/Carport							
Porch, Patio, Deck, Fireplace(s), etc.							
Fence, Pool, etc.							
Net Adj. (total)		☐ + ☐ - $		☐ + ☐ - $		☐ + ☐ - $	
Adjusted Sales Price of Comparable		% Net % Grs. $		% Net % Grs. $		% Net % Grs. $	

Comments on Sales Comparison (including the subject property's compatibility to the neighborhood, etc.): ________

ITEM	SUBJECT	COMPARABLE NO. 1	COMPARABLE NO. 2	COMPARABLE NO. 3
Date, Price and Data Source for prior sales within year of appraisal				

Analysis of any current agreement of sale, option, or listing of the subject property and analysis of any prior sales of subject and comparables within one year of the date of appraisal:

INDICATED VALUE BY SALES COMPARISON APPROACH .... $ ________

INDICATED VALUE BY INCOME APPROACH (If Applicable) Estimated Market Rent $ ________ /Mo. X Gross Rent Multiplier ________ = $

RECONCILIATION

This appraisal is made ☐ "as is" ☐ subject to the repairs, alterations, inspections, or conditions listed below ☐ subject to completion per plans and specifications.

Conditions of Appraisal: ________

Final Reconciliation: ________

The purpose of this appraisal is to estimate the market value of the real property that is the subject of this report, based on the above conditions and the certification, contingent and limiting conditions, and market value definition that are stated in the attached Freddie Mac Form 439/Fannie Mae Form 1004B (Revised ________).

I (WE) ESTIMATE THE MARKET VALUE, AS DEFINED, OF THE REAL PROPERTY THAT IS THE SUBJECT OF THIS REPORT, AS OF ________ (WHICH IS THE DATE OF INSPECTION AND THE EFFECTIVE DATE OF THIS REPORT) TO BE $ ________.

APPRAISER		SUPERVISORY APPRAISER (ONLY IF REQUIRED):	
Signature		Signature	☐ Did ☐ Did Not Inspect Property
Name		Name	
Date Report Signed		Date Report Signed	
State Certification #	State	State Certification #	State
Or State License #	State	Or State License #	State

Freddie Mac Form 70 6-93 12CH. — PAGE 2 OF 2 — Fannie Mae Form 1004 6-93

Laser Generated Form by EFS Software 1-800-438-8727

Valuation

The *valuation* section of the appraisal indicates how the appraiser arrived at the opinion of value. Generally accepted appraisal standards require that the appraiser consider three approaches to the determination of value: the cost, market, and income approaches. The appraiser then weighs—mathematically or subjectively or both—the information from each approach to arrive at an opinion on the value of the property.

Cost Approach

The **cost approach** is based on the premise that a buyer will not pay more for a property than he or she would for a comparable property with the same utility. Thus, the value of the property cannot be greater than the cost of replacing it with a comparable property. The steps in the cost approach are as follows:

1. Estimate the value of the land as vacant.
2. Estimate the cost of replacing the improvement as new.
3. Estimate depreciation for the improvement. Three types are estimated: (a) physical deterioration (deferred maintenance, peeling paint, sagging shutters, etc.); (b) functional obsolescence (bad floor plan, no air conditioning in South Florida, etc.); or (c) economic obsolescence (changing neighborhood characteristics, busy street, change in flight path for nearby airport, etc.).
4. Subtract 3 (the depreciation estimate) from 2 (the replacement estimate).
5. Add 1 (land value) and 4 (the replacement-less-depreciation value) to arrive at the total value.

SIDEBAR

Cost Approach Example

The Sawyer house is 18 years old. The home has 1,240 square feet, and building costs in that area are currently about $100/sq. ft. The lot is worth $30,000.

1. Land value: $30,000
2. Cost to replace the improvement would be 1,240 sq. ft. × $100/sq. ft: $124,000. This would be the current value of the house, new. But this house is 18 years old, so we need to depreciate the value.
3. Depreciation estimate. Taking into account physical deteri oration, functional obsolescence, and economic obsolescence, the appraiser estimates the depreciation to be $24,000. (*Note:* The appraiser could have also used a straight-line depreciation formula based on the age of the house and its expected life.)
4. Subtracting the depreciation estimate the replacement cost, we get the *depreciated value of the house:* $124,000 – $24,000 = $100,000.
5. Add the depreciated value of the house to the value of the land to get the total estimated property value: $100,000 + 35,000 = $135,000.

In estimating depreciation, *physical and functional obsolescence* are generally internal to the property and may be *curable*. A problem is considered curable if the cost to remedy it is less than the value added by making the repair. *Economic obsolescence* is external to the property and is generally *incurable* because it is caused by factors beyond control of the individual homeowner—heavy street traffic, for example. Not all external factors are detrimental, however. A property that adjoins a golf course, for example, is favorably affected.

The general limitation of the cost approach is that cost is not necessarily equal to value. For example, if you built an expensive home in an industrial district you might soon discover that your home's cost exceeds its value.

> **SIDEBAR**
>
> **Market Approach Example**
>
> The Burton family residence is a four-bedroom, 2.5-bath frame home in a five-year-old development. The home has 1,850 square feet and is in very good condition. To use the market approach to estimate a value for the home, the appraiser obtained data on two "comparable" properties. The information on all three properties is shown in Table 11-1.
>
> After adjustments, the values of the comparable properties are $227,900 and $254,000. The estimate of the market value of the subject property is $241,000.

Market Approach

The **market approach** is based on the premise that the selling prices of similar properties (comparables) in the neighborhood are good indicators of value. The appraiser generally obtains data for at least three comparable properties. The appraiser adjusts the data for differences in physical characteristics of the comparable properties relative to the subject property. For example, the appraiser may deduct $1,300 from the value of a comparable property because it has a fireplace and the subject property does not. Typically, appraisers make several adjustments. In addition to physical characteristics, the appraiser examines factors such as location, time on the market, and financing. The appraiser should make certain that the comparables do not involve unusual financing that could result in an overappraisal for the subject property.

Table 11-1
Market Approach to Valuation of Burton Home

	Burton Home	Comparable 1	Comparable 2
Price	(to be determined)	$235,900	$265,500
Construction	Wood frame	Wood frame	Wood frame
Age	5	10 *Adjustment:* Subtract $8,000 for age.	5
Condition	Very Good	Very Good	Fair *Adjustment:* Subtract $10,000 for difference in condition.
Bedrooms	4	4	3 plus den
Bathrooms	2.5	2.5	2.25 *Adjustment:* Subtract $1,500 for quarter bath.
Square feet	1,850	1,750 *Adjustment:* Subtract $1,300 for size.	1,850
Special features	None	Fireplace *Adjustment:* Add $1,300 for fireplace.	None
Adjustments		$235,900 –8,000 –1,300 +1,300 *Adjusted price:* $227,900	$265,500 –10,000 –1,500 *Adjusted price:* $254,000

Income Approach

The **income approach** says that the value of the property is a function of the income that accrues or can accrue to it. This approach arrives at a value by "capitalizing" the potential rent on the property using either an income multiplier, called a **gross rent multiplier**, or an *overall capitalization rate*. For example, if a similar property produces $10,000 per month in gross rent and the appropriate gross rent multiplier (value divided by gross monthly rent) is 10, then the estimated value for the property is $1,200,000. The gross rent multiplier is determined by dividing the sale prices of recently sold comparable properties by the rent paid (income) on those properties.

Alternatively, the appraiser may use the *overall capitalization rate* (or "cap rate") to determine value. The overall cap rate is the reciprocal of the income multiplier and is defined as net operating income divided by the value of the property. Again, comparable properties are generally used to determine the overall cap rate. Thus, if a property has net operating income of $10,000 per year and the applicable capitalization rate is 10 percent, the indicated value of the property is $100,000.

SIDEBAR

Income Approach Example

Suppose a subject income-producing property has net operating income (NOI) of $40,000. Three recently sold properties considered to be equally comparable to the subject property have been identified. The following information is known about the comparable properties:

Comparable	NOI	Selling Price	Capitalization Rate
1	$38,500	$394,900	38,500/394,900 = 9.75%
2	$40,500	$405,000	40,500/405,000 = 10%
3	$42,000	$409,750	42,000/409,750 = 10.25%
			Average = 10%

Value of subject Property = $40,000/0.10 = $400,000

Reconciliation

The estimates of value produced by the three approaches are not usually identical. The appraiser considers each estimated value and arrives at a final estimate. This is called the *reconciliation* phase of the appraisal. At this point, the appraisal becomes more "subjective art" than "exact science" as the appraiser evaluates the reliability of each estimate based on such factors as quality and quantity of data. For example, an appraiser of an older home might give more weight to the market approach valuation than to the cost approach. Likewise, an appraiser might give more weight to the income approach when considering a four-unit multifamily dwelling than when considering a single-family home.

Let's say an appraiser obtains the following three estimates for the Leatherburys' home:

Market approach:	300,000
Cost approach:	380,000
Income approach:	240,000

Now let's say this appraiser decides that the relative significance of those three approaches is not equal. The appraiser decides to base 10 percent of the decision on the income approach, 30 percent on the cost approach, and 60 percent on the market approach. Here's how this would work:

Market approach:	$300,000 × 0.60 = $180,000
Cost approach:	$380,000 × 0.30 = $114,000
Income approach:	$240,000 × 0.20 = $ 48,000
Reconciled valuation (add the three weighted numbers)	$342,000

Summary

The steps involved in loan processing and closing are designed to reassure the parties to the transaction that their interests are protected. The buyer will want a clear (unencumbered) title to the property. The lender will want security for the loan and assurance that the buyer will make the required payments. The lender will also want assurance that the value of the collateral (property) will be preserved—which he obtains through an accurate appraisal and, in some cases, by advance payment of property taxes and hazard insurance.

The lender also will desire insurance against events that would cause a loss. Such events could result from a borrower default (mortgage insurance) or a clouded title that would jeopardize the lender's interest (title insurance). The insurance agencies take steps necessary to verify that sufficient information has been gathered to assess the risk of default and loss. The next chapter provides more information on mortgage insurance and title insurance.

At each step throughout the process, verifications of relevant facts, data, or information by outside parties are required. The entire process can be viewed as one in which each party takes the necessary steps to protect against loss.

Key Terms and Definitions

appraisal—An estimate or opinion of value supported by factual data by a qualified person. Also, the process by which this estimate is obtained.

cost approach—An appraisal technique used to establish value by first estimating the cost to reproduce the facility, then deducting for depreciation and finally adding the value of the land.

gross rent multiplier—The sales price of recently sold properties divided by the annual rent generated by those properties.

income approach—One of three traditional means of appraising property, based on the assumption that value is equal to the present value of future rights to income. Others are comparable sales and cost of construction.

market approach—Also called comparable sales method. A method of appraisal valuation that estimates value based on the recent sale of properties with comparable characteristics.

market value—The value that a property would sell for between a willing seller and a willing buyer, both having full information about the property.

Review Questions

1. List and explain the steps in loan processing related to evaluating a property.
2. What is the importance of an appraisal in loan processing?
3. List and briefly explain the three basic appraisal methods.
4. Who decides if an appraisal report is acceptable?
5. How does an appraiser reconcile differences in results from the three appraisal methods applied to a single property?

Problems to Solve (Answers may be checked against the Answer section)

1. The Colliers' lakeside house has 2,240 square feet. Building costs in that area are currently about $140/sq. ft. The appraiser estimates depreciation to be $18,000. The lot is worth $45,000. According to the cost approach to valuation, what is the estimated property value?
2. The Scott family residence is a three-bedroom, two-bath, 10-year-old home. The home has 1,800 square feet and is in very good condition. To use the market approach to estimate a value for the home, the appraiser obtained data on two "comparable" properties. The information on all three properties is shown in Table 11-2. Calculate the adjustments for each of the comparables and then estimate the market approach valuation for the Scott house.

Table 11-2
Market Approach to Valuation of Scott Home

	Scott Home	Comparable 1	Comparable 2
Price	(to be determined)	$181,900	$205,500
Age	10	10	5 *Adjustment:* Add $8,000 for age.
Condition	Very good	Fair *Adjustment:* Subtract $8,000 for difference in condition.	Very good
Bedrooms	3	3	3
Bathrooms	2	2	2.25 *Adjustment:* Add $1,500 for quarter bath.
Square Feet	1,800	1,750 *Adjustment:* Subtract $1,300 for size.	1,800
Special Features	None	None	Fireplace *Adjustment:* Add $1,300 for fireplace.
Adjustments		Calculate the adjustments here.	Calculate the adjustments here.

Estimate of Scott family residence market value: ___________

Chapter 12

Closing and Insurance

Chapter Outline

Learning Objectives

After reading this chapter you will be able to:

- List the information required to complete a standard settlement statement.
- Name and describe the four principal types of mortgage default insurance that protect lenders against losses that result from borrower default and subsequent foreclosure.
- Describe the similarities and differences of the FHA and VA insurance programs.
- Compare private mortgage insurance programs to the government programs.
- Define title insurance and indicate what losses it is intended to cover.

Key Terms

abstract
American Land Title Association
cloud on title
co-insurance
direct endorsement program
lender's policy
loan processing
loan-to-value ratio
mortgage insurance premium (MIP)
owner's policy
private mortgage insurance (PMI)
self-insurance
suit to quiet title
title
title insurance
title search
underwriting

Introduction

The closing of the real estate transaction includes a final analysis of the buyer's loan application, disclosure of information required by various government regulations and lender guidelines, completion of a final settlement statement, transfer of title to the property, and issuance of insurance. In addition to homeowner's insurance, both title insurance and mortgage default insurance may be required. Mortgage default insurance is exactly what its name implies—it insures the lender against loss if the borrower defaults on a loan. Likewise, title insurance insures the new homeowner and the lender against claims by others to the title (ownership) of the property.

Closing

Analysis of the Application

This stage of **loan processing** involves a complete analysis of the financial position of the borrower and the disclosure of information required by the Real Estate Settlement Procedures Act, (RESPA), Regulation Z, and the Equal Credit Opportunity Act (ECOA). RESPA requires that lenders provide, in advance, general information about the settlement costs and, within three days of receiving the application, a statement of the estimated costs of settlement and monthly payments. Also within this three-day period, the lender must provide the borrower with a good-faith estimate of the cost of the loan over its term, including an estimate of the annual percentage rate (APR). The lender must provide the *actual* APR and total finance charges at or prior to settlement.

The Federal Housing Administration (FHA) and Veterans Administration (VA) use a joint application form for mortgages they insure. The Federal National Mortgage Association (FNMA) and the Federal Home Loan Mortgage Corporation (FHLMC) have their own preferred form for loans that will be sold to them. Some lenders prefer to take all loan applications on their own form and then transfer the data to the appropriate application form. The Department of Housing and Urban Development (HUD) requires that FHA loans include a face-to-face meeting between lender and borrower at some time during the application stage.

Some of the more important items collected on the application form include the type of loan applied for, terms of the loan applied for, purpose of the loan (construction loan, construction-permanent loan, existing property), names in which the title will be held, down payment and settlement charges, and borrower information. Important borrower information includes gross monthly income, other income, monthly housing expense, previous employment data, assets, liabilities, net worth, previous credit references, and a schedule of other real estate owned.

In the application analysis phase of the loan process, the lender is concerned with two factors: (1) the borrower's ability to make the down payment (and the source of that down payment) and monthly payments on the loan and (2) the accuracy of the financial data provided on the loan application. To address the first concern, the lender examines the borrower's liquid assets, the amount and stability of the borrower's income relative to housing expenses, and the past credit history of the borrower. On the second point, the lender must verify the accuracy of the financial data by contacting independent, third- party sources.

To verify the credit standing of the applicant, the lender obtains a credit report from a local credit-reporting agency or credit bureau. If the applicant lived in another area within the last two years, then a credit report from that area will be required. The credit report will indicate any failure of the applicant to make timely payments to other creditors that report to the bureau. The lender also will determine if there are any outstanding liens or judgments against the applicant.

Submission for Insurance

Most loans are insured to protect the lender from loss due to default on the loan. Mortgage default insurance and title insurance are discussed in greater detail later in this chapter.

When the verification of borrower information has been made and if no major problems appear, the lender will submit the loan for insurance. The FHA and VA have a common form for the submission. Most of the items on the form are self-explanatory, but a few comments are in order. If FHA credit approval is applied for, the lender indicates which of the many FHA insurance programs is applicable. Information on housing expenses, such as interest, hazard insurance, property taxes, utilities, and maintenance, is included in the application. Information on the borrower's income assets and liabilities also is included. The FHA is particularly concerned with the financial position of the borrower and his or her ability to meet the monthly housing expenses.

For FHA approval, the lender will submit a package consisting of the following documents:

1. Mortgage credit analysis worksheet,
2. Application for commitment of insurance,
3. Copy of the sales contract,
4. All verifications of deposits,
5. All verifications of employment,
6. Credit reports,
7. Verifications of indebtedness, and
8. Other supporting documents, such as a sales contract on the borrower's former residence, schedule of payments on a graduated-payment mortgage, any buy-down escrow agreement, and evidence of security for secondary financing.

Many lenders participate in the FHA's **direct endorsement program**. Under this program, the lender essentially performs the underwriting process. To become a *direct endorser*, a lender will submit 15 or so test cases that the FHA will check. If no substantial differences appear between the decisions of the lender and the FHA decisions for the test cases, approval will be granted for direct endorsement of subsequent loans. A lender who is a direct endorser is essentially an agent of the FHA, but may still hire independent appraisers or use an FHA appraiser. A direct endorser can cut out several days' worth of loan processing time.

If the application for insurance is accepted, the FHA will issue its commitment to insure the loan, a mortgage insurance certificate. The certificate will indicate the maximum mortgage amount (which may include the financing of the mortgage insurance premium), the interest rate on the loan, and the monthly payment. The commitment will have an expiration date beyond which the loan cannot be closed. If the commitment is conditional on modifications of the loan arrangement, the expiration date is six months after issue for existing properties and one year for new properties. For firm commitments, the expiration date is the expiration date of the conditional commitment, or 90 days from the date of the firm commitment, whichever is later.

Transferring Title and Settlement Statement

Loan closing includes two separate, but related, transactions: (1) title to the property passes from the seller to the buyer; and (2) the buyer signs a promissory note. The closing involves preparing and assembling the legal documents necessary to carry out the closing transaction in the jurisdiction. In some areas of the country, a closing agent prepares the documents. In other areas, the lender prepares the documents and forwards them to a closing agent to complete the process. In still other locations, the lender prepares the documents, carries out the closing, and records the documents.

The *promissory note* represents the borrower's promise to repay the loan. It states the terms of the loan, including the loan amount, interest rate, payments, due date, and so forth. See Chapter 7 for further information on notes.

For most jurisdictions, a *mortgage* or *deed of trust* is the security instrument used. FNMA and FHLMC use a joint form; the FHA and VA have somewhat different forms, due to the nature of their programs. The mortgage or deed of trust includes some of the same basic information as the note and, in addition, provides a legal description of the property. It also describes what constitutes a default and what will happen in the event of a default.

The *deed* conveys title to the property from the seller to the buyer. It is crucial that the sellers identified in the deed as the grantors are the same as the owners of record, and that the buyers indicated as the grantees are the same as the borrowers identified in the mortgage or deed of trust. The property identified on the deed also must be the same as the one described on the mortgage.

The *settlement statement* is a record of the actions occurring at the closing. The record is kept on form HUD-1, a standardized settlement statement designed to comply with RESPA. See Figure 12-1 for a sample of the HUD-1 form. See the appendix to Chapter 12 for a blank form with detailed line item instruction.

The *commitment* should be part of the closing file. If an FHA commitment is involved, the borrower must sign certain certifications.

A *truth-in-lending disclosure (Regulation Z)* must be given to the borrower and must include the major financial terms of the loan.

Disbursement of funds can be handled in any of several ways. The lender may give the closing agent checks payable to the ultimate recipients (title company, mortgage insurer, real estate agent, and so forth). Alternatively, the lender can give the closing agent one check for the full amount of the loan and payable to the agent. The agent then issues checks to the recipients.

SIDEBAR

The Completed HUD-1 Settlement Form

Figure 12-1 shows a completed sample of the HUD-1 settlement statement. As shown, page 1 of the form provides information on the parties involved: the buyer, seller, and lender. Page 1 also provides a summary of the borrower's (Section J) and seller's (Section K) transactions, including the total funds due from the borrower and total funds due to the seller at closing. For the borrower, the contract price (line 101) is given, along with the borrower's settlement costs (line 103). Any monies paid on the borrower's behalf, such as earnest money (line 201) and the amount of the new mortgage (line 202), are also shown. Line 301 gives the total funds due from the borrower at closing. Subtracting line 302, which shows funds paid by/for the borrower, results in line 303, which is the amount of money the borrower has to bring to the closing.

The summary of the seller's transaction in Section K gives the contract price (line 401), along with any adjustments for seller prepaid items. Items such as the settlement charges (line 502) and loan payoff (line 504) are subtracted to produce the cash settlement to the seller at closing. Line 602 shows the actual amount of money going to the seller at closing.

Page 2 of the settlement form shows the settlement charges for the borrower and seller. Some typical items for the borrower are loan origination fee, mortgage insurance, appraisal, credit report, and underwriting fee. The lender requires some items to be paid or deposited in advance. These include prepaid interest, insurance premiums, and property taxes. There may also be charges related to the title search or title insurance. Finally, the borrower will pay for document recording fees and documentary stamps on the mortgage.

As page 2 shows, the typical settlement charges for the seller include the broker's commission, documentary stamps on the deed, and a pest inspection. Line 1400 gives the total settlement charges for both the borrower and the seller. Any of this amount that has not been prepaid is required to be paid at closing.

Figure 12-1 Sample HUD-1 Form for Settlement Statement

A. **Settlement Statement**

U.S. Department of Housing and Urban Development

OMB Approval No. 2502-0265

B. Type of Loan

1. ☐ FHA 2. ☐ FmHA 3. ☒ Conv. Unins. 4. ☐ VA 5. ☐ Conv. Ins.	6. File Number: 1162	7. Loan Number: 8205	8. Mortgage Insurance Case Number:

C. Note: This form is furnished to give you a statement of actual settlement costs. Amounts paid to and by the settlement agent are shown. Items marked "(p.o.c.)" were paid outside the closing; they are shown here for informational purposes and are not included in the totals.

D. Name & Address of Borrower:	E. Name & Address of Seller:	F. Name & Address of Lender:
James T. Buyer 1208 Oak Street Hometown, USA	URA Seller	ABC Mortgage 106 Main Street Hometown, USA

G. Property Location:	H. Settlement Agent:	
1854 Pine Street Hometown, USA	Bill Settley Place of Settlement: ABC Mortgage	I. Settlement Date: 07/25/01

J. Summary of Borrower's Transaction		K. Summary of Seller's Transaction	
100. Gross Amount Due From Borrower		**400. Gross Amount Due To Seller**	
101. Contract sales price	225,000.00	401. Contract sales price	225,000.00
102. Personal property		402. Personal property	
103. Settlement charges to borrower (line 1400)	7,120.21	403.	
104.		404.	
105.		405.	
Adjustments for items paid by seller in advance		**Adjustments for items paid by seller in advance**	
106. City/town taxes to		406. City/town taxes to	
107. County taxes to		407. County taxes to	
108. Assessments 7/25/01 to 12/31/01	43.83	408. Assessments 7/25/01 to 12/31/01	43.83
109.		409.	
110.		410.	
111.		411.	
112.		412.	
120. Gross Amount Due From Borrower	232,164.04	**420. Gross Amount Due To Seller**	225,043.83
200. Amounts Paid By Or In Behalf Of Borrower		**500. Reductions In Amount Due To Seller**	
201. Deposit or earnest money	10,000.00	501. Excess deposit (see instructions)	
202. Principal amount of new loan(s)	180,000.00	502. Settlement charges to seller (line 1400)	15,530.00
203. Existing loan(s) taken subject to		503. Existing loan(s) taken subject to	
204.		504. Payoff of first mortgage loan 1st Star Mtg	186,870.14
205.		505. Payoff of second mortgage loan	
206.		506.	
207.		507.	
208.		508.	
209.		509.	
Adjustments for items unpaid by seller		**Adjustments for items unpaid by seller**	
210. City/town taxes to		510. City/town taxes to	
211. County taxes 01/01/01 to 07/25/01	1,502.82	511. County taxes 01/01/01 to 07/25/01	1,502.82
212. Assessments to		512. Assessments to	
213.		513.	
214.		514.	
215.		515.	
216.		516.	
217.		517.	
218.		518.	
219.		519.	
220. Total Paid By/For Borrower	191,502.82	**520. Total Reduction Amount Due Seller**	203,902.96
300. Cash At Settlement From/To Borrower		**600. Cash At Settlement To/From Seller**	
301. Gross Amount due from borrower (line 120)	232,164.04	601. Gross amount due to seller (line 420)	225,043.83
302. Less amounts paid by/for borrower (line 220)	(191,502.82)	602. Less reductions in amt. due seller (line 520)	(203,902.96)
303. Cash ☒ **From** ☐ **To Borrower**	40,661.22	**603. Cash** ☒ **To** ☐ **From Seller**	21,140.57

Section 5 of the Real Estate Settlement Procedures Act (RESPA) requires the following: • HUD must develop a Special Information Booklet to help persons borrowing money to finance the purchase of residential real estate to better understand the nature and costs of real estate settlement services; • Each lender must provide the booklet to all applicants from whom it receives or for whom it prepares a written application to borrow money to finance the purchase of residential real estate; • Lenders must prepare and distribute with the Booklet a Good Faith Estimate of the settlement costs that the borrower is likely to incur in connection with the settlement. These disclosures are manadatory.

Section 4(a) of RESPA mandates that HUD develop and prescribe this standard form to be used at the time of loan settlement to provide full disclosure of all charges imposed upon the borrower and seller. These are third party disclosures that are designed to provide the borrower with pertinent information during the settlement process in order to be a better shopper.

The Public Reporting Burden for this collection of information is estimated to average one hour per response, including the time for reviewing instructions, searching existing data sources, gathering and maintaining the data needed, and completing and reviewing the collection of information.

This agency may not collect this information, and you are not required to complete this form, unless it displays a currently valid OMB control number.

The information requested does not lend itself to confidentiality.

Previous editions are obsolete — Page 1 of 2 — form **HUD-1** (3/86) ref Handbook 4305.2

Figure 12-1 Sample HUD-1 Form for Settlement Statement (Continued)

L. Settlement Charges	Paid From Borrowers Funds at Settlement	Paid From Seller's Funds at Settlement
700. Total Sales/Broker's Commission based on price $ 225,000.00 @ 6.000 % = 13,500.00		
Division of Commission (line 700) as follows:		
701. $ 6,750.00 to Capital Realty		
702. $ 6,650.00 to Smith Realty		
703. Commission paid at Settlement		13,500.00
704. TRANSACTION FEE		295.00
800. Items Payable In Connection With Loan		
801. Loan Origination Fee 0.125 % to ABC Mortgage	225.00	
802. Loan Discount %		
803. Appraisal Fee to		
804. Credit Report to		
805. Lender's Inspection Fee		
806. Mortgage Insurance Application Fee to ABC Mortgage	360.00	
807. Assumption Fee		
808. TAX SERVICE FEE to ABC Mortgage	80.00	
809. UNDERWRITING FEE to ABC Mortgage	200.00	
810. FLOOD CERT FEE	14.00	
811.		
900. Items Required By Lender To Be Paid In Advance		
901. Interest from 07/25/2001 to 08/01/2001 @$ 36.2500 /day 7 days	253.75	
902. Mortgage Insurance Premium for months to		
903. Hazard Insurance Premium for 1 year to National Ins	550.00	
904. years to		
905.		
1000. Reserves Deposited With Lender		
1001. Hazard insurance 3 months@$ 45.83 per month	137.49	
1002. Mortgage insurance months@$ per month		
1003. City property taxes months@$ per month		
1004. County property taxes 11 months@$ 222.98 per month	2,452.78	
1005. Annual assessments months@$ per month		
1006. Aggregate Anal. Adj. to ABC Mortgage	183.31-	
1007. months@$ per month		
1008. months@$ per month		
1100. Title Charges		
1101. Settlement or closing fee to ABC Mortgage	100.00	
1102. Abstract or title search to Corbitt Title Co.	100.00	
1103. Title examination to Corbitt Title Co.	75.00	
1104. Title insurance binder to		
1105. Document preparation to		
1106. Notary fees to		
1107. Attorney's fees to		
(includes above items numbers:)		
1108. Title insurance to Corbitt Title Co.	1,225.00	
(includes above items numbers:)		
1109. Lender's coverage $ 180,000.00 - 25.00		
1110. Owner's coverage $ 225,000.00 - 1,200.00		
1111. FL 9 (Simultaneous) to Corbitt Title Co.	122.50	
1112. ALTA 8.1, ALTA 5.1 to Corbitt Title Co.	50.00	
1113.		
1200. Government Recording and Transfer Charges		
1201. Recording fees: Deed $ 6.00 ; Mortgage $ 87.00 ; Releases $	93.00	
1202. City/county tax/stamps: Deed $ 1,575.00 ; Mortgage $ 630.00	630.00	1,575.00
1203. State tax/stamps: Deed $; Mortgage $ 360.00	360.00	
1204.		
1205.		
1300. Additional Settlement Charges		
1301. Survey to Bob's Survey, Inc.	225.00	
1302. Pest inspection to Larry's Pest Control		100.00
1303. COURIER to ABC Mortgage		60.00
1304.		
1305.		
1400. Total Settlement Charges (enter on lines 103, Section J and 502, Section K)	7,120.21	15,530.00

Previous editions are obsolete — Page 2 of 2 — form **HUD-1** (3/86) ref Handbook 4305.2

Recording of the deed and the mortgage gives constructive notice to the public that the buyer is the new owner of the property and that the mortgagee (lender) has a lien on the property. Recording is not necessary to enforce any claims made regarding the transfer of the property or the indebtedness.

The final step is the payment of the mortgage insurance. The lender instructs the closing agent to issue a check payable to the Secretary of Housing and Urban Development for the full amount of the **mortgage insurance premium (MIP)**. The check will accompany a Mortgagee's One-Time MIP Transmittal Form.

We next discuss mortgage default insurance and title insurance. We start with a description and comparison of three default insurance plans: VA, FHA, and private mortgage insurance (PMI). These plans are different in terms of their eligibility requirements, costs (premiums), loan limits, underwriting procedures, and coverage. We will also discuss the purpose, nature, and cost of title insurance.

Mortgage Default Insurance

Four principal types of mortgage default insurance protect lenders against losses that result from borrower default and subsequent foreclosure. One type provides *partial coverage*, in which the insurer will cover losses up to a certain percentage of the original amount of the loan. If the coverage is 20 percent, all claims up to $20,000 on a $100,000 loan would be covered. A second type provides for *full coverage*. Under full coverage, all lender losses are covered. A third type is *co-insurance*. With **co-insurance** all losses up to a certain portion of the loan are covered. Losses above this amount are shared between the lender and the insurer in the same ratio. Thus, if the coverage ratio is 20 percent and there is a $30,000 loss on a $100,000 loan, the lender will cover $22,000 of the loss ($20,000 plus 20 percent of the remaining $10,000 of the loss). The fourth type of mortgage insurance is *self-insurance*. With **self-insurance**, lenders absorb the default risk themselves.

The cost of mortgage insurance is typically borne by either the borrower (in the case of FHA and PMI) or the federal government (VA). Also, the borrower may have no choice about carrying mortgage insurance since the lender may list it as a requirement for making the loan. For example, the insurance guarantee on a VA loan is provided at no cost except for a funding fee paid by the borrower at the time the loan is originated. This funding fee is not optional. On FHA loans and loans covered by private mortgage insurance, the borrower pays an up-front fee and a yearly premium. Because FHA insurance covers the entire loan amount, historically the premium had to be paid by the borrower for the entire life of the loan. This has changed and is discussed below. Payment of the premium is mandatory. For conventional mortgages that have loan-to-value ratios greater than 80 percent, private mortgage insurance is required.

Government Insurance

The two government mortgage insurance programs come from the VA and the FHA. The VA is a partial insurance program that covers losses up to a certain proportion of the loan amount. The FHA is a full insurance program that covers all losses. Most private mortgage insurance is co-insurance.

Veterans Administration

Veterans Administration insurance was created by the Serviceman's Readjustment Act of 1944 with Section 501 of the GI Bill of Rights. The VA was elevated to cabinet rank in 1989. The VA provides a guarantee program that assists eligible veterans and their immediate families (generally the spouse) in acquiring a home with little or no down payment. The veteran must occupy the home as his or her primary residence. Veterans on overseas active duty may purchase a home as a primary residence for his or her immediate family. The VA guarantees (insures) a portion of the loan to the lender depending on the amount of the veteran borrower's eligibility. The VA does not protect the veteran against losses of any kind.

Eligibility

To be eligible for a VA loan, veterans must serve a minimum time on active duty. The time runs from 90 days for "hot" wars to six years for the reserves and national guard. In general, service during peacetime requires 181 days of continuous active duty for eligibility. A veteran not on active duty must hold a discharge other than dishonorable. Unmarried surviving spouses of individuals who died while in service or as the result of a service-connected disability are generally eligible for a VA loan.

A veteran's Certificate of Eligibility certifies his or her *entitlement*. As of October 1994, the maximum available entitlement is $50,750. In contrast, the maximum entitlement at the inception of the program in 1944 was $2,000. As housing prices have increased over the years, Congress has likewise increased the entitlement limit.

The VA guarantees the lender against losses up to 25 percent of the original loan, or $50,750, whichever is less. This establishes a maximum loan amount of $203,000. Most VA loans are sold to Ginnie Mae, which requires at least a 25 percent guarantee. Ginnie Mae will purchase VA loans with original principal balances up to this amount.

Loan Assumptions

VA loans approved prior to March 1, 1988, are fully assumable. VA loans approved after that date are assumable subject to credit qualification of the buyer. For the earlier loans, the veteran is liable for the default of the buyer (who assumes the loan) unless the veteran obtains a release of liability. For the later loans, the buyer must assume full liability to repay the loan, including the indemnity liability of the VA. In either case, the VA loan must have an entitlement attached to it. Thus, when a property is sold to a nonveteran, the selling veteran's entitlement remains with the property. Entitlement can only be restored by replacing it with another entitlement or by repaying the mortgage.

Note that restoration of entitlement is different from release of liability. For example, a veteran may allow the mortgage to be assumed by a nonveteran who qualifies. In this case the nonveteran could assume liability for the loan, giving the veteran a release of liability. However, the veteran's entitlement would continue to be encumbered by the loan. Furthermore, veterans who previously have used their entitlement may have an unused portion, which they may apply to the purchase of another residence, even though the initial loan has not been paid off.

Down Payment

The funding fee associated with a VA guarantee varies with the amount of the down payment. With 0 to less than 5 percent down payment, the funding fee is 2 percent of the loan amount. With at least 5 percent but less than 10 percent down payment, the fee is 1.5 percent. With a 10 percent or greater down payment, the fee is 1.25 percent. The fee is higher for reservists and for mortgage refinancing. It is waived for veterans entitled to compensation for service-connected disabilities. The fee may be included in the loan amount, provided the total does not exceed the VA limit. Existing single-family homes and two- to four-unit dwellings are eligible for VA insurance as long as the veteran occupies the property after the closing. New units are not eligible unless the builder has received prior approval or provides the veteran with an approved 10-year warranty.

Other Characteristics

The VA will also guarantee qualifying graduated-payment loans. Because of the negative amortization feature of such loans, the veteran must make a down payment. Also, the rate on the loan may be slightly higher than on a standard loan. In 1992, the VA began an adjustable-rate mortgage program. The loans are one-year adjustable loans using the Treasury bill yield index with annual and life-of-loan interest rate caps of 1 and 5 percent, respectively, and a margin of 2.00.

Since 1992, the VA has been allowed to charge market interest rates and discount points. Any discount points paid by the borrower cannot be added to the loan amount. Previously, the VA director set interest rates and the borrower could pay no points except the funding fee.

Federal Housing Administration

The National Housing Act created the FHA in 1934 to encourage improvement in housing standards and conditions. The primary function of the FHA is and has always been to provide a system of mutual mortgage insurance. The FHA has been part of HUD since 1965. Its mortgage insurance programs are designed to protect private lenders against losses caused by defaults by borrowers. Like the VA, the FHA does not protect the borrower against losses of any kind, nor does it lend government funds directly. The FHA has more than 50 different programs providing loans for home purchases, home improvement, nursing homes, mobile home parks, and multifamily projects, among others.

Along with typical mortgage financing, the FHA will make construction-permanent loans to assist builders by allowing loan approvals prior to construction. Also, the FHA will issue reverse annuity mortgages, which allow borrowers to convert equity into a monthly income or a line of credit. Borrower requirements for this type of loan are the following: (1) have attained at least 62 years of age, (2) own the property, (3) occupy the property as a principal residence, and (4) participate in a consumer information session. This type of loan has no income qualifications and no repayment as long as the home is occupied as a principal residence by the borrower. Closing costs may be financed, and financing is available for one- to four-unit properties.

FHA coverage is different from the VA guarantee. The FHA insures the full amount of the loan against default and foreclosure. To control risk, FHA places a limit on the amount of the loan that it will insure. It takes into consideration the borrower's income, credit and work history, funds available for settlement, and monthly housing expense. FHA insurance is open to any qualified resident of the United States. Citizenship is not required, but the property must be the borrower's principal residence and must be located in the United States.

The interest rate and discount points are negotiable with the lender. Either the buyer or the seller can pay discount points. Prior to November 30, 1984, FHA had set a maximum rate that a lender could charge and prohibited the buyer from paying the points, except for a one-point origination fee. These limits were intended to protect borrowers. In reality, however, when the market rate exceeded the set FHA rate, lenders charged points on FHA loans in order to equalize the rates. Because the borrower could not pay the points, they were charged to the seller—who often raised the price of the house. This policy created such distortions in the credit market that the FHA abandoned the practice in favor of the current policy.

FHA Loan Limits

At one time, the upper limit on the loan amount was nationally uniform. This caused a shortage of FHA insurance in areas where housing was particularly expensive, such as Hawaii, Alaska, and portions of California. As a result, loan limits are now allowed to vary depending on the cost of housing for a given area. Currently the high cost limit is $160,950 for a single-family home, but in many high-cost areas the limit is set at 95 percent of the median house price in the standard metropolitan area (SMA) or county. For non-high-cost areas, the limit is 48 percent of the Fannie Mae/FHLMC conforming loan limits. This loan limit is set in January of each year and in 1999 was $240,000. This amounts to $115,200 for a single-family home. Limits for Alaska, Guam, Hawaii, and the Virgin Islands may be adjusted up to 150% of loan limits. The limits are higher for multifamily properties—and the FHA will finance properties with as many as four units as long as one unit is owner occupied.

Loan Assumptions

Prior to December 1, 1986, all FHA loans were simple assumptions. This meant that the buyer did not have to qualify to assume the mortgage. Furthermore, there was no release of liability for payments for the seller unless requested and unless the purchaser agreed to assume such liability. This remains the status of loans that originated prior to December 1, 1986. For loans that originated between that date and December 14, 1989, rules that regulate assumptions changed. For these loans, assumptions made within one year of origination required a creditworthiness review of the persons seeking to assume the mortgage. The period was extended to two years if the assuming parties did not intend to occupy the residence. Loans made to, or assumed by, nonowner occupants are called *investor loans*.

For loans that originated subsequent to December 14, 1989, the rules governing assumptions were changed again. For the entire life of the loan, a creditworthiness review is required of all borrowers seeking to assume the loan. Furthermore, no nonowner occupants (investors) may assume any of these loans. That is, the assumptor must be an owner-occupant.

Refinancing

FHA loans can be refinanced, and cash can be obtained on owner-occupied properties up to 85 percent of the acquisition cost (appraised value plus closing costs). A borrower can refinance out of an insured, graduated-payment loan, but not into one. In March 1989, the FHA announced its Streamline Refinance Plan (SRP) for very-high-rate mortgages (15 percent and above). Under this plan, the FHA offered refinancing with little paperwork and with the refinancing costs included in the new loan. Alternatively, the borrower could refinance without any costs whatsoever by obtaining a new loan with a rate slightly above the market rate. Because mortgage rates at the time were approximately 10 to 11 percent, the plan offered borrowers tremendous savings on their payments.

Loan-to-Value Ratios

Of the FHA's several loan programs, the most popular is the Section 203b program. This program insures standard 30-year fixed-rate mortgages on one- to four-family houses. The FHA had set the maximum **loan-to-value ratio** at 97 percent of the first $25,000 and 95 percent of the remainder up to $125,000 (after which it goes to 90 percent), based on the lesser of the appraised value or selling price (including closing costs). The Omnibus Budget Reconciliation Act of 1990 (OBRA) modified the National Housing Act to set additional limits on the loan-to-value ratio under this program. For a property with an appraised value of $50,000 or less, the maximum loan-to-value ratio is 98.75 percent of the appraised value or the sales price (excluding closing costs), whichever is less. For properties with an appraised value of more than $50,000, the maximum loan-to-value ratio is 97.5 percent of the lesser of the above two values. Thus, two calculations must be made. If the FHA rules result in the lower amount, then the closing costs are considered to be included in the financing. Note, however, that in 1991 HUD announced additional regulations that limited the portion of closing costs that could be financed to 57 percent.

The Section 245a program is the FHA's graduated payment mortgage plan. The borrower can qualify with less monthly income, but the down payment requirement is larger than the standard Section 203b loan because of the negative amortization. Depending on the plan selected, the payments will increase annually for 5 or 10 years and for various growth rates.

Mortgage Insurance Premium

Prior to 1984, the FHA charged an annual premium (paid monthly) over the life of the loan. The annual premium was 0.5 percent of the outstanding balance. This amount was divided by 12 and added to the monthly payment. If a loan was prepaid, the borrower ceased to make premium payments but did not receive a refund of any sort.

From 1984 to 1991, the annual premium was dropped and the FHA charged a one-time, up-front premium only (except for loans on condominiums, which continued to have a monthly premium). The one-time mortgage insurance premium was either paid in cash at closing or financed into the mortgage. If financed into the mortgage, the premium was 3.8 percent of the amount of the loan. If paid in cash at closing, the premium was 3.661 percent of the amount of the loan.

In 1990, a new law established a phased-in reduction of the rate to a permanent 2.25 percent. This portion of the premium was renamed the *up-front MIP*. The permanent rate became effective in 1994. However, starting January 1, 2001, the upfront premium was reduced from 2.25 percent to 1.50 percent. The up-front premium can be financed and is the same whether it is paid in cash or financed into the mortgage. The new law also reinstated the annual premium so that currently the FHA borrower pays both an up-front premium and an annual premium.

Because the up-front premium is a lump-sum payment that covers the life of a loan, it is subject to a partial refund when the loan is prepaid. The FHA calculates the refund using a scale based on the number of years the loan has been outstanding. No refund is paid on a loan that has been assumed.

The amount of the reinstated annual premium is 0.5 percent of the outstanding balance. The length of time the premium must be paid depends on the amount of the down payment. With a loan-to-value (LTV) ratio of less than 90 percent, the annual premium is assessed for the first 11 years of the loan life. With a loan-to-value ratio of 90 through 95 percent, the premium must be paid for the full 30 years. If a mortgage has a loan-to-value ratio greater than 95 percent, the premium charge jumps to 0.55 percent and must be paid for the full life of the loan. Also, starting January 1, 2001, new borrowers for the first time can suspend the annual insurance premium when the mortgage is paid down to 78 percent of the purchase price. The insurance coverage would continue. Table 12-1 shows the fee structure since 1991. (This fee structure is also applicable to graduated-payment loans.) The fee structure gradually transfers the cost of insurance from an up-front to a "pay-as-you-go" basis. This change lowered the initial cost of purchasing a residence.

Rural Housing Service

The Rural Housing Service (formerly the Farmers Home Administration) has a guaranteed housing loan program that provides mortgage financing for rural areas. The program provides financing for new home loans, construction-to-permanent loans, and loans to purchase existing homes, including repairs/ improvements. Typical advantages of this program are (1) 100 percent loan-to-value ratio, (2) no mortgage insurance, (3) closing costs and the guarantee fee can be financed in many cases, (4) conventional appraisals are used, (5) not limited to first-time home buyers, and (6) 29 and 41 percent payment-to-income

Table 12-1
FHA Mortgage Insurance Premiums

Fiscal Year	Up-Front MIP (%)	LTV Ratio	Annual Premium	Term of Annual Premium (years)
1991–1992	3.80	89.99 and under	0.50	5
	3.80	90.00–95.00	0.50	8
	3.80	95.01 and over	0.50	10
1993–1994	3.00	89.99 and under	0.50	7
	3.00	90.00–95.00	0.50	12
	3.00	95.01 and over	0.50	30
1995–2000	2.25	89.99 and under	0.50	11
	2.25	90.00–95.00	0.50	30
	2.25	95.01 and over	0.55	30
2001–present	1.50	same as 1995–2000	same as 1995–2000	same as 1995–2000

ratios. The program does impose some restrictions—no swimming pools are allowed and financing does not cover manufactured homes. The program also limits the maximum loan amount.

Private Mortgage Insurance

Private mortgage insurance (PMI), provided by private companies, insures lenders against losses caused by borrower default. The industry dates to the early 1900s, when title companies would acquire and resell mortgages—sort of a small secondary market. To make the market work, the loans were sold with a guarantee of payment as well as a guarantee of title. By the time of the Great Depression, mortgage guaranty firms numbered into the hundreds, and many of them were undercapitalized. Years of rising real estate values had insulated them from default risk. The Depression, however, created huge numbers of defaults, and many mortgage insurance companies were unable to honor their commitments.

The widespread failure of the mortgage insurance companies was one of the motivations for the creation of FHA insurance. After World War II, the VA program joined the FHA insurance program. Both government programs, aimed at low- to moderate-income homebuyers, placed limits on the amount of the loan. Bureaucratic rules also led to occasional delays in processing. Because of the limitations of government insurance, conventional loans occupied a significant part of the mortgage market.

Private mortgage insurance reemerged in the late 1950s in Wisconsin with the formation of the Mortgage Guaranty Insurance Corporation (MGIC, pronounced "magic"). Other firms followed, and by the 1970s, a dozen or so large and mostly well-capitalized firms were offering mortgage insurance. The restructured industry was based on solid capital requirements. Although PMI is regulated by individual state agencies, all states require that insurers hold large reserves for possible losses. In addition to reserves for normal losses, PMI companies must maintain a reserve sufficient to weather a severe economic recession or catastrophic depression.

The co-insurance factor of PMI provides an incentive for lenders to try to mitigate losses as much as possible, since, after they reach the limit, they share the bulk of additional default losses. Each PMI company has what is called a *master policy*, which governs the terms and conditions of the individual insurance policies. These master policies contain additional provisions intended to control losses. Some typical provisions include the following:

The lender shall pursue whatever foreclosure process is the quickest, unless the procedure precludes the possibility of pursuing a deficiency judgment.

Voluntary conveyance of title, or a deed-in-lieu-of-foreclosure is encouraged, so as to avoid the legal expense of a foreclosure.

Attorney's fees are limited to 3 percent of the total claim (this prevents lenders from running up legal expenses for any attorney "friends").

The lender must make any repairs on the property to bring it to a condition that existed at the time the policy was taken out. This prevents the lender from neglecting the property to the detriment of the insurer.

Figure 12-2 shows the procedures for the filing and resolution of a claim to a mortgage insurer (MI). For example, a loan is considered in default after three or four monthly payments have been missed. At that time, the lender must file a notice of default with the insurance company. If the loan is not brought current by the borrower, then the lender will seek to take title to the property, either through foreclosure or voluntary conveyance. After title is obtained, the lender will either sell the property for more than the amount of debt (and there is no loss), sell the property for less than the amount of debt and submit a claim to the MI, or not sell the property but submit a preliminary claim. In the latter case, the MI will have two options: (1) to pay the lender the percentage of the liability established by the policy or (2) to pay the claim in full and take title to and sell the property.

Fee Structure

The fee structure for private mortgage insurance is somewhat different from that of government insurance. PMI requires a relatively small up-front fee and an annual charge. If, after some years, the lender decides not to renew the policy, the annual fees cease. This fee structure has caused problems for the PMI industry. One such problem is the adverse selection problem. This means that

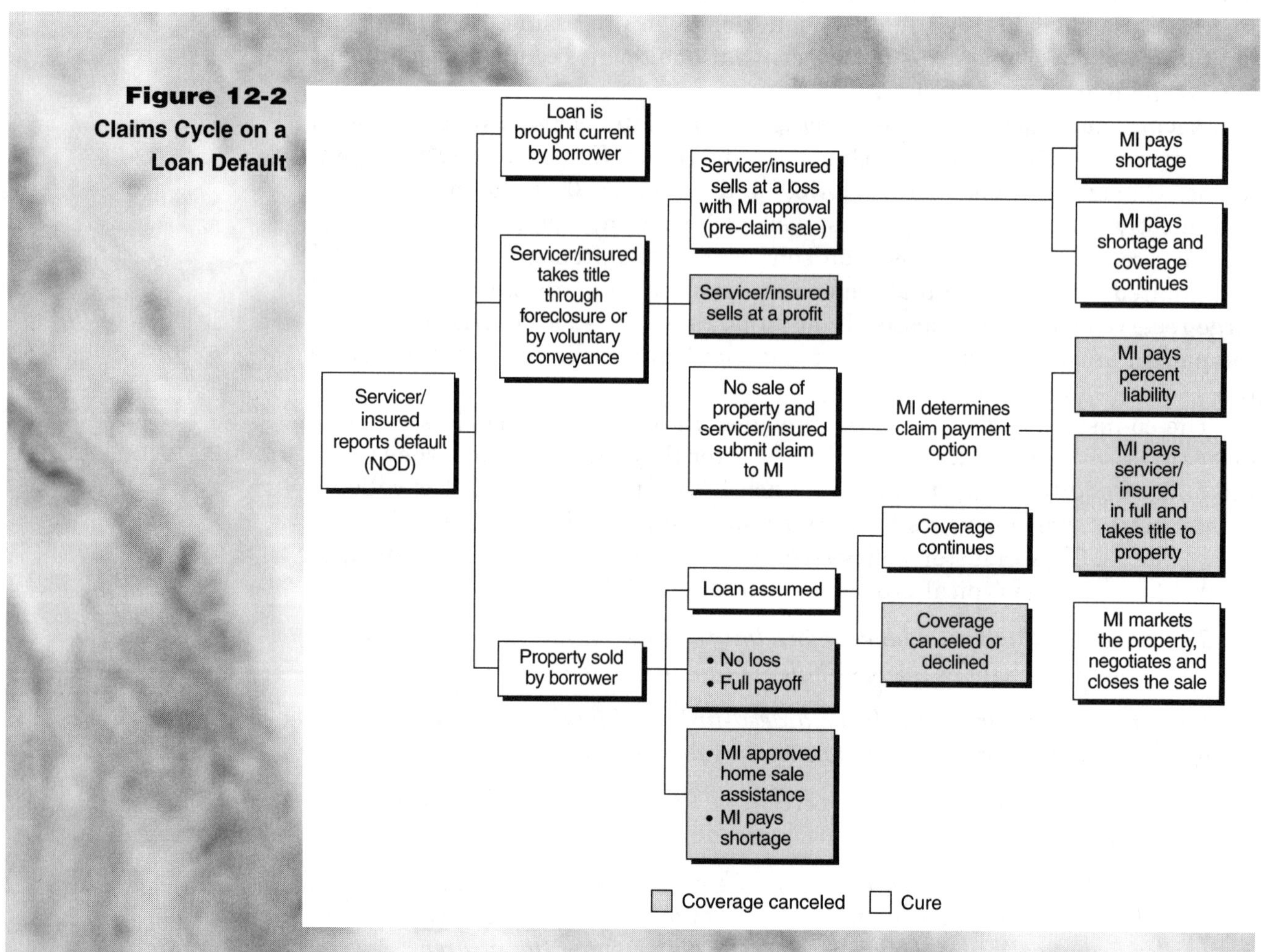

Figure 12-2 Claims Cycle on a Loan Default

lenders have a tendency to cancel mortgage insurance on loans that, after the fact, turn out to be low risk. Local property prices may have risen significantly, for example. If loans continue to be risky, lenders continue to keep the policy in force by making payments (insurance companies cannot cancel insurance). Thus, after a period of time, insurance companies lose business on the good loans, but keep it on the riskier ones.

Cancellation of Mortgage Insurance

The Homeowners' Protection Act of 1998 affords greater rights to the homeowner in canceling mortgage insurance when and if the amount of the loan falls sufficiently to provide protection to the lender in terms of greater amounts of equity. Effective for loans made on or after July 29, 1999, the act mandates several disclosures that the lender must make at the time the loan is originated. Basically, at the time of the loan the lender must disclose an amortization schedule of the loan and indicate the point at which the loan-to-value ratio (based on the original value of the house) reaches 80 percent. The lender must also advise the borrower of his or her right to cancel the mortgage insurance at that point. The lender must also indicate that the private mortgage insurance will be automatically canceled at the point the loan-to-value ratio reaches 78 percent.

Where the lender pays the premium directly to the PMI company, the lender must provide to the borrower information on the benefits and costs of lender-paid versus borrower-paid mortgage insurance. The lender must also indicate that lender-paid insurance usually results in a higher interest rate on the loan.

Finally, the act requires the lenders to, annually, remind borrowers of their cancellation rights and give them the phone number and address of the servicer of the loan.

Comparison of Government and Private Mortgage Insurance Programs

The government and private mortgage insurance programs have some similarities and many differences. The government programs have restrictions on the size of the loan that is insured, whereas PMIs do not. Also, while PMIs dominate the high-priced end of the mortgage insurance market, they still compete with FHA and VA insurance in the moderate price range. The VA has a modified co-insurance feature to the extent that the lender absorbs all losses above the insured amount. PMI companies engage in locational **underwriting** and can charge different premiums according to the risk of the loan, particularly the loan-to-value ratio. While the FHA insurance program charges annual premiums based on the loan-to-value ratio, the VA has a one-time, uniform, up-front fee. Both make insurance available irrespective of the location of the property. As stated above, PMI firms charge an initial fee plus an annual charge. If the lender drops insurance, the PMI premium stops.

Both FHA insurance and PMI cancel the premium when the mortgage is paid in full. In both cases, furthermore, the coverage can be dropped once the equity has reached a certain percent of the value of the property.

Table 12-2
Mortgage Insurance Comparison

	FHA	VA	PMI
Limit on size of loan	Yes	Yes	No
Co-insurance feature	No	Modified	Yes
Uniform premium	Yes	N/A	No
Underwriting	No	No	Yes
Very low down payment loans	Yes	Yes	No
Fee structure	Partial up-front and annual	Up-front, one-time	Partial up-front and annual
Available for new houses	Yes	Generally no	Yes

Table 12-2 provides a summary of the key characteristics of the FHA, VA, and private mortgage insurance.

Title Insurance

Real estate property passes from one owner to another through a *transfer of the title* to the property. A **title** conveys legal rights to possess and use the property. The buyer wants a bundle of legal rights to the property that is as complete and unencumbered as possible. The government, of course, may always restrict or deny certain property rights through its police powers. It has, for example, the ability to restrict the use of the property through zoning ordinances, the right to take the property for public purposes (eminent domain or expropriation), the right to require that all or portions of the property be used for public services (easements for utilities, for example), and the right to place taxes on property for revenue generation. Beyond these government powers, however, the buyer desires an unencumbered, "clear" title, free from restrictions by private parties.

Some parts of the country use a title **abstract** to show the title history of a property. The buyer's and seller's attorneys review and approve the abstract at the time of sale. However, an abstract is just a chronological list of the recorded documents on the property. It does not represent a thorough search of title nor does it insure against any defects in the title. This approach to providing a check on the title to the buyer is, therefore, used less and less. Increasingly, buyers and lenders require *title insurance*.

Title insurance is obtained when property ownership is transferred. It insures against the risk that clear title may not be transferred to the buyer. It does not insure against any loss that may result from government restriction of property rights, such as zoning legislation or eminent domain. Also, title insurance does not insure against future events.

Title insurance also involves **title search**, a process that reviews each title transfer of the property throughout its history. The search reviews public records for occasions where clear title to property may not have been transferred. Most people think that clear title to property may be endangered by some ancient event in the history of the property. They envision the discovery of a document that shows a fraudulent transfer by an unscrupulous long-lost relative sometime in the 1800s, or that an ancient treaty with Native Americans was misinterpreted, or a land grant from an early Spanish king was never really made, or a land patent to an early colonist contained errors in its description. They look on title insurance as protection against such claims. Title insurance may cover such events, but that is not its primary purpose. Most failures to transfer clear title occur as a result of much more recent events.

Another common misconception is that title insurance is generally not necessary. Some people reason that if the seller of the property had a title search and received clear title when he purchased the property, then the title must still be unencumbered. Nothing could be further from the truth. Most encumbrances or obstacles to a transfer of clear title are recent and subsequent to the last transfer. The most obvious is a mortgage (deed of trust) that exists because the present owner financed the purchase of the real estate. But other encumbrances also may exist. There may be a second mortgage, taken out subsequent to the last transfer of the property. A lien may be on the property as a result of the failure of the present owner to pay local property taxes. The Internal Revenue Service may have placed a lien on the property if the owner has not paid his federal income taxes. There could be a mechanic's lien on the property if the owner had repairs or additions made and did not pay the contractor. There may even be a lien for failure to pay water or sewage bills. Furthermore, these liens can appear quickly and may be quite recent. A title search is designed to discover these encumbrances. Except for current property taxes accrued but not yet payable, these encumbrances will be listed on a preliminary title search and must be removed (generally by paying them) when title is transferred.

When title to a property is transferred, a title company conducts a title search and issues a title insurance policy. An experienced professional conducts the title search and reports on the quality of the title. If the search reveals any problems, the loan process stops until the problems are resolved (see later section titled "Clouds on Title").

A "standard" title insurance policy is sometimes used, but more frequently now insurers use a policy called the **American Land Title Association (ALTA)**. The dozen or so national title insurance companies use the ALTA policy because it has broader coverage. An ALTA policy insures the lender and the new owner separately against certain losses. Both parties are insured for losses if (1) title to the property is vested with the wrong party; (2) a lien or encumbrance remains after the transfer; (3) title is unmarketable; (4) the land physically abuts one or more streets, yet the owner fails to receive ordinary access rights; (5) the mortgage is unenforceable; (6) the lien of the mortgage is shown incorrectly as far as its order of priority; or (7) an assignment of the mortgage is invalid. Some additional risks, such as coverage for mining claims or unrecorded easements or liens, can be covered by an expanded ALTA policy, which FNMA, FHLMC, and GNMA and other secondary mortgage market entities often require.

If a property is purchased without financing (all cash), the new owner does not have to purchase title insurance. He can assume the risk. If he does purchase insurance, it will involve an **owner's policy**. In this case, only items (1) through (4) above will be covered.

A lender, on the other hand, will require the new owner to purchase a **lender's policy** that will cover the additional factors (5) through (7) above. Also, the lender's policy will cover losses that result from known liens or other encumbrances discovered in the search process. Because of the additional coverage, the lender's policy is somewhat more expensive than the owner's policy. The amount of the coverage is usually equal to the amount of the loan, which can be less than the value of the property.

Torrens System of Title

The Torrens system of title search only searches back to the last title search. This system assumes that the last search was complete and accurate. This saves time and lowers cost. Nonetheless, only a few states have adopted its use to any degree—Minnesota, Massachusetts, and Hawaii. Some other states permit its use, but the Torrens system is not the one used most often. Possibly converting to this system would be costly for some states and title insurance companies.

Clouds on Title

When the search of a property's title reveals a problem or fault, the lender will require that the fault be cured before making the loan. A problem with a title is called a **cloud on title**. Examples of such problems include a tax or other lien, an encroachment, or missing (or wrong) signatures. All clouds on title must be cleared before the loan process will proceed. Sometimes the borrower files a **suit to quiet title**, asking the court to remove or correct a title fault.

Title Insurance versus Property Insurance

Title insurance is different from other types of insurance (property and casualty insurance, for example) in several respects. First, title insurance covers losses caused by events that occurred prior to the payment of the premium. Property and casualty, life, and health insurance usually cover losses that occur subsequent to the payment of the premium. Second, the title insurance company or its agent will make every effort to ensure that losses do not occur as a result of past events in the chain of title. The largest element of cost for title insurers is searching the public records for encumbrances and evidence of errors in the transfer of title prior to the current transaction.

Losses from claims are much less, however. As a percent of revenues, claims may run 40 to 90 percent for property and casualty companies. For title insurance companies, claim losses run between 4 and 7 percent of premium income. Thus, the bulk of the premium for title insurance covers the cost of searching the records or maintaining their own records.

Summary

Lenders who desire to insure their loans against the risk of loss have a choice of government or private insurance programs. In either case, the loans must meet the qualifications of the insurers. The FHA and VA set loan-to-value and size limits on loans they insure. For this reason, many large loans are insured by private mortgage insurers (PMIs). The VA provides partial coverage, while the FHA provides full coverage for all losses. PMI insurance covers up to an agreed-on proportion of the loan. If the loss exceeds this proportion, the lender and insurer share the additional loss. This is a co-insurance relationship.

Title insurance insures the lender (and borrower) against a loss due to a defect in the title. Borrowers' policies do not insure against liens or defects on the property known to exist before its sale. Lenders' policies insure against loss from any lien or defect that exists prior to the sale, known or unknown.

Key Terms and Definitions

abstract of title—A condensed written history of title transactions and recorded instruments or condition bearing on the title to designated real estate.

American Land Title Association (ALTA)—A national association, founded in 1907, representing 2,100 title abstractors, title insurance companies, title insurance agents, and associate members. It is the role and responsibility of the title industry and its ALTA members to guarantee the safe, efficient transfer of real property and to provide protection for consumers and lenders alike. The association speaks for the title industry and establishes standard procedures and title policy forms.

cloud on title—Any conditions revealed by a title search that adversely affect the clear title to real estate. A cloud on title is usually removed through a suit to quiet title.

co-insurance—A sharing of insurance risk between insurer and owner depending on the relation of the amount of the policy and a specified percentage of the actual value of the property insured at the time of loss.

direct endorsement program—An FHA program whereby qualified lenders are authorized to approve borrowers prior to all information being provided to the FHA.

lender's policy—Title insurance that, among other assurances, covers all losses that may occur from any encumbrance or lien that pre-existed change of title, known or unknown.

loan processing—The steps involved in creating a loan from application through closing.

loan-to-value ratio—The amount of the loan divided by the value of the house.

mortgage insurance premium (MIP)—The charge paid by a mortgagor for mortgage insurance either to FHA or a private mortgage insurance company. On an FHA loan, the payment is 3.8 percent of the loan balance.

owner's policy—Title insurance that, among other assurances, covers losses that may occur *only* from *known* pre-existing encumbrances or liens.

private mortgage insurance (PMI)—Insurance written by a private (nongovernmental) company protecting the mortgage lender against loss caused by a mortgage default or foreclosure.

self-insurance—A lender that incurs all risk of default loss on his or her portfolio of loans.

suit to quiet title—A court proceeding whereby the court is asked to declare that clear title rests with the party bringing the action.

title—The legally recognized ownership interest in a property.

title insurance—Insurance that preexisting encumbrances on the property are removed at or prior to closing.

title search—A search of the public records to discover any liens or other impediments to a transfer of an unencumbered title.

underwriting—The process of analyzing risk and determining an appropriate charge for taking on the risk. It involves a review of borrower's credit, value of security, and certain legal documents.

Review Questions

1. What two transactions take place in the loan closing?
2. What is a settlement statement?
3. List the information required to complete a standard settlement statement.
4. What documents must be recorded and why?
5. Define and explain the four different types of mortgage insurance coverage. Give an example of each.
6. List three similarities and three differences of the FHA and VA insurance programs.
7. How does the FHA determine its premium on its standard (Section 203b) program?
8. Compare private mortgage insurance programs to the government programs.
9. Define title insurance and indicate what losses it is intended to cover.
10. Distinguish between an owner's (borrower's) and a lender's title policy in terms of coverage.
11. Compare title insurance with property and casualty insurance.
12. Compare title insurance with an abstract of title.

Problems to Solve (Answers may be checked against the Answer section)

1. Assume the following information on a residential loan default:

Value of house at foreclosure sale	$100,000
Balance of loan at time of last payment	120,000
Original loan amount	125,000
Delinquent interest payments	4,000
Foreclosure costs	
Attorney fees	5,000
Court expense	300
REO expenses	
Maintenance	800
Hazard insurance	400
Property taxes	550
Repairs	700

Determine the amount of the loss for which the lender will receive reimbursement if the loan was insured or guaranteed by (a) the FHA, (b) the VA, or (c) a typical PMI with a 15 percent coverage ratio. In each case indicate the proportion of the loss that would not be covered and, thus, must be borne by the lender.

2. For Problem 1, what would the value of the house have to be, other things unchanged, for the lender to bear no portion of the loss under a private mortgage policy?
3. Alternatively for Problem 1, if the value of the house remains at $100,000, what would the private mortgage insurance coverage ratio have to be in order for the lender to bear no portion of the loss?
4. Complete the blank HUD-1 form in Appendix 12 (pages 218–219), using the following information:

Mr. Henry Martin purchases a home with a sales price of $260,000. He makes a $10,000 deposit. His loan is a conventional loan for $200,000 at a rate of 7.0 percent. The loan is not insured. The lender charges a 1 percent origination fee, 2.5 discount points, $200 appraisal fee, $50 credit report fee, interest adjustment of $435, and a loan collection establishment fee of $65.

Henry's first payment is due on October 1.

The seller has a first mortgage at 9.5 percent interest in the amount of $118,600, which is paid to September 1. The seller also has a second mortgage of $20,000 at 14 percent interest, also paid to September 1. The settlement date is August 15.

The premium for hazard insurance for a new policy is $540.

The title company charges a mortgagee's (lender's) title insurance premium of $686 and an owner's title insurance premium of $300 and an escrow fee of $600. The seller will pay the owner's title insurance premium, but the escrow fee will be split equally between seller and buyer.

The real estate broker charges the seller a 6 percent commission. Other costs include recording fees of $25 to the buyer and $25 to the seller. In addition, the termite inspection cost of $40, a carpet allowance of $2,000, and a home warranty policy premium ($250) will be paid by the seller.

Suggested Reading

Ambrose, B. and C. Capone. "Cost–Benefit Analysis of Single-Family Foreclosure Alternatives." *Journal of Real Estate Finance and Economics* 13, 1996, pp. 105–120.

Clauretie, T. M. and M. Jameson. "Residential Loan Renegotiation: Theory and Evidence." *Journal of Real Estate Research* Vol. 10, 1995 pp. 153–161.

Clauretie, T. M., and T. Herzog. "The Effect of State Foreclosure Laws on Loan Losses: Evidence From the Mortgage Insurance Industry." *Journal of Money, Credit and Banking* 22(2) 1990, pp. 221–233.

Dennis, M. W. *Residential Mortgage Lending*. Upper Saddle River, N.J.: Prentice Hall, 1989, Chap. 16.

Melicher, R. W., and M. Unger. *Real Estate Finance*. Cincinnati, Ohio: South-Western College Publishing, 1989 Chap. 1.

Plotkin, I. H. *On the Theory and Practice of Rate Review and Profit Measurement in Title Insurance*. Cambridge, Mass.: Arthur D. Little, Inc., 1978.

Sirmans, C. F. *Real Estate Finance*, 2nd ed. New York: McGraw-Hill, 1989, Chap. 3.

Stowe, A. M. "Servicing FHA Single-Family Loans." *Mortgage Banking* 57(8), (1997), 91–97.

Touche, Ross & Co. *The Cost of Mortgage Foreclosure: Case Studies of Six Savings and Loan Associations*. Washington, D.C.: Author, 1975.

Wiedemer, J. P. *Real Estate Finance*, 7th ed., Upper Saddle River, N.J.: Prentice Hall, 1995, Chap. 5.

Related Web Sites

Information on risk mitigation for lenders, investors, and REITs.
http://www.boston-financial.com

Comprehensive guide for buying a home.
http://www.maxsol.com

Provides information for buyers and sellers of homes plus a nationwide referral network for finding real estate agents.
http://www.reinfonet.com

For information about the Federal National Mortgage Association and the housing finance system.
http://www.fanniemae.com

For information about the Federal Home Loan Mortgage Corporation.
http://www.freddiemac.com

For housing information (FHA included) and consumer alerts from the Department of Housing and Urban Development.
http://www.hud.gov

For information on VA mortgages.
http://www.va.gov

Examples of information required for loan processing.
http://www.mortgages.infopages.net

Appendix 12: HUD-1 Settlement Statement and Instructions for Completing

The following are line item instructions for completing Sections A through L of the HUD-1 settlement statement, required under Section 4 of RESPA and Regulation X of the Department of Housing and Urban Development. This form is to be used as a statement of actual charges and adjustments to be given to the parties in connection with the settlement. The instructions for completion of the HUD-1 are primarily for the benefit of the settlement agents who prepare the statements and need not be transmitted to the parties as an integral part of the HUD-1. There is no objection to the use of the HUD-1 in transactions in which its use is not legally required.

Instructions for completing the individual items on the HUD-1 form:

Section A. This section requires no entry of information.

Section B. Check appropriate loan type and complete the remaining items as applicable.

Section C. This section provides a notice regarding settlement costs and requires no additional entry of information.

Sections D and E. Fill in the names and current mailing addresses and zip codes of the Borrower and the Seller. Where there is more than one Borrower or Seller, the name and address of each one is required. Use a supplementary page if needed to list multiple Borrowers or Sellers.

Section F. Fill in the name, current mailing address and zip code of the Lender.

Section G. The street address of the property being sold should be given. If there is no street address, a brief legal description or other location of the property should be inserted. In all cases give the zip code of the property.

Section H. Fill in name, address, and zip code of settlement agent; address and zip code of "place of settlement."

Section I. Date of settlement.

Section J. Summary of Borrower's Transaction. Line 101 is for the gross sales price of the property being sold, excluding the price of any items of tangible personal property if Borrower and Seller have agreed to a separate price for such items.

A. **Settlement Statement**

U.S. Department of Housing and Urban Development

OMB Approval No. 2502-0265

B. Type of Loan

1. ☐ FHA 2. ☐ FmHA 3. ☐ Conv. Unins. 4. ☐ VA 5. ☐ Conv. Ins.	6. File Number:	7. Loan Number:	8. Mortgage Insurance Case Number:

C. Note: This form is furnished to give you a statement of actual settlement costs. Amounts paid to and by the settlement agent are shown. Items marked "(p.o.c.)" were paid outside the closing; they are shown here for informational purposes and are not included in the totals.

D. Name & Address of Borrower:	E. Name & Address of Seller:	F. Name & Address of Lender:

G. Property Location:	H. Settlement Agent:	
	Place of Settlement:	I. Settlement Date:

J. Summary of Borrower's Transaction		K. Summary of Seller's Transaction	
100. Gross Amount Due From Borrower		**400. Gross Amount Due To Seller**	
101. Contract sales price		401. Contract sales price	
102. Personal property		402. Personal property	
103. Settlement charges to borrower (line 1400)		403.	
104.		404.	
105.		405.	
Adjustments for items paid by seller in advance		**Adjustments for items paid by seller in advance**	
106. City/town taxes to		406. City/town taxes to	
107. County taxes to		407. County taxes to	
108. Assessments to		408. Assessments to	
109.		409.	
110.		410.	
111.		411.	
112.		412.	
120. Gross Amount Due From Borrower		**420. Gross Amount Due To Seller**	
200. Amounts Paid By Or In Behalf Of Borrower		**500. Reductions In Amount Due To Seller**	
201. Deposit or earnest money		501. Excess deposit (see instructions)	
202. Principal amount of new loan(s)		502. Settlement charges to seller (line 1400)	
203. Existing loan(s) taken subject to		503. Existing loan(s) taken subject to	
204.		504. Payoff of first mortgage loan	
205.		505. Payoff of second mortgage loan	
206.		506.	
207.		507.	
208.		508.	
209.		509.	
Adjustments for items unpaid by seller		**Adjustments for items unpaid by seller**	
210. City/town taxes to		510. City/town taxes to	
211. County taxes to		511. County taxes to	
212. Assessments to		512. Assessments to	
213.		513.	
214.		514.	
215.		515.	
216.		516.	
217.		517.	
218.		518.	
219.		519.	
220. Total Paid By/For Borrower		**520. Total Reduction Amount Due Seller**	
300. Cash At Settlement From/To Borrower		**600. Cash At Settlement To/From Seller**	
301. Gross Amount due from borrower (line 120)		601. Gross amount due to seller (line 420)	
302. Less amounts paid by/for borrower (line 220)	( )	602. Less reductions in amt. due seller (line 520)	( )
303. Cash ☐ From ☐ To Borrower		**603. Cash ☐ To ☐ From Seller**	

Section 5 of the Real Estate Settlement Procedures Act (RESPA) requires the following: • HUD must develop a Special Information Booklet to help persons borrowing money to finance the purchase of residential real estate to better understand the nature and costs of real estate settlement services; • Each lender must provide the booklet to all applicants from whom it receives or for whom it prepares a written application to borrow money to finance the purchase of residential real estate; • Lenders must prepare and distribute with the Booklet a Good Faith Estimate of the settlement costs that the borrower is likely to incur in connection with the settlement. These disclosures are manadatory.

Section 4(a) of RESPA mandates that HUD develop and prescribe this standard form to be used at the time of loan settlement to provide full disclosure of all charges imposed upon the borrower and seller. These are third party disclosures that are designed to provide the borrower with pertinent information during the settlement process in order to be a better shopper.

The Public Reporting Burden for this collection of information is estimated to average one hour per response, including the time for reviewing instructions, searching existing data sources, gathering and maintaining the data needed, and completing and reviewing the collection of information.

This agency may not collect this information, and you are not required to complete this form, unless it displays a currently valid OMB control number.

The information requested does not lend itself to confidentiality.

Previous editions are obsolete

Page 1 of 2

form **HUD-1** (3/86)
ref Handbook 4305.2

L. Settlement Charges

	Paid From Borrowers Funds at Settlement	Paid From Seller's Funds at Settlement
700. Total Sales/Broker's Commission based on price $ @ % =		
Division of Commission (line 700) as follows:		
701. $ to		
702. $ to		
703. Commission paid at Settlement		
704.		
800. Items Payable In Connection With Loan		
801. Loan Origination Fee %		
802. Loan Discount %		
803. Appraisal Fee to		
804. Credit Report to		
805. Lender's Inspection Fee		
806. Mortgage Insurance Application Fee to		
807. Assumption Fee		
808.		
809.		
810.		
811.		
900. Items Required By Lender To Be Paid In Advance		
901. Interest from to @$ /day		
902. Mortgage Insurance Premium for months to		
903. Hazard Insurance Premium for years to		
904. years to		
905.		
1000. Reserves Deposited With Lender		
1001. Hazard insurance months@$ per month		
1002. Mortgage insurance months@$ per month		
1003. City property taxes months@$ per month		
1004. County property taxes months@$ per month		
1005. Annual assessments months@$ per month		
1006. months@$ per month		
1007. months@$ per month		
1008. months@$ per month		
1100. Title Charges		
1101. Settlement or closing fee to		
1102. Abstract or title search to		
1103. Title examination to		
1104. Title insurance binder to		
1105. Document preparation to		
1106. Notary fees to		
1107. Attorney's fees to		
(includes above items numbers:)		
1108. Title insurance to		
(includes above items numbers:)		
1109. Lender's coverage $		
1110. Owner's coverage $		
1111.		
1112.		
1113.		
1200. Government Recording and Transfer Charges		
1201. Recording fees: Deed $; Mortgage $; Releases $		
1202. City/county tax/stamps: Deed $; Mortgage $		
1203. State tax/stamps: Deed $; Mortgage $		
1204.		
1205.		
1300. Additional Settlement Charges		
1301. Survey to		
1302. Pest inspection to		
1303.		
1304.		
1305.		
1400. Total Settlement Charges (enter on lines 103, Section J and 502, Section K)		

Previous editions are obsolete

Page 2 of 2

form **HUD-1** (3/86)
ref Handbook 4305.2

Line 102 is for the gross sales price of any items of tangible personal property excluded from Line 101. Personal property could include such items as carpets, drapes, stoves, refrigerators, etc. What constitutes personal property varies from state to state. Manufactured homes are not considered personal property for this purpose.

Line 103 is used to record the total charges to Borrower detailed in Section L and totaled on Line 1400.

Lines 104 and 105 are for additional amounts owed by the Borrower or items paid by the Seller prior to settlement but reimbursed by the Borrower at settlement. For example, the balance in the Seller's reserve account held in connection with an existing loan, if assigned to the Borrower in a loan assumption case, will be entered here. These lines will also be used when a tenant in the property being sold has not yet paid the rent, which the Borrower will collect, for a period of time prior to the settlement. The lines will also be used to indicate the treatment for any tenant security deposit. The Seller will be credited on Lines 404–405.

Lines 106 through 112 are for items which the Seller had paid in advance, and for which the Borrower must therefore reimburse the Seller. Examples of items for which adjustments will be made may include taxes and assessments paid in advance for an entire year or other period, when settlement occurs prior to the expiration of the year or other period for which they were paid. Additional examples include flood and hazard insurance premiums, if the Borrower is being substituted as an insured under the same policy; mortgage insurance in loan assumption cases; planned unit development or condominium association assessments paid in advance; fuel or other supplies on hand, purchased by the Seller, which the Borrower will use when Borrower takes possession of the property; and ground rent paid in advance.

Line 120 is for the total of Lines 101 through 112.

Line 201 is for any amount paid against the sales price prior to settlement.

Line 202 is for the amount of the new loan made by the Lender or first user loan (a loan to finance construction of a new structure or purchase of manufactured home where the structure was constructed for sale or the manufactured home was purchased for purposes of resale and the loan is used as or converted to a loan to finance purchase by the first user). For other loans covered by Regulation X which finance construction of a new structure or purchase of a manufactured home, list the sales price of the land on Line 104, the construction cost or purchase price of manufactured home on Line 105 (Line 101 would be left blank in this instance) and amount of the loan on Line 202. The remainder of the form should be completed taking into account adjustments and charges related to the temporary financing and permanent financing and which are known at the date of settlement.

Line 203 is used for cases in which the Borrower is assuming or taking title subject to an existing loan or lien on the property.

Lines 204–209 are used for other items paid by or on behalf of the Borrower. Examples include cases in which the Seller has taken a trade-in or other property from the Borrower in part payment for the property being sold. They may also be used in cases in which a Seller (typically a builder) is making an "allowance" to the Borrower for carpets or drapes which the Borrower is to purchase separately. Lines 204–209 can also be used to indicate any Seller financing arrangements or other new loan not listed in Line 202. For example, if the Seller takes a note from the Borrower for part of the sales price, insert the principal amount of the note with a brief explanation on Lines 204–209.

Lines 210 through 219 are for items which have not yet been paid, and which the Borrower is expected to pay, but which are attributable in part to a period of time prior to the settlement. In jurisdictions in which taxes are paid late in the tax year, most cases will show the proration of taxes in these lines. Other examples include utilities used but not paid for by the Seller, rent collected in advance by the Seller from a tenant for a period extending beyond the settlement date, and interest on loan assumptions.

Line 220 is for the total of Lines 201 through 219.

Lines 301 and 302 are summary lines for the Borrower. Enter total in Line 120 on Line 301. Enter total in Line 220 on Line 302.

Line 303 may indicate either the cash required from the Borrower at settlement (the usual case in a purchase transaction) or cash payable to the Borrower at settlement (if, for example, the Borrower's deposit against the sales price (earnest money) exceeded the Borrower's cash obligations in the transaction). Subtract Line 302 from Line 301 and enter the amount of cash due to or from the Borrower at settlement on Line 303. The appropriate box should be checked.

Section K. Summary of Seller's Transaction. Instructions for the use of Lines 101 and 102 and 104–112 above, apply also to Lines 401–412. Line 420 is for the total of Lines 401 through 412.

Line 501 is used if the Seller's real estate broker or other party who is not the settlement agent has received and holds the deposit against the sales price (earnest money) which exceeds the fee or commission owed to that party, and if that party will render the excess deposit directly to the Seller, rather than through the settlement agent, the amount of excess deposit should be entered on Line 501 and the amount of the total deposit (including commissions) should be entered on Line 201.

Line 502 is used to record the total charges to the Seller detailed in Section L and totaled on Line 1400.

Line 503 is used if the Borrower is assuming or taking title subject to existing liens which are to be deducted from sales price.

Lines 504 and 505 are used for the amounts (including any accrued interest) of any first and/or second loans which will be paid as part of the settlement.

Line 506 is used for deposits paid by the Borrower to the Seller or other party who is not the settlement agent. Enter the amount of the deposit in Line 201 on Line 506 unless Line 501 is used or the party who is not the settlement agent transfers all or part of the deposit to the settlement agent in which case the settlement agent will note in parentheses on Line 507 the amount of the deposit which is being disbursed as proceeds and enter in column for Line 506 the amount retained by the above described party for settlement services. If the settlement agent holds the deposit insert a note in Line 507 which indicates that the deposit is being disbursed as proceeds.

Lines 506 through 509 may be used to list additional liens which must be paid off through the settlement to clear title to the property. Other payoffs of Seller obligations should be shown on Lines 506–509 (but not on Lines 1303–1305). They may also be used to indicate funds to be held by the settlement agent for the payment of water, fuel, or other utility bills which cannot be prorated between the parties at settlement because the amounts used by the Seller prior to settlement are not yet known. Subsequent disclosure of the actual amount of these post-settlement items to be paid from settlement funds is optional. Any amounts entered on Lines 204–209 including Seller financing arrangements should also be entered on Lines 506–509.

Instructions for the use of Lines 510 through 519 are the same as those for Lines 210 to 219 above.

Line 520 is for the total of Lines 501 through 519.

Lines 601 and 602 are summary lines for the Seller. Enter total in Line 420 on Line 610. Enter total in Line 520 on Line 602.

Line 603 may indicate either the cash required to be paid to the Seller at settlement (the usual case in a purchase transaction) or cash payable by the Seller at settlement. Subtract Line 602 from Line 601 and enter the amount of cash due to or from the Seller at settlement on Line 603. The appropriate box should be checked.

Section L. Settlement Charges.

For all items except for those paid to and retained by the Lender, the name of the person or firm ultimately receiving the payment should be shown. In the case of "no cost" or "no point" loans, the charge to be paid by the lender to an affiliated or independent service provider should be shown as P.O.C. (Paid Outside of Closing) and should not be used in computing totals. Such charges also include indirect payments or back-funded payments to mortgage brokers that arise from the settlement transaction. When used, "P.O.C." should be placed in the appropriate lines next to the identified item, not in the columns themselves.

Line 700 is used to enter the sales commission charged by the sales agent or broker. If the sales commission is based on a percentage of the price, enter the sales price, the percentage, and the dollar amount of the total commission paid by the Seller.

Lines 701–702 are to be used to state the split of the commission where the settlement agent disburses portions of the commission to two or more sales agents or brokers.

Line 703 is used to enter the amount of sales commission disbursed at settlement. If the sales agent or broker is retaining a part of the deposit against the sales price (earnest money) to apply towards the sales agent's or broker's commission, include in Line 703 only that part of the commission being disbursed at settlement and insert a note on Line 704 indicating the amount the sales agent or broker is retaining as a "P.O.C." item.

Line 704 may be used for additional charges made by the sales agent or broker, or for a sales commission charged to the Borrower, which will be disbursed by the settlement agent.

Line 801 is used to record the fee charged by the Lender for processing or originating the loan. If this fee is computed as a percentage of the loan amount, enter the percentage in the blank indicated.

Line 802 is used to record the loan discount or "points" charged by the Lender, and, if it is computed as a percentage of the loan amount, enter the percentage in the blank indicated.

Line 803 is used for appraisal fees if there is a separate charge for the appraisal. Appraisal fees for HUD and VA loans are also included on Line 803.

Line 804 is used for the cost of the credit report if there is a charge separate from the origination fee.

Line 805 is used only for inspections by the Lender or the Lender's agents. Charges for other pest or structural inspections required to be stated by these instructions should be entered in Lines 1301–1305.

Line 806 should be used for an application fee required by a private mortgage insurance company.

Line 807 is provided for convenience in using the form for loan assumption transactions.

Lines 808–811 are used to list additional items payable in connection with the loan including a CLO Access fee, a mortgage broker fee, fees for real estate property taxes or other real property charges.

Lines 901–905. This series is used to record the items which the Lender requires (but which are not necessarily paid to the lender, i.e., FHA mortgage insurance premium) to be paid at the time of settlement, other than reserves collected by the Lender and recorded in 1000 series.

Line 901 is used if interest is collected at settlement for a part of a month or other period between settlement and the date from which interest will be collected with the first regular monthly payment. Enter that amount here and include the per diem charges. If such interest is not collected until the first regular monthly payment, no entry should be made on Line 901.

Line 902 is used for mortgage insurance premiums due and payable at settlement, except reserves collected by the Lender and recorded in the 1000 series. A lump sum mortgage insurance premium paid at settlement should be inserted on Line 902, with a note that indicates that the premium is for the life of the loan.

Line 903 is used for hazard insurance premiums which the Lender requires to be paid at the time of settlement except reserves collected by the Lender and recorded in the 1000 series.

Lines 904 and 905 are used to list additional items required by the Lender (except for reserves collected by the Lender and recorded in the 1000 series) including flood insurance, mortgage life insurance, credit life insurance and disability insurance premiums. These lines are also used to list amounts paid at settlement for insurance not required by the Lender.

Lines 1000–1008. This series is used for amounts collected by the Lender from the Borrower and held in an account for the future payment of the obligations listed as they fall due. Include the time period (number of months) and the monthly assessment. In many jurisdictions this is referred to as an "escrow", "impound", or "trust" account. In addition to the items listed, some Lenders may require reserves for flood insurance, condominium owners' association assessments, etc.

After itemizing individual deposits in the 1000 series using single-item accounting, the servicer shall make an adjustment based on aggregate accounting. This adjustment equals the difference between the deposit required under aggregate accounting and the sum of the deposits required under single-item accounting. The adjustment will always be a negative number or zero. The settlement agent shall enter the aggregate adjustment amount on a final line in the 1000 series of the HUD-1 statement.

During the phase-in period, an alternative procedure is available. If a servicer has not yet conducted the escrow account analysis to determine the aggregate accounting starting balance, the settlement agent may initially calculate the 1000 series deposits for the HUD-1 settlement statement using single-item analysis with a one-month cushion (unless the mortgage loan documents indicate a smaller amount). In the escrow account analysis conducted within 45 days of settlement, the servicer shall adjust the escrow account to reflect the aggregate accounting balance.

Lines 1100–1113. This series covers title charges and charges by attorneys. The title charges include a variety of services performed by title companies or others and includes fees directly related to the transfer of title (title examination, title search, document preparation) and fees for title insurance. The legal charges include fees for Lender's, Seller's or Buyer's attorney, or the attorney preparing title work. The series also includes any fees for settlement or closing agents and notaries. In many jurisdictions the same person (for example, an attorney or a title insurance company) performs several of the services listed in this series and makes a single overall charge for such services. In such cases, enter the overall fee on Line 1107 (for attorneys), or Line 1108 (for title companies), and enter on that line the item numbers of the services listed which are covered in the overall fee. If this is done, no individual amounts need be entered into the borrower's and seller's columns for the individual items which are covered by the overall fee. In transactions involving more than one attorney, one attorney's fees should appear on Line 1107 and the other attorney's fees should be on Line 1111, 1112 or 1113. If an attorney is representing a buyer, seller, or lender and is also acting as a title agent, indicate on line 1107 which services are covered by the attorney fee and on line 1113 which services are covered by the insurance commission.

Line 1101 is used for the settlement agent's fee.

Lines 1102 and 1103 are used for the fees for the abstract or title search and title examination. In some jurisdictions the same person both searches the title (that is, performs the necessary research in the records) and examines title (that is, makes a determination as to what matters affect title, and provides a title report or opinion). If such a person charges only one fee for both services, it should be entered on Line 1103 unless the person performing these tasks is an attorney or a title company in which case the fees should be entered as described in the general directions for Lines 1100–1113. If separate persons perform these tasks, or if separate charges are made for searching and examination, they should be listed separately.

Line 1104 is used for the title insurance binder which is also known as a commitment to insure.

Line 1105 is used for charges for preparation of deeds, mortgages, notes, etc. If more than one person receives a fee for such work in the same transaction, show the total paid in the appropriate column and the individual charges on the line following the word "to."

Line 1106 is used for the fee charged by a notary public for authenticating the execution of settlement documents.

Line 1107 is used to disclose the attorney's fees for the transaction. The instructions are discussed in the general directions for Lines 1100–1113. This line should include any charges by an attorney to represent a buyer, seller or lender in the real estate transaction.

Lines 1108–1110 are used for information regarding title insurance. Enter the total charge for title insurance (except for the cost of the title binder) on Line 1108. Enter on Lines 1109 and 1110 the individual charges for the Lender's and owner's policies. Note that these charges are not carried over into the Borrower's and Seller's columns, since to do so would result in a duplication of the amount in Line 1108. If a combination Lender's/owner's policy is purchased, show this amount as an additional entry on Lines 1109 and 1110.

Lines 1111–1113 are for the entry of other title charges not already itemized. Examples in some jurisdictions would include a fee to a private tax service, a fee to a county tax collector for a tax certificate, or a fee to a public title registrar for a certificate of title in a Torrens Act transaction. Line 1113 should be used to disclose services that are covered by the commission of an attorney acting as a title agent when Line 1107 is already being used to disclose the fees and services of the attorney in representing the buyer, seller, or lender in the real estate transaction.

Lines 1201–1205 are used for government recording and transfer charges. Recording and transfer charges should be itemized. Additional recording or transfer charges should be listed on Lines 1204 and 1205.

Lines 1301 and 1302 are used for fees for survey, pest inspection, radon inspection, lead-based paint inspection, or other similar inspections.

Lines 1303–1305 are used for any other settlement charges not referable to the categories listed above on the HUD-1, which are required to be stated by these instructions. Examples may include structural inspections or presale inspection of heating, plumbing, or electrical equipment. These inspection charges may include a fee for insurance or warranty coverage.

Line 1400 is for the total settlement charges paid from Borrower's funds and Seller's funds. These totals are also entered on Lines 103 and 502, respectively, in sections J and K.

Note: HUD forms, instructions, and other documents can be found at www.hudclips.org.

Chapter 13

Modern Finance

Chapter Outline

Learning Objectives

After reading this chapter you will be able to:

- Describe how a tax-deferred exchange and an installment sale agreement allow real estate investors to alter their portfolios without having the value reduced by tax payments.
- List the property requirements for an exchange.
- Describe how an installment allows the seller to defer payment of taxes on capital gains.

Key Terms

boot
contract price
gross profit percentage
imputed interest rate rule
installment sale
related-persons rule
tax-deferred exchange

Introduction

When a real estate transaction is classified as an outright sale, the capital gain from the sale must be reported and is taxed in full. This can be the case even if the seller does not receive the entire selling price. For example, if a seller sold a property and passed the deed to the buyer but took back a mortgage from the buyer for all or some of the purchase price, the transaction is still classified as an outright sale. In this case, the seller would be taxed on the entire capital gain from the sale even though payment is being received in increments over time.

Several arrangements address the need to minimize the tax burden of the sale of a property. Chief among these are tax-deferred exchanges and installment sales.

Tax-Deferred Exchange

By using Section 1031 (of the Internal Revenue Service Code) provisions for a **tax-deferred exchange**, an investor may exchange one or more properties for another. Several basic requirements must be met for an exchange to qualify as tax deferred. The new properties must be "like-kind" properties, but virtually all real estate properties are considered like-kind. Owners may exchange farmland for apartment complexes, or office buildings for warehouses.

The Section 1031 or so-called tax-deferred exchange rule has important implications for real estate investors. Under Section 1031 an investor may permanently defer the gain on investment real estate properties. As long as the investor keeps exchanging properties instead of selling, the equity buildup is not taxed. At the investor's death, the basis of the properties will automatically adjust to market value, eliminating all capital gains.

Basic Requirements

Section 1031 has four basic requirements:

1. Both the relinquished and the acquired property must be held for productive use in a trade or business or for investment. Thus, owner-occupied residences are not eligible for a like-kind exchange.
2. The property exchanged and the one received must be of like-kind. For real estate, this involves almost any type of property.
3. The exchange must actually occur. The owner cannot sell one property for cash and immediately use the cash proceeds to purchase another property. There can be no intervening sale of the relinquished property, no matter how quickly the new acquired property is purchased.

4. The basis in the acquired property will be equal to the basis in the relinquished property. The calculation of the basis must be adjusted if any non-real-estate property, or "boot," is involved.

Three-Party Exchanges

What happens when an owner identifies a new property to acquire, but the owner of the identified property does not wish to exchange it for the property in question? One solution is the three-party exchange. Assume that Mrs. Andrews owns a property A and desires to exchange it for property B. Mr. Benthall, who owns property B, however, has no interest in owning Mrs. Andrews' property. In a three-party exchange, someone interested in property A is found, Ms. Chatham, for example. Now Ms. Chatham who really wants property A actually buys property B and then exchanges it for property A. All parties end up with the property they want: The third party, Ms. Chatham, gets property A. The original owner of property A, Mrs. Andrews, gets property B. The owner of property B, Mr. Benthall, gets cash.

Delayed Exchanges

What happens when a third-party buyer for property A is available who wants to own property A immediately, before the owner of property A can identify another desirable property? In this case, the solution may be a delayed exchange. The owner of property A (Mrs. Anderson, in our example) would transfer title (not sell) to the third party (Ms. Chatham) who, in turn, would agree to transfer a property identified by the owner of property A at some time in the future. In such a case, the third-party buyer usually would deposit a sufficient sum of money in escrow to purchase the identified property at a later date. In this type of exchange, the owner of property A simply transfers title to the third party and says "Some time in the future, I will identify other properties that you can purchase and deliver their title to me."

Boot

In a like-kind exchange, the real estate properties exchanged will not always have identical values. For example, the owner of a property worth $10 million may wish to exchange it for another property worth $8 million plus $2 million in cash. The cash is the **boot**. *Boot* is a general term for property in an exchange that is not like-kind. In this case, the boot is a taxable portion of the exchange. If the investor is in the 30 percent tax bracket, then the tax due will be $600,000. This is still better than the $3 million tax bill that the seller would incur if the property were sold outright.

Boot is not limited to cash. It can be any non-like-kind property, including the relief of a mortgage obligation. Using the previous example, assume that there is a $1 million mortgage on the property to be relinquished. If the owner of the property to be exchanged (worth $8 million) exchanges that property and pays off the mortgage on the relinquished property plus $1 million, then the boot will consist of $1 million in cash and $1 million in mortgage relief.

Additional Requirements

Numerous technical requirements must be met for a like-kind exchange to avoid taxation. Those who contemplate such an exchange are wise to seek the counsel of a tax specialist or a specialist in such exchanges. Most large urban areas have several such specialists who belong to a society or group of real estate exchangers.

Three requirements must be met to satisfy a delayed tax-deferred exchange:

1. The owner of the relinquished property must identify the replacement property within the identification period. The identification period begins on the date the relinquished property is transferred and ends 45 days thereafter. If more than one property is involved in the exchange, the period begins with the first transfer of a property.
2. The exchange must be completed within a specified exchange period. The exchange period begins on the date of the transfer of the relinquished property and ends 180 days later or on the due date of the tax return for the taxable year, whichever occurs sooner.
3. The owner of the relinquished property must not be in constructive receipt of the proceeds from the transfer of the property.

Multiple Property Tests

In a delayed transaction it can be difficult, if not impossible, to identify the property to be acquired within 45 days. IRS rules permit the owner to identify several prospective properties within this time period, provided the three-property test, the 200 percent test, or the 95 percent test are met.

The *three-property test* permits property owners to identify any three other properties to be exchanged without regard to their fair market values. The *200 percent* test limits the identified properties to 200 percent of the fair market value of the properties relinquished. The *95 percent test* applies if the first two criteria are not met. Under this rule, the identification requirement is still met if at least 95 percent of the identified property is actually received by the termination of the 180-day exchange period.

Other Considerations

Incidental property may be involved in an exchange. This type of property is usually personal property (such as furniture and fixtures), but can be included in the real estate package as long as its value does not exceed 15 percent of the aggregate value of the replacement property. If the property to be acquired does not exist but is to be constructed, then the regulations require that as much detail as possible about the property be described within the identification period. Variations due to typical production changes are allowed. However, any additional construction after the property is received is not considered like-kind property; rather, it will be considered boot. For the 200 percent test, the fair market value of the property to be produced is its value at the time it is to be received.

Recall that the owner of the property to be relinquished cannot receive money from the transaction. Yet, in a delayed transaction, what happens if the other party fails to deliver title to the property as required under the exchange agreement? In this case, the property owner may require that the other party deposit a sum of money in an escrow account to guarantee delivery of the property. Tax rules allow this arrangement as long as the property owner has not received any cash on the delivery of the property to be relinquished.

Tax-deferred exchanges have obvious benefits for property owners who desire to change their type of real estate investment without having to pay taxes and thereby reduce the size of their investment portfolio. Like so many other tax regulations, the rules involved in the tax-deferred exchange can be complicated. Property owners who anticipate an exchange are advised to seek professional guidance in structuring the transaction to ensure compliance with the applicable regulations.

SIDEBAR

Tax-Deferred Exchange Example

Suppose that Investor A purchased a triplex five years ago that is currently worth $150,000. The property has an adjusted basis of $75,000 and Investor A owes $67,500 on the mortgage. She is seeking to buy a larger property and has found a fourplex offered for sale by Investor B. The fourplex is valued at $300,000 and is subject to a $217,500 mortgage. Table 13-1 shows the process of Investor A and Investor B doing a tax-deferred exchange. In doing the exchange, the equities must balance, which may require a boot or maybe refinancing one of the mortgages.

The recognized gain of $0 for Investor A shows that the $66,000 realized gain is completely deferred. The effect on the tax basis of the new property now owned by Investor A is shown on the last line ($234,000). The $66,000 gain on the old property has been subtracted from the new property's $300,000 value. While this lowers the property's depreciable basis, Investor A has more cash. Furthermore, she has achieved her goals of disposing of the old property while deferring the tax on the gain. She has also acquired a property worth more than the old one.

Table 13-1
Tax-Deferred Exchange Calculations

	Investor A	Investor B
A. Equities Must Balance		
Market value of property given	$150,000	$300,000
– Mortgage balance	– 67,500	–217,500
= Equity given	82,500	82,500
+ Boot (unlike property)	+ 0	+ 0
= Total	82,500	82,500
B. Realized Gain		
Market value of property given	150,000	300,000
– Selling expenses	– 9,000	– 18,000
– Adjusted basis	– 75,000	– 270,000
= Realized gain	66,000	12,000
C. Recognized Gain		
Net mortgage relief	0	150,000
– Boot given	– 0	– 0
– Selling expenses	– 9,000	– 18,000
+ Boot received	+ 0	+ 0
= Net boot received	0	132,000
Recognized gain (lesser of realized gain or net boot received)	0	12,000
D. Tax Basis of Property Received		
Adjusted basis	75,000	270,000
– Boot received	– 0	– 0
– Old mortgage	– 67,500	– 217,500
+ Boot given	+ 0	+ 0
+ Selling expenses	+ 9,000	+ 18,000
+ Mortgage on new property	+ 217,500	+ 67,500
+ Recognized gain	+ 0	+ 12,000
= Tax Basis of New Property	234,000	150,000

Installment Sale Financing

When a property is sold, it is treated as an outright sale if the seller pays income tax on the full capital gain in the year of sale. An alternative method of sale is the **installment sale**, which occurs when the seller takes back a promissory loan from the buyer. The financing provided by the seller may take a first, second, or later mortgage position. Ordinarily the IRS would consider the receipt of a promissory note as taxable income, the same as cash. This would require payment of taxes in the year of sale. However, a section in the tax code allows different treatment for a qualified installment sale.

To qualify as an installment sale, the seller must receive at least one payment after the year of the sale. In a typical scenario, the seller receives a down payment in the year of sale followed by a series of payments over the installment period.

Installment sales are used most frequently on income properties in order to postpone taxes and can be used only when a gain results from the sale. Losses incurred on the sale of business assets must be deducted in the year of sale, and losses from property held for personal use are not tax deductible.

Because this financing results in a series of payments, the seller is taxed only on the portion of capital gain received with each payment. The major task in an installment sale is distinguishing with each payment the portions of taxable profit and the return of original investment. The capital gains percentage is called the **gross profit percentage**. It is calculated as a percentage of the **contract price**. Once determined, the gross profit percentage stays constant and is applied to each payment received to determine the taxable portion of that payment.

Previously, the installment method was optional. If payments were to be received by the seller, the seller had to elect installment method if desired. Currently, however, under these circumstances the installment method is required. If sellers want the sale to be treated as an outright sale, they must elect out. A sale can be treated as an outright sale, with taxes paid on the full capital gain in the year of sale, even if the seller receives the proceeds from the sale over future periods.

Another useful tax rule is the **related-persons rule**, which says if an installment sale is made to a related person (defined as spouse, children, parents, and grandparents; brothers and sisters do not qualify) who, in turn, sells the property within a 2-year period, the original seller must recognize the balance of the gain at the time the related person makes the sale. One exception to this rule is an involuntary conversion by the related person.

Installment sales are also subject to the **imputed interest rate rule**. A seller might have an incentive to set an interest rate below the market rate and raise the contract price to make up for the lost interest. This transforms the income from interest to capital gains, which may have more favorable tax treatment. To prevent use of this strategy, the IRS instituted the imputed interest rule, which assigns a portion of the income as interest rather than capital gain income for tax purposes based on an "imputed" minimum interest rate. This rule is addressed in the system of applicable federal rates, which was established by Congress in 1985. This is not designed to be a form of credit control or the setting of interest rates.

Other Considerations in an Installment Sale

In the preceding example, the debt is fully amortized over the installment period of two years. In some cases, however, the note may be amortized over a longer period than the installment agreement. This results in a balloon payment in the last year of installment receipts. This is usually done to make the debt service payments more affordable. This would have the effect of rearranging the cash flows from the installment receipts. Also, if a sale is greater than $150,000 and the seller has a large amount of other debt, the seller may have to recognize additional gain through the allowable installment indebtedness rule.

Summary

Tax-deferred exchanges of real estate property and installment sales are two popular ways in which property owners alter their real estate investment portfolio without having its value reduced by tax payments. In a tax-deferred exchange, the owner of the relinquished property must receive another property of like kind in exchange within 180 days of relinquishing the property. An installment sales agreement is an alternative to the outright sale and allows the seller to defer payment of taxes on capital gains by electing to receive a series of installment payments.

SIDEBAR

Installment Sale Example

Suppose that Joan Smith sells property to Mark Jones for $150,000 in a two-year installment agreement with 40 percent down and the balance financed at 10 percent. The adjusted basis of the property is $80,000 with accumulated depreciation of $45,500. Smith has selling expenses of $5,000 and is in a 28 percent marginal tax bracket. The property has been depreciated on a straight-line basis and the buyer will make annual debt service payments. What is the seller's income, specifically, after-tax cash flows (ATCFs), in the year of sale and from the installment receipts?

These cash flows are calculated in Table 13-2. The calculation in the upper left corner (part A) shows that the ATCF in the year of sale is $48,890. It is the down payment minus selling expenses and taxes. The tax liability in the year of sale is shown in part B. The entry excess of mortgage over adjusted basis and selling expenses is applicable if the transaction includes the assumption of a loan by Jones from Smith. If there is no loan assumption, this entry is zero. If there is an assumption, the sum of adjusted basis plus selling expenses is subtracted from the balance of the assumed mortgage. A positive difference is entered in the table. If this difference is negative or zero, then the entry is zero. Calculating the tax also requires the profit percentage, which is shown in part C. The profit percentage is the total gain (selling price minus selling expenses minus adjusted basis) divided by the contract price and is shown to be 0.4333. Note that selling expenses are not deducted in calculating the contract price. The total gain from the sale is calculated normally by subtracting selling expenses and adjusted basis from the selling price.

The tax rate on the gain from the sale is calculated to be 23.50 percent. This is a weighted average of the tax on depreciation recapture (25 percent) and the tax on long-term capital gain (20 percent). The depreciation is 70 percent of the total gain and is prorated equally across the installment period. The total gain from the sale is $65,000 of which the depreciation recapture portion is $45,500. The remaining portion of $19,500 is classified as long-term capital gain.

The columns on the right side show the ATCFs for the installment receipts and the corresponding tax liabilities. Part D gives the after-tax cash flow each year from the installment receipts. For year 1, this is $44,973. Part E calculates the tax on installment receipts. The principal portion of the payment must be distinguished from the interest portion because of different tax treatment (interest is taxed as ordinary income) and in order to determine the portion of principal that is taxable in a given year. Thus, the total tax in a given installment period is the sum of the tax on interest and the tax on taxable principal.

Table 13-2
After-tax Cash Flows from Installment Sale Agreement

A. ATCF in Year of Sale	
Down payment	$60,000
– Selling expenses	– 5,000
– Taxes	–6,110
= ATCF	$48,890
B. Tax in Year of Sale	
Down payment	$60,000
+ Excess of mortgage over Adj. basis and selling expenses	+ 0
= Total payment in year of sale	$60,000
× Profit percentage	×0.4333
= Taxable portion of gain	$25,998
× Tax rate on gain	×0.235*
= Taxes in year of sale	$6,110
C. Profit Percentage	
Sale price	$150,000
– Selling expenses	– 5,000
– Adjusted basis	–80,000
= Total capital gain	$65,000
Sale price	$150,000
– Mortgage balance assumed	–0
+ Excess of mortgage over Adj. basis and selling expenses	+ 0
= Contract price	$150,000

D. ATCF from Installments	Year 1	Year 2
Debt service payment	$51,857	$51,857
+ Balloon payment	+ 0	+ 0
– Tax on installment	–6,884	–6,120
= ATCF	$44,973	$45,737
E. Taxes on Installments		
Repayment of principal	$42,857	$47,143
+ Balloon payment	+ 0	+ 0
= Principal portion	42,857	47,143
× Profit percentage	×0.4333	×0.4333
= Taxable principal	18,570	20,427
× Tax rate on principal	× 0.235*	× 0.235*
= Tax on principal	4,364	4,800
Interest earned	9,000	4,714
× Marginal tax rate	× 0.28	× 0.28
= Tax on interest	2,520	1,320
Tax on principal	4,364	4,800
+ Tax on interest	2,520	1,320
Tax on installment	$6,884	$6,120

Total gain/contract price = profit percentage 65,000/150,000 = 0.4333

*Tax rate on gain = (0.70)(0.25) + (0.30)(0.20) = 0.235. The depreciation recapture is 70 percent of the total gain and is prorated equally across the installment period.

Key Terms and Definitions

boot—Property that is not like-kind in a like-kind exchange. Cash is an example.

contract price—In an installment sale, it is the selling price minus the balance of any mortgage assumed plus the excess of this mortgage balance over the sum of adjusted basis and selling expenses.

gross profit percentage—The percentage of each payment which is capital gain.

imputed interest rate rule—IRS rule that establishes a minimum interest rate that must be charged based on market conditions.

installment sale—The selling of an appreciated property on terms rather than for cash so as to postpone the payment of capital gains taxes on the profits.

related-persons rule—If a property in an installment sale to a related person is sold within two years, the original seller must recognize the remaining capital gain at the time of sale.

tax-deferred exchange—Exchanging one or more properties for another and deferring the payment of capital gains tax.

Review Questions

1. What is the purpose of allowing like-kind exchanges of real estate properties?
2. Indicate two main criteria that must be met for a like-kind exchange of real estate property to satisfy the rules of a tax-deferred exchange.
3. What is the gross profit percentage in an installment sale and why is it important?
4. Explain the treatment of an assumed mortgage in an installment sale.

Problem to Solve (Answer may be checked against the Answer section)

1. Mr. Lunt sells property to Mr. Deen for $250,000 on a three-year installment basis. Mr. Deen will pay 30 percent down and the balance will be financed over a five-year period at 8 percent interest with *annual* payments. Mr. Lunt's original purchase price was $160,000 with acquisition costs of $10,000. He has made no capital improvements, and his accumulated depreciation is $37,000 on a straight-line basis. Mr. Lunt has selling expenses of $8,000 and is in a 28 percent tax bracket. Calculate Mr. Lunt's after-tax cash flow in the year of sale and the ATCFs from the installment receipts.

Part IV

Government Regulations and Programs

Part IV addresses various roles of the federal government in residential real estate finance. Chapter 14 addresses the regulation of mortgage lending, including the purpose of the laws and the consequences that may apply for failure to follow them. Chapter 15 describes the major federal programs that are in place to assist low- and moderate-income families in obtaining housing.

Chapter 14

Federal Regulation of Mortgage Lending

Chapter Outline

Learning Objectives

After reading this chapter you will be able to:

- Describe how the federal government regulates the practice of residential mortgage lending.

- Identify the various laws regulating residential mortgage lending.
- Explain the purpose of the laws and what motivated them.
- Describe the consequences that may apply for failure to follow the various regulations.

Key Terms

abusive practices
annual percentage rate (APR)
Community Reinvestment Act
computerized loan origination systems
Consumer Credit Protection Act (Truth-in-Lending)
Equal Credit Opportunity Act
Home Mortgage Disclosure Act
Real Estate Settlement Procedures Act
redlining
Regulation Z
Uniform Settlement Statement

Introduction

Every real estate professional should have knowledge of and understand how the federal government regulates mortgage lending. By *regulate* we mean the passing of laws that either prohibit, encourage, or require certain practices. The prohibited practices generally concern discrimination by mortgage lenders against any protected class of individuals. The federal government defines protected classes of borrowers according to their gender, race, national origin, religion, and status as a person with a disability. Thus, the target of prohibited practices is discrimination (refusal to take an application or grant a loan) by a lender against an individual because of his or her race, gender, national origin, and so forth. Discrimination against individuals is not the only prohibited practice, however. The federal government prohibits anticompetitive practices by those involved in the lending and settlement process. By settlement process we mean the "paperwork" by which a housing transaction is completed. A housing transaction usually involves several tasks: a transfer of the deed, removal of liens, provision for title insurance and mortgage insurance, the establishment of an escrow account for property taxes and hazard insurance, and so forth. Several individuals or firms are involved in this process, and some may have the incentive to behave in a manner that inhibits competition. As we will see below, the federal government recognizes this opportunity for anticompetitive behavior and prohibits certain relationships between those involved in the settlement process.

Encouraged or required practices include the disclosure of information involved in the lending and the settlement processes. The federal government believes that consumers should have available all of the relevant financial information needed to make an informed and rational decision. Also, lenders are encouraged, by legislation, to make mortgage loans available to minority communities or to communities that may have been underserved without such legislation.

Antidiscrimination Legislation

Three major pieces of legislation guide lender behavior relative to discrimination in lending. The **Equal Credit Opportunity Act** prohibits lenders from discriminating on the basis of race, national origin, gender, age, or marital status. The **Home Mortgage Disclosure Act** requires lenders to report on the areas within their market where they make loans. This report requirement discourages lenders from avoiding certain neighborhoods when making loans. Finally, the **Community Reinvestment Act** requires lenders to define their market area and take an assertive role in lending to all citizens in all neighborhoods within their market area.

Equal Credit Opportunity Act

The Equal Credit Opportunity Act (ECOA) of 1974 extended the civil rights momentum of the 1960s to credit markets. Though not strictly limited to consumer credit, the ECOA concentrates on this area of the capital market. The ECOA grew out of hearings held in 1972 on discrimination against women in the credit market. Witnesses testifying at the hearings of the National Commission on Consumer Finance (NCCF) in May of that year indicated that (especially) married women faced difficulties in obtaining credit. Later in that year the NCCF report was cited by the Senate Committee on Banking, Housing, and Urban Affairs as justification for federal legislation. The Senate developed a version of a bill, which became law in October 1974. This version prohibited discrimination in credit markets based on gender and marital status. Subsequently, the House of Representatives Committee on Banking, Currency, and Housing sought an expansion of the bill to include discrimination on the basis of age, race, national origin, religion, and color. The Senate amended this bill by adding yet two more protected classes: those receiving income from welfare and those who had, in good faith, exercised their rights under the ECOA. The revised bill became law in March 1976. The act requires lenders to notify applicants of a decision within 30 days of an application for credit and to provide written reasons for any denial of credit.

One difficulty with interpreting and enforcing this legislation has been differentiating between those decisions and other behaviors that are discriminatory (such as denial of credit) and those that represent legitimate efforts of lenders to screen applicants for credit. The act assigns the task of judging these behaviors to the Federal Reserve Board (FRB). In Regulation B, the board states that it is illegal to discriminate by treating one candidate for credit "less favorably" than another. Accurately defining and interpreting discriminatory behavior, however, is a difficult task.

Three approaches to defining or identifying discriminatory lending behavior are to determine effects, intent, and practices. Under the effects method, discrimination is said to exist if members of minority groups are underrepresented in the class of credit recipients; that is, if they represent a smaller proportion of those receiving credit than they do in the general population. Under the intent approach, discrimination is held to have existed if a lender intends to treat minority groups less favorably. Finally, the practices approach to discrimination holds that discriminatory behavior exists when a lender fails to adhere to a set of guidelines governing the do's and don'ts of the lending procedure. For example, FRB guidelines prohibit the use of "Mr." and "Mrs." on credit application forms and require that a married woman's credit history be considered independently of that of her spouse. Failure to adhere to these practices may result in a finding of discriminatory behavior. Lenders are careful to avoid any prohibited practices in taking and evaluating credit applications.

Legitimate credit screening may result in fewer credit approvals for members of minority groups than their proportion in the general population. If, for example, income is a legitimate screening device and black families have, on average, less income than white families, then the result is that black families will be underrepresented in the creditworthy group. This is so, even though race is not a screening factor. These circumstances make the effects approach to discrimination difficult to interpret and enforce. In addition, strict compliance with an effects approach would result in more credit being granted to unworthy candidates (based on income) and less to worthy candidates. In turn, the total cost of credit (through a greater number of defaults) to all groups would increase.

A lender's intent is difficult to determine, and lenders are not likely to admit discriminatory intent. The federal government, therefore, focuses on the practices approach to regulate discrimination and enforce the ECOA [although Regulation B does mention the effects test in a footnote to Section 202.6(a)]. Thus, under the ECOA, a lender's discrimination against individuals on the basis of race, for example, is illegal. Furthermore, a lender who simply refuses to make any loan whatsoever in certain neighborhoods is engaging in a practice called **redlining**. In years past, lenders used redlining (literally) to delineate "risky" neighborhoods in which they would not make loans. Lenders were wary of so-called "transitional" neighborhoods, those that were changing from one predominant ethnic group to another. Lenders envisioned a risk of declining property values in such neighborhoods. Since a house serves as a collateral for the mortgage loan, any event that would cause property prices to fall would represent a risk to lenders. To prevent redlining, Congress passed the Home Mortgage Disclosure Act and the Community Reinvestment Act.

Home Mortgage Disclosure Act and Community Reinvestment Act

The Home Mortgage Disclosure Act (HMDA) of 1975 and the Community Reinvestment Act (CRA) of 1978 are closely related to the ECOA. These acts reflect the concern of the federal government that all citizens have access to credit markets, regardless of the neighborhood in which they wish to live. The first act discourages lending institutions from avoiding certain neighborhoods, and the second encourages them to evaluate and actively lend in their defined community.

The Home Mortgage Disclosure Act requires a lender with assets exceeding $10 million to compile a report on the distribution of its loans, by number and dollar amount, within and outside any Standard Metropolitan Statistical Area where it has a main or branch office. The report must indicate the distribution of loans by census tract, and the lender must make it available for public inspection. The 1990 census data must be used for all loans made after January 1, 1992. State-chartered institutions are exempt from the disclosure requirements if they are subject to state laws that are substantially similar to HMDA requirements.

The 1989 Financial Institutions Reform, Recovery, and Enforcement Act (FIRREA) included some major changes in the HMDA. The changes expanded coverage to include mortgage lenders not affiliated with depository institutions and to include data on home improvement loans. In addition, the changes required institutions to report the race, sex, and income of mortgage and home improvement loan applicants and borrowers. Depository institutions with less than $30 million in assets are exempt from these additional provisions, however. In 1991 the Federal Reserve Board issued revised rules that required reporting of data on home-improvement loan refinancing and on rejected loan applications submitted through brokers or correspondents. The revisions made it clear that civil money penalties could be imposed for violations of the act.

The Community Reinvestment Act requires all federally regulated financial institutions (primarily commercial banks, savings and loan associations, and mutual savings banks) to publicize their lending activities within their community. Under the act an institution must do the following:

1. Define its "community" by preparing a map, indicating the area from which it accepts deposits and to which it makes loans.
2. List and make available to the public and regulators the types of credit services available.
3. Post a notice in its place of business indicating that its lending practices are being evaluated by their federal regulator and that the public can appear and make comments at any hearing for the purpose of authorizing any expansion.
4. Make a periodic report (community support statement) to its regulator concerning its efforts to serve the credit needs of its community.

Based on the community support statement, federal regulators can make written evaluations of an institution's record of meeting the credit needs of the community. They can deny a request for expansion to any institution that fails to comply with these provisions.

By amendments made under FIRREA, each evaluation has a public and confidential section. Under the public portion, the regulatory agency will rate the institution's record of meeting the community's credit needs as outstanding, satisfactory, in need of improvement, or in substantial noncompliance. The confidential portion is designed to protect the identity of complainants. In 1991, the Federal Housing Finance Board ruled that the Federal Home Loan Bank (FHLB) System could deny access to long-term FHLB advances (loans) by member thrifts that have poor evaluations. If an institution has an outstanding or satisfactory evaluation of its statement, it will be deemed to be in compliance. If it receives a lower evaluation, it must indicate how it expects to cure the deficiencies in an action plan. Access to long-term FHLB advances will be restricted if an institution's community-support action plan is disapproved or fails to substantially meet the goals of the action plan within one year.

The reason for these acts is that Congress was concerned that discriminatory lending practices could take place other than at the point of loan application. Specifically, citizen groups had long charged that lenders discriminated by using redlining.

Those who defended the practice claimed that lenders were simply identifying neighborhoods where the risk of mortgage lending was greater than normal. Default risk is greatest where property values are likely to decline (see Chapter 10 for further information on default risk). The risk is greater if the borrower lacks assets that the lender can pursue in satisfaction of any deficiency. The combination of falling property prices and low levels of wealth are typical of neighborhoods that are in transition from predominantly white to a mixture of white and racial minorities. Property values are likely to stabilize when the transition is complete and a racial minority predominates in the neighborhood. If lenders were not averse to default risk, then the redlining practice would appear to be racially motivated.

Critics of redlining claim that the practice not only discriminates against the population segment that most needs access to credit, but that it also contributes to the decline of neighborhoods. They argue that the inaccessibility of mortgage funds reduces demand for properties and causes their values to fall. Owners, in turn, have little incentive to maintain their properties. In addition, they are denied access to home improvement loans. The result is a deterioration of properties within the redlined area. Whether redlining causes deterioration in neighborhoods or deterioration causes redlining is a difficult cause-and-effect relationship to untangle. Proponents on each side of the issue have their own points of view.

A related issue is the practice of "FHAing" a neighborhood. Critics of redlining argue that lenders would originate predominantly or only FHA mortgages within a redlined area. However, if certain areas do have a greater risk of default, then issuing mostly FHA mortgages would be a reasonable response by a lender. The FHA fully insures lenders against all elements of loss. For conventional loans the lender would either be self-insured, if he held the loan in his own portfolio, or would require private mortgage insurance (PMI). Private mortgage insurance is a co-insurance relationship, however, and under the PMI contract, the lender absorbs a portion of the loss (much like the deductible on your automobile insurance).

Critics of FHAing argue that this practice contributes to neighborhood decay. They claim that, because all elements of loss are covered and the FHA often acts slowly in resolving their claims, many properties in default are left to deteriorate and become targets of vandalism.

Whatever the merits of the arguments on each side of the issue, Congress saw the issue as one of civil rights rather than one of risk management. With this perspective predominating, Congress sought a prohibition against the practice of redlining.

Legislation Requiring Information

Regulation of Settlement Procedures

As stated above, various aspects of the real estate settlement process—the process of transferring title from a home seller to a homebuyer—provide the potential for abuse. Homebuyers borrow money infrequently, have little knowledge of the value of the settlement services provided, and have little incentive or opportunity to "comparison shop" for settlement services. As a result, Congress felt it necessary to pass consumer protection legislation that would require disclosure of the costs of settlement prior to the settlement itself. The result was the **Real Estate Settlement Procedures Act**.

Real Estate Settlement Procedures Act

Congress enacted the Real Estate Settlement Procedures Act (RESPA) of 1974 in response to consumer complaints concerning the costs of completing a residential property transaction. Not only were the costs of settlement becoming expensive, but many consumers expressed frustration over understanding and controlling the various cost elements. The heart of this legislation mandates that reasonable estimates of all settlement charges be made known prior to settlement. A listing of the possible settlement charges provides an idea of the confusion faced by the typical borrower. Such charges might include an appraisal fee, a credit report fee, inspection fee (termites, for example), mortgage insurance premium, notary fees, title insurance, title search fee, document preparation fee, prepaid interest, attorneys' fees, recording fee, real estate transfer fee (sometimes called document stamps), sales commissions, and service charges.

Another concern of consumers was the "kickback" potential in the settlement process. Lenders in search of business might be tempted to give kickbacks to real estate salespersons in exchange for directing homebuyers to them. Title companies might, in turn, give kickbacks to the lender for directing business to them, and so forth. Since the average homebuyer is initially unaware of all of the players in the settlement procedure, the area is ripe for consumer abuse. Consumer groups felt that some of the settlement services were overpriced, either in terms of the value to the borrower or the cost of supplying the service. RESPA was designed to make markets more competitive by requiring the dissemination of information to consumers and prohibiting certain practices, particularly kickbacks.

Disclosure Requirements

RESPA mandates three disclosure requirements. First, at the time of the loan application, the lender must give the borrower a booklet that completely details RESPA and lists the information that must be disclosed. The booklet, which is provided by the Department of Housing and Urban Development (HUD), explains the settlement process and outlines the standard practices and procedures. The booklet also indicates the remedies that are available to the loan applicant in the event the settlement fails to conform to RESPA requirements.

The second disclosure requirement is a "good-faith estimate" of the settlement charges that are likely to be assessed against the borrower. If a range of values is provided for a particular service, then the range must be based on actual experience. Lenders also must disclose any special relationship that exists between them and another service provider. For example, if the lender uses only one attorney to review the settlement, then the lender must disclose any business relationship that may exist between them. Figure 14-1 shows a typical good faith estimate.

The **Uniform Settlement Statement** is the third disclosure required by RESPA. This disclosure, made on a form provided by HUD, contains a list of all the charges to be made against the borrower and a complete accounting of all disbursements to be made at settlement. The borrower has the right to review this statement prior to the date of settlement. The Uniform Settlement Statement must be accurate and must contain no estimates of values. Lenders must retain a copy for at least two years and cannot charge any fee or other assessment for completing the form.

Figure 14-1 Good Faith Estimate

GOOD FAITH ESTIMATE

Lender:	Sales Price:
Address:	Base Loan Amount:
	Total Loan Amount:
Applicant(s):	Interest Rate:
	Type of Loan:
Property Address:	Preparation Date:
	Loan Number:

The information provided below reflects estimates of the charges which you are likely to incur at the settlement of your loan. The fees listed are estimates - actual charges may be more or less. Your transaction may not involve a fee for every item listed.

The numbers listed beside the estimates generally correspond to the numbered lines contained in the HUD-1 or HUD-1A settlement statement which you will be receiving at settlement. The HUD-1 or HUD-1A settlement statement will show you the actual cost for items paid at settlement.

800	**ITEMS PAYABLE IN CONNECTION WITH LOAN:**		**1100**	**TITLE CHARGES:**	
801	Origination Fee @ % + $	$	1101	Closing or Escrow Fee	$
802	Discount Fee @ % + $	$	1102	Abstract or Title Search	$
803	Appraisal Fee	$	1103	Title Examination	$
804	Credit Report	$	1105	Document Preparation Fee	$
805	Lender's Inspection Fee	$	1106	Notary Fee	$
806	Mortgage Insurance Application Fee	$	1107	Attorney's Fee	$
807	Assumption Fee	$	1108	Title Insurance	$
808	Mortgage Broker Fee	$			$
810	Tax Related Service Fee	$			$
811	Application Fee	$			$
812	Commitment Fee	$			$
813	Lender's Rate Lock-In Fee	$			$
814	Processing Fee	$			$
815	Underwriting Fee	$	**1200**	**GOVERNMENT RECORDING AND TRANSFER CHARGES:**	
816	Wire Transfer Fee	$	1201	Recording Fee	$
		$	1202	City/County Tax/Stamps	$
900	**ITEMS REQUIRED BY LENDER TO BE PAID IN ADVANCE:**		1203	State Tax/Stamps	$
901	Interest for days @ $ /day	$	1204	Intangible Tax	$
902	Mortgage Insurance Premium	$			$
903	Hazard Insurance Premium	$			$
904	County Property Taxes	$			$
905	Flood Insurance	$			$
		$	**1300**	**ADDITIONAL SETTLEMENT CHARGES:**	
		$	1301	Survey	$
1000	**RESERVES DEPOSITED WITH LENDER:**		1302	Pest Inspection	$
1001	Hazard Ins. Mo. @$ Per Mo.	$			$
1002	Mortgage Ins. Mo. @$ Per Mo.	$			$
1004	Tax & Assmt. Mo. @$ Per Mo.	$			$
1006	Flood Insurance	$			$
		$		**TOTAL ESTIMATED SETTLEMENT CHARGES:**	$
	"S"/"B" designates those costs to be paid by Seller/Broker.			"A" designates those costs affecting APR.	

TOTAL ESTIMATED MONTHLY PAYMENT:		**TOTAL ESTIMATED FUNDS NEEDED TO CLOSE:**	
Principal & Interest	$		
Real Estate Taxes	$	Payoff Payment	$
Hazard Insurance	$	Estimated Closing Costs	$
Flood Insurance	$	Estimated Prepaid Items / Reserves	$
Mortgage Insurance	$	Total Paid Items (Subtract)	$
Other	$	Other	$
TOTAL MONTHLY PAYMENT	$	CASH FROM BORROWER	$

THIS SECTION IS COMPLETED ONLY IF A PARTICULAR PROVIDER OF SERVICE IS REQUIRED. Listed below are providers of service which we required you to use. The charges indicated in the Good Faith Estimate above are based upon the corresponding charge of the below designated providers.

ITEM NO.	NAME & ADDRESS OF PROVIDER	TELEPHONE NO.	NATURE OF RELATIONSHIP

These estimates are provided pursuant to the Real Estate Settlement Procedures Act of 1974, as amended (RESPA). Additional information can be found in the HUD Special Information Booklet, which is to be provided to you by your mortgage broker or lender, if your application is to purchase residential property and the Lender will take a first lien on the property.

Under RESPA the lender must also disclose to the borrower whether or not the lender intends to sell the mortgage. Along these lines the lender must also disclose the percentage of its loans that it has sold in the last 12 months and the percentage it expects to sell in the next 12 months.

RESPA covers all first mortgages that are secured by one- to four-family residences and made by a federally regulated or insured lender. It does not cover mortgaged property in excess of 25 acres, home improvement loans, loans to finance the purchase of land where no proceeds are used to construct a dwelling, construction loans to developers, or the execution of a land sales contracts.

Regulation of Abusive Practices

RESPA deals with potentially abusive practices, such as kickbacks, required use of certain title services, and unduly large escrow accounts. RESPA requires that the payment of money or something of value be for actual services rendered (that is, not a kickback). If payment exceeds the value of services provided, then it is assumed that a kickback has been provided. **Abusive practices** are monitored closely, especially in cases where one of the parties can direct business to certain service providers. Real estate salespersons often can direct the homebuyer to a certain lender. That lender, in turn, can often direct the borrower to a particular attorney, appraiser, or title company. Payments from lenders to realtors are suspect, as are payments from attorneys, appraisers, and title companies to lenders.

RESPA prohibits any lender or other requirement that the borrower obtain title insurance from a certain title company. It also limits the amount of funds that can be required in an escrow account. Generally, no more than one-twelfth of the annual taxes and hazard insurance can be included in the monthly payment. Lenders may require that an additional amount be placed in escrow to cover any unexpected increases in taxes or insurance. This contingency is limited to one-sixth the current estimate of a reasonable annual charge.

Remedies Under RESPA

RESPA does not provide for an equitable remedy or a right of rescission. Nothing in the act affects the validity or enforceability of any sale, contract for the sale of real estate, or any loan agreement. The act provides for damages for the abusive practices violations. In such cases the damaged party can recover attorneys' fees and treble damages. There is also a criminal penalty for abusive practices. Finally, if the laws within a given state provide greater protection than RESPA, those laws will be the ones in effect.

RESPA's Effect on Real Estate Sales

After RESPA was passed, technological developments and changing market structure created conflicts of interest within the mortgage-origination sector of the market. Advances in computer technology gave birth to **computer loan origination systems** (CLOs). CLOs allowed borrowers to view, and in some cases apply for, loans from an extensive list provided by lenders. The ability of borrowers to select loans by computer led some large institutional lenders to align themselves with real estate sales firms in order to capture the borrower at the point of first contact. Traditional mortgage lenders, particularly mortgage bankers, saw the new alignments between the large institutional investors and the real estate sales firms as a threat to their market share. They claimed that such arrangements had the potential to violate Title 8 of RESPA.

CLOs, introduced in the early 1980s, are of two types. One type is a "loan information network" that allows all lenders the opportunity to display their loans and rates to potential borrowers. Borrowers view the alternative loans and then make separate contact with the lender. The loan listings are updated periodically, either by the lenders or the staff employed by the CLO system. The listings usually are displayed on a computer in a participating realtor's office. Another type of CLO is the "integrated origination and processing system." These networks contain loan applications that are completed on a computer screen and transmitted to a centralized processing and underwriting station for approval. The real estate salesperson takes the application information from the borrower at the point of sale. This type of CLO system also may allow the salesperson to track the loan through its processing stages. This type of CLO generally has some sort of a prequalification program that is used to gain an initial indication of the likelihood that the loan will be approved.

CLOs are either private networks or open networks. Private networks only offer the loans chosen by the sponsor of the network, and only affiliated originators may use the system. Open networks allow any lender who pays a participation fee to list loans on the system and receive processed loans. Private networks have been the object of criticism by those who think they may lead to violations of RESPA.

One example of a controversial private network is Citicorp's Mortgage Power Program. This program began in 1981 on a limited, regional basis and, by 1990, accounted for approximately 5 percent of the national first mortgage market. The program lined up participating realtors and offered loans at attractive terms to homebuyers. In effect, Citicorp used the program to reach the homebuyer at the first point of contact, the real estate salesperson. By marketing its loans in this manner, Citicorp avoided large marketing costs, including those hard costs (bricks-and-mortar) required to open offices throughout the country. Because of these lower marketing costs, Citicorp was able to offer loans with fewer or no origination points or other fees. The participating real estate sales firms were able to charge a fee for their service and still remain competitive.

Critics of the Citicorp program claimed the relationship was a form of disguised referral fees. Instead of charging points for the loans and sending a portion to the referring real estate sales firm, Citicorp simply reduced its origination fees and allowed the real estate firm to substitute its own charges. Participants claimed that the charges made by the real estate sales firms were compensation for financial advice and loan consultation—charges allowed under RESPA. Citicorp, in fact, sought the opinion of HUD before implementing their program on a nationwide basis. In 1986 the general counsel of HUD issued an opinion that Mortgage Power did not violate RESPA.

Citicorp's position was buttressed by two court cases, *United States v. Graham Mortgage Corp.* and *Eisenberg v. Comfed Mortgage.*[1] In these cases the courts basically said it was not clear that HUD had intended that the definition of settlement charges include the origination of a loan. One can understand how traditional lenders would be threatened by a mortgage origination system that attracts the consumer at the point of sale and give sales firms the incentive to divert loan business to large institutional investors.

---

[1] 564 F. Supp. 1239 (E.D. Mich. 1983), rev'd 740 2nd 414 (6th Cir. 1984), reh'g den.

In 1992 HUD issued a rule that allowed companies to pay employees for referrals to affiliated firms as long as customers were informed about the affiliation. In response to pressure from lenders (the Mortgage Bankers Association filed a lawsuit) the Clinton administration requested that HUD revise the rules. The revision, issued in 1994 and proposed as a final rule in 1996, revoked the 1992 rule allowing referrals. It did, however, create several exemptions. The 1996 rule allowed, for example, a managerial employee to be compensated if a certain percentage of her clients do business with affiliated firms. She cannot be paid on a per-referral basis. Also, a nonmanagerial employee who does not provide settlement services (stock broker, for example) can be paid for referrals. Finally, a financial services representative who markets services for several companies can be paid on a commission basis but cannot perform settlement services.

This 1996 rule also eliminates exemptions for CLOs where the borrower pays the fee, but allows all CLO fees (by borrowers, lenders, or others) if the fee reasonably relates to the value of services provided. The revisions incorporated in the 1996 rule brought more complaints from settlement providers and HUD delayed implementation until July 1997. Finally, the 1996 revisions included a policy statement that defined acceptable services of a CLO. The statement indicated that a CLO may:

1. Provide information concerning products or services.
2. Prequalify a prospective buyer.
3. Provide consumers with an opportunity to select ancillary services.
4. Provide prospective borrowers with information regarding the rates and terms of loan products.
5. Collect and transmit information on properties for evaluation by lenders.
6. Provide loan origination, processing, and underwriting services.
7. Make final funding decisions. Table 14-1 shows the advantages and disadvantages of CLO systems as perceived by advocates and opponents.

Information on Financing Costs

The federal government has also determined that consumers in search of a mortgage would benefit from more information on the financing costs of these loans.

Table 14-1
Advantages and Disadvantages of CLOs

Advantages	Disadvantages
Less costly form of loan origination for lenders	Danger of steering business and paying referral fees (kickbacks)
Access to more geographically dispersed markets	Less professional loan counseling and less quality control
Incentives for aggressive rate competition	Loss of lender identity
Side-by-side loan comparisons for borrowers	Closing off of a sizable portion of the market to traditional lenders
Reduces processing and approval time	

When the lender requires the borrower to pay discount points, origination fees, and mortgage insurance the actual cost of the loan can be greater than expected. In other words, even though the loan may carry an interest rates of, say, 8 percent, after considering points, origination fees, and other charges that actual "effective" rate of interest will often be greater. Because most borrowers lack the financial sophistication to determine the "effective" rate (called the annual percentage rate), federal legislation requires lenders to provide this and other financial information. The financial disclosures are included in legislation passed in 1968 called the Consumer Credit Protection Act or the Truth-in-Lending Act.

Consumer Credit Protection Act

Title I of the **Consumer Credit Protection Act** of 1968, containing the Truth-in-Lending law, and the Fair-Credit Billing Acts require lenders to provide full information about any loan they grant to a customer. The act gives the board of governors of the Federal Reserve System the authority to set standards and regulate this portion of the act. The regulatory requirements established by the board, referred to as **Regulation Z**, became effective July 1, 1969. They apply to both consumer loans (installment and revolving credit) and to residential mortgages. Loans exempt from Regulation Z include commercial and agricultural loans, loans from a securities dealer to a customer to purchase securities (margin account), student loans, and loans over $25,000 not secured by real property. Residential loans covered by the act include those used to purchase a one- to four-family dwelling, including condominiums, mobile homes, and trailers. Loans for transactions involving dwellings with more than four units are considered commercial and are not covered by the regulations. Also, an owner-seller of a single-family residence who extends credit to a purchaser is not required to conform to the regulations. The regulations do apply to second mortgages. The regulations are not intended to set maximum or minimum loan terms but rather to ensure the consumer is made fully aware of the essential terms of any loan. The motive is to provide consumers with sufficient and early information so that they may shop and compare charges among various loans.

Disclosure must be made in writing and in a form the borrower may keep. Disclosures must be made prior to the consummation of the loan or within three business days after the lender receives an application for the loan. This three-day period coincides with the same period that a lender has to provide good-faith estimates of settlement costs under RESPA. If the lender does not know the precise credit terms, the lender must make the disclosures based on the best information reasonably available and must indicate which items are estimates.

The two most important loan features that must be revealed to the consumer are the total finance charges and the annual percentage rate of interest (APR). These two items must be made more "conspicuous" than any other items of disclosure.

Total Finance Charges

Total finance charges are the total of all charges over the life of the loan and include interest charges, origination fees (points), discount points, appraisal and credit report fees, premiums for creditor life and accident insurance (should the borrower die, the mortgage balance will be paid), and mortgage insurance premiums. Not included in finance charges are any fees that would be associated with the sale of the property, even if no mortgage were involved. These typically include application fees, charges for delinquent payments or default, sales taxes, transfer taxes, recording fees, attorney fees, title examination fees, deed preparation fees, and the like. In some cases the lender may charge the seller of the property "points" for extending a mortgage to the buyer. Such charges are not considered finance charges under Regulation Z, even if the seller of the property raises its price to recoup the cost of the points. The same is true for any other seller-paid fees, such as mortgage insurance premiums.

In addition to the amount of the total finance charges, the lender must disclose the number, amount, and due date of each payment. Disclosure also is required for any prepayment penalties, delinquency and penalty charges, and prepaid finance charges. Prepaid finance charges represent an interest charge for the first partial month payment until regular payments begin.

Annual Percentage Rate

The **annual percentage rate** (APR) is the effective yield on a loan. The APR will be greater than the contract rate of interest when there are up-front finance charges, such as origination and discount points. To understand how the APR is calculated, first consider a simple mortgage with no finance charges other than the contract rate of interest of, say, 10 percent. The contract rate establishes the payment. When additional finance charges are considered, the monthly payment remains the same and the lender may quote the same contract rate, 10 percent. Origination and discount points will have the effect of reducing the amount of the effective loan amount below the face value. The right side of the equation is the monthly payment annuity. If the left side (loan amount) is reduced, then the equation will no longer be in balance. Raising the

Mortgage Math: Calculation of APR

The monthly payment on a $100,000 loan at 10% is $877.57. This means that

$$\$100{,}000 = \frac{877.57}{(1+.00833)^1} + \frac{877.57}{(1+.00833)^2} + \frac{877.57}{(1+.00833)^3} + \ldots + \frac{877.57}{(1+.00833)^{360}}$$

Now, if $4,000 is charged for points and origination fees combined, then the left side of the equation becomes $96,000. The equation would be out of balance if the right side were not reduced. This reduction is accomplished by raising the value of the interest rate in the denominators as follows:

$$\$96{,}000 = \frac{877.57}{(1+.00874)^1} + \frac{877.57}{(1+.00874)^2} + \frac{877.57}{(1+.00874)^3} + \ldots + \frac{877.57}{(1+.00874)^{360}}$$

Now, .00874 per month times twelve months is 10.5 percent annually. So the charge of four discount points results in an APR of 10.5 percent, one-half percent greater than the contract rate.

discount rate restores the balance. The discount rate that restores the balance is the annual percentage rate. It is found just as the internal rate of return is calculated in traditional capital budgeting problems or commercial real estate investment analysis. As in those cases, lenders have no set formulas that will conveniently yield the APR. Computer programs are available to search for the correct APR.

The regulations require that the APR reported to the borrower be within 0.125 percent of the true APR (0.25 percent for adjustable-rate mortgages). Thus, if a fixed-rate mortgage had an APR of 10.57 percent and the lender reported it as 10.5 percent, she would be within the allowed tolerance. A lender may be absolved from any error that is made if the calculation was made through the use of a calculation tool (for example, a computer program) used in good faith. To be absolved, the lender must have taken reasonable steps to verify the accuracy of the calculation tool.

Now, the lender calculates the APR of a 30-year loan on the basis of a borrower holding the loan for the full 30-year period. If the borrower repays the loan prior to its maturity, the actual cost increases. The discount and origination points are "spread out" over a fewer number of years. For loans prepaid early in their life, the actual cost can be substantially greater than the contract rate. The actual cost is inversely related to the holding period of the loan. Regulation Z does not require that these other costs be disclosed, only the one based on a 30-year holding period. Depending on the borrower's expected holding period for a loan, the APR revealed by the lender can lead to an incorrect choice of loans.

SIDEBAR

Loans A and B have different contract rates and up-front points. The actual APRs for each loan as a function of the holding period are shown in Figure 14-2.

Mortgage A has the lower "Reg. Z" APR (based on the term of the loan, *N*). If the borrower plans to hold the loan less than *T** years, mortgage A will have the higher actual APR. Most borrowers are likely not sophisticated enough to make these subtle distinctions. Yet, there is no current requirement that a loan's APR based on different holding periods be disclosed.

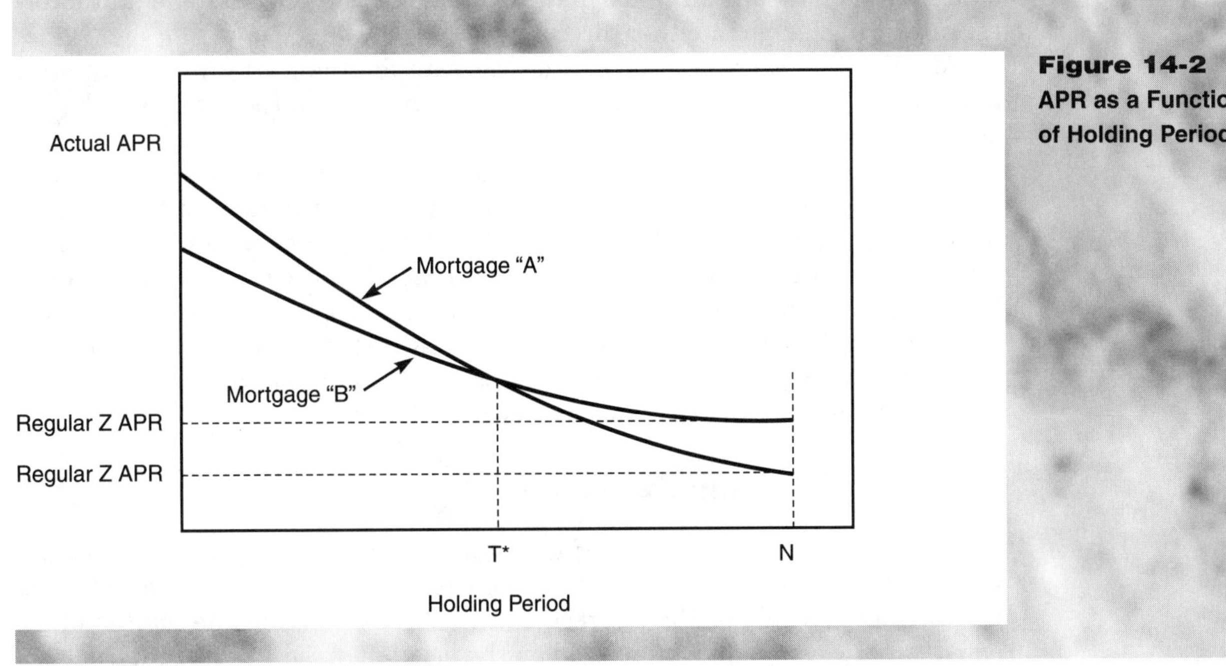

Figure 14-2
APR as a Function of Holding Period

Regulation Z and Alternative Mortgage Instruments

Special rules apply to a wide variety of the alternative mortgage instruments, some of which were discussed in the previous chapters, including graduated-payment mortgages, adjustable-rate mortgages, shared appreciation mortgages, buy-down mortgages, and home equity loans.

Graduated-Payment Mortgages

Consider a graduated-payment mortgage with a five-year graduation period and a 7.5 percent yearly increase in payments. The loan amount is \$44,900 and carries a 14.75 percent rate of interest. Finance charges include two discount points (\$898) and an initial mortgage-insurance premium of \$225. The following equation can be used to compute the APR:

$$\begin{aligned} \$43{,}777 = {} & \$446.62/(1 + r/12)^{1} + \ldots + \$479.67/(1 + r/12)^{13} + \ldots \\ & + \$515.11/(1 + r/12)^{25} + \ldots + \$553.13/(1 + r/12)^{37} + \ldots \\ & + \$593.91/(1 + r/12)^{49} + \ldots + \$673.68/(1 + r/12)^{61} + \ldots \\ & + \$673.68/(1 + r/12)^{360} \end{aligned}$$

The resulting APR is 15.37 percent. The lender must advise the borrower that any negative amortization is a finance charge and not part of the amount financed.

Adjustable-Rate Mortgages

The major problem with estimating the APR on adjustable-rate mortgages (ARMs) is that the future payments are not known with certainty. They will go up or down with movements in the index. Disclosure of finance charges is generally based on the initial terms of the loan. Lenders cannot assume that interest rates will change in either direction.

Many ARMs carry a reduced interest rate for the initial period. In such cases the APR is computed as a time-weighted average of the rates over the life of the loan.

The lender also must disclose general information about its ARM loans, including the margin; the index used and where information on the index is published (such as *The Wall Street Journal*); the frequency with which the rate can change; any caps on the interest rate change, either periodically or over the life of the loan; any cap on the payment change; and any provision for negative amortization. The lender also is required to provide the borrower with an example showing how payments on its ARM loan would have changed over a recent period of time. Historical indexes are used for this purpose.

Shared Appreciation Mortgages

With this type of loan, the lender receives a share of the appreciation in the value of the property in return for a reduction in the initial rate of interest. Because the amount of the appreciation is unknown when the loan is originated, all disclosures must be based on the original, fixed interest rate.

Mortgage Math: ARM Example

Consider an ARM with a 2 percent margin, originated when the index is 10 percent. The contract rate, if fully indexed, would be 12 percent. The lender may agree to a first-year rate of 9 percent. In this case the APR, assuming no other finance charges, would be 11.90 percent, based on the first year at 9 percent and the remaining years at 12 percent. If the loan were for $100,000, the lender would have to disclose that there would be 12 payments of $804.62, and 348 payments of $1,025.31.

	Years	Interest Rate	Total
	1	9	9
	29	12	348
Totals	30		357

Weighted average = 357/30 = 11.9

Buy-Down Mortgages

In certain transactions the seller or another third party may agree to pay an amount to the lender in order to reduce the borrower's payments or to reduce the interest rate for a portion of the loan's term. If the lower rate is reflected in the terms of the contract, then the disclosures must take the buy-down into account. As with ARMs, the APR must be a composite rate that takes into account the lower initial rate and the higher subsequent rate. Payment disclosures also must reflect the two levels. If the lower rate is not reflected in the contract (as might be the case where a side contract is made between the party providing the buy-down and the borrower), then the disclosure provided by the lender cannot reflect the buy-down. The effect of all borrower buy-downs must be included in the disclosure.

Home Equity Loans

Home equity loans (HELs) are usually open-ended; the borrower can "take down" amounts as needed up to a level determined by the value of the equity in the property. There is no amortization schedule, but the loan will generally stipulate minimum monthly payments. The rate on HELs is almost always variable and tied to some money market index, such as short-term Treasury yields. HELs can be best described as open-ended, nonamortizing, adjustable-rate mortgages.

Disclosure regulations require that the lender inform the borrower that the lender will acquire a security interest in the home. The lender also must inform the borrower that certain conditions may allow the lender to terminate the loan (require full payment of the balance), deny any further extensions of credit, or reduce the credit limit. One such condition would be the failure to meet repayment terms as determined by agreement between the lender and borrower. Payment terms also must be disclosed, including the periodic rate, how the rate is determined, and a statement that paying only the interest charge will not reduce the principal of the loan.

The lender also must provide an example of how payments would behave based on a $10,000 extension of credit and the most recent 15-year history of the index value. The example must reflect all significant loan terms, such as negative amortization, rate carryover, rate discounts, and rate and payment limitations that would have been affected by the index movement during that period. The board of governors of the Federal Reserve System made several additional minor changes in disclosure requirements as a result of the Home Equity Loan Consumer Protection Act of 1988. Lenders are no longer required to provide HEL disclosures to a borrower as a result of the latter's inquiry into credit other than a HEL. Also, fees charged to a borrower who voluntarily closes out an HEL account prior to its scheduled maturity need not be disclosed. Because hazard insurance is already carried on the property securing most HELs, the lender need not disclose the amount of insurance premiums but only that property insurance is required.

Other Regulation Z Requirements

Under Regulation Z the borrower has the right to rescind the credit transaction within a short period after it has been consummated. This right allows the cancellation of any agreement that the borrower may have been pressured into accepting. The borrower may cancel the transaction within three business days or the receipt of a notice of rescission, whichever occurs later. If a complete and accurate disclosure of the finance charges as required by the regulation has not been made, then the three-day rescission period is extended until such disclosures have been made. The borrower may not waive the right of rescission unless a financial emergency arises, and then he may do so only in writing. There can be no preprinted forms for this purpose. The right of rescission does not apply to first mortgages on residential properties where the borrower is not a natural person (if the borrower is a corporation, for example) or if the loan is for a business purpose. Also, the borrower does not have a right to rescind a mortgage transaction for other than a principal dwelling. A borrower cannot rescind a loan made to purchase a second, or a vacation, home.

Regulation Z also prescribes certain practices for advertising in the print media (newspaper, billboards, fliers, window displays, and the like). If the advertisement contains any information about a single financing term, such as the down payment, installment payments, number of payments, or length of the loan, then it must also disclose all the other terms, including the cash price; down payment; number, amount, and due dates of payments; and the annual percentage rate of interest. Furthermore, such information cannot be relegated to the "fine print" section of the advertisement.

Finally, Regulation Z provides for both civil remedies and criminal penalties. The civil remedy is an amount equal to twice the finance charge involved (but not less than $100 nor more than $1,000), plus attorneys' fees and court costs. Additional damages suffered by the borrower also can be recovered. If, for example, the borrower obtains a loan with an advertised APR of 10 percent and it turns out that the lender miscalculated and the actual APR is 11 percent, the borrower may claim damages. Specifically, the borrower might have been able to obtain another loan with a true APR of 10 percent. The borrower can seek reimbursement for the difference in the finance charges. Criminal penalties for noncompliance (a misdemeanor) include one year in jail or a $5,000 fine, or both. Lenders can avoid the civil and criminal penalties if the violation was the result of a miscalculation, but the borrower may still seek damages.

Summary

The influence of the federal government on housing and housing finance issues is pervasive. Legislation is concerned with making housing more affordable, making borrowers more knowledgeable, making the market for housing and housing finance more efficient, and moving toward the elimination of discrimination. Two sets of laws, in particular, are concerned with making more information available to the consumers on the one hand and prohibiting discrimination on the other.

Laws enacted to increase knowledge include RESPA, which requires advanced disclosure of all the costs associated with the settlement (sale) process, and the Consumer Credit Protection Act, which requires lenders to provide advanced information on the cost of a mortgage, including the all important actual rate of interest (APR) charged.

Laws enacted to prohibit discrimination in lending include the Equal Credit Opportunity Act, the Home Mortgage Disclosure Act, and the Community Reinvestment Act. The ECOA, initiated by complaints of discrimination against women, includes prohibitions against other discrimination as well. The HMDA and the CRA are laws that encourage and monitor lenders in an effort to provide more housing financing to minorities and to impoverished neighborhoods.

Key Terms and Definitions

abusive practices—Prohibited lender practices, usually in terms of discrimination, that are constant, pervasive, and extensive.

annual percentage rate—The annual rate of interest on a loan after consideration for additional loan charges such as origination points, discount points, and mortgage insurance.

Community Reinvestment Act—A federal act that encourages banks to define their communities and take proactive efforts to increase lending in underserved markets.

computerized loan organization systems—Networks of lenders that offer their loan products, which can be accessed by computers.

Consumer Credit Protection Act (truth-in-lending)—A federal law that requires lenders to provide information about their loans, in particular, the annual percentage rate and the total finance charges over the life of the loan.

Equal Credit Opportunity Act—A federal law that prohibits lenders from discriminating on the basis of gender, race, or national origin.

Home Mortgage Disclosure Act—A federal law that requires lenders to disclose the geographic locations of their loans within their service areas in an attempt to prevent lenders from redlining.

Real Estate Settlement Procedures Act—A federal law that requires lenders to provide borrowers with the cost of the various settlement (sale) costs prior to and at the actual transaction.

redlining—A lender practice of refusing to make loans in what they may regard as high-risk neighborhoods. It comes from the practice of drawing a red line around the high-risk neighborhoods on a map.

Regulation Z—The regulation of the Federal Reserve Board that applies to the Consumer Credit Protection Act requirement that lenders disclose the APR and total finance charges associated with their loans.

Uniform Settlement Statement—A statement of the costs associated with the settlement (sale) of a property as required by RESPA.

Review Questions

1. What is the motivation behind the Equal Credit Protection Act?
2. Indicate three ways discriminatory lending practices can be defined. How does Regulation B attempt to define such practices?
3. What is the motivation behind the Home Mortgage Disclosure Act?
4. what is the motivation behind the Real Estate Settlement Procedures Act?
5. What is the effect of a mortgage prepayment on the actual APR?
6. Why do origination points and/or discount points increase the APR?
7. What are the two main disclosures required by the Consumer Credit Protection Act?

Problems to Solve (Answers may be checked against the Answer section)

1. Assuming a 30-year $100,000 loan at 9 percent annual rate:
   a. what would the monthly payment be?
   b. what would the APR be if the total origination and discount points were
      (1) zero points?
      (2) two points?
      (3) four points?
2. Assume four discount points in the previous problem. What would the actual or effective APR be if the loan were paid off at the end of ten years?

Related Web Site

A good source of consumer credit is:
http://www4.law.cornell.edu/uscode/15/ch41.html.

Chapter 15

Federal Subsidies and Grants for Housing

Chapter Outline

Learning Objectives

After reading this chapter you will be able to:

- Describe the major federal government programs that are in place to assist low- and moderate-income families in obtaining housing.
- Discuss the motivation behind the programs.
- List the restrictions and requirements placed on the recipients of the benefits by the federal government.

Key Terms

Community Development Block Grant (CDBG)
Department of Housing and Urban Development (HUD)
entitlement community
Fair Housing Act
HOME Investment Partnerships Program
homeless assistance
Section 108 Loan Guarantee Program
subsidized public housing

Introduction

As we have seen elsewhere, real estate finance is significantly affected by a host of government policies and programs. Some of those programs have been developed specifically to help our families that have low to moderate incomes obtain housing.

Department of Housing and Urban Development

Nearly all of the assistance to low- and moderate-income families that is provided by the federal government is done through the **Department of Housing and Urban Development (HUD)**. HUD programs assist families in obtaining shelter in both single-family and multi-family properties through direct grants and subsidies. It also works to enforce fair housing laws and develop the inner cities. The department was created as part of President Lyndon Johnson's War on Poverty and given cabinet status on November 9, 1965, but its history extends back to the National Housing Act of 1934.

HUD currently lists its goals as:

- Fighting for fair housing (that is, fighting discrimination against protected classes such as race, gender, handicapped, and so forth)
- Increasing the affordability of housing for low- and moderate-income families
- Reducing homelessness
- Promoting jobs and economic opportunity (especially in economically depressed areas such as the central cities)
- Empowering people and communities

HUD Programs

To meet its goals, the following programs are offered by HUD:

Community Development Block Grants. These grants help communities with economic development and housing rehabilitation

Subsidized Housing, Section 8. Provides certificates or vouchers for low-income families.

Subsidized Public Housing. Provides affordable housing for low-income families.

Homeless Assistance. Provided through local communities and nonprofit organizations.

HOME Investment Partnership Act Block Grants. These grants help develop and support affordable housing for low-income families.

Fair Housing Act. Provides enforcement of fair housing laws that prohibit discrimination.

Mortgage and Loan Insurance. Provided as discussed in Chapter 12.

Support of secondary mortgage market activities. Support is provided through the activities of the Government National Mortgage Association (GNMA or Ginnie Mae, a wholly owned federal corporation within HUD, which is discussed in detail in Chapter 3).

Community Development Block Grant Program

HUD's **Community Development Block Grant (CDBG)** program was established in 1974 to help states and local communities develop their economically depressed areas. CDBG funds are awarded to states and local areas on a formula basis and may be used for a wide array of economic activities, not just residential housing. They can be used to aid low- and moderate-income individuals and families, prevent or rehabilitate slum or blight conditions, and meet urgent needs that may threaten the health and safety of the local citizens. Funds can be used to acquire real property, renovate housing, improve public facilities such as water, sewer, streets and neighborhood centers, promote activities related to energy conservation and renewable energy resources, and promote job creation activities.

The CDBG formula allocates 70 percent of its funds to **entitlement communities** (larger cities with populations over 50,000 and central cities and urban counties with populations of at least 200,000) and 30 percent to states, which then distribute the funds to smaller communities. HUD determines the amount of each entitlement grant by a statutory dual formula that uses several objective measures of community needs, including the extent of poverty, population, housing overcrowding, age of the housing stock and population growth lag in relationship to other metropolitan areas. In fiscal year 1996, $4.6 billion in CDBG grants was distributed to 1,005 entitlement communities and states. Of this amount $1.6 billion was used for public facilities and $1.46 billion was used for housing activities.

To receive a CDBG entitlement grant, the grantee must develop and submit to HUD a consolidated plan. The jurisdiction identifies its goals and considers other HUD programs in the plan (such as the HOME Investment Partnerships and Emergency Shelter Grants).

CDBG Section 108 Loan Guarantee Program

The **Section 108 Loan Guarantee Program** provides communities with financing for economic development, housing rehabilitation, public facilities, and large-scale physical development projects. Eligible activities include economic development activities under CDBG, acquisition of real property, rehabilitation of publicly owned real property, construction and reconstruction of public facilities, and public works and site improvements.

Assisted Housing: Vouchers and Certificates

HUD assists low-income households with rental subsidies in the private sector, primarily through what is known as Section 8 vouchers and certificates. The Section 8 program is handled through the Office of Public and Indian Housing. Families needing help with meeting their rental payments apply for Section 8 assistance through their local public housing agency.

Under the Section 8 voucher program, families have a freedom of choice in selecting the housing they wish to occupy. The rental unit must meet acceptable health and safety levels before the housing agency can approve payments to landlords under either the voucher or the certificate program. The housing agency inspects the property and approves the lease. The Office of Public and Indian Housing provides the funds for the rental voucher through a program that is managed by the local public housing agencies (PHAs). The latter are created by state law, administered through local governments, and work with the Office of Public and Indian Housing.

Under the Section 8 certificate program, rent subsidies pay the owner of the rental unit the difference between what the tenants can afford and the market rental rate. The maximum market rents are adjusted on a periodic basis to reflect increased costs of rent and utilities. Rental certificate holders generally pay either 30 percent of their monthly *adjusted* income or 10 percent of their *gross* income toward rent and utilities. Eligibility for a rental voucher or certificate is determined by the local housing agency and is based on total annual gross income and family size. In general, the family's income cannot exceed 50 percent of the median income for the county or the metropolitan area in which the family chooses to live. Median income levels for each area are published by HUD and vary by location. Overall, more than 3 million households received Section 8 rental assistance in fiscal year 1996.

In rural communities the Department of Agriculture provides rental assistance programs, home improvement and repair loans and grants, and self-help housing loans to low-income individuals and families.

Subsidized Public Housing for Low-Income Households

HUD's **subsidized public housing** programs provide direct payment to local PHAs to develop and operate housing for low-income families. In fiscal year 1996, HUD distributed more than $6.2 billion to approximately 3,350 local public housing authorities, which, in turn, provided public housing and services to approximately 1.3 million households. Some of the support includes the following:

- Funds for modernization under a *Comprehensive Grant Program* (CGP) for large PHAs (more than 250 units) as well as under the *Comprehensive Assistance Improvement Program* (CIAP) for smaller PHAs. The funds in both these programs are used to improve the physical condition of PHA properties.
- The *Tenant Opportunity Program* (TOP), a set-aside within the modernization program discussed above. TOP funds are used to promote resident organization and management of the properties in which they reside.
- *Operating subsidies* that assist the local PHAs in the cost of operating and maintaining the facilities that they own.

- *Drug elimination grants*, which are allocated to PHAs on an as-needed basis to help fight drugs.

Homeless Assistance

HUD provides funds to state and local governments (as well as other nonprofit organizations) to assist homeless individuals and families. The funds are used to help move the homeless from the streets to a temporary shelter, supportive housing, and back into the mainstream of life. These efforts have their origin in the Stewert B. McKinney Homeless Assistance Act of 1987. This act provides for direct HUD grants to communities to help them deal with homelessness. The **homeless assistance** is carried out through the Office for Community Planning and Development (CPD). The CPD administers the *Shelter Plus Care* program that provides rental assistance for the homeless. Recipients must provide supportive services equal to the value of the assistance.

CPD also administers the *Supportive Housing* program, which supplies grants to state and local governments to provide short-term transitional housing for homeless individuals, especially those with mental afflictions or with AIDs. Finally, the *Emergency Shelter Grants* program provides funds to states, counties, and territories to be used to renovate and rehabilitate older buildings so that they can be used to shelter the homeless.

HOME Investment Partnerships Program

The **HOME Investment Partnerships Program**, administered by the CPD, was created by the 1990 Cranston-Gonzalez National Affordable Housing Act. It provides funds for participating jurisdictions to increase the supply of affordable housing for low-income families. The funds are distributed on a formula basis and are administered on the local level through community development departments and housing finance agencies.

Participating jurisdictions must provide a 25 percent match for housing activities supported by HOME. The matching funds must come from nonfederal sources and may include donated materials or labor.

HUD establishes Home Investment Trust Funds for each locality. The trust fund provides a line of credit that the jurisdiction can draw on as needed.

States are automatically eligible for HOME funds, whereas local jurisdictions are conditionally eligible for at least $500,000 under the formula. Local jurisdiction can use the funds to provide home purchase or rehabilitation financing assistance to low-income homeowners or new homebuyers. Funds can also be used to demolish dilapidated housing to make room for a new HOME-assisted development. The funds can also be used to provide rental assistance to low-income households for up to two years. In fiscal year 1998, HUD allocated $1.5 billion to this program.

Fair Housing Act Enforcement

HUD's programs to prevent discrimination in housing through public education and enforcement are administered by the Assistant Secretary for Fair Housing and Equal Opportunity (FHEO). In addition to investigating and resolving complaints of discrimination under the fair housing laws, FHEO conducts compliance reviews of HUD funds recipients, ensures equal employment opportunity and affirmative action within HUD, and ensures that HUD programs provide equal opportunity. Under its Fair Housing Assistance Program (FHAP), FHEO assists state and local governments in becoming certified as having "substantially equivalent" fair housing laws. The FHEO operates the Fair Housing Initiatives Program (FHIP), which provides funds to public and private agencies so that they may assist HUD in its enforcement activities such as testing, investigations, and complaint resolution. FHIP also conducts education programs to alert the public to activities that constitute a violation of the **Fair Housing Act**.

Mortgage Loan Insurance Program

HUD administers the Federal Housing Administration (FHA) mortgage program. This program offers mortgage insurance to many homebuyers who would otherwise not qualify for private mortgage insurance. Often many homebuyers, especially first-time homebuyers, cannot afford the large down payment required for conventional loans and private mortgage insurance. The FHA insurance program allows these homebuyers to purchase homes with mortgage insurance.

The Assistant Secretary for Housing–Federal Housing Commissioner administers approximately 10 mortgage insurance programs. As of the end of 1996, the FHA had insurance in force on 6.5 million single-family residences totaling $401 billion. The FHA also assists in providing affordable rental housing by insuring loans to developers and builders of multifamily properties. As of the end of 1996, FHA had insurance in force on 15,935 properties totaling $48.6 billion.

Summary

The federal government, through the Department of Housing and Urban Development, offers various forms of housing assistance to low-income households. Through HUD programs, these families have opportunities to occupy adequate housing that would not otherwise be within reach of their financial resources. HUD also provides funds for the general improvement of the conditions of the neighborhoods within which low-income households reside. Several different programs have the same or overlapping goals. States and local jurisdiction must develop a comprehensive plan that considers all of the sources of funds and all of the goals from the various HUD programs. Details of the programs change from year to year and recent updates can be found on the Internet at http://www.hud.gov/.

Key Terms and Definitions

Community Development Block Grant (CDBG)—HUD program that provides funds to cities and urban counties on a formula basis to entitled communities to carry out a wide range of community development projects.

Department of Housing and Urban Development (HUD)—Established by the Housing and Urban Development Act of 1965, HUD supersedes the Housing and Home Finance Agency. It is responsible for the implementation and administration of government housing and urban development programs. The broad range of programs includes community planning and development, housing production and mortgage credit (FHA), equal opportunity in housing, and research and technology.

entitlement community—Communities entitled to receive annual grants under the CDBG program. The entitlement community is generally made up of central cities within SMSAs, other cities with populations of at least 50,000, and urban counties with populations of at least 200,000.

Fair Housing Act—Act passed in 1968 to prohibit discrimination in the sale or rent of housing on the bases of race, color, religion, or national origin. Gender was added by the Housing and Community Development act of 1974.

HOME Investment Partnerships Program—A grant to states and localities that communities may use in partnership with local nonprofit groups to fund activities that build, buy, and rehabilitate affordable housing for rent or ownership for low-income households.

homeless assistance—Grants for rental assistance for the homeless.

Section 108 Loan Guarantee Program—A loan guarantee program for public entities such as cities and urban counties, the proceeds of which are to be used for various programs under the CDBG.

subsidized public housing—Various programs of the federal government to help low-income households pay market rent.

Review Questions

1. List the main goals of HUD.
2. List the major federal government programs that are in place to assist low- and moderate-income families in obtaining housing.
3. What is the primary goal of HUD's CDBG program?
4. What is an entitlement community?
5. What is the function of the Section 108 Loan Guarantee Program?
6. What portion of rent does the Section 8 certificate program pay?
7. Describe five programs supported by HUD through subsidized public housing.
8. For what purposes can local jurisdictions use HOME Investment Partnerships Program funds?
9. What are the goals and duties of the FHEO?
10. What is the main role of the FHA mortgage program?

Related Web Sites

Up-to-date information about HUD programs is available on the Internet at http://www.hud.gov and www.hudclips.org.

Answers to Chapter Problems

CHAPTER FOUR

1. 7%
2. real rate is 3%
3. 9%

CHAPTER FIVE

1. old bank $1,000 (1.06)^5 = $1,338.23
   new bank $1,000 (1+.06/12)^60 = $1,348.85
   difference = $10.62
2. option two 7.77%
   option three 7.72%
3. $129,402
4. $38,311.39
5. $24,166.14
6. a. 15.24%
   b. 25.68%
7. $61,486.41
8. a. $1,727.14 per acre
   b. 5.76%
9. a. $13,121.08
   b. $1,062.19
10. 0.20X = $8,318.83,
    X = $41,594
11. $610.20
12. $12,800 per acre
13. $71,186
14. $36,324
15. $83,527

16. a. $7,347
    b. $7,430
    c. $82.73
    d. Option A = 8%
       Option B = 8.24%

CHAPTER EIGHT

1. $702.06
2. $71,356
3. a. $965.55
   b. $900
   c. $11,586.60 – $820 = $10,766.60
   d. $117,303
   e. $32,062.80
4. 8.75%
5. a. $798.81
   b. $91,429
   c.

	Total Paid Annually	Interest	Repayment of Principal	End of Year Balance
1	$9,585.74	$8,999.93	$585.81	$94,414
2	$9,585.74	$8,941.79	$643.95	$93,770
3	$9,585.74	$8,877.89	$707.86	$93,062
4	$9,585.74	$8,807.62	$778.11	$92,284
5	$9,585.74	$8,730.40	$855.34	$91,429

6. a. Loan 1 8.551%
      Loan 2 8.721%
      Loan 3 8.861%
   b. Loan 1 8.948%
      Loan 2 9.008%
      Loan 3 9.004%
   c. Loan 1 9.415%
      Loan 2 9.472%
      Loan 3 9.466%
7. a. $789.81
   b. $882.10
   c. $775.27
   d. $729.67
8. a. 11.63%
   b. 10.61%
   c. 9.18%
   d. 10.11%
9. a. 334 months
   b. 197 months
   c. 322 months
   d. never

10. a. \$8,840 or 8.84%
    b. \$7,444 or 76.76%
    c. \$16,747 or 13.39%
    d. 27.49%
11. a. \$96,574.15
    b. \$85,563.12
    c. \$78,130.57

CHAPTER NINE

1. a. \$877.57
   b. 0.00698* × \$100,000 = \$698.23 *from table in text
   c. \$421.60
   d. \$733.76
2. a. \$803.39 (amortize \$99,164 at 9% for 348 months)
   b. \$875.11 (amortize \$99,164 at 10% for 348 months)
   c. \$875.11
3. a. \$768.91
   b. \$875.81
   c. 10.327%
4. a. \$483.14, \$492,80, and \$507.59
   b. 8.11%
   c. 8.86%
5. FRM = 10.537%
   ARM = 10.885%
6. \$6,581.98
7. a. payment savings = \$105.76/mo. Present value = \$12,105
      Cost = \$6,953 Net present value = \$5,152 Refinance!
   b. Net present value = \$7,903 + \$1,109 – \$6,953 = \$1,249 Refinance!
   c. Net present value = –\$7,984 – \$7,863 + \$22,741 = \$6,894 Refinance!

CHAPTER TEN

1. **Conventional loan**
   PITI = \$2,834.54, PITI plus car loan = \$4,074.54
   \$2,834.54 = 0.28 × X, so X = \$10,123.36
   \$4,074.54 = 0.36 × X, so X = \$11,318.14

   FHA loan
   PITI + association dues = \$2,934.54
   PITI + association dues + car loan = \$4,174.54
   \$2,934.54 = 0.29 × X, so X = \$10,119.10
   \$4,174.54 = 0.41 × X, so X = \$10,181.80

CHAPTER ELEVEN

1. \$340,600
2. comparable one = \$181,900 + \$8,000 + \$1,300 = \$191,200
   comparable two = \$205,500 – \$8,000 – \$1,500 – \$1,300 = \$194,700
   average = \$192,950

CHAPTER TWELVE

1. FHA total exposure = \$120,000 + \$4,000 + \$5,000 + \$300 + \$800 + \$400 + \$550 + \$700
   = \$131,750
   loss = \$131,750 – \$100,000
   = \$31,750
   portion borne by lender = 0%

   VA payment is 25% of loan amount or the amount of loss whichever is less. Payment = \$31,250; lender loses \$500 or 1.57% of the total loss

   PMI exposure = \$120,000 + \$4,000 + \$3,720 (3% rule) +\$300 +\$550 +\$400 + \$800
   = \$129,000
   Loss = 31,750
   Payment = minimum of 0.15 × \$129,000 or \$129,000 – \$100,000
   = minimum of \$19,350 or \$29,000
   = \$19,350
   lender loses \$31,750 – \$19,350 = \$12,400 = 39.05%
2. Loss = Exposure less the value of the House (L = E – H)
   Claim = 0.15 × Exposure (C = 0.15 × E)
   Exposure = \$129,770
   = 120,000 + 4,000 + 3,720 + 300 + 550 + 40 + 800
   For no Loss, Claim must equal Loss (C = L)
   so E × J = 0.15 × E
   or 0.85 × E = H
   or 0.85 × \$129,770 = \$110,305
   Answer = \$110,305
3. Exposure = \$129,770
   Loss = \$29,770
   \$29,770 = 0.23 × \$129,770
   Answer = 23%

CHAPTER THIRTEEN

1. Calculation of profit:

sales price	\$250,000
less selling expense	(\$8,000)
less adj. basis	(\$133,000)
total gain	\$109,000

Sales price	$250,000
Exc. of mort. over adj. basis and selling exp.	0
Less mortgage balance assumed	0
Equals contract price	$250,000
Profit percentage =	0.436 (109,000/250,000)

Taxes on Installment Receipts

	1	2	3
principal portion	$29,830	$32,216	$34,794
plus balloon	$0	$0	$78,160
total principal	$29,830	$32,216	$112,954
times profit percentage	0.436	0.436	0.436
taxable principal	$13,006	$14,046	$49,248
times tax rate on principal	0.217*	0.217	0.217
tax on principal	$2,822	$3,048	$10,687
interest earned	$14,000	$11,614	$9,036
times marginal rate	0.28	0.28	0.28
tax on interest	$3,920	$3,252	$2,530
total tax	$6,742	$6,300	$13,217

*= (0.34)(0.25) + (0.66)(0.20) = 217

After-Tax Cash Flows

	1	2	3
before tax cash flows	$43,830	$43,830	$43,830
balloon payment	$0	$0	$78,160
less taxes	($6,742)	($6,300)	($13,217)
after-tax cash flow	$37,088	$37,530	$108,773

CHAPTER FOURTEEN

1. a. $804.62
   b. 1. 9%
      2. 9.22%
      3. 9.46%
2. Balance in year 10 = $89,429.74
   APR = 9.64%

GLOSSARY

ability-to-pay default theory The theory that mortgage defaults occur because the mortgagor is unable to meet the monthly payment.

abstract of title A condensed written history of title transactions and recorded instruments or condition bearing on the title to designated real estate.

abusive practices Prohibited lender practices, usually in terms of discrimination, that are constant, pervasive, and extensive.

adjustment rate cap A limit on the contract rate of interest (for a particular adjustment period) on an adjustable-rate mortgage. Commonly referred to as rate cap.

adjustable-rate mortgage (ARM) A type of mortgage in which the interest rate adjusts periodically according to a preselected index, such as Treasury bill rates, and a margin. This adjustment results in the mortgage payment either increasing or decreasing. Limits can be set on the amount by which interest rates or payments can change.

American Land Title Association (ALTA) A national association, founded in 1907, representing 2,100 title abstractors, title insurance companies, title insurance agents, and associate members. It is the role and responsibility of the title industry and its ALTA members to guarantee the safe, efficient transfer of real property and to provide protection for consumers and lenders alike. The association speaks for the title industry and establishes standard procedures and title policy forms.

amortization schedule A schedule showing the amount of each payment and the portion that is interest and the portion that is principal.

annual percentage rate (APR) The annual rate of interest on a loan after consideration for additional loan charges such as origination points, discount points, and mortgage insurance.

annuity A series of equal payments.

annuity due An annuity where the payments are made at the beginning of each payment period.

appraisal An estimate or opinion of value supported by factual data by a qualified person. Also, the process by which this estimate is obtained.

biweekly mortgage A mortgage with payments due every two weeks, totaling 26 payments per year.

boot Property that is not like-kind in a like-kind exchange. Cash is an example.

borrower qualification and loan underwriting The process of assessing the riskiness of a loan according to the financial position of the borrower.

building and loan association Early financial intermediary established to provide financing for neighborhood home loans.

callability risk The risk that a debt instrument, including a mortgage, will be paid off prior to maturity if the market rate of interest falls.

capital market A market where securities (stocks and bonds) with maturities greater than one year are traded.

cloud on title Any conditions revealed by a title search that adversely affect the clear title to real estate. A cloud on title is usually removed through a suit to quiet title.

co-insurance A sharing of insurance risk between insurer and owner depending on the relation of the amount of the policy and a specified percentage of the actual value of the property insured at the time of loss.

collateralize A security that has another asset that "backs" or guarantees payment of interest and principal.

collateralized mortgage obligation (CMO) A multiple-class, pay-through bond, first issued by the FHLMC in June 1983. CMOs are secured by a pool of mortgages or a portfolio of pass-through securities. The CMO provides a type of call protection and pays principal and interest semiannually rather than monthly, as a pass-through security does.

Community Development Block Grant (CDBG) HUD program that provides funds to cities and urban counties on a formula basis to entitled communities to carry out a wide range of community development projects.

Community Reinvestment Act A federal act that encourages banks to define their communities and take proactive efforts to increase lending in underserved markets.

compounding The process where interest is added to the principal amount periodically so that subsequent interest is earned not only on the original principal but on the added interest as well.

compounding annually The process of compounding on an annual basis—that is, interest is added at one-year intervals.

computerized loan organization systems Networks of lenders that offer their loan products, which can be accessed by computers.

conforming conventional loan A loan whose terms, such as the loan-to-value, comply with the requirements of the GSE's.

conforming mortgage A mortgage whose terms, such as its loan-to-value ratio and amount, must conform to the requirements of the three federal agencies before those agencies will agree to purchase them.

Consumer Credit Protection Act (truth-in-lending) A federal law that requires lenders to provide information about their loans; in particular, the annual percentage rate and the total finance charges over the life of the loan.

contract price In an installment sale, it is the selling price minus the balance of any mortgage assumed plus the excess of this mortgage balance over the sum of adjusted basis and selling expenses.

cost approach An appraisal technique used to establish value by first estimating the cost to reproduce the facility, then deducting for depreciation and finally adding the value of the land.

cost of funds index (COFI) Index for an adjustable-rate mortgage based on the average of interest rates paid by thrifts to their depositors (their cost of funds).

credit enhancement The process whereby the issuer of a mortgage-related security adds support to the underlying assets by contributing capital or overcollateralizing the assets.

debt instrument A security such as a promissory note or a bond that outlines the terms of the loan.

deed of trust (trust deed) A type of security instrument conveying title (in trust) to a third party (trustee). It is used to secure the payment of a note. A conveyance of the title land to a trustee as collateral security for the payment of a debt with the condition that the trustee shall reconvey the title to the borrower (trustor) upon the payment of the debt. The trustee has the power to sell the real estate and pay the debt in the event of a default on the part of the debtor.

default risk The risk of incurring a loss on a loan as a result of a default.

deficiency judgment A judgment levied against the borrower personally (personal assets) for the difference between the mortgage debt (including payments in arrears) and the liquidation value of the property.

deficit entity A household, business, or government that has current expenditures in excess of current income and must obtain funds from surplus entities.

Department of Housing and Urban Development (HUD) Established by the Housing and Urban Development Act of 1965, HUD supersedes the Housing and Home Finance Agency. It is responsible for the implementation and administration of government housing and urban development programs. The broad range of programs includes community planning and development, housing production and mortgage credit (FHA), equal opportunity in housing, and research and technology.

direct endorsement program An FHA program whereby qualified lenders are authorized to approve borrowers prior to all information being provided to the FHA.

direct transfer of funds The transfer of funds from a surplus entity to a deficit entity without the use of an intermediary.

discount point A fee charged by a lender at closing or settlement that results in increasing the lender's effective yield on the money borrowed. An amount equal to 1 percent of a loan's principal.

discounting The process of establishing an amount of money at present, that, with added interest, will equal a given amount of money in the future or a future value.

effective cost (yield) The rate of interest actually incurred when the mortgage is paid off before its scheduled maturity.

entitlement community Communities entitled to receive annual grants under the CDBG program. The entitlement community is generally made up of central cities within SMSAs, other cities with populations of at least 50,000, and urban counties with populations of at least 200,000.

Equal Credit Opportunity Act A federal law that prohibits lenders from discriminating on the basis of gender, race, or national origin.

equitable right of redemption The common law right to redeem property during the foreclosure period by paying past due amounts. In some states the mortgagor has a statutory right to redeem property after a foreclosure sale. This is limited to several months or a year.

equity default theory theory that states that mortgage defaults occur only if there is negative equity in the property.

equity interest Ownership in a business, usually through ownership of stock.

Fair Housing Act Act passed in 1968 to prohibit discrimination in the sale or rent of housing on the bases of race, color, religion, or national origin. Gender was added by the Housing and Community Development act of 1974.

Farmers Home Administration (FmHA) An agency within the Department of Agriculture that operates principally under the Consolidated Farm and Rural Development Act of 1921 and Title V of the Housing Act of 1949. This agency provides residential property financing to farmers and other qualified borrowers who are unable to obtain loans elsewhere.

Federal Agricultural Mortgage Corporation (FAMC) A corporation created by the Agricultural Credit Act and intended to act similarly to the GNMA and FNMA, but for farm mortgages.

federal credit agency Federally sponsored and/or supported agency that supports various activities such as housing or agriculture through credit availability.

Federal Financing Bank (FFB) A federal bank established by the federal Financing Bank Act of 1973 to consolidate and reduce the government's cost of financing a variety of federal agencies and other borrowers whose obligations are guaranteed by the federal government.

Federal Home Loan Mortgage Corporation (FHLMC) A private corporation authorized by Congress with an independent board of directors to provide secondary mortgage market support for conventional mortgages. It also sells participation certificates secured by pools of conventional mortgage loans. Popularly known as Freddie Mac, it is under the oversight of HUD.

Federal Housing Administration (FHA) Its main activity is the insuring of residential mortgage loans made by private lenders. FHA is a division of HUD, which sets standards for construction and underwriting and charges a fee, generally 3.8 percent of the loan amount.

Federal National Mortgage Association (FNMA) A privately owned corporation created by Congress to support the secondary mortgage market. It purchases and sells residential mortgages insured by the FHA or guaranteed by the VA, as well as conventional home mortgages. Popularly known as Fannie Mae, it is under the oversight of HUD.

fiducia In Roman times acted as a deed-of-trust.

fiduciary A person in a position of trust and confidence for another.

Financial Accounting Standards Board (FASB) An independent, private entity that establishes standards for financial accounting and reporting and derives its authority from the SEC.

fixed-rate mortgage A mortgage for which the interest rate does not change.

fully amortized mortgage A mortgage that has a portion of the principal paid so that there is no remaining balance with the last payment.

fully indexed rate The rate of interest on an adjustable-rate mortgage when no discount or teaser rate applies.

future value of an annuity An amount of money to be received at a future date.

gage A deposit or pledge to ensure fulfillment of an agreement.

Government National Mortgage Association (GNMA) Nicknamed Ginnie Mae, this HUD agency operates as a participant in the secondary mortgage market. It is involved with special government financing programs for urban renewal projects, elderly housing, and other high-risk mortgages. GNMA also carries out the liquidation and special assistance functions performed by the Federal National Mortgage Association prior to its reorganization in 1968. The association is involved with the mortgage securities pool and the tandem plan.

government-sponsored enterprise (GSE) Refers to the three federal housing agencies: GNMA, FNMA, and FHLMC.

graduated payment mortgage (GPM) A residential mortgage designed to overcome the tilt effect. The monthly mortgage payments start at a level below that on an FRM and increase at a predetermined rate with later payments above that on an FRM. They may level off at some predetermined point.

grantor trust When the owner of real property, called the grantor, conveys title of the property to a trust.

gross profit percentage The percentage of each payment which is capital gain.

gross rent multiplier The sales price of recently sold properties divided by the annual rent generated by those properties.

guaranteed mortgage certificate (GMC) A bond-like instrument issued by Freddie Mac that represents ownership in a large pool of residential mortgages. Principal is returned annually and interest is paid semi-annually.

guarantor A person or entity that guarantees the performance of a loan taken out by another party.

home equity loan A second loan on a house based on existing equity.

HOME Investment Partnerships Program A grant to states and localities that communities may use in partnership with local nonprofit groups to fund activities that build, buy, and rehabilitate affordable housing for rent or ownership for low-income households.

Home Mortgage Disclosure Act A federal law that requires lenders to disclose the geographic locations of their loans within their service areas in an attempt to prevent lenders from redlining.

Home Owners Loan Corporation (HOLC) An agency formed in 1933 to help stabilize the economy. HOLC issued government-guaranteed bonds to lenders for delinquent mortgages and then refinanced homeowner indebtedness.

homeless assistance Grants for rental assistance for the homeless.

hypotheca An instrument allowing lenders, in Roman times, to take possession of property in the event of actual default.

imputed interest rate rule IRS rule that establishes a minimum interest rate that must be charged based on market conditions.

income approach One of three traditional means of appraising property, based on the assumption that value is equal to the present value of future rights to income. Others are comparable sales and cost of construction.

index A rate of interest, such as a Treasury-bill rate, used to measure periodic interest rate adjustments for an adjustable-rate mortgage.

inflation risk The risk that inflation will cause a decline in the purchasing power of the future dollars to be received from an investment.

initial period discount See teaser rate.

installment sale The selling of an appreciated property on terms rather than for cash so as to postpone the payment of capital gains taxes on the profits.

interest only (IO) A security that gives the owner the right to all of the interest payments from a pool of mortgages.

lender's policy Title insurance that, among other assurances, covers all losses that may occur from any encumbrance or lien that preexisted change of title, known or unknown.

life-of-loan rate cap The maximum rate of interest allowed under the terms of an adjustable rate-mortgage. Commonly referred to as life cap.

liquidity risk The risk that an asset may not be easily and rapidly sold for cash at its current value.

loan processing The steps involved in creating a loan from application through closing.

loan-to-value ratio The amount of the loan divided by the value of the house.

margin The number of basis points a lender adds to an index to determine the interest rate of an adjustable-rate mortgage.

market approach Also called comparable sales method. A method of appraisal valuation that estimates value based on the recent sale of properties with comparable characteristics.

market value The value that a property would sell for between a willing seller and a willing buyer, both having full information about the property.

mark-to-market A procedure where an asset (or liability, but usually an asset) is revalued periodically (can be as frequently as daily) on the books of the holder.

maturity risk The increase in risk due to the increase in the maturity of a debt obligation due to possible changes in interest rates or inflation rates.

maturity value The value of an investment when it matures, such as the face value of a bond at maturity.

money market The market where short-term (less than one year) debt obligations are exchanged.

mortgage A conveyance of an interest in real property given as security for the payment of a debt.

mortgage activity Origination of loans by lenders and the purchase and sale of those loans in the secondary mortgage market.

mortgage constant A value that when multiplied by the initial loan amount will produce the amount of the payment.

mortgage debt Amount of loans made for the purchase of real estate property.

mortgage insurance premium (MIP) The charge paid by a mortgagor for mortgage insurance either to FHA or a private mortgage insurance company. On an FHA loan, the payment is 3.8 percent of the loan balance.

mortgage payment The amount due on each payment date.

mortgage-backed bond (MBB) A bond or debt instrument that is backed by a pool (large group) of mortgages and for which the cash flow of the mortgages serves as the source of repayment.

mortgage-backed security (MBS) A security purchased by investors that is secured by mortgages. Such securities are also known as pass-through securities since the debt service paid by the borrower is passed through to the purchaser of the security.

mortgage-related security A security backed or collateralized by a pool of mortgages.

mortgagor A borrower who pledges property through a mortgage to secure a loan.

negative amortization A loan payment schedule in which the outstanding principal balance goes up, rather than down, because the payments do not cover the full amount of interest due. The unpaid interest is added to the principal.

nonrecourse In the event of a default by the borrower this is a provision that prevents a lender from pursuing any assets of the borrower other than the property that serves as collateral for the loan.

ordinary annuity An annuity where the payments are made at the end of each payment period.

owner's policy Title insurance that, among other assurances, covers losses that may occur only from known pre-existing encumbrances or liens.

participation certificate (PC) Mortgage-backed security issued by FHLMC that is backed by mortgages purchased from eligible sellers. Called PC because seller retains some interest (5 or 10 percent) in the mortgages sold to FHLMC.

pass-through security A security issued by the Government National Mortgage Association that provides for the interest and principal to pass through to the holder of the security.

payment-to-income ratios The borrower's monthly payment on a mortgage divided by his or her monthly income.

pigus—The same as hypothea, except the lender could take possession in the event of anticipated default.

prepayment The payment or pay-off of the balance of a mortgage before the end of its term.

prepayment fee (penalty) The dollar amount levied against a borrower by a lender for paying off a loan before its maturity date. Also known as a prepayment penalty.

prepayment protection mortgage (PPM) A mortgage with a prepayment penalty.

price level adjusted mortgage (PLAM) A loan that adjusts the outstanding balance by the actual inflation rate.

primary market The market where financial securities are first originated

prime loan Prime loans are those made to well-qualified borrowers.

principal only (PO) A security that gives the owner the right to all of the principal payments (both scheduled amortization and prepayments) from a pool of mortgages.

private mortgage insurance (PMI) Insurance written by a private (nongovernmental) company protecting the mortgage lender against loss caused by a mortgage default or foreclosure.

promissory note A written instrument that is evidence of a loan and contains provisions for the repayment of the loan.

rate of return Expressed as a percentage and usually on an annual basis represents the interest received from an investment.

real estate employment Total persons employed in the real estate industry, which includes brokers, salespersons, lenders, title companies, appraisers, and so forth.

real estate mortgage investment conduit (REMIC) A type of mortgage-backed security that allows for income to be taxed only to the holders of the bond and not to the entity holding the mortgages.

Real Estate Settlement Procedures Act A federal law that requires lenders to provide borrowers with the cost of the various settlement (sale) costs prior to and at the actual transaction.

real rate of interest The nominal interest received less the rate of inflation. Example: If you receive 8 percent annual interest on a bond but inflation is 5 percent annually, your real rate received is 3 percent annually.

reconveyance The transfer of the title of real estate from one person to the immediately preceding owner. It is used when the performance of debt is satisfied under the terms of a deed of trust.

recourse The right of the holder of a note secured by a mortgage or deed of trust to look personally to the borrower or endorser for payment, not just to the property.

redlining A lender practice of refusing to make loans in what they may regard as high-risk neighborhoods. It comes from the practice of drawing a red line around the high-risk neighborhoods on a map.

refinance To repay one or more existing mortgage loans by simultaneously borrowing funds through another mortgage loan.

Regulation Z The regulation of the Federal Reserve Board that applies to the Consumer Credit Protection Act requirement that lenders disclose the APR and total finance charges associated with their loans.

related-persons rule If a property in an installment sale to a related person is sold within two years, the original seller must recognize the remaining capital gain at the time of sale.

reverse annuity mortgage (RAM) A financing arrangement whereby a lender pays the borrower a fixed annuity or periodic payment based on a percentage of the property's value.

secondary market The market where existing securities are exchanged.

secondary mortgage market A market where existing mortgages are bought and sold. It contrasts with the primary mortgage market, where mortgages are originated.

Section 108 Loan Guarantee Program A loan guarantee program for public entities such as cities and urban counties, the proceeds of which are to be used for various programs under the CDBG.

securities market A market where securities such as corporate stocks and bonds, government bonds, and mortgages are bought and sold.

security An instrument that memorializes the transfer of funds.

self-insurance A lender that incurs all risk of default loss on his or her portfolio of loans.

senior/subordinated pass-through A mortgage pass-through security issued in two classes. The subordinated class absorbs the payment risk for both classes.

statutory right of redemption The right of a borrower after a foreclosure sale to reclaim her property by repaying her defaulted loan.

subprime loans Subprime loans are those made to borrowers with some past credit problems such as frequent delinquent payments and/or previous foreclosures and bankruptcies.

subsidized public housing Various programs of the federal government to help low-income households pay market rent.

suit to quiet title A court proceeding whereby the court is asked to declare that clear title rests with the party bringing the action.

surplus entity A household, business, or government that has current income in excess of current expenditures and will transfer the excess to deficit entities.

tax-deferred exchange Exchanging one or more properties for another and deferring the payment of capital gains tax.

teaser rate A below market rate of interest for an initial period of time only on an adjustable-rate mortgage.

thrifts Savings and loan associations, mutual savings banks, and credit unions.

title The legally recognized ownership interest in a property.

tilt effect The effect of a rise in interest rates whereby the real payments on a standard fixed-rate mortgage are much greater at the beginning of the loan than at the end.

title insurance Insurance that preexisting encumbrances on the property are removed at or prior to closing.

title search A search of the public records to discover any liens or other impediments to a transfer of an unencumbered title.

tranche Refers to a class of securities within a CMO. Each class will have a different interest rate and maturity date.

underwriting The process of analyzing risk and determining an appropriate charge for taking on the risk. It involves a review of borrower's credit, value of security, and certain legal documents.

Uniform Settlement Statement A statement of the costs associated with the settlement (sale) of a property as required by RESPA.

INDEX